The Weary Titan

The Weary Titan

Britain and the Experience of Relative Decline,

1895–1905

Aaron L. Friedberg

Princeton University Press

PRINCETON, NEW JERSEY

Copyright © 1988
by Princeton University Press
Published by Princeton University Press,
41 William Street, Princeton, New Jersey 08540
In the United Kingdom:
Princeton University Press, Guildford, Surrey

Publication of this book has been aided by
the Whitney Darrow Fund
of Princeton University Press
This book has been composed in Baskerville

Clothbound editions of
Princeton University Press books
are printed on acid-free paper,
and binding materials are chosen for strength
and durability. Paperbacks,
although satisfactory for personal collections,
are not usually suitable
for library rebinding

Printed in the United States of America
by Princeton University Press,
Princeton, New Jersey

Library of Congress Cataloging-in-Publication Data

Friedberg, Aaron L., 1956–
  The weary titan : Britain and the experience of relative decline.
1895–1905 / Aaron L. Friedberg.
    p.   cm.
  Bibliography: p.
  Includes index.
  ISBN 0-691-05532-7
    1. Great Britain—Foreign relations—1901–1910.   2. Great Britain—
Foreign relations—1837–1901.   3. Great Britain—Economic
conditions—19th century.   4. Great Britain—Economic conditions—
20th century.   5. Great Britain—History, Military—19th century.
6. Great Britain—History, Military—20th century.   7. Great Britain—
Economic policy.   8. Great Britain—Military policy.   I. Title.
DA570.F75   1988
941.081—dc19   88-9937
                                                        CIP

For my parents
Joan Brest Friedberg
and
Simeon Adlow Friedberg

The Weary Titan staggers under the too vast orb of its fate.
—Joseph Chamberlain, 1902 Colonial Conference

Contents

Six. Change, Assessment, and Adaptation / 279

Seven. Britain and the Experience of Relative Decline / 292

Tables and Maps

Preface

Like most books, this one is a product of its times. Like many, it is also intended to serve more than one purpose. As the reader will soon discover, much of what follows is an attempt to reconstruct and to analyze the deliberations and decisions of a small group of turn-of-the-century British statesmen, military officers, and bureaucrats. Because of the enormous difficulty of the challenges they faced, their story has a certain intrinsic drama and interest. The purpose of this study is not, however, purely or even primarily to provide a record of past events. As I will argue, the essential problems that confronted Britain's leaders at the end of the nineteenth century were not unique to their particular time and place. The questions of how statesmen come to understand and seek to respond to their circumstances are universal ones. More specifically, how leaders measure relative national power and how they become aware of and react to shifts in the position of their own country are puzzles that, I will try to show, lie at the very heart of most theories of international politics.

Along with its historical and theoretical motivations, this book is also driven by a pressing contemporary concern. At least since the end of the 1960s, Americans have been divided by a debate over where their country stands, where it is going, and what role it should seek to play in the world. One central theme in this ongoing discussion has been the question of whether (and if so why) the United States has experienced a relative decline in its power. The matter has been taken up by academics, journalists, and politicians. Public anxiety over the apparent erosion of America's relative military capabilities and general political stature helped to determine the outcome of the 1980 presidential election. A parallel concern for the nation's economic future has manifested itself with increasing force as the decade has progressed. The debate over decline and the pressures that have helped to force it to the surface seem unlikely to subside; indeed, they will probably continue to shape the evolution of American national strategy for at least the remainder of this century.

Although there are certain obvious differences in size, economic base, population, location, natural resources, domestic political structure, weapons technology, and historical experience, there are also an impressive number of similarities between the United States today and Great Britain at the beginning of this century. Both either are or were essentially insular, liberal democratic, capitalist, "great" powers with interests and commitments scattered around the globe. Toward the middle of the nineteenth century Britain enjoyed considerable advantages in wealth and production over its nearest rivals and held a firm lead in the dominant form of military power. One hundred years later something similar could be said of the United States. By certain gross measures, in the last thirty years of the nineteenth century there was a decline in Britain's relative stature as other countries increased their capabilities even more rapidly than Britain could expand its own. Again, similar observations have been made about the most recent phase of American history.

There is no simple prediction or lesson to be derived from these facts. To take the most obvious possibility, just because the erosion of Britain's position continued (albeit by fits and starts) from the end of the nineteenth century down through the twentieth does not mean that the United States will necessarily suffer a similar fate. Not all relative declines are irreversible, nor does a loss of relative advantage inevitably lead to a change in absolute status.

With this caveat in mind, it can be noted that similarities in objective circumstances seem also to have given rise to similar strategic problems and internal controversies in Great Britain and the United States. The questions that informed Englishmen were asking themselves at the beginning of this century will have a familiar ring to American ears: Are we now passing through a period of relative national decline? How can we tell? If it is occurring, is that decline inevitable? Does it reflect our unusual (and transient) good fortune during the past thirty or forty years, or is it the result of mistakes and misguided policies? Is our international economic position being eaten away, and what, if anything, can we do about it? Should we adhere to a policy of free trade or should we adopt protectionism? Are we approaching the limits of our national financial resources? Can we afford to maintain vast foreign commitments while at the same time improving the welfare of our citizens? What are the implications for our world role and, in particular, for the structure of our alliances of having lost clear "strategic" superiority? Do our commitments now exceed our capabilities? Do we have sufficient ground forces to support our friends and allies overseas against the vast armies of hostile land powers? Can we sustain our present posture without resorting to conscription, higher taxes, or other burdensome impositions on our domestic population?

This study will not directly address these questions in their present-day, American form, nor do I think that contemporary controversies can be resolved solely through an examination of past events. Nevertheless, I do believe that such an investigation can help us to step aside from our own debates and disagreements, to understand better both the limitations of the concepts we use to interpret our situation and the elusive reality that lies beneath our formulations, and, perhaps, to see more clearly the choices and the dangers we face. Such perspective is not easy to come by. I hope that the reader will find some in what follows.

In writing this book I have incurred an unusually long list of debts. Professors Samuel Huntington and Stanley Hoffmann supported the project from its earliest stages and have provided me with every manner of assistance and guidance along the way. Professor Judith Shklar has also been a valued source of advice and encouragement.

Andrew Marshall planted the seeds from which this book grew. I am very pleased to add one more item to the long list of studies for which he has been directly or indirectly responsible.

I am grateful to Benjamin Berman, Eliot Cohen, John Dilulio, Kurt Guthe, Robert Jervis, Jane Katz, Yuen Foong Khong, Andrew Marshall, Mary Ann McGrail, Ethan Nadelmann, Stephen Rosen, and Adrienne Sirken for reading and commenting on various chapters. Michael Doyle, John Gooch, Stanley Hoffmann, Samuel Huntington, Paul Kennedy, Robert Keohane, Jack Snyder, Zara Steiner, and Martin Wiener read the entire manuscript in one version or another and provided me with many useful suggestions. I wish to thank all of these people, although by mentioning their names I do not mean to imply that all or indeed any of them endorse what I have written. I alone am responsible for the contents of this book and, in particular, for any errors it may contain.

Generous fellowships from the Krupp, Olin, and MacArthur foundations allowed me to complete my research and writing far more quickly and easily than would otherwise have been possible. A year as a fellow in the Ford Foundation's program in European Society and Western Security at the Harvard Center for International Affairs gave me time to prepare the manuscript for publication. I am truly grateful to these organizations for their support.

I wish to thank the following libraries and individuals for granting me permission to quote from documents in their possession or under their control: Nigel Arnold-Forster (H. O. Arnold-Forster Papers); the British Library (Arthur Balfour Papers); the University of Birmingham Library (Joseph and Austen Chamberlain papers); the Masters, Fellows, and Scholars of Churchill College in the University of Cambridge and Lord Fisher (Admiral Sir John Fisher Papers); Mr. R. H. Harcourt Williams, librarian at Hatfield House, and Lord Salisbury (Papers of the Third Marquess of Salisbury); India Office Library (Lord George Hamilton Papers); National Maritime Museum (Admiral Cyprian A. G. Bridge Papers); Bodleian Library, Oxford University, and the earl of Selborne (Second Earl of Selborne Papers); and the Public Record Office (War Office, Admiralty, Treasury Department, and Cabinet papers).

Portions of this book have been published previously in "Britain Faces the Burdens of Empire: The Financial Crisis of 1901–1905," *War and Society* 5, no. 2 (1987), and "Britain and the Experience of Relative Decline," *Journal of Strategic Studies* 10, no. 3 (1987). I appreciate the cooperation of these journals in permitting me to use material that first appeared in their pages.

Meg Alexander prepared two maps for the book with skill and dispatch.

Finally, my deepest thanks must go to my friends, to Adrienne, who came in at the end and at the beginning, and to all the other members of my family. Their love has sustained me in this as in every endeavor.

Princeton, N.J.
December 1987

Abbreviations

AC	Austin Chamberlain Papers, Birmingham University Library
Adm.	Admiralty Papers
BM, Add. Mss.	British Museum, Additional Manuscripts
BRI	Sir Cyprian A. G. Bridge Papers, National Maritime Museum Library
Cab.	Cabinet Papers
FO	Foreign Office Papers
H.H. Mss. 3M	Hatfield House Manuscripts, Papers of the Third Marquess of Salisbury
IOL	India Office Library
JC	Joseph Chamberlain Papers, Birmingham University Library
PRO	Public Record Office
T	Treasury Papers
WO	War Office Papers

The Weary Titan

International Relations Theory
and the Assessment
of National Power

Historians who live in democratic ages are not only prone to attribute
each happening to a great cause but also are led to link facts together to
make a system. . . . As it becomes extremely difficult to discern and analyze the reasons which, acting separately on the will of each citizen, concur in the end to produce movement in the whole mass, one is tempted
to believe that this movement is not voluntary and that societies uncon-
sciously obey some superior dominating force. . . . Thus historians who
live in democratic times do not only refuse to admit that some citizens
may influence the destiny of a people, but also take away from the
peoples themselves the faculty of modifying their own lot.
—Tocqueville, *Democracy in America*

How do statesmen think about power and, in particular, how do
they seek to measure the relative power of the nations they lead?
How do individuals and entire governments become aware of
changes (and especially unfavorable ones) in the relative power of
their own country? How do nations seek to adapt to such shifts? In
other words, what is the relationship between changing power and
changing assessments, on the one hand, and shifting assessments
and evolving state policies, on the other?

These would appear to be questions of considerable theoretical
and practical significance, yet they are generally little studied and
poorly understood. The first section of this chapter will be devoted
to an examination of several of the major existing bodies of theoretical literature on international relations. These writings either
ignore the question of how relative power is actually measured,
gloss over it, or highlight the problem without resolving it. Despite
a general lack of direct attention, there are nevertheless two models
of the processes of assessment and adaptation implicit in the existing

3

literature, and these will be discussed in the second major portion of this chapter. Questions of method will be addressed in a final section in which the overall structure of this study and the organization of its four central chapters will be laid out and explained.

Theories of International Relations
Structural Realism

Perhaps the most influential approach to the study of international relations in recent years has been that referred to as "structural realism" or "neorealism."[1] Adherents of this school believe that world politics can best be understood at what they call the "systemic level of analysis."[2] The most important characteristic of an international system in this view is its structure, and that, in the formulation put forward by Kenneth Waltz, is determined by the principle on which the system is organized, the functions of the units of which it is composed, and the distribution of "capabilities" among those units.[3]

General definitions aside, the units that make up (modern) international systems are nation-states, and the principle that governs them is that of anarchy. In practice, therefore, the structure of such anarchic systems is determined by the way in which power is distributed among states. Structural realists hold that the shape of a particular system will strongly determine the behavior of the states that make it up; structure (like anatomy), in this view, is akin to destiny. Changes in structure will also, quite logically, lead to generally predictable changes in behavior.

The appeal of structural theories lies in their parsimony and their promise of predictive power. Conversely, the weakness of such systems of explanation is their tendency to collapse into a materially driven determinism. In the words of one noted political scientist: "It has been a peculiar tendency of recent social science to disparage the importance of learning, cognitive ideas, and understanding. Few theories incorporate these concepts as major explanatory variables."[4] This observation applies particularly to structural realism, which has little or nothing to say about how statesmen think and, in particular, how they think about power.

---

[1] For a discussion of the concept see Keohane, "Theory of World Politics: Structural Realism and Beyond," in Finifter, ed., *Political Science: The State of the Discipline*, pp. 503–40. See also the essays in Keohane, ed., *Neorealism and Its Critics*.

[2] On the idea of levels of analysis see Singer, "The Level-of-Analysis Problem in International Relations," pp. 77–92.

[3] The definition is from Waltz, *Theory of International Politics*, pp. 100–101.

[4] Krasner, "Regimes and the Limits of Realism: Regimes as Autonomous

Waltz presents balance-of-power theory as an expression of the importance of structure in world politics. Under conditions of anarchy (and assuming a desire for self-preservation) the major states that define the structure of an international system will tend to act so as to counterbalance one another. If one state behaves aggressively or begins to augment its power relative to the others, some of them will usually form an alliance to defend themselves. This inclination is a strong one and can bring together countries that would otherwise have nothing in common. As Waltz puts it: "We find states forming balances of power whether or not they wish to."[5]

But is balancing inevitable? There would not appear to be any reason, either logical or empirical, for believing that this must be the case. As Arnold Wolfers observes in his criticism of the more traditional forms of "automatic" or "self-regulating" balance-of-power theories:

> Some weak countries seek safety by getting on the bandwagon of an ascending power, hoping somehow to escape complete subjugation once their powerful "friend" has gained supremacy. Other countries are so absorbed with their internal affairs or so unheeding of national power that the effects of their policies on the distribution of power, whether helping to preserve or upset the balance, are purely accidental.[6]

Waltz tends to downplay the possibility of what he calls "bandwagoning,"[7] but he does not go so far as to suggest that balances *must* form or that the behavior of any particular state will be completely determined by the shape of the system in which it operates. Ultimately Waltz is careful to avoid the trap of structural determinism. Balance-of-power theory, he argues, explains "the constraints that confine all states. The clear perception of constraints provides many clues to the expected reactions of states, but by itself the theory cannot explain those reactions. They depend not only on international constraints but also on the characteristics of states."[8]

Variables," in Krasner, ed., *International Regimes*, p. 368. On the problem of determinism in modern political science see Almond and Genco, "Clouds, Clocks, and the Study of Politics," pp. 489–522.

[5] Waltz, *Theory of International Politics*, p. 125.

[6] Wolfers, *Discord and Collaboration*, p. 124. Hedley Bull makes a similar point: "states threatened by a potential dominant power have the option of failing to counterbalance it" (*The Anarchical Society*, p. 104).

[7] Waltz, *Theory of International Politics*, p. 126. For the argument that "balancing" is more likely than "bandwagoning" see Walt, *The Origins of Alliances*, esp. pp. 17–49, 262–85.

[8] Ibid., p. 122.

This seems both sensible and familiar, but it leaves a number of important unanswered questions. What are the internal characteristics that determine how a state will respond to external pressures? And who is possessed of the "clear perception of constraints" to which Waltz refers? Is it the remote, omniscient analyst or the statesman forced to make decisions without benefit of hindsight or perfect information?

Shifts in the distribution of power within an international system may be "real" in some sense, but they may fail to have any impact unless and until they are perceived. A nation whose leadership does not realize that its power is declining relative to that of another country will probably not feel compelled to enter into protective alliances with third parties. A knowledge of how such conclusions are reached and acted upon would appear to be essential to any complete balance-of-power theory, regardless of the language in which it is couched.

Similar criticisms can be made of the cluster of theories that forms another variant of structural realism. In 1973 Charles Kindleberger advanced the notion that the stability and openness of an international economic system is critically dependent on its structure. Specifically, Kindleberger suggested that stability requires hegemony. Only when one country is both willing and able to take on the role of leadership will a lasting free-trade regime be possible. If the hegemonic power loses either its desire or its capacity to manage the system, then, barring the emergence of a successor, protectionism and general economic disorder will result.[9]

Kindleberger's initial hypothesis has been elaborated into what has become known as the theory of "hegemonic stability" by political scientists concerned with understanding the effects of what they see as the recent loss of American world economic leadership.[10] Attention to the general problem of hegemonic decline has also sparked renewed interest in cyclical theories of global politics. Robert Gilpin, for example, writes that all of history can be understood in terms of the rise and fall of successive hegemons. As one state grows and matures it begins to face challenges from newer

[9] Kindleberger, *The World in Depression, 1929–1939*, esp. pp. 19–30, 291–308.

[10] See, for example, Krasner, "State Power and the Structure of International Trade," pp. 317–43; Keohane, "The Theory of Hegemonic Stability and Changes in International Economic Regimes, 1967–1977," in Holsti, ed., *Change and the International System*, pp. 131–62; McKeown, "Tariffs and Hegemonic Stability Theory," pp. 73–91; Stein, "The Hegemon's Dilemma: Great Britain, the United States, and the International Economic Order," pp. 355–86; Russett, "The Mysterious Case of Vanishing Hegemony," pp. 207–31.

competitors. Eventually the question of world leadership will be resolved by war. But, Gilpin points out,

> the conclusion of one hegemonic war is the beginning of another cycle of growth, expansion, and eventual decline. The law of uneven growth continues to redistribute power, thus undermining the status quo established by the last hegemonic struggle. Disequilibrium replaces equilibrium, and the world moves toward a new round of hegemonic conflict.[11]

An earlier and less developed version of this idea was advanced as the theory of the "power transition" by A. F. K. Organski. Again, differential rates of economic growth are held to be the motive force that drives a simple but seemingly inescapable mechanism:

> At any given moment the single most powerful nation on earth heads an international order. . . . In the present period, the most powerful nation has always been an industrial nation. . . . As new nations industrialized, the old leader was challenged. . . . Ordinarily, such challenges by newcomers result in war. . . . One could almost say that the rise of such a challenger guarantees a major war.[12]

What both the economic and the more broadly political theories of hegemonic stability and decline have in common is their strong deterministic quality.[13] It is often claimed that a change in the structure of the international system (i.e., in the distribution of power within it) *must* produce certain specified consequences, whether the onset of protectionism or the outbreak of a major war. The intervening mechanisms of perception, analysis, and decision are usually either overlooked or their outcomes are considered to be preordained.

Once again, there would seem to be strong logical and historical reasons for questioning the explanatory and predictive power of theories that move directly from international structures to state behavior. What reason is there for assuming, for example, that the rulers of a present or prospective world economic leader will be

---

[11] Gilpin, *War and Change in World Politics*, p. 210.

[12] Organski, "The Power Transition," in Rosenau, ed., *International Politics and Foreign Policy*, p. 370. This excerpt is drawn from Organski's book *World Politics*, which was originally published in 1958.

[13] For a critique of the determinism of "basic force" versions of the hegemonic stability theory see Keohane, *After Hegemony: Cooperation and Discord in the World Political Economy*, esp. pp. 31–46.

able to detect the shifts in industrial power that (in theory) must compel their nation to abandon or adopt a managerial role? (Why then did Britain continue to advocate free trade even after the nation had lost its position of industrial primacy at the end of the nineteenth century, and why was the United States so slow to take up Britain's mantle during the 1920s and 1930s?) If shifts in military capabilities are readily detectable, why do declining powers often fail to launch preemptive attacks on their rising competitors? When unfavorable shifts are quickly identified, will war be the inevitable result? (How then were England and America able to avoid a war of hegemonic succession during the early years of the twentieth century?)

Structural considerations provide a useful point from which to begin analysis of international politics rather than a place at which to end it. Even if one acknowledges that structures exist and are important, there is still the question of how statesmen grasp their contours from the inside, so to speak, of whether, and if so how, they are able to determine where they stand in terms of relative national power at any given point in history. It would appear that, right or wrong, such estimates will go a long way toward shaping state behavior and, in particular, toward determining national responses to structural change.

Mathematical Realism

Where structural realism essentially ignores the problem of assessment, another strand of contemporary thinking about world politics glosses it over with simplifying assumptions. Efforts to construct mathematical models of international interactions, such as competitions in armaments or alliance formation or war, usually substitute retrospective, "objective" measures of relative national power for the judgments made by contemporary statesmen.

The most fully developed example involves the attempt of students of arms races to establish the existence of a direct, predictable, quantifiable relationship between the defensive efforts of pairs of potentially hostile states.[14] For modeling purposes, theo-

---

[14] This relationship is typically expressed as a pair of equations:

$$\Delta X = kY - aX + g$$
$$\Delta Y = lX - bY + h$$

where X and Y are either the military expenditures or the arms stocks of the two states, $-a$ and $-b$ are "fatigue coefficients" that represent the burden of earlier decisions to buy arms, and g and h are some measure of the hostility that each state feels toward the other. Clearly, as Y's spending (or level of preparedness) increases, X's will tend to do so also. For reviews of the mathematical arms-race literature see Busch, app., "Mathematical Models of Arms Races," in Russett, *What Price Vigilance? The Burdens of National Defense,* pp. 193–233; Luterbacher, "Arms Race Models: Where Do We Stand?"

rists generally assume that there is some single, observable, and mutually agreeable surrogate for military power (whether spending or equipment stocks) on which both sides will focus and to which each participant must respond. In other words, the effort to evaluate enemy capabilities, which is at least implicitly identified as central to the process under investigation, is assumed to be a simple and direct procedure. It seems clear, however, that the inner workings of competing states are not nearly so straightforward or transparent as this picture suggests. Figures on foreign military spending are notoriously controversial and unreliable, and physical indicators of capability can sometimes be even less dependable. This may be so under the best of circumstances, but it is especially likely to be the case when the enemy is doing what he can to conceal his own preparations for war. The apparent complexity of the assessment process in real life may help to explain some of the failings of existing arms race models.

Calculations of relative capability must also, presumably, play a part in the processes through which leaders decide whether or not to enter into an alliance or begin a war.[15] Here again, attempts at modeling typically substitute crude surrogates for the actual assessments of decision-makers.[16] Although these may reflect accurately the thinking of national leaders, there is no a priori reason for believing that they will always do so. The more modelers differ from statesmen in their assumptions about the best way to measure power, the less likely it is that their models will accurately capture reality.

Classical Realism

The centrality of the problem of assessing national power is a familiar theme in the work of more traditional, "realist" writers on

---

pp. 199–217; Rattinger, "Econometrics and Arms Races: A Critical Review and Some Extensions," pp. 421–39; Russett, "International Interactions and Processes," in Finifter, ed., *Political Science*, pp. 543–53. Another more recent and perhaps more promising branch of the arms-race literature uses deductive, game theoretic techniques to model military competitions and to assess the impact of complicating factors like imperfect intelligence (Downs, Rocke, and Siverson, "Arms Races and Cooperation," pp. 118–46).

[15] For a discussion of the assessment problem as it relates to theories of alliance formation see Holsti, Hopmann,

and Sullivan, *Unity and Disintegration in International Alliances: Comparative Studies*, pp. 4–14.

[16] One study measures total population, iron production, and military personnel to create a "Composite Index of National Capability" (CINC). This index is then tested as a predictor of "war-proneness." No mention is made of whether real statesmen actually use this index or of what the causal link might be between their calculation of capabilities and their inclination to make war (Bremer, "National Capabilities and War Proneness," in Singer, ed., *The Correlates of War* 2:57–82).

international relations. Indeed, the formulation of accurate assessments is widely held to be the single most important prerequisite of successful statesmanship. In praising the wartime leadership of Pericles, for example, Thucydides reports as his primary virtue that "he appears to have accurately estimated what the power of Athens was."[17] Similarly, after discussing what he calls "the elements of national power,"[18] Hans Morgenthau advises that "it is the task of those responsible for the foreign policy of a nation. . . . to evaluate correctly the bearing of these factors upon the power of their own nation and of other nations as well, and this task must be performed for both the present and the future."[19]

Correct assessments are assumed by realists to be a first step in the critical process through which ends are brought into alignment with means. Thus Henry Kissinger writes in *A World Restored* that "the test of a statesman . . . is his ability to recognize the real relationship of forces and to make this knowledge serve his ends."[20] Along the same lines, Walter Lippmann observed in 1943 that "a foreign policy consists in bringing into balance, with a comfortable surplus of power in reserve, the nation's commitments and the nation's power. The constant preoccupation of the true statesmen is to achieve and maintain this balance."[21]

Power calculations may be important not only to the decision-makers of each individual state but to the successful functioning of the system of states as a whole. In the view of many realists, it is only when national leaders can adequately appreciate existing and potential power relationships that they will act so as to preserve a balance among themselves. Edward Gulick, in his study *Europe's Classical Balance of Power*, lists the presumed existence of a "rational system of estimating power" as one of the foundations upon which the eighteenth- and nineteenth-century European state system was based.[22] As Gulick puts it, "The estimation of power was, and is, one of the common mental processes of balance-of-power statesmen."[23]

But how (and how easily) are these common operations performed? Realists have traditionally assumed that assessment is not

---

[17] Thucydides, *The Peloponnesian War*, p. 163.

[18] Geography, natural resources, industrial capacity, military preparedness, population, national character, national morale, and the quality of diplomacy and government (Morgenthau, *Politics Among Nations*, pp. 112–49).

[19] Ibid., p. 150.

[20] Kissinger, *A World Restored*, p. 325.

[21] Lippmann, *U.S. Foreign Policy: Shield of the Republic*, p. 9.

[22] Gulick, *Europe's Classical Balance of Power*, p. 24.

[23] Ibid., p. 28.

only important but also difficult. "It is an ideal task," Morgenthau concludes, "and hence incapable of achievement."[24] "Erroneous power estimates have plagued nations at all times and have been the cause of many national calamities," writes Arnold Wolfers. "Neither the difficulties nor the importance of accuracy in the estimates of power can be exaggerated."[25]

All this still leaves the question of means and methods unresolved. When it comes to explaining how statesmen actually do their difficult job, the classical realists appear to lose interest and move on to other, more tractable subjects. For the most part, the complexities of the problem are noted and the matter is simply dropped. Thus Hans Morgenthau concludes that

> the task of assessing the relative power of nations for the present and for the future resolves itself into a series of hunches, of which some will certainly turn out to be wrong, while others may be proved by subsequent events to have been correct.[26]

In a similar vein, Gulick writes that

> statesmen, whether accurate in their estimates or not, must measure power, regardless of the primitive character of the scales at their disposal. . . . One may, then, dismiss the question of "power" with the admission, on the one hand, that it is impossibly complex and the assertion, on the other hand, that the statesmen themselves were reduced to making guesses. These guesses have themselves become historical facts.[27]

Even if they were substantially correct, these statements would not be very satisfying, if only because all forms of guessing are not equally imprecise. It is possible to concede that judgments about changing power relationships may represent imperfect knowledge and even that they may be based on guesses or hunches without abandoning interest in understanding how they come to be formulated. In fact, because the weighing of relative power appears to be so central to foreign policy decision making, those concerned with developing theories of international politics should not be content to dismiss assessment as easily as has often been done in the past.

[24] Morgenthau, *Politics Among Nations*, p. 153.
[25] Wolfers, *Discord and Collaboration*, p. 112.
[26] Morgenthau, *Politics Among Nations*, p. 154.
[27] Gulick, *Europe's Classical Balance of Power*, p. 28.

Two Models of Assessment and Adaptation

There has, of course, been a tremendous amount written about power and its measurement. Much of the literature on this subject is abstract and analyzes the relationships between pairs of unspecified "actors."[28] More recently, efforts have also been made to look at the problem from a specifically international point of view.[29] What is striking about virtually all of this work is that it aims to demonstrate how power *should* be evaluated by detached, rational observers rather than to determine how it has been or is being weighed by residents of the real political world.

Despite this lack of direct attention, there are nevertheless two schematic sketches of the related processes of assessment and adaptation embedded in the various theoretical works discussed above. In fact, one or the other of these implicit models can be found at the core of most major theories of international relations. As will be discussed, however, while they provide a set of useful reference points, both alternative accounts are, in important ways, inadequate.

Calculative Model

National leaders are often assumed to think of power as a stock of one or more commodities, in much the same way as do the mathematical modelers and many of the international power theorists. The number, variety, and weighting of items included on the list of resources varies from one analyst to the next. Some concentrate only on tangible quantities like state area, population, government revenue, defense spending, trade, and the size of a nation's armed forces.[30] Others try to capture the intangible elements that they

[28] Among the important articles are Simon, "Notes on the Observation and Measurement of Political Power," pp. 500–516; Dahl, "The Concept of Power," pp. 201–15; Harsanyi, "Measurement of Social Power, Opportunity Costs, and the Theory of Two-Person Bargaining Games," pp. 67–79; Nagel, "Some Questions About the Concept of Power," pp. 120–37.

[29] See, for example, Knorr, *Power and Wealth: The Political Economy of International Power;* Hart, "Three Approaches to the Measurement of Power in International Relations," pp. 289–305; Keohane and Nye, *Power and Interdependence: World Politics in Transition;* Baldwin, "Power Analysis and World Politics," pp. 161–94; Goldmann and

Sjostedt, eds., *Power, Capabilities, Interdependence: Problems in the Study of International Influence.* Perhaps the most interesting distinction to emerge both here and in the literature cited above is that between power as resources and power as control.

[30] See Ferris, *The Power Capabilities of Nation-States.* Another author uses a single index that combines military resources (numbers of men under arms and defense expenditures as a proportion of total world military capabilities), industrial power (share of world pig iron or ingot steel production and share of world industrial fuel consumption), and human potential (share of a given international system's total population and urban population) (Bueno de Mes-

consider to be important and that, by implication, either are or ought to be included in the calculations of real statesmen.[31]

An assessment process based on calculation would presumably be uncomplicated and might, indeed, be fairly mechanical. Governments would keep track of their own critical resources and could be expected at all times to know such things as the size of their army (or navy or population) and the capacity of their national economy. By keeping similar statistics for all other countries (or at least for those of importance either as actual or potential allies and enemies), a state's leaders could be reasonably certain of knowing their relative standing at any given moment. Assessment would then be simply a matter of counting and comparison.[32]

Dynamic measurements of changes in the distribution of power would be only slightly more complex. Through periodic or continuous updating of statistics, shifts in relative capabilities could be readily detected. And so, according to one author, the problem of estimating changing relative national power should be "not much different than estimation of market share for the firm."[33] Decisive shifts would, in this view, be readily recognizable.

The clear implication of the calculative model is that assessment of changes in relative power can, should, and therefore probably will be, accompanied by appropriate adjustments in national policy. This assumption is sometimes stated directly. Quincy Wright, for example, notes that most balance-of-power theories rest on the belief "that statesmen in pursuing a balance-of-power policy do so intelligently—that they measure the factors involved . . . accurately and guide their behavior by these calculations."[34]

Elsewhere, as in most structural realist formulations, assessment through rational calculation plays the part of a reliable but invisible transmission belt connecting objective change to adaptive behavior. Here, as Robert Keohane points out, whether the proponents of structural realism acknowledge it or not,

---

quita, *The War Trap*, pp. 101–109).

[31] Thus Hans Morgenthau includes "national character" and "national morale" on his list (see note 18, above). Ray Cline has suggested that power can be expressed as an equation in which $P = (C + E + M) \times (S + W)$. Here C (critical mass) equals population plus territory; E and M are economic and military capability; and S and W are some impressionistic measure of strate-

gic purpose and national will (Cline, *World Power Assessment, 1977*, p. 34).

[32] The logical result of such calculations may be a table of the sort Cline compiles in which he gives every country in the world a power "score," from 3 (Cuba) to 523 (USSR) (Cline, *World Power Assessment*, pp. 173–74).

[33] Doran, "War and Power Dynamics: Economic Underpinnings," p. 422.

[34] Wright, *A Study of War* 2:754.

the link between system structure and actor behavior is forged by the rationality assumption, which enables the theorist to predict that leaders will respond to the incentives and constraints imposed by their environments. Taking rationality as constant permits one to attribute variations in state behavior to various characteristics of the international system. Otherwise, state behavior might have to be accounted for by variations in the calculating ability of states.[35]

In any case, the calculative model suggests that adaptation to changes in relative power should be essentially continuous. The path described by state policy is therefore likely to be a smooth and straight line with no lags or zigzags.[36]

Perceptual Model

Classical realism, with its emphasis on the intellectual problems of statesmanship and on the sometimes tragic quality of international political life, contains within it an alternative to the calculative model of assessment. Writers like Morgenthau and Wolfers point out the difficulties of measuring power in practice and suggest that errors in judgment are not only possible but perhaps even likely. Such mistakes can have severe consequences, as when they cause a state to fail to form a balancing alliance or when they result in its mistakenly waging war against a stronger opponent. One author has even asserted that "it is the problem of accurately measuring the relative power of nations which goes far to explain why wars occur."[37]

The essence of this view is captured in a remark by the great English statesman Lord Bolingbroke:

> The precise point at which the scales of power turn . . . is imperceptible to common observation . . . some progress must be made in the new direction, before the change is perceived. They who are in the sinking scale . . . do not easily come off from the habitual prejudices of superior wealth, or power, or skill, or courage, nor from the confidence that these prejudices inspire. They who are in the

---

[35] Keohane, "Theory of World Politics," in Keohane, ed., *Neorealism and its Critics*, p. 167.

[36] The overall picture here is of the state as a "cybernetic mechanism," reacting to stimuli reaching it along certain specified channels in ways intended to ensure a stable relationship between "entity" and "environment." See Deutsch, *The Nerves of Government;* also Steinbrunner, *The Cybernetic Theory of Decision: New Dimensions of Political Analysis;* Rosenau, *The Study of Political Adaptation.*

[37] Blainey, *The Causes of War,* p. 114.

rising scale do not immediately feel their strength, nor assume that confidence in it which successful experience gives them afterwards. They who are the most concerned to watch the variations of this balance, misjudge often in the same manner, and from the same prejudices. They continue to dread a power no longer able to hurt them, or they continue to have no apprehensions of a power that grows daily more formidable.[38]

Whereas in the calculative model facts and figures are the raw materials of assessment, here statesmen are seen to deal in less precise but more lingering images, both of other countries and of their own.

The manner in which decision-makers come to form such perceptions has been the subject of considerable analytical attention.[39] Not surprisingly, much of what has been written in this area concentrates on the question of how statesmen form beliefs about the intentions and capabilities of others.[40] In contrast, as one scholar has recently pointed out, "national self images" have received a good deal less direct scrutiny.[41]

A belief in the relative weakness of one's own country or in the strength of another is presumably at least partly the result of past events. Kenneth Boulding has speculated that the citizens of a country as a whole may come to share a historical "national image" that extends "backward into a supposedly recorded or perhaps mythological past and forward into an imagined future." It is "the consciousness of *shared* events and experiences" like war, writes Boulding, that is "of the utmost importance . . . in the creation and sustenance of the national image."[42]

The literature on perceptions suggests that, however they come to be formed, the beliefs of national leaders (including, presumably, their beliefs about the relative power of states in the international system) are slow to change. Boulding argues that such ad-

[38] Quoted in Gulick, *Europe's Classical Balance of Power*, p. 29.

[39] Best and probably most influential is the work of Jervis, especially *Perception and Misperception in International Politics*. For a discussion of the literature and an analysis of recent findings see George, *Presidential Decisionmaking in Foreign Policy: The Effective Use of Information and Advice*, pp. 25–80. See also Jonsson, ed., *Cognitive Dynamics and International Politics*.

[40] See, for example, the essays by William Scott and Ralph White in Kelman, ed., *International Behavior: A Social-Psychological Analysis*. See also articles in *Image and Reality in World Politics*, a special issue of the *Journal of International Affairs*; Holsti, "Cognitive Dynamics and Images of the Enemy: Dulles and Russia," in Finlay, Holsti, and Fagen, eds., *Enemies in Politics*, pp. 25–96; Stoessinger, *Nations in Darkness: China, Russia, America*.

[41] Lebow, *Between Peace and War*, p. 195.

[42] Boulding, "National Images and International Systems," pp. 122–23.

justments occur rarely, if at all,[43] while John Stoessinger asserts that change is possible only as the consequence of some monumental disaster.[44]

Students of cognitive processes have focused on crises or dramatic events as the most likely agents of attitude change. Drawing on evidence from behavioral psychology, Robert Jervis concludes that individuals are able to dismiss or absorb bits of "discrepant information" that might call an accepted belief into question if they arrive slowly and one at a time. Conversely, bad news is usually hardest to handle when it comes in large batches. For this reason Jervis believes that "in politics, sudden events influence images more than do slow developments."[45]

This view has a certain intuitive appeal, but it is by no means undisputed. In a study of public opinion that may also have some relevance to the analysis of elite attitudes, Karl Deutsch and Richard Merritt conclude that even spectacular events usually do not result in massive or permanent shifts in collective beliefs. Cumulative events tend to have a larger influence over long periods of time ("perhaps two decades or more"), but, the authors find, "often it takes the replacement of one generation by another to let the impact of external changes take its full effect."[46]

Similarly, in their study *Conflict Among Nations*, Glenn Snyder and Paul Diesing assert that the "immediate images" that national leaders have of their opponents in a crisis may fluctuate without affecting "background images," the ways in which elites view each other's countries more generally. These deeper beliefs "usually do not change, and then only marginally during the course of a crisis."[47] Over the short term, according to Snyder and Diesing, "change in background image for a government usually results from a change of regime, or a shift in the balance of power within a regime, not from individuals changing their minds."[48] In general, "adjustment of background images occurs through changes of personnel."[49]

[43] Boulding, "The Learning and Reality-Testing Process in the International System," p. 10.

[44] "Most national leaders," he writes, "will not examine their prejudices and stereotypes until they are shaken and shattered into doing so" (Stoessinger, *Nations in Darkness*, p. 194).

[45] Jervis, *Perception and Misperceptions*, p. 308. On the gradual, onion-peeling process of attitude change see Jervis, pp. 288–315.

[46] Karl Deutsch and Richard Merritt, "Effects of Events on National and International Images," in Kelman, ed., *International Behavior*, pp. 182–83.

[47] Snyder and Diesing, *Conflict Among Nations: Bargaining, Decision Making, and System Structure in International Crises*, p. 329.

[48] Ibid.

[49] Ibid., p. 332.

Although there are obviously important differences regarding the means by which change can occur (whether through sudden shocks, or changes in personnel, or even in entire generations), there does seem to be agreement that central beliefs or images are remarkably resistant to modification.[50] If assessment is a matter of images and self-images and if beliefs about relative national power are like others that have been studied, then there is good reason to expect that changes in assessments will lag behind real shifts in the distribution of power. Adaptation is therefore also likely to be delayed and to come in discrete chunks rather than as a continuous stream of minor corrections. Where the calculative model postulates steady adjustment to change, a model based on perception predicts periods of quiescence punctuated by bursts of activity. Instead of a straight line, in this view the path of policy is more likely to resemble a step-function.

Method
Structure of the Study

Taken together, the next four chapters are intended to constitute a single case study of assessment and adaptation under conditions of relative decline. At best this investigation can shed light on only one-half of the larger problem of reactions to shifts in international position. Responses to relative *increases* in national power will have to be considered elsewhere.[51] Moreover, the case examined here is one in which there appears in retrospect to have been both an objective erosion in power and a reasonably open, contemporary debate over what was occurring.[52] Cases in which real change went essentially unnoticed, or in which erosion was feared but seems not to have occurred, are also worth considering.[53]

Within these boundaries there are obvious limits to the generalizations that can be derived from the study of any single, unique group of events.[54] The four central chapters that follow lay out one

---

[50] Alexander George summarizes the findings from the psychological literature by pointing out that "while . . . beliefs can change, what is noteworthy is that they tend to be relatively stable" (George, *Presidential Decisionmaking*, p. 57).

[51] Among the possible cases would be Germany and the United States during the last quarter of the nineteenth century.

[52] France during the 1920s and 1930s might be another, similar, example.

[53] Britain in the mid-1930s presents one conceivable case of blindness. The United States in the early 1950s is a possible instance of unwarranted anxiety.

[54] As Harry Eckstein has pointed out, the simultaneous examination of several cases permits the more rapid formulation of "candidate generalizations." On the other hand, "unlike

set of specific answers to the broad questions with which this chapter began. In chapter 6 these will be compared with the two sets of hypothetical answers provided by the calculative and perceptual models. This comparison illuminates the inadequacies of each and points toward a more refined general understanding of the processes of assessment and adaptation.

Put briefly, an investigation of the British case suggests the importance of organizational, intellectual, and domestic political factors in explaining how nations respond to shifts in relative power. There is strong reason to expect that in modern states the assessment process will be decentralized rather than concentrated in one agency or individual. Instead of a single discussion about some aggregated notion of national power, there are likely to be several parallel debates about the different components of that power going on simultaneously. Each of these will involve elements of both rational calculation and perception or belief. Specifically, this study highlights the central role of simplifying, but sometimes misleading, indicators in both public and intragovernmental discussions of the various forms of national power.

Official estimates of where a country stands may change neither continuously nor in single large jumps but, rather, disjointedly and unevenly. For example, widely shared concern over relative military decline may precede worries about eroding national economic power. In each field, shifts are likely to result not simply from exogenous shocks or random personnel changes but rather from a prolonged process of bureaucratic discussion and, sometimes, public political debate. This process is driven by gradual developments in the thinking of "change agents," middle- and upper-level officials whose views begin to deviate from the norm and who are able to receive a wider hearing only at moments of intense crisis.

National adaptation is a function both of the overall pattern of official assessments and of the division of domestic political power. Recognition of decline inside the government and agreement on how best to respond may come more quickly in some areas than in others. Even in those sectors where an internal consensus can be reached a national government may lack the political power to im-

---

wide-ranging comparative studies, [individual] case studies permit intensive analysis that does not commit the researcher to a highly limited set of variables, and thus increases the probability that critical variables and relations will be found. The possibility of less superficiality in research . . . also plays a role here." On the possibilities and limitations of single case studies in the development of theories see Eckstein, "Case Study and Theory in Political Science," in Greenstein and Polsby, eds., *Handbook of Political Science* 7 : 79–138; quote from p. 106.

plement its preferred policies. The net result is likely to be a mixture of action in some areas and inaction in others. Instead of either failing to adjust at all or responding with a coherent national strategy, Britain reacted to the early evidence of its relative decline in a fragmented and only partially coordinated way. As will be argued in chapter 6, there are reasons to believe that what was true of England at the turn of the century may be true as well of other countries at other times. The validity of such generalizations will have to be established through an examination of additional case studies.

Structure of Chapters 2–5

At the turn of the twentieth century (and, in particular, during the period 1895 to 1905),[55] Britain's leaders talked a good deal about national power in general. More specifically, they were concerned with what I have called economic, financial, sea, and military[56] power—Britain's relative position in the international economy, its capacity to pay for an adequate defense, its control of the seas, and its ability to defend the land borders of the empire. Although these elements were separated to a considerable degree, none of them was treated in complete isolation from the others. Accepting a division that contemporary statesmen themselves employed, I will consider each kind of power in turn (rather than following a simple chronological scheme), while trying to show how interconnections were made.[57]

Each of the next four chapters is organized in roughly the same fashion. All are centered around a debate or decision that occurred during the years 1895–1905, although, as will become apparent, the intellectual and historical background to these events often

[55] This decade of troubled peace, punctuated in the middle by the Boer War, was characterized by an intense and wide-ranging discussion of Britain's relative power. As such it presents an unusual opportunity to examine the processes of assessment and adaptation during a period that is now recognized as one of relative decline. These end points also mark a clear political epoch during which two consecutive Conservative governments (staffed at high and low levels by many of the same people) ruled the country. Looked at in historical perspective, these ten years may be thought of as comprising a distinct sequence of frames in the decades-long "feature film" of British decline. In the next four chapters these frames will be magnified, scrutinized, and dissected.

[56] "Military" is used here in the way the British used it at the time—to refer to ground forces as compared with naval forces.

[57] Because my first concern is with assessment and because I found no evidence that Britain's leaders thought in terms of a separate category of "diplomatic power," I have chosen an approach that differs from the more traditional, historical treatments of the period. Instead of focusing on diplomacy as an independent category, internal discussions of ongoing negotiations with other states are presented here as the occasion for debates over relative power, and treaties emerge, in several cases, as one of a number of adaptive responses to changing assessments.

extended many years into the past. It was in the course of these discussions over practical policies that the assumptions of the participants came most clearly to the surface. After analyzing each specific debate, every chapter will conclude with a return to the three central questions about power measurement, changing assessments, and national adaptation raised at the opening of this chapter.

In studying a series of controversies that took place over eighty years ago I have found myself confronted by a tension between the demands of objectivity and judgment. On the one hand, I have tried to treat my subjects fairly. By this I mean simply that I have attempted to put myself in their shoes, trying as best I could to understand how they thought and how the problems they defined for themselves must have appeared at the time. On the other hand, I cannot and do not seek to avoid evaluating the performance of those whom I am describing. For this reason I have not hesitated to judge them against the standard of a future that was necessarily hidden from their view. At the close of this book, in chapter 7, I will have some general remarks about the overall quality of Britain's response to relative decline. In addition, each of the next four chapters is aimed in part at solving a retrospective puzzle: Why were Britain's leaders unable or unwilling to do anything about the relative decline in its economic power? Why, after the turn of the century, did they come to the incorrect conclusion that the limits of the nation's financial resources had been reached? Why, despite the obvious gravity of that decision, did they surrender worldwide sea supremacy with so little anguish? Why, in the face of clear warnings, did they refuse to consider realistically the enormous problems posed by the emerging threat of large-scale land warfare?

No one who thinks carefully about these questions should come away with the soothing conclusion that Britain's leaders at the turn of the century were nothing more than a pack of short-sighted blunderers. In the face of enormous economic, technical, military, and political changes, they struggled to preserve their nation's place in the world. Perhaps they could have done better. They could almost certainly have done worse. In judging them, modern critics might well ask what they should have done differently.

Economic Power:
The Loss of Industrial
Preeminence

[T]he habits of political discussion which induce us to catalogue for purposes of debate the outward signs that distinguish . . . the standing from the falling state, hide the obscurer, but more potent, forces which silently prepare the fate of empires. National character is subtle and elusive; not to be expressed in statistics, nor measured by the rough methods which suffice the practical moralist or statesman. And when through an ancient and still powerful state there spreads a mood of deep discouragement, when the reaction against recurring ills grows feebler . . . when learning languishes, enterprise slackens, and vigour ebbs away, then . . . there is present some process of social degeneration, which we must perforce recognise, and which, pending a satisfactory analysis may conveniently be distinguished by the name of "decadence."
—Arthur J. Balfour
  Lecture on "Decadence" at Newnham College,
  January 1908

Like many politicians, Joseph Chamberlain chose his hometown as the place from which to begin a major public campaign. Unlike most, however, Chamberlain's immediate objective was not the acquisition of high office, but rather the preservation of his country's position as the preeminent world industrial power.

On 15 May 1903, the former mayor of Birmingham returned to the city where he had begun his career some thirty years before to address a large crowd at the town hall. As colonial secretary in the Conservative coalition government that had held power since 1895, Chamberlain was guaranteed an attentive, respectful audience. In contrast with his more stolid, aristocratic colleagues, Chamberlain was also a dynamic, colorful, and sometimes unpredictable public speaker. Even at the age of sixty-seven, the colonial secretary was considered to be one of the most exciting and powerful figures in British politics.[1]

As he had done on many previous occasions, Chamberlain began by reminding his listeners of the tremendous importance of the empire that lay beyond Britain's shores. The just-completed Boer War, in which colonial assistance had been so crucial, was only the most recent indication of the benefit to be derived from strong imperial ties. If those bonds were permitted to weaken, allowing each of the components of the empire to drift off in its own direction, the results could be disastrous for Britain. "Think what it means to your power and influence as a country," Chamberlain warned, "think what it means to your trade and commerce."[2]

The time had come to take dramatic steps to ensure that Britain and its colonies would not be pulled apart by the centrifugal forces at work in the new century. Specifically, Chamberlain proposed that preparations be made for the creation of some kind of imperial economic union. As a necessary first step toward integration, Britain should consider the imposition of import duties on foreign goods that would give an advantage to colonial products. There could be no denying that such a measure would involve at least a partial abandonment of the free-trade principles that had guided the country through sixty years of unprecedented economic progress. But times had changed. Britain was faced with "an absolutely new situation," one that could be met successfully only after accepted beliefs had been exposed to rigorous reexamination.[3]

Chamberlain's "Demand for an Enquiry" speech marked the beginning of an intense controversy that ultimately broke his health, ended his active career, split his adopted party, and restored the Liberals to office after ten years of opposition and frustration. As high political drama the story of these events is unmatched, but there was more involved than a mere clash of party platforms or a scramble for elective office. The so-called tariff reform debate that began in 1903 has been described as "the first great debate on Britain's economic future after the passing of her mid-Victorian supremacy."[4] At one level the issues involved were practical—whether

---

[1] The standard biography is the six-volume work *The Life of Joseph Chamberlain,* begun by J. L. Garvin and completed by J. Amery. In addition, see M. Balfour, *Britain and Joseph Chamberlain;* Browne, *Joseph Chamberlain: Radical and Imperialist;* P. Fraser, *Joseph Chamberlain: Radicalism and Empire, 1868–1914;* and Strauss, *Joseph Chamberlain and the Theory of Imperialism.*

[2] Quoted in Amery, *The Life of Joseph Chamberlain* 5:186. (For the complete text see Boyd, ed., *Mr. Chamberlain's Speeches* 2:130–39.)

[3] Ibid., p. 191.

[4] Rempel, *Unionists Divided: Arthur Balfour, Joseph Chamberlain, and the Unionist Free Traders,* p. 9.

to begin a system of imperial preference at all or to use tariffs to retaliate against European and American protectionism. As Chamberlain clearly recognized, there were also questions of ideology at stake. His proposals ran counter to a belief in the virtues of free trade that was widely, if not universally, accepted in every stratum of British society.

At the most important level, the debate over tariff reform involved an effort to assess Britain's economic performance and to compare its power and prospects with those of other states. Then, as now, such an undertaking was far from simple or straightforward. The productive mechanism of a modern industrial nation is a vast arrangement of millions of moving parts. To understand its workings and fix its capacity at any given moment is difficult enough. Predicting how it will function in the future and comparing its operation with those of other, different mechanisms is an even greater challenge. But given the close relationship between economic or industrial capabilities and the capacity to create other forms of power, there can be no doubt of the importance to statesmen of such projections.

Several months after his Birmingham speech Chamberlain told an audience in Glasgow of a recent trip he had made to the Continent.

> I have been in Venice . . . which had at one time a commercial supremacy quite as great in proportion as anything we have ever enjoyed. Its glories have departed.
> . . . When I was there last I saw the great tower of the Campanile. . . . The other day, in a few minutes, the whole structure fell to the ground. Nothing was left of it but a mass of ruin and rubbish. I do not say to you, gentlemen, that I anticipate any catastrophe so great or so sudden for British trade; but I do say that I see signs of decay; that I see cracks and crevices in the walls of the great structure, that I know that the foundations upon which it has been raised are not broad enough or deep enough to sustain it. Now, do I do wrong, if I know this—if I even think I know it—do I do wrong to warn you?[5]

Why did Chamberlain think that he knew these things about Britain's trade and about the country's economic condition more

[5] Speech at Glasgow, 10/7/03, quoted in Amery, *The Life of Joseph Chamberlain* 6:461.

generally? Why did other intelligent contemporary observers disagree so passionately with his diagnosis and with the prescriptions he offered? And why, ultimately, was he unable to persuade his countrymen of the need for dramatic change in national habits and policies?

Background
Losing the Lead

With almost a century of hindsight and the help of modern economic science, it is obvious that the forty years before World War I marked a critical turning point for Great Britain. Whereas in 1870 only England and Belgium could be described as highly industrialized, by 1900 this was no longer the case.[6] The new German nation, the United States, and, to a lesser extent, France, Russia, and Japan were all embarked on a course of sustained, modern economic development. With the passage of time the vast gap that had once separated Britain from all its competitors narrowed and, in some cases, disappeared altogether.

In absolute terms Britain continued to flourish and, indeed, to prosper as it had never done before. Between 1870 and 1900 the country's gross national product grew from £1.317 billion to £2.084 billion, and national income per capita rose from £29.9 to £42.5.[7] London was still the world's financial center,[8] and Britain continued to dominate world trade. In this important latter category, however, there was a measure of relative decline. By one modern-day estimate Britain's share of international commerce fell from 25 percent in 1880 to 21 percent in 1900. During the same period the German share rose from 9 to 12 percent, and the American portion increased from 10 to 11 percent.[9] Looking just at world trade in manufactures, the economic historian S. B. Saul reckons that between 1899 and 1913 Britain slipped from 34 to 31 percent while Germany increased from 23 to 27.5 percent and America's share grew from 11.5 to 13 percent.[10]

[6] Hinsley, "Introduction," in Hinsley, ed., *The New Cambridge Modern History* 11:3.

[7] Mathias, *The First Industrial Nation: An Economic History of Britain, 1700–1914*, pp. 457–58, 467–68.

[8] In 1875, by one estimate, Britain exported £1,050 million of capital; in 1900 the figure stood at £2,400 million. Whether this was a good thing for England can be, and was in fact, debated (Hinsley, Introduction, p. 4). The precise magnitude of Britain's overseas investments remains a subject of lively controversy. See Platt, *Britain's Investment Overseas on the Eve of the First World War: The Use and Abuse of Numbers*.

[9] Wilson, "Economic Conditions," in Hinsley, ed., *The New Cambridge Modern History*, p. 56.

[10] Saul, *Studies in British Overseas Trade, 1870–1914*, pp. 22–23.

The economic picture was not uniformly bleak, but what is apparent in retrospect is that in one critical area of production after another Britain was being displaced by other countries, and especially by Germany and the United States. While British steel output grew significantly at around the turn of the century, for example, that of its principal rivals increased even more dramatically. According to W. A. Lewis, between 1890 and 1907 Britain's output rose from 3.6 to 6.5 million tons. The United States (which had slipped past Britain during the 1880s) went from 4.3 to 23.4 million tons. Starting from a smaller base of 2.2 million, the Germans were able to increase production fivefold to 11.9 million tons.[11] In pig iron Britain surrendered its lead to the United States between 1880 and 1890,[12] and by 1906 Germany, too, had drawn ahead.[13] In 1870 the British produced three times as much coal as their nearest competitors (the Germans), but between 1890 and 1900 the United States expanded its output from 143 to 244 million tons while Britain went from 184 to 228 million tons. By 1914 the British and German figures for coal production were just about equal.[14]

Although contemporary observers had no way of knowing for certain, Britain's rivals were now growing at an overall rate far faster than its own. By one estimate the average annual growth rate in England from the 1860s to the 1880s was 2.4 percent. For the period 1885–1905 this figure fell to 1.9 percent.[15] The economist D. J. Coppock calculates British growth from 1870 to 1913 at 1.6 percent per year and estimates that the United States grew at a rate of 5 percent per annum for the equivalent period while Germany expanded at a 4.7 percent annual rate.[16] A. E. Musson has fixed the annual growth rate in manufactured goods for the period 1873–1913 at 1.8 percent for the United Kingdom, 3.9 percent for Germany, and 4.8 percent for the United States.[17]

The reasons for this difference in growth rates are still a topic of lively debate among economic historians, but its consequences are no longer in dispute.[18] As David Landes has put it, during the period leading up to the First World War there was "a shift from monarchy to oligarchy, from a one-nation to a multi-nation indus-

[11] Lewis, "International Competition in Manufactures," p. 580.

[12] Taylor, *The Struggle for Mastery in Europe, 1848–1918*, p. xxx.

[13] Mitchell, *European Historical Statistics, 1750–1975*, pp. 414–15.

[14] Taylor, *Struggle for Mastery in Europe*, p. xxix.

[15] Mathias, *The First Industrial Nation*, p. 459.

[16] Coppock, "The Causes of the Great Depression, 1873–1896," p. 227.

[17] Musson, "The Great Depression in Britain, 1873–1896: A Reappraisal," p. 208.

[18] Some of the explanations for this phenomenon will be briefly considered in the conclusion to this chapter.

Table 2-1
Percentage Shares of World Manufacturing Production

Period	US	Germany	Britain	France	Russia
1870	23.3	13.2	31.8	10.3	3.7
1881–1885	28.6	13.9	26.6	8.6	3.4
1896–1900	30.1	16.6	19.5	7.1	5.0
1906–1910	35.3	15.9	14.7	6.4	5.0
1913	35.8	15.7	14.0	6.4	5.5

Source: League of Nations, *Industrialization and Foreign Trade*, p. 13.

trial system."[19] In the new oligarchy Great Britain was no longer even first among equals (see Table 2-1). Coppock estimates that in 1870, Britain, the United States, and Germany held 32-, 23-, and 13-percent shares, respectively, of total world production; in 1913 the proportions had changed to 14, 36, and 16 percent.[20] Musson makes similar calculations, indicating the last decade of the nineteenth century as the time during which leadership in manufacturing output passed from Britain to the United States.[21]

This, as nearly as can be discerned, is the reality with which Britain found itself confronted at the beginning of the twentieth century. To understand how that reality was perceived at the time, it is necessary first to ask how contemporary Englishmen thought about the problems of industry, trade, and economic change.

The Dogma of Free Trade

Given the magnitude of their success it is hard to imagine how the mid-Victorians could have avoided a certain smugness. They were proud of their governmental institutions and of the domestic stability that seemed to derive from them, of their Christian culture, their presumably advanced state of moral development, and, increasingly as the notion came into vogue, of their Anglo-Saxon "racial" origins.[22] By the middle of the nineteenth century there

[19] Landes, "Technological Change and Development in Western Europe, 1750–1914," in Habakkuk and Postan, eds., *The Cambridge Economic History of Europe* 6:475.
[20] Coppock, "Causes of the Great Depression," p. 227.
[21] Musson, "The Great Depression in Britain," pp. 208–209.
[22] On mid-Victorian achievements and arrogance see Watson, "The Brit-

ish Parliamentary System and the Growth of Constitutional Government in Western Europe," and Furley, "The Humanitarian Impact," in Bartlett, ed., *Britain Pre-eminent: Studies of British World Influence in the Nineteenth Century,* pp. 101–51. See also Hyam, *Britain's Imperial Century, 1815–1914: A Study of Empire and Expansion*, pp. 15–69, and Gordon, *The Moment of Power*, pp. 113–43.

was a widespread belief (among Englishmen, at least) that Britain had both the capability and the right, indeed the positive obligation, to remake mankind in its own image. Lord Palmerston, foreign secretary and later prime minister, expressed these sentiments with typical bluntness. "We stand at the head of moral, social and political civilization," he said. "Our task is to lead the way and direct the march of other nations."[23]

Underlying this self-confidence, providing the most visible evidence of Britain's superiority to other nations and giving the country the means and the desire to exert its will overseas, was the awesome productive engine of the British domestic economy. Britain was in fact what most Britons at the time probably considered it to be, "the workshop of the world," able to produce and profit more prodigiously than any other nation on earth. This self-descriptive phrase conveyed an image made up of several interlocking components.

First, it was widely recognized that Britain's exalted position rested on its relative level of technological advancement. The nation was in the vanguard of the forces of progress that were transforming the world. This fact was dramatically demonstrated at the Crystal Palace Exposition held in London in 1851, where locals and foreign visitors could view the fruits of the industrial revolution and especially steam engines and locomotives of British design.[24] The so-called Great Exhibition has been described as "the supreme festival of [the] belief of the age in itself,"[25] but it was also more specifically a profound expression of English self-confidence. Queen Victoria described the inauguration of the exhibition as "the *greatest* day in our history, the *most beautiful* and *imposing* and *touching* spectacle ever seen."[26] Several months earlier, as preparations for the grand opening were being completed, the queen had summed up her feelings and doubtless those of many of her subjects. "We are capable," she confided to her diary, "of doing anything."[27]

The "workshop of the world" was not, as the words of the phrase suggested, turned in upon itself. Because the British manufacturer possessed such a lead in the most sophisticated techniques and

---

[23] Hyam, *Britain's Imperial Century,* p. 49.

[24] For an anecdotal account see Morris, *Heaven's Command,* pp. 195–200. David Landes identifies this event as marking "the apogee of Britain's career as the 'workshop of the world,'" but he also notes the presence of some impressive foreign exhibits, particularly a two-ton block of cast steel manufactured by the Krupp works (Landes, *The Unbound Prometheus,* pp. 124, 179).

[25] Oakeshott, *Commerce and Society: A Short History of Trade and Its Effect on Civilization,* p. 258.

[26] Morris, *Heaven's Command,* p. 197.

[27] Ibid., p. 196.

equipment, he was able for a time to outproduce and underbid his overseas competitors. Drawing on the rest of the world for raw materials and food, the nation as a whole could fabricate and export low-cost, high-quality machinery and consumer goods. The net result of these exchanges was that Britain dominated global commerce (a position of advantage that many Englishmen considered to be theirs by "divine prerogative"[28]) and accumulated wealth more rapidly than any other country.

What reasons did contemporary British observers give for their superior material success? The nation's citizens may well have thought of themselves as more vigorous, more inventive, more in harmony with the wishes of the Almighty, than any of their competitors. But judging by the outcome of some of the more important public debates of the period, most of them also believed that their good fortune resulted in the first instance from wise policy, in particular from the triumph of laissez-faire notions of political economy.

Following the publication of Adam Smith's treatise, *An Inquiry into the Nature and Causes of the Wealth of Nations*, in 1776, the idea that minimal government interference in trade and production meant maximum wealth and well-being gained ground at a rapid pace. Smith's theories regarding the benefits of free trade were embellished by scholars like David Ricardo, and they entered the popular vocabulary through the speeches and pamphlets of Richard Cobden and John Bright.[29] By the middle of the century, after a series of intense struggles that tended both to demonstrate and to increase the political power of the new middle classes, most existing government constraints on commerce and, in particular, on overseas trade had been removed. What had begun as "a purely utilitarian and piecemeal movement, thriving on the mild modification of import duties," had become "a doctrinaire force making for complete freedom of trade, backed by a whole philosophy of commercial liberalism and a new popular faith in the virtues of free competitive enterprise."[30]

---

[28] Oakeshott, *Commerce and Society*, p. 251.

[29] The *locus classicus* of laissez-faire thinking concerning international trade is book 4 of Smith's *Wealth of Nations*, "Of Systems of Political Economy." See also Ricardo, *On the Principles of Political Economy and Taxation*. One collection of Cobden's addresses was published at the height of the tariff reform controversy as Cobden, *Speeches on Free Trade*. A useful sampling of laissez-faire thought can be found in Bullock and Shock, *The Liberal Tradition*.

[30] Thomson, *England in the Nineteenth Century*, pp. 77–78. For a fascinating account of the rise and fall of the "liberal creed" see Polanyi, *The Great Transformation: The Political and Economic Origins of Our Time*.

It is possible to exaggerate the uniformity and intensity of Britain's acceptance of the doctrine of free trade. Powerful agricultural interests had to be overcome before import restrictions on food could be removed, and many of those who had opposed repeal of the so-called Corn Laws never reconciled themselves to the new system. Some who benefited from free trade in the 1850s and 1860s turned against it when conditions changed in subsequent decades. Moreover, as will become evident, certain important political figures retained philosophic doubts about the presumed virtues of laissez-faire economics generally and free trade in particular. But there could be no arguing with visible evidence of success. In 1842, before the repeal of several major import duties, Britain's exports were valued at slightly less than they had been at the close of the Napoleonic Wars, around £47 million. By 1870 the nation was selling £200 million worth of goods to overseas consumers.[31] A large part of the credit for this substantial growth seemed clearly to lie with legislation adopted in the intervening period that, by eliminating tariffs, had lowered production costs and increased the efficiency of British industry. As one of Chamberlain's biographers has put it, by the latter part of the nineteenth century, "whatever the historic reality, public opinion . . . was convinced that [England's] unexampled prosperity had been due to Free Trade."[32]

The apostles of free trade believed that commerce was a "grand panacea" for the world's ills.[33] By promoting global exchange they believed themselves to be unleashing a force that would eventually overwhelm national differences and unify mankind.[34] But even hard-headed nationalists who had no time for the cosmopolitan visions of the true believers in free trade were convinced of its benefits. Britain seemed to have profited disproportionately from the general reduction in tariffs that had followed its own abandonment of import duties. There was little reason to think that it could not continue to do so, dominating world trade and maintaining its lead in industry as far ahead into the future as anyone could possibly foresee.

In fact, a good deal of Britain's early success had to do with its

[31] Thomson, *England in the Nineteenth Century*, p. 83.
[32] Amery, *The Life of Joseph Chamberlain* 5:220.
[33] The phrase is Cobden's, ibid., p. 32.
[34] Thus in one famous speech against the Corn Laws, Richard Cobden declared: "I see in the Free Trade principle that which shall act on the moral world as the principle of gravitation in the universe, drawing men together, thrusting aside the antagonisms of race, and creed, and language and uniting us in the bonds of eternal peace" (speech at Manchester, 1/15/46, in Cobden, *Speeches on Free Trade*, p. 187).

substantial head start over other countries. In any case, the classical theory of free trade made no promises of permanent national advantage. Unencumbered exchange meant optimum efficiency and maximum *global* welfare, but it did not guarantee the lasting predominance of any one political unit. The free play of economic forces would undoubtedly result in shifts in comparative advantage in certain crucial industries, and it might also cause one nation to displace another as the leader in overall production and wealth. These were theoretical fine points with which most free traders did not concern themselves.

Inklings of Decline

By the beginning of the 1870s many Englishmen probably believed that "all was for the best in the best of all possible worlds."[35] Not everyone was so complacent, however. As Britain's economic orbit approached its apogee, worried voices began to be heard from a number of quarters. The disparate critical analyses that first appeared in the 1870s and 1880s and would reemerge at the turn of the century tended to resolve themselves into two distinct but related strands: some observers worried that Britain was about to be surpassed (in ways not always clearly specified) by states of enormous size; others began to question whether a continued policy of free trade would be sufficient to maintain the country's early industrial advantage.

Gigantism

The latter half of the nineteenth century seemed likely to be an era of bigness. The 1860s and early 1870s had been marked by a bitter struggle to preserve the unity of the American republic, the creation of a new Italian state, and the emergence of Germany. Russia was engaged in the steady expansion of its empire to the east. Thoughtful observers could not help but notice that the most dynamic powers appeared to be those which were geographically extensive. In its issue for 20 December 1869 the *Pall Mall Gazette* pointed out that "the tendency of men's minds everywhere has been to the aggregation of small and the better consolidation of large States, and neither in Europe, nor in America does the course of events seem to promise well for the continued independence of weaker powers."[36]

Big states were strong states and little ones, weak. Moreover, big

[35] Hobsbawm, *Industry and Empire*, p. 126.

[36] Quoted in Bodelsen, *Studies in Mid-Victorian Imperialism*, p. 85.

states tended "naturally" to swallow up their smaller neighbors. It was a vision of international life that anyone who had heard of Darwin would find familiar, if not necessarily congenial. Precisely why it was that bigness and power should be so strongly correlated was not always spelled out at first, although later the linkage would be drawn more explicitly between extensive empires and substantial, secure markets. Presumably the connection was indirect, with greater surface area implying a larger population and a more generous endowment of natural resources. "Little England" was merely, in the words of a later imperial enthusiast, "an island off the northwest coast of Europe . . . that . . . has an area of 120,000 square miles and a population of 30 odd million."[37] As such it was at a clear disadvantage relative to the newly emerging superstates. Whatever the magnitude of its existing superiority, there was real reason to fear that Britain might not be so much overtaken as transcended by its rivals.

To many Britons, the answer to this new challenge seemed first of all to lie in consolidation of the existing white, English-speaking portions of the empire. Early versions of this argument were used to oppose the drift toward imperial separation that was alleged to have characterized the decade of the 1860s. Gladstone's administration of 1868–1874 came in for particularly intense criticism, and the Government's colonial secretary, Lord Granville, was accused of trying to speed the process by which the colonies might eventually become independent of the motherland. Such a policy was fully in keeping with the dominant liberal doctrine, which held that overseas possessions were costly, burdensome, and unnecessary. At best, they were regarded as possible trading partners (although the benefits of commerce could be enjoyed by both parties without one formally ruling the other); at worst, they required expensive garrisons and periodic interventions to save them from misguided adventures. The response to these claims from the growing imperialist camp was that existing policies ignored the opinions of Britain's kinsmen overseas, lacked grandeur, and, most important, tended to cut England off from a much needed source of additional power.[38]

[37] John Seeley, quoted in ibid., p. 165.

[38] For the development of British imperialist thinking see (in addition to Bodelsen) James Butler, "Imperial Questions in British Politics, 1868–1880," and Ronald Robinson, "Imperial Problems in British Politics, 1880–1895," in Benians, Butler, Carrington, eds., *The Cambridge History of the British Empire* 3:17–64, 127–80. See also Porter, *The Lion's Share: A Short History of British Imperialism, 1850–1970;* Thornton, *The Imperial Idea and Its Enemies: A Study in British Power;* Tyler, *The Struggle for Imperial Unity (1868–1895).*

Support for imperial unification came from a variety of sources, but it tended always to have the same idea at its core: the consolidation of smaller units meant size, which meant, in turn, power. In 1869 Charles Dilke (soon to become an influential Liberal MP) published a popular book on his travels through the empire in which he urged the unification of the Anglo-Saxon "race." "It is no exaggeration," he wrote, "that in power the English countries would be more than a match for the remaining nations of the world."[39] Dilke hoped that what he called "Greater Britain" might triumph where Great Britain alone could not.

The writer James Anthony Froude was anxious to preserve the "vigor" of the English people, a quality he feared was being choked by overcrowding of the industrial homeland. The "boundless room" for expansion that the colonies provided would "reproduce the old English character and the old English strength over an area of a hundred Britains." If bound together by "a common cord of patriotism," Canada, Australia, New Zealand, the Cape Colony, and England could match even the United States. But, Froude warned, "if we cannot rise to the height of the occasion, the days of our greatness are numbered. We must decline in relative strength, decline in purpose and aim, and in the moral temperament which only the consciousness of a high national mission confers."[40]

The fullest and most influential expression of this theme of strength through unity would come several years later when the period of rapid territorial expansion (as opposed to the mere consolidation of the existing empire discussed in the 1860s and 1870s) was about to get under way. John Seeley, a professor at Cambridge University, put forward the notion in an 1881 lecture that the fundamental tendency in English history was toward the acquisition of territory and the increase of national power. This trend was not continuous, since Britain had obtained and lost an empire before. Nor was it inevitable; wise decisions were needed to ensure its continuance. As Seeley explained, his generation had two choices: to consolidate the English-speaking colonies (in which case England would "take rank with Russia and the United States in the first rank of state, measured by population and area, and in a higher rank than the states of the Continent") or to permit those colonies to become completely independent nations.[41]

In the often-quoted summation to his second course of lectures

[39] Dilke, *Greater Britain*, p. 545.
[40] Froude, "England's War (1871)," in *Short Studies on Great Subjects*, p. 399.

[41] Seeley, *The Expansion of England: Two Courses of Lectures*, p. 19.

(given in 1882), Seeley identified the federal system of government, steam, and electricity as the developments that made possible
states on a larger scale than had previously been imagined. And
he predicted that the day was not long distant when Russia and
the United States would "surpass in power the states now called
great as much as the great country-states of the sixteenth century
surpassed Florence." If Britain failed to consolidate its empire, it
would be reduced "to the level of a purely European Power looking
back, as Spain does now, to the great days when she pretended to
be a world-state."[42]

One public figure touched quite deeply by the writings of men
like Seeley, Froude, and Dilke was Joseph Chamberlain.[43] Three
years after becoming mayor of Birmingham in 1873, he was elected
to Parliament and, as a Liberal, served in Gladstone's 1880 cabinet
as president of the Board of Trade. Within six years, however,
Chamberlain had broken with his party over the question of Irish
home rule. From that point on he became an increasingly visible
and vocal spokesman for imperial unification and, somewhat later,
for the seizing of additional territory in the "unclaimed" tropical
regions of the world. In 1887 Chamberlain decided that, if he ever
held high office again, he wanted to be colonial secretary.[44] It was
the empire, he felt quite certain, that held the key to England's
future.

Protectionism

Britain's triumphant example and, as time passed, its exports of
investment capital and machine goods served to stimulate the development of other modern economic powers. In an ironical but
important way, therefore, the early success of the world's "first industrial nation" helped to set the stage for its subsequent relative
decline.[45]

The proliferation of industrialism had not advanced very far before some anxious Englishmen began to notice the presence of potential competitors. As early as the 1840s, a select parliamentary
committee on "Import Duties and the Exportation of Machinery"

[42] Ibid., p. 350.

[43] Chamberlain referred to Seeley
and Froude in his later speeches and,
according to his biographer, was so
impressed with Seeley's *Expansion
of England* that he sent his eldest son
Austen to Cambridge to study with
the great man (Garvin, *The Life*

of Joseph Chamberlain 3:9).

[44] Garvin reports that Chamberlain
confided this ambition to his future
wife in 1887 (ibid.).

[45] On this point see Peter Stearns,
"Britain and the Spread of the Industrial Revolution," in Bartlett, ed., *Britain Pre-eminent*, pp. 7–30.

had remarked on Prussian efforts to imitate British machines.[46] Concern over changing circumstances is also reflected in an 1856 pamphlet by Richard Burn of Manchester entitled *The Darkening Cloud*.[47] Burn, whose arguments have been described as foreshadowing "with astonishing accuracy" those that would be made in later years, called attention to Britain's tendency to import more than it exported and its growing dependence on foreign sources of food.[48]

In the prevailing climate of optimism and self-assurance, warnings like these were not taken very seriously, and the cheery complacency of the majority must have been infuriating to those less certain of what lay ahead. To the claim that there was no evidence of difficulty or decay, the *Annual Register* for 1866 and 1867 gave two answers: "The first that when signs become clearly visible, the catastrophe will perhaps have ceased to be avertible, the other, that there may be signs already, though not precisely the same that have appeared before the decadence of other great empires." The basis of British power was the country's advantage in industry and commerce; "if she forgets this, she is lost . . . to the extent of having to give up her lead, and ceasing to be a first-rate power."[49]

For obvious reasons, the economic Jeremiahs of the late 1860s and early 1870s went largely unheeded.[50] These were years in which business was good and exports (led by the rapid development of demand for railway equipment on the American continent) were booming.[51] In the early 1870s Britain was averaging £230 million in exports per year, greater than the combined total of the United States and Germany.[52] But the year 1873 marked the beginning of difficulties that were to stretch well into the 1890s. For the first time in nine years the annual trade returns showed a drop in the value of British exports, and from 1873 to 1877 the decline continued.[53]

---

[46] See Austen Albu's introduction to Williams, *Made in Germany*, p. xiii.

[47] Burn, *The Darkening Cloud: Or England's Commercial Decline and the Depression of Our National Industry from the Inroads of Foreign Competition.*

[48] Brown, *The Tariff Reform Movement in Great Britain, 1881–1895*, p. 4.

[49] Hyam, *Britain's Imperial Century*, p. 98.

[50] Tyler gives two more examples of the genre: In 1870, a D. Grant wrote that England had lost "the singularity of her position" and that the country's dream of being the workshop of the world was already a thing of the past. Two years later Jehu Mathews published a study of imperial federation that suggested that there were "sound reasons for fearing that England's commercial supremacy might already be in danger" (Tyler, *The Struggle for Imperial Unity*, p. 12).

[51] Saul, *Studies in British Overseas Trade*, p. 17.

[52] Hoffman, *Great Britain and the German Trade Rivalry, 1875–1914*, p. 7.

[53] Saul, *Studies in British Overseas Trade*, p. 18.

There was a recovery at the close of the decade, followed by another slump after the 1880s began.

Taken as a whole, the years between 1872 and 1896 are usually referred to as the "Great Depression." Expanded worldwide production of industrial and agricultural goods helped to keep prices and profits down, making for an uncertain business climate, slower overall growth, and periodic high unemployment. At first the downturn seemed temporary, but after several years uneasiness began to mount.[54] In Britain the diminished expansion in exports was the symptom that caused most concern.[55] Although exports picked up after 1879, the rate of growth was not what it once had been. A periodic swell in foreign demand was followed in 1884–1886, 1891–1894, and 1896–1898 by a renewed slump.[56]

Across Europe governments responded to hard times by reimposing or raising tariffs that had been lowered during the brief period of Continental enthusiasm for free trade.[57] The intent of such policies was to protect domestic producers from foreign imports, but the larger effect was to retard recovery in those countries (like Britain) which relied heavily on exports. In all, trading conditions were far less favorable than they had been during the 1850s and 1860s.

The Great Depression's impact on the development of thinking inside Britain needs to be considered from four different angles. In the first place, the onset of difficulties encouraged a wide-ranging public discussion of trade, trade policy, and the health and prospects of the economy in general. Out of this there emerged a critique of free trade, which provided much of the intellectual foundation for Chamberlain's 1903 tariff reform campaign. Public criticism provoked an official response that was generally (although not uniformly) optimistic. The debate over the benefits of free trade also helped to shape the attitudes of important figures in the Conservative party. Finally, it marked the emergence and general acceptance of certain statistical indicators of economic performance that were to dominate subsequent discussion.

Free Traders versus Fair Traders. Critics of laissez faire maintained that Britain's domestic economy and its foreign trade were both

[54] Hoffman, *Great Britain and the German Trade Rivalry*, p. 14.

[55] Brown, *The Tariff Reform Movement*, p. 11.

[56] Zebel, "Fair Trade: An English Reaction to the Breakdown of the Cobden Treaty System," pp. 164–65.

[57] France raised its tariffs in 1872 and 1882, Germany did so in 1879, and Russia, in 1883 and 1887. Tariff levels were already high in the United States but rose still higher in the 1890s (ibid., p. 162).

being undermined by the government's failure to respond in kind to foreign protectionism. This charge had three specific counts: first, it was alleged that the closing of overseas markets was causing severe harm to export businesses; second, cheap imports were blamed for destroying Britain's agriculture and weakening its industry; finally, it was claimed that the net imbalance in the nation's trade of imports over exports was draining the country of capital. Under a regime of "one-sided free trade," Britain was losing its earlier advantages and being surpassed as the world's leading industrial power.

The pained outcries of landowners and businessmen most directly affected by poor trading conditions first made the economic outlook a topic for public consideration. In August 1877 the Bradford *Chronicle and Mail* fretted that "our trade with America has fallen . . . and with Germany the fall is, if anything, greater. . . . Unless the nations of Europe and the United States can be induced to treat with us on fair terms . . . our foreign trade, as regards Bradford, is doomed to decay."[58] This lament was taken up more generally in the charter of the National Fair Trade League, which in 1881 called for the imposition of import duties on foreign manufactured goods. Such duties were viewed by the league as bargaining tools, to be reduced once other countries agreed to lower their barriers against British goods.[59]

Demands for retaliatory protection were based on the assertion that exports had been stagnating, a notion that the defenders of free trade were inclined to reject. In a lecture before the Statistical Society in 1882, the chief of the Board of Trade's statistical department, Robert Giffen,[60] criticized the evidence put forward by the fair traders to support their claims. In the recent controversy, Giffen complained, there had been "a great rush of figures, indicating that those who use them have hardly the rudiments of statistical ideas, whether true or false."[61] Giffen noted that claims of a decline in exports often failed to account for shifts in the price of materials from which finished goods were manufactured. If those prices fell (as they had in the case of raw cotton, for example), then so too

[58] Brown, *The Tariff Reform Movement*, p. 11.

[59] Zebel, "Fair Trade," pp. 167–69.

[60] Sir Robert Giffen (1837–1910) was a former assistant editor of the *Economist* (1868–1876) and a well-known author and advocate of free trade. He held his job at the Board of Trade for twenty-one years, keeping track of government trade statistics from 1876 to 1897.

[61] Giffen, *The Use of Import and Export Statistics*, pp. 1–2.

would the value of certain exports. This did not mean, however, that trade was necessarily suffering.[62]

Whatever was happening to exports, there could be no mistaking the flood of foreign imports that had begun to arrive in increasing volume and diversity on Britain's shores. Cheap raw materials and (since the repeal of the Corn Laws) food had provided vital fuel for the earlier stages of the industrial revolution. By the second half of the century, however, the opening of vast areas of the American plains to cultivation and the development of railroads and refrigerator ships to bring goods to market were helping to drive high-cost British producers of grain and meat out of business.[63] The migration of agricultural production to areas that had a comparative advantage was something that the theorists of free trade had long since accepted as both inevitable and (because of its benefits for consumers and nonagricultural producers) even desirable. But the full playing out of the process left Britain dependent on foreign producers and, in a world still made up of separate and sometimes hostile nation-states, vulnerable to supply disruptions and possible naval blockades. This was a condition that frightened farmers, of course, but that also gave pause to some who had no immediate, material interest in agriculture.[64]

During the last decades of the century it was not only food and raw materials but also manufactured goods that increasingly found their way into the homes and workplaces of average Britons. This fact became especially noticeable after the passage of the 1887 Merchandise Marks Act, which forced foreign exporters to label goods sold in the United Kingdom with the name of the country of manufacture. For the first time Englishmen began to realize how much they were buying from overseas.[65] In 1896 Ernest Williams, a journalist for the *New Review,* tapped a deep wellspring of anxiety over

[62] Ibid., pp. 17–18. See also Giffen's 1887 essay on "The Recent Rate of Material Progress in England," in the collection of his works entitled *Economic Inquiries and Studies* 2:99–144.

[63] In the late 1860s the United Kingdom still produced three-quarters (by value) of all the grain, meat, dairy products, and wool it consumed. By the late 1870s this had fallen to little more than one-half (Musson, "The Great Depression in Britain," p. 225).

[64] Even those most directly affected were slow to realize what was happen-

ing. Benjamin Brown reports that it was not until the 1890s that foreign competition rather than bad weather and bad luck was accepted as the principal cause of the depression in agriculture (*The Tariff Reform Movement,* p. 146). By the turn of the century there was widespread concern that free trade had left England dangerously exposed to blockade and starvation. See, for example, Lilly, "Collapse of England," pp. 771–84.

[65] Hoffman, *Great Britain and the German Trade Rivalry,* p. 234.

this new situation with articles and, later, a best-selling book.[66] Britain was pictured as being inundated with German machines, tools, household goods, and even children's toys. Several years later a rather pale imitation by F. A. McKenzie detailed in similar fashion the challenge posed by *The American Invaders.*[67]

The most cursory perusal of the trade returns during the last third of the century revealed one fact about which there was very little debate. From the 1860s at least, the value of imports had consistently exceeded the value of exports. By ordinary assumptions such a situation should not have been possible. Yet Britain seemed to be buying more than it was selling overseas. How was the difference being made up, if not with earnings from exports? The answer seemed to be that, under the system of "free imports," the nation was living off its capital, exporting securities to finance current spending. Presumably this could not go on forever.

Robert Giffen referred in the early 1880s to one version of the alarmist argument that purported to prove that the country had accumulated £1,000 million in debts, which, if their repayment should ever be demanded, would bring about a financial collapse.[68] Such claims seem to have driven the levelheaded Giffen practically to distraction. In any case, he spent a good deal of time and effort during the 1880s, 1890s, and beyond arguing that the supposed "excess of imports" was the result of peculiarities in the trade returns. By failing to record "invisible exports" (such as the substantial earnings derived from shipping and insurance) and by not accounting for earnings from overseas investments, the returns badly misstated Britain's position.[69] In fact, as Giffen would argue later, a correct assessment of the situation would show that "the excess of imports about which so many people are concerned does not at all imply that we are diminishing our capital abroad. It merely shows that our charges to foreign countries . . . are much greater than the so-called exports which appear in our trade returns."[70]

Official Analysis. Free traders and fair traders clashed in the press and in Parliament, but there were no real changes in government policy. For the most part the successive Liberal and Conservative regimes of the 1880s and 1890s exhibited what one historian has

---

[66] See Williams, *Made in Germany.*

[67] McKenzie, *The American Invaders: Their Plans, Tactics, and Progress.*

[68] Giffen, "Use of Import and Export Statistics," p. 20.

[69] Ibid., pp. 20–46. See also a book by the free trader Jeans, *England's Supremacy,* pp. 109–10.

[70] Giffen, "Are We Living on Capital?" in *Economic Inquiries and Studies,* p. 287.

called a "peculiar and sustained" official optimism about trade and economic conditions.[71] The authorities did periodically feel a need to give public justification for their inaction, however, and these utterances provided a soothing counterpoint to the sound and fury of public debate. In 1885, under pressure from the fair traders, the Conservative prime minister Lord Salisbury appointed a commission to report on the "Depression of Trade and Industry."[72] The final report of the royal commission was issued in 1886, and it contains a delicate blend of good news, bad news, and moral uplift that was to set the tone for subsequent official pronouncements.

The commission concentrated on four key sectors (iron, textiles, shipbuilding, and agriculture), but, taking the nation as a whole, it concluded that "the production of commodities generally and the accumulation of capital . . . has been proceeding at a rate more rapid than the increase of population."[73] Britain was getting wealthier but at the same time there could be no doubt that profits and agricultural prices were falling. For these unpleasant features of the contemporary situation, the commission provided a whole range of possible explanations, from worldwide overproduction to a tight money supply.[74] Demand in the home market had been hurt by the drop in agricultural purchasing power and by the penetration of foreign-made goods. Trade restrictions on the Continent had suppressed profits in export industries even further, and foreigners were cutting into traditional British markets in Africa and Asia.

On this last point the commission sounded a tentative note of alarm. What was happening overseas might not be simply temporary. "In neutral markets, such as our own colonies and dependencies, and especially in the East, we are beginning to feel the effects of foreign competition in quarters where our trade formerly enjoyed a practical monopoly. The increasing severity of this competition both in our home and in neutral markets is especially noticeable in the case of Germany."[75]

The German challenge raised the larger question of British

[71] D. C. M. Platt explains this as being due in large part to the continuing commitment to noninterference of most career bureaucrats. "The official," he writes, "was not a free agent. . . . His views were likely to be laissez-faire and Free Trade." This was especially true at the Board of Trade, where almost everyone was "a member of the Cobden Club . . . a Free Trader to the core" (*Finance, Trade, and Politics in British Foreign Policy, 1815–1914,* p. 104).

[72] Brown, *The Tariff Reform Movement,* p. 64.

[73] "Royal Commission on the Depression of Trade and Industry: Final Report," *Parliamentary Papers* 23 c4893 (1886), p. xi.

[74] Ibid., pp. xvii–xviii.

[75] Ibid., p. xx.

competitivenesss. As so many other observers were to do, the commissioners blamed "the trading class of this country" for "falling off
. . . from the more energetic practice of former periods."[76] What
was needed was not protectionism but more old-fashioned vigor.
The search for new markets and the effort to hold onto existing
ones would have to receive "much more attention . . . [from] our
mercantile classes" if Britain's commercial position was to be maintained "in the face of the severe competition to which it is now
exposed."[77]

In their recommendations, the majority of the commission urged
greater emphasis on technical and foreign language education,
some increase in the gathering of trade-related information by diplomatic and consular officials overseas, and the accumulation of
more statistics on home trade.[78] The commissioners seem to have
been uncertain just how serious or long-term Britain's problems
were. On the one hand, they were resigned to a measure of inevitable relative decline:

> We cannot, perhaps, hope to maintain, to the same extent
> as heretofore, the lead which we formerly held among
> the manufacturing nations of the world. Various causes
> contributed to give us a position far in advance of other
> countries, which we were able to hold for many years; but
> those causes could not have been expected to operate per-
> manently, and our supremacy is now being assailed on all
> sides.

On the other hand, England was still England:

> We have still the same physical and intellectual qualities
> which gave us so commanding a lead; and we see no rea-
> son why, with care, intelligence, enterprise and thorough-
> ness, we should not be able to continue to advance.[79]

In the end it still seemed a bit difficult to take Britain's challengers
seriously. After all, the commissioners asserted, it was largely care-
lessness that had permitted "foreign rivals, with less natural facilities for production, to compete with us in markets which have been,
and might again be, our own."[80]

Over the course of the next ten years, the Board of Trade made
occasional reports to Parliament comparing the foreign trade of
Britain with that of other countries. These were more narrowly

---

[76] Ibid.
[77] Ibid., pp. xxiv–xxv.
[78] Ibid., p. xxiv.
[79] Ibid.
[80] Ibid., p. xxiii.

focused than the report of the royal commission, and they tended to confirm its more optimistic judgments while calling into question some of its warnings. In this vein, in 1888, Robert Giffen reported on a Board of Trade examination of the available statistics, undertaken "to throw light on . . . the alleged greater relative progress which the imports and exports of certain foreign countries . . . have made."[81]

Using figures collected on a common basis to correct for peculiarities in national bookkeeping techniques, Giffen claimed that, between 1875–1877 and 1884–1885, British exports had increased by 8 percent. During the same period those of Germany had risen 16 percent and those of the United States, 35 percent, while French exports had fallen 13 percent.[82] Even if not as rapidly as that of some of its rivals, Britain's export trade *was* increasing. Giffen blamed the use of anecdotal evidence from consular reports for creating "the popular impression . . . that German trade is gaining ground everywhere at the expense of English exports." In fact, Giffen concluded, "our predominance in the great common markets remains substantially what it was ten years ago."[83]

In 1894, under a Liberal government, Giffen made the same argument in a continuation of his earlier report. Comparing 1884–1885 with 1890–1892, Giffen found export increases of 10, 5, 14, and 26 percent for Britain, Germany, France, and the United States, respectively.[84] The conclusion to be derived from these figures was that "there is no weakening in the hold of the United Kingdom (in comparison with its chief competitors) upon either the import or the export trade of the world."[85] At the same time, Giffen's own estimates revealed the possibly disturbing fact that Britain's trade was not growing as rapidly as that of at least two of its rivals.

Conservative Misgivings. For Conservative and Liberal governments alike, the accepted official posture was one of guarded optimism. No responsible politician, whatever his views, was yet willing to challenge openly the country's faith in free trade. Nevertheless, the fair-trade agitation of the 1880s and 1890s did have an important impact on the thinking of the two leading figures of the Con-

---

[81] "Statistical Tables Relating to the Progress of the Foreign Trade of the United Kingdom, and of Other Countries, in Recent Years, with Report to the Board of Trade Thereon," *Parliamentary Papers* 1043 c5297 (1888), p. 3.

[82] Ibid.

[83] Ibid., p. 10.

[84] "Statistical Tables Relating to the Progress of the Foreign Trade of the United Kingdom, and of Other Countries, in Recent Years," *Parliamentary Papers* 80 c7349 (1894), p. 3.

[85] Ibid., p. 14.

servative party: Robert Cecil, third marquess of Salisbury, and his nephew Arthur James Balfour.

Salisbury and Balfour had similar backgrounds, attitudes, temperaments, and qualities of mind.[86] They were both aristocratic, wealthy, eccentric, well-educated, and possessed of intellectual interests outside politics. Salisbury dabbled in scientific experimentation and maintained a fully equipped laboratory on the grounds of his estate, while Balfour published several scholarly works on philosophic subjects and at one time considered a career as a university professor.

Balfour was his uncle's protégé and close political ally, serving him first as a private secretary under Disraeli and, in successive Salisbury administrations (1885–1886, 1886–1892, 1895–1902), as secretary of the Local Government Board, secretary of state for Scotland and Ireland, and lord of the Treasury. On becoming prime minister for the last time in 1895, Salisbury made Balfour his deputy and gave him the post of Conservative party leader in the House of Commons. When he stepped aside in 1902, the old man made certain that his nephew would take up where he had left off.

Both Balfour and Salisbury had longstanding doubts about the laissez-faire gospel. It seemed to them somewhat vulgar and excessively materialistic, and it had the dubious distinction of having been the tool with which Britain's new middle classes forced themselves into national politics. Salisbury was unwilling on both practical and intellectual grounds to accept any absolute doctrine that claimed to apply equally in every situation. During the 1881 fair-trade debate he wrote: "In spite of any formula, in spite of any cry of Free Trade, if I saw by raising the duties on luxuries, or threatening to raise it, I could exercise pressure on a foreign power, inducing it to lower rates and give relief, I should pitch orthodoxy and formulae to the winds and exercise pressure."[87]

Similarly, Balfour (who as a young man had been a close friend of the family of Liberal leader William Gladstone) became a Conservative because he objected to John Stuart Mill's sweeping philosophic stance.[88] In an article published in the early 1880s, Balfour

[86] The standard biography of Salisbury is Cecil, *Life of Robert, Marquis of Salisbury.* Also helpful are Pinto-Duschinsky, *The Political Thought of Lord Salisbury, 1854–68,* and Smith, ed., *Lord Salisbury on Politics.* On Balfour see Dugdale, *Balfour: A Life of Arthur James Balfour.* See also Judd, *Balfour and the British Empire;* Young, *Arthur James Balfour;* Zebel, *Balfour: A Political Biog-*

raphy. For good short sketches see Churchill, *Great Contemporaries,* pp. 61–75, 237–57. See also Tuchman, *The Proud Tower,* pp. 1–69.

[87] Brown, *The Tariff Reform Movement,* p. 60.

[88] Egremont, *Balfour: A Life of Arthur James Balfour,* p. 42. See also A. Balfour, *Chapters of Autobiography,* p. 85.

criticized Richard Cobden for placing excessive emphasis on material factors, and he hinted that the early protectionists might not have been entirely incorrect. Opponents of Corn Law repeal had been attacked as holding views that were self-serving and manifestly false. "But at this moment the vast majority of the civilized world advocate false economic theories of precisely the same kind; and . . . [they] imagine those theories to be to their advantage."[89] Could all of them be wrong, Balfour wondered, and only Britain correct?

In the emerging view of the Conservative leadership, trade was to be treated in the same manner as every other issue of public policy, empirically and on a case-by-case basis.[90] Protection might be justified if conditions demanded it. The question was whether Britain's economic situation had changed sufficiently to warrant modification of a traditional policy. On this point both Salisbury and Balfour were far more willing to consider the possible accuracy of pessimistic assessments than were their firmly free-trade contemporaries in either party.

What kept the Conservatives from traveling too far down the road toward protectionism was more a shrewd calculation of political realities than any unwillingness to examine accepted beliefs. After the Liberal party split in 1886, the so-called Liberal Unionists (who favored developing the empire but continued to believe in free trade) moved into alignment with the Conservatives. Salisbury was anxious not to offend his new allies with any radical departure from accepted commercial policy. Although he toyed with the possibility of tariff "retaliation" during the 1890s, Salisbury kept a careful restraint on any movement toward broader protective measures.[91] After the turn of the century, Balfour tried with less success to continue his uncle's policies. Ultimately Balfour's failure had precisely the result that had been predicted: it split the Conservatives and reunited the Liberals.

Facts and Figures. Underlying the discussion of tariffs and retaliation was a growing feeling of unease about Britain's relative economic performance and position. If, as the fair traders claimed, the country was allowing its lead to be eaten away by the rising industrial powers, then there might very well be reason to consider changes in national policy. But how could the truth of the matter be established?

---

[89] A. Balfour, "Cobden and the Manchester School," in his *Essays and Addresses,* p. 201.

[90] Brown, *The Tariff Reform Movement,* p. 63.

[91] Ibid., pp. 65–83.

One of Chamberlain's biographers has written that "it is difficult in this over-documented age to realize how little statistical information was available even to Government Departments at the turn of the century."[92] The development of economic ideas and techniques did not allow for the calculation of total domestic (let alone foreign) national income, and there was therefore no reliable way of estimating growth rates or comparing overall economic capabilities across national boundaries.[93] In addition to these conceptual problems, laissez-faire assumptions restricted to a very limited number those economic issues that fell within the official purview. As a result there were precious few reliable figures available on prices, production in various sectors, investment, capital movements, or even total employment.

Virtually the only statistics kept over a long period of time were the Customs Department's record of imports and exports.[94] These showed fluctuations in the volume, value, and direction of Britain's overseas trade and, as Giffen's Board of Trade reports demonstrated, they could also be used to make rough comparisons of the progress of commerce in different countries. As discussion of the nation's condition progressed, the trade returns emerged as *the* indicator of Britain's economic performance. The famed Cambridge economist Alfred Marshall would later explain this development in a letter to Arthur Balfour: "The statistics of foreign trade are specially definite and accessible; and since the fluctuations of business confidence and activity are reflected in foreign trade among other

---

[92] Amery, *The Life of Joseph Chamberlain* 5:284.

[93] The absence of such aggregate figures was lamented at the time. Thus in 1903 a Government report observed that in order to determine the state of the economy, "the best single figure for our purposes, if it were available, would be the total volume or value of the production of the year. Unfortunately, no such figure can be given, and the existing statistics of production for particular industries (e.g. coal and iron) are too limited in range to enable sound inferences to be drawn as to the rate of increase or decrease of productive industry as a whole" (PRO, Cab. 37/64/20, "Memorandum on the Present Position of Employment and Trade," Board of Trade, 3/30/03).

[94] Amery asserts that "there were no statistics except the trade returns" (*The*

Life of Joseph Chamberlain 5:220). This is not strictly true. By the end of the century the government was able to assemble a number of raw measures of economic activity, including the amounts of coal, pig iron, and various metals produced, cotton consumed, gross property and profits assessed for income tax purposes, Bank of England discount rates, food item prices, and numbers of paupers and amounts of poor relief paid out each year. These could be used to show that the economy was still growing (something that all but the most fanatical protectionists were usually prepared to accept), but they were good for little else. See "Statistical Tables Showing the Progress of British Trade and Production, 1854–95," *Parliamentary Papers* 76 c8211 (1896). See also PRO, Cab. 37/64/20.

things, the habit has grown up of using export statistics as a prima facie indication of the time and extent of such fluctuations."[95]

By themselves the trade statistics were not even a very good measure of Britain's total overseas commerce, let alone its overall economic activity. As one Government report cautioned:

> [The] test of our economic position . . . most widely employed is that afforded by the total value or volume of our foreign trade, taken as a whole, or of the exports of British produce. These figures are of great value . . . when taken in conjunction with others, though, taken singly they are subject to many qualifications not always sufficiently considered. Thus they represent only a comparatively small fraction of the total trade transactions of the year, and the expansion or contraction of this margin may not always harmonize with the expansion or contraction of production as a whole. . . . A large part of the external transactions of the United Kingdom, e.g. the movement of securities, the earnings of shipping, insurance of ships and cargoes, etc. do not figure or only figure partially in the trade accounts.[96]

Despite such warnings, by 1903 the trade returns had come to be accepted as a sort of common currency by all parties to the debate over the nation's economic health. As will be discussed, this fact had certain important, distorting effects on the way in which that discussion unfolded. Trade figures may have been better than no figures at all, but as a tool for capturing the complexities of the period through which Britain was passing, they were clearly inadequate.

Crisis
Opening Moves, 1895–1897

By the time he reached the Colonial Office in 1895, Joseph Chamberlain was already convinced that dramatic steps would have to be taken if Britain was to retain its economic position. While serving as president of the Board of Trade under Gladstone in 1882, he had begun to develop doubts about the wisdom of continuing a policy of "one-sided free trade."[97] These misgivings had only grown during the intervening decade of relatively poor economic conditions.

[95] PRO, T 168/54, "Memorandum on Fiscal Policy and International Trade," Alfred Marshall, 8/31/03.

[96] PRO, Cab. 37/64/20.
[97] Amery, *The Life of Joseph Chamberlain* 5:210.

At the same time, as has been described, Chamberlain was also increasingly fascinated by the potential of a united and perhaps even an enlarged British Empire. Gradually these two strands seem to have come together in his mind to form a coherent image of the future. The British Isles as such might be too small to compete economically with the new, monolithic superstates. But if Britain could forge its empire into a single commercial unit (albeit one made of widely scattered components), the country would be a match for all comers. In pursuit of this vision, Chamberlain was led to a plan of action that he would follow, with twists, turns, and occasional false starts, for the remainder of his life.

The economic downturn that characterized the early 1890s helped to win Conservative and some Liberal support for the formal annexation of new territories, mostly in the "unclaimed" tropical regions of Africa. There was growing concern that the imperial "scramble" that had begun in earnest in the 1880s would result in ever larger portions of the world being sealed off behind protective barriers. Not only the mother countries but the increasingly sizable empires under their control might then be diminished as markets for British trade.[98] The need (as the Liberal Imperialist leader Lord Roseberry put it) to "stake out claims for posterity" and hold open areas that might otherwise be swallowed by hostile powers became a staple of imperialist rhetoric.

Less spectacular than expansion but in some ways more intractable was the problem of imperial consolidation. During the 1880s various schemes for political, military, and economic federation had been put forward, but all faced serious objections either at home or in the colonies. At the first Colonial Conference, held in 1887, a South African delegate had proposed that all components of the empire (including Britain) impose some common tariff on imports of nonimperial goods. Colonies that already had import duties to generate revenues and protect their infant industries would simply add on the new tariff.[99] Such a plan was presumably intended to promote imperial trade and a feeling of unity while generating revenue for maintaining the British fleet at distant colonial stations.

Whatever the specifics, for Britain a discussion of economic union meant serious consideration of protective tariffs, and this was a divisive subject that Salisbury preferred to avoid. In his role

[98] Robinson, "Imperial Problems in British Politics," p. 161.

[99] Tyler, *The Struggle for Imperial Unity*, p. 167. For details of the so-called Hofmeyr proposal see Jebb, *The Imperial Conference*, pp. 63–69. In 1894 there were also suggestions from the colonies for a system of imperial preference (Garvin, *The Life of Joseph Chamberlain* 3:178).

as host the prime minister therefore sought to steer the conference toward less ambitious projects.[100] Chamberlain was not yet a member of the Government, but he was sympathetic to the call for commercial federation, and in 1888 he told an audience that it was "the duty of every statesman to do all in his power to maintain and increase" the intraimperial trade upon which "a great part of our population is dependent at the present moment."[101] Nevertheless, Chamberlain recognized that there was as yet little chance that the British public would support any kind of preferential (and hence protective) scheme.[102]

One of Chamberlain's first acts on taking over as colonial secretary was to seek evidence with which to persuade his colleagues and his countrymen of the need for commercial unification. In November the Colonial Office issued a circular requesting that each of the colonies provide information regarding the penetration of "foreign" (i.e., non-British) goods into their markets. "I am impressed," Chamberlain wrote the various governors, "with the extreme importance of securing as large a share as possible of [our] mutual trade . . . for British producers and manufacturers, whether located in the Colonies or in the United Kingdom."[103] The results eventually collected showed some increase in the share of colonial trade conducted with foreigners, but there was none of the dramatic evidence of decline and disaster for which Chamberlain must secretly have hoped.[104]

If statistics failed to rouse the country, then more tangible political events might very well do the trick. At the beginning of the next year Chamberlain seized on the crises in relations with Germany and the United States to promote the idea of union in general and economic union in particular.[105] In January of 1896 he noted that

---

[100] Ibid., p. 121. See also his opening remarks of 4/4/87 in "Proceedings of the Colonial Conference 1887," *Parliamentary Papers* 56 c5091 (1887).

[101] Speech at the Devonshire Club, 4/9/88, in Boyd, ed., *Mr. Chamberlain's Speeches* 1 : 322.

[102] In 1890 he is reported to have told a Canadian visitor interested in an imperial preference plan that public opinion would be against it (Zebel, "Joseph Chamberlain and the Genesis of Tariff Reform," p. 131).

[103] Chamberlain's despatch of 11/28/95 is contained in "Trade of the British Empire and Foreign Competition: Despatch From Mr. Chamberlain to the Governors of Colonies and the

High Commissioner of Cyprus and Replies Thereto," *Parliamentary Papers* 60 c8449 (1897), p. 16.

[104] From 1884 to 1894 the foreign share of total colonial imports had increased by only 6 percent, from around 26 percent to roughly 32 percent. Britain's principal competitors here as elsewhere were the United States and Germany. The key to their success, the report concluded somewhat haughtily, was their willingness to provide "low class" products, but there was every likelihood that these would be followed someday by higher-quality goods (ibid., pp. 2–12).

[105] These events will be discussed briefly in chapter 4.

the hostility and jealousy of other nations had left Britain in a state of "splendid isolation" and urged that everything possible be done to "improv[e] our communications, by developing our commercial relations, [and] by cooperating in mutual defence."[106] Two months later he advised that if the problem of unification was to be dealt with "in a practical spirit," it would have to be approached "on its commercial side."[107]

Still riding the wave of imperial good feeling, in June Chamberlain came forward with his own federation plan. He was now prepared openly to identify a commercial union as the necessary first step in creating a more united empire, one more like Germany or the United States. Toward this end, the colonial secretary proposed the creation of a "British Zollverein or Customs Union." Within the limits of the empire there would be "free trade," but each of its elements could impose whatever duties seemed suitable on the products of foreign powers. Britain, for its part, would place tariffs on those goods (like meat, wool, and sugar) in which the colonies specialized.[108]

If Chamberlain was right and only a more economically unified empire would allow Great Britain to predominate well into the twentieth century, then his plan had a certain appeal. That there would be costs associated with a "British Zollverein" was undeniable. Even modest duties on imports of food and raw materials would raise the cost of living for English consumers and increase the production expenses of domestic manufacturers. The colonies, on the other hand, would have to give up an important source of revenue and lower the barriers to British goods behind which they had been nurturing their own industries, thereby exposing themselves to the full weight of the mother country's productive might.[109]

The poor conditions in trade and industry that characterized 1896, and the widespread public attention to Britain's relative economic position coincident with Chamberlain's proposals, gave at least the hope of their success at home.[110] In August the president

---

[106] Speech in London, 1/21/96, in Boyd, ed., *Mr. Chamberlain's Speeches* 2:362.

[107] Speech before the Canada Club, 3/25/96, quoted in Garvin, *The Life of Joseph Chamberlain* 3:179–80.

[108] Speech before the Congress of Chambers of Commerce of the Empire, 6/9/96, in Boyd, ed., *Mr. Chamberlain's Speeches* 2:367–71.

[109] See Tyler, *The Struggle for Imperial Unity*, pp. 164–71.

[110] It was during the summer of 1896 that journalist Ernest Williams gained great attention by warning that "the industrial glory of England is departing and England does not know it" (*Made in Germany*, p. 1). According to Ross Hoffman, "Mr. Williams' alarmist views shook England as no similar piece of writing had done. The press of the summer of 1896 was full of *Made in Germany*" (Hoffman, *Great Britain and the German Trade Rivalry*, p. 247).

of the Board of Trade, Charles Ritchie, responded to the commotion by requesting that his staff undertake a detailed study comparing Britain with its principal competitors. Aware of the limited utility of the import-export tables for long-range projections, Ritchie advised that it would be "desireable that [an] examination should not be confined, as in the Returns at present published by the Board of Trade, to the statistics of the countries from which imports are received and to which exports are sent, but that any figures in the possession of the Board should be comprehensively dealt with."[111]

The report that followed from this directive concentrated on France, Germany, and the United States, and it contained a wide array of population and production statistics along with the usual trade indicators. On a variety of important issues the board's conclusions were not much different from those reached by the Royal Commission on the Depression eleven years earlier. Britain was still considered to be ahead of its rivals, competition was acknowledged, and self-help was prescribed as the appropriate response. In certain ways, however, the protectors of free-trade orthodoxy were now more willing to admit the existence of possibly unfavorable trends.

Although Britain was far ahead of either Germany or the United States in its "power of manufacture for export," these countries appeared to be experiencing more rapid growth. "Beginning from a lower level, each country is for the moment travelling upwards more rapidly than we who occupy a much higher eminence." Moreover, assuming continued peace, Germany, America, and to some extent France seemed "certain to increase their rate of upward movement." Pressure on Britain's position could therefore be expected to grow more intense with the passage of time; the question was no longer one of temporary setbacks but rather of permanent, structural change. "Their competition with us in neutral markets, and even in our home markets, will probably, unless we ourselves are active, become increasingly serious. Every year will add to their acquired capital and skill and they will have larger and larger additions to their population to draw upon."[112]

Still, there was no reason to adopt a mercantilist view of the world in which gains for others necessarily involved a loss for Britain. Richer neighbors should mean more trade and hence more

[111] Letter from Ritchie to Sir Courtenay Boyle, 8/19/96, in "Board of Trade Memorandum on the Comparative Statistics of Population, Industry and Commerce in the United Kingdom and Some Leading Foreign Countries," *Parliamentary Papers* 83 c8322 (1897), p. 1.
[112] Ibid., p. 29.

wealth. But if Britain hoped to keep up, the country would have to try harder than in past years. "The change of conditions must be recognised, and we can scarcely expect to maintain our past un-doubted pre-eminence, at any rate without strenuous effort and careful and energetic improvement in method." [113]

On the question of how this improvement could be assured, the board's staff held firmly to the truths that had sustained its prede-cessors. "The solution of the question of how best to develop and increase our competing power is one to which the State can only give limited assistance. . . . What the Government can do is to fa-cilitate the supply of accurate and carefully collected information and in the discharge of this duty . . . we are somewhat behind-hand." [114]

Perhaps a wider array of government statistics would have done more than merely aid the progress of British trade. As things stood, there simply was no evidence to sustain a uniformly gloomy view of the nation's prospects and little to convince agnostics of the need for anything so uncertain as Chamberlain's unification plan. The tendency to worry about the economy seemed to some to be rather foolish. Lord Salisbury claimed to find the nation's penchant for panic bewildering and faintly amusing. "I have often thought how strange is the contrast between men in their individual and in their collective capacities," the prime minister told an audience in the spring of 1897.

> The individual Briton is the boldest, the most disregard-ing man as to danger you can find anywhere on earth. . . . The collective Briton, however, is as timorous as a woman; he sees danger everywhere. If a nation increases its ex-ports for a single year, the downfall of British trade is at hand. If any nation finds an outlet for its trade . . . in-stead of rejoicing at the amount of natural resources which is produced for human industry, he says there is a rival to whom our fall will be due. [115]

By summer it was clear that Chamberlain's proposal could not overcome the opposition that it had stimulated both at home and in the colonies. At the Colonial Conference that he had called for June to coincide with the Queen's Jubilee, Chamberlain avoided raising

---

[113] Ibid.
[114] Ibid.
[115] Speech to the Associated Cham-bers of Commerce, 3/10/97, quoted in Hoffman, *Great Britain and the German Trade Rivalry*, p. 224.

the whole subject of an imperial Zollverein, preferring instead to concentrate on schemes for military and political integration.[116]

For the next five years Chamberlain would preserve a noticeable silence on "imperial free trade" and on the general question of Britain's economic condition. This was due partly to his increasing preoccupation with problems of foreign and colonial policy. In addition, the setbacks of his first years in office seem to have convinced him that there was an uphill battle to be faced in persuading the country to accept his vision of the future. According to his biographer, Chamberlain decided in 1897 that "if he moved again with power for closer union, he would have to stake himself upon a revolutionary effort to reverse altogether the national commercial policy of Cobden and Peel."[117] A frontal assault on free trade would require, in turn, proof that the doctrine had failed or that it was no longer adequate. Chamberlain would have to find some way of convincing the nation that its relative economic decline was real and serious, that what had happened already was only a prelude to an absolute loss of industrial preeminence, and that these disturbing trends could be reversed only by the prompt adoption of appropriate policies.

Opportunity Knocks, 1902

Events that could not be foreseen in 1897 gave Chamberlain the chance to reopen his crusade. In October 1899 mounting tensions between Boer and English settlers in South Africa erupted into open fighting. At first it appeared that the conflict would be quickly resolved by a crushing display of armed imperial might. By December, however, the British army had suffered serious setbacks. Reinforcements were dispatched, and what had begun as a skirmish blossomed into ferocious, full-scale war. Conventional operations continued for over a year, giving way gradually to a brutal form of guerrilla warfare that dragged on until the spring of 1902.[118]

By the time the war ended, Britain was in the throes of a severe financial crisis. To raise desperately needed revenues the government had been forced to boost taxes and to impose new duties on certain imports and exports. In April 1902 the chancellor of the Exchequer announced that imported grain would now be subject

---

[116] See his introductory remarks of 6/24/97 in Keith, ed., *Selected Speeches and Documents on British Colonial Policy* 2 : 216–19. See also the account of the Conference in Garvin, *The Life of*

Joseph Chamberlain 3 : 188–92.
[117] Garvin, *The Life of Joseph Chamberlain* 3 : 194.
[118] For an extremely detailed account see Pakenham, *The Boer War*.

to a tariff of the sort that had last been used in the 1860s. This was a controversial step and, in the eyes of the free traders, a dangerous measure, because it could easily be misinterpreted as a move back toward protectionism. The purpose of the new duty, as government officials were eager to point out, was simply to generate funds and not to shield domestic farmers from foreign competition.[119]

To Chamberlain the new tariff was a gift from heaven. Once again a national emergency had brought home the importance to Britain of its empire; once again an interest in strengthening imperial ties coincided with a downturn in the nation's trade.[120] This time, however, there was an instrument for action readily at hand. Instead of proposing "free trade within the Empire" with all its complications, Chamberlain could now simply suggest that Britain make a slight change in preexisting policies. The duty on imported corn was already in place. Why not eliminate it for grain grown inside the empire? If the colonies chose, they could respond by lowering their tariffs on British exports of manufactured goods. The result would not be a true "Imperial Zollverein," but it would be a step in the right direction.

In May 1902 Chamberlain publicly broached the subject of "reciprocal preference." His reason for doing so, as he made quite plain to his audience, was a deep concern over the economic future of Britain.

> The position of this country is not one without anxiety to
> statesmen and careful observers. The political jealousy
> . . . the commercial rivalry more serious than anything we
> have yet had, the pressure of hostile tariffs, . . . the pres-
> sure of [state] subsidies, it is all becoming more weighty
> and more apparent. . . . Even the industries and com-
> merce which we thought to be peculiarly our own, even
> those are in danger.[121]

The only way to meet these challenges was by drawing the empire more closely together, something that might be impossible if Britain held rigidly to a policy of free trade.

> If by adherence to economic pedantry, to old shibboleths,
> we are to lose opportunities of closer union. . . . If we do
> not take every chance in our power to keep British trade

[119] The financial crisis will be discussed in detail in chapter 3.

[120] Zebel, "Joseph Chamberlain and the Genesis of Tariff Reform," p. 156.

[121] Speech at Birmingham, 5/16/02, quoted in Amery, *The Life of Joseph Chamberlain* 5 : 17.

in British hands, I am certain we shall deserve the disasters which will infallibly come upon us.[122]

Chamberlain's new plan received only the most lukewarm endorsement from his Government colleagues. Having bowed to the need for revenue-raising tariffs on corn, the Board of Trade was now prepared to grant that offering preference to the colonies might be desirable as a "concession to sentiment." In other words, the political benefits of modest differential tariffs could conceivably be worth their economic cost to the British consumer. But any push for full integration would require the colonies to make serious cuts in their own tariffs, something that they were unlikely to want to do. Besides, given that Britain only carried on one-third of its trade within the empire, steps designed to limit all foreign imports seemed likely to do the country more harm than good.[123]

The question of reciprocity was brought to a head at the third Colonial Conference, held in London during July 1902. Following a precedent that Canada had established independently in 1897, the colonial governments agreed among themselves to grant unilateral preference to all imported British goods. The mother country was urged to respond in kind but reciprocal action was not demanded.[124]

Chamberlain was ecstatic. The time had come, he wrote to the South African high commissioner, to "take some new steps of a rather sensational kind."[125] Accordingly, Chamberlain urged the cabinet to remit the duty on imports of Canadian grain and proposed that he be authorized to make a tour of the self-governing colonies to see if similar arrangements could not be worked out.

Having been in power as prime minister for only four months, Arthur Balfour was understandably reluctant to give full endorsement to Chamberlain's plans. As he explained in a memorandum to the king: "It is suggested that, while retaining the shilling duty on corn, as regards *foreign* importation, our *Colonies* should be allowed

[122] Speech at Birmingham, 5/16/02, quoted in Gollin, *Balfour's Burden: Arthur Balfour and Imperial Preference,* p. 25.

[123] PRO, Cab. 37/62/120, "Memorandum on Preferential Trade Arrangements with the Colonies," Gerald Balfour, President of the Board of Trade, 6/30/02. The Board of Trade calculated that in 1901 England had imported £416.5 million from foreign countries and £105.5 million from the colonies. Exports for the same year stood at £175 million to nonimperial nations and £105 million to the colonies (PRO, Cab. 37/62/113, "Statistics of Trade of the United Kingdom with the Various Colonies and Possessions," Board of Trade, 6/18/02).

[124] Amery, *The Life of Joseph Chamberlain* 5:54.

[125] Chamberlain to Alfred Milner, 9/4/02, quoted in ibid., p. 80.

to import it free. There is a very great deal to be said in favour of this proposal. But it raises very big questions indeed . . . and the Government which embarks upon it provokes a big fight." [126] Despite Balfour's misgivings and strong objections from Charles Ritchie (now chancellor of the Exchequer),[127] on 19 November the cabinet gave provisional acceptance to the colonial secretary's plan; later that month he departed for South Africa.[128]

When Chamberlain returned to England in March 1903, he discovered that the Government's position had been changed in his absence. By threatening to resign and leave the budget request for the upcoming year in a shambles, Ritchie had succeeded in persuading Balfour to reverse course and abandon reciprocal preference.[129] When the new budget was introduced in April, the chancellor of the Exchequer announced that the duty on corn had been eliminated entirely after only one year's service. It was this betrayal and Ritchie's public insistence that the government would never abandon free trade that caused Chamberlain to give his "call for an inquiry" speech in Birmingham on 15 May 1903.

Internal Debate, June–September 1903

The colonial secretary's speech was followed by several weeks of increasingly heated discussion in the press and in Parliament. Worried that his cabinet was about to be split between the so-called Unionist Free Traders (led by the Liberal Unionist duke of Devonshire) and Chamberlain's supporters, Arthur Balfour moved to impose a "ministerial truce," which would prohibit further public declarations on fiscal policy. Under the terms of this agreement, which went into effect at the beginning of June, ministers were to forgo "further explicit statements of individual opinion" while the government was "allowed officially to collect information upon the effects of the proposed policy." [130]

For the next four months the cabinet struggled to come to some common understanding of the overall economic situation and some agreement, however narrow, on the ways in which it could best be met. Officials from the Board of Trade and the Treasury were con-

[126] Ibid., p. 117.
[127] Ritchie objected that preference for Canada meant "the abandonment of the principle . . . which was established more than half a century ago" and raised the probability that the Conservatives would be blamed for raising food prices (PRO, Cab. 37/63/148, "Preferential Treatment," brief for the chancellor of the Exchequer, 10/31/02, pp. 3, 7).
[128] Ibid., p. 123.
[129] Gollin, *Balfour's Burden*, p. 31. See also Rempel, *Unionists Divided*, pp. 25–27.
[130] Balfour to Devonshire, 6/4/03, quoted in Rempel, *Unionists Divided*, p. 38.

sulted and, in addition, both Balfour and Chamberlain sought the views of outside experts.[131] From these discussions there emerged three distinct assessments of Britain's condition (Chamberlain's, the governmental free traders', and Balfour's) and three matching prescriptions for policy. Unable to obtain a consensus, the prime minister was eventually forced to purge the cabinet of both its extremes in order to strike out on his own course.

Chamberlain's Assessment

Without Chamberlain, as Balfour would observe rather ruefully, a debate over tariff policy might have been delayed a little longer. There was little hope, however, that it could have been suppressed forever. "The question of 'Fiscal Reform,' which has now burst into so violent a flame, is not new," the prime minister wrote to Devonshire, "it has feebly smouldered for many years. . . . Chamberlain's action has precipitated the crisis; has made it more acute, and more dangerous; but it could not I think in any case have been long postponed."[132] Clearly it was the colonial secretary who drove the tariff reform debate, and it was to his views that others in the Government were forced to respond.

As noted, Chamberlain's general understanding of the situation facing Britain had been set quite early, perhaps as early as the 1880s. Without its colonies and the markets, money, and manpower they could provide, England would soon be displaced as the world's greatest power. Imperial federation and, in particular, economic unification were thus essential for national survival. Unification, whether through a customs union or some system of preferential treatment, required that the nation modify its traditional policy of free trade. In other to shake the prevailing belief in laissez faire, Chamberlain realized that he would have to prove that it was no longer operating to Britain's benefit. He was thus brought at last into an inescapable confrontation with the facts. Chamberlain knew what he wanted them to say or, to be more fair, he knew what they *must* say. Now he would have to use them to persuade others of a relative decline in the nation's economic power that might not yet

[131] Chamberlain would eventually assemble a brain trust that included the economists Sir Vincent Caillard, W. A. S. Hewins, W. J. Ashley, and William Cunningham as well as the geographer Sir Halford Mackinder. See Amery, *The Life of Joseph Chamberlain* 5:288–90, and Rempel, *Unionists Divided,* p. 65. For Hewins's own account of his role see Hewins, *The Apologia of an Imperialist,* pp. 62–109. Balfour consulted economists Percy Ashley and Alfred Marshall.

[132] BM, Add. Mss. 49770, Balfour to Devonshire, 8/27/03.

be fully tangible. As he admitted to the economist Robert Giffen, "Figures are most dangerous things in the hands of inexperienced people, still I must work with the tools I have, and although I am sceptical, even of Official returns, I cannot well be accused of unfairness if I adopt them."[133]

Like his principal opponents, Chamberlain rested his case squarely on the evidence contained in the trade returns. From these he concluded first and most importantly that "British exports have been stagnant for ten years." Moreover, he asserted that the figures "would have shown an immense decline but for the increase of Colonial trade and the larger export of Coal."[134] Colonial absorption of imports from Britain was well and good, so long as it could be preserved. Britain's increasing reliance on coal exports, however, indicated to Chamberlain and his allies that the country was slipping as a provider of manufactured goods and becoming increasingly dependent on the sale of an expendable raw material.[135]

Under the existing policy of free imports, England's home markets were exposed to the dumping of foreign goods sold at below cost by the great industrial combines of Europe and the United States. For this reason Chamberlain predicted that "British industries will be in the most serious danger when Germany and America have large over-production." The solutions to all these problems were evident in the successful policies of other powers. "Tariffs and Preference, which might remedy [these] evils, are consistent with a growth and progress of protected nations enormously greater than our own."[136]

Although he presented his bill of particulars as the "four facts [we have] to go upon,"[137] Chamberlain's third and fourth points, at least, were pure speculation. They nevertheless indicate the direction in which his thinking had developed by the summer of 1903. Preferential treatment of colonial food products was necessary to ensure imperial markets for British manufactured goods. Now that he had raised the dread subject of tariffs, Chamberlain was prepared to push his argument one step further. Protection might be necessary not only to promote unity or even (as the fair traders had always claimed) to provide the Government with an instrument of

[133] JC 18/18/66, Chamberlain to Robert Giffen, 11/2/03.
[134] Chamberlain to duke of Devonshire, 7/25/03, quoted in Amery, *The Life of Joseph Chamberlain* 5:364.
[135] W. J. Ashley, one of Chamberlain's principal advisers, explained that "in exporting coal, Great Britain is evidently living upon its capital, for it can never be replaced" (Ashley, *The Tariff Problem*, p. 104).
[136] Amery, *The Life of Joseph Chamberlain* 5:364.
[137] Ibid.

retaliation against foreign powers; it might actually, in and of itself, be a good thing for British industry.

This view was reflected in a plan prepared by two of Chamberlain's few allies inside the bureaucracy. In a memorandum circulated in early July, G. L. Ryder and T. J. Pittar of the Customs Department observed that British imports had grown in value by 50 percent in the preceding thirty years while the value of the nation's exports had increased only 10 percent. Even this last figure was suspect, because, as Chamberlain also noted, "the portion of our exports that consists of a Capital asset, viz: Coal, has grown much more than other exports." To cope with the situation and to head off further damage, Ryder and Pittar proposed a 3-percent duty on food (half of which would be remitted in the case of colonial imports) and a 7-percent tariff on all imported manufactured goods, to be increased as necessary. In order to lessen the strain that might be imposed on the working man by higher food duties, existing taxes on certain consumer items like tea would be simultaneously reduced.[138] This was essentially the plan that Chamberlain would put forward in the fall after he had left the Government.

The Free Traders' Assessment

Chamberlain approached the available evidence with a firm conviction that Britain was declining. His principal opponents carried with them an equally strong belief that, whatever else might be true, protection was a bad thing. Where the colonial secretary was inclined to see indications of decay, the Government's free traders, in the cabinet and the various bureaucracies, looked for signs of hope or at least for evidence that what was happening was the inevitable result of the operation of natural forces.

In general, the members of the cabinet who opposed protection agreed with the secretary of state for Scotland, Lord Balfour of Burleigh, that "the onus of proof lies on those who propose . . . change." [139] By the end of the summer, in the view of the free traders, that proof had simply not been forthcoming. The investigation

[138] BM, Add. Mss. 49780, "Can Our Import Duties Be So Modified As to Become a Means of Promoting Our Export Trade, and Lightening the Present Charge on the Food of the People?" Ryder et al., 7/13/03. An earlier version of this plan is contained in a memorandum entitled "Mr. Chamberlain's Scheme of Preferential and Protective Duties," circulated on 7/4/03. It appears likely that Chamberlain drew on these papers in his subsequent letter to the duke of Devonshire quoted above.

[139] PRO, Cab. 37/65/54, "Memorandum on Fiscal Policy by Balfour of Burleigh," Balfour of Burleigh, 8/19/03.

initiated by Balfour had yielded little of value. As the duke of Devonshire complained to the prime minister in August,

> The inquiry to which I assented and which I understood
> was to be undertaken was an inquiry into the results of
> fifty years of a policy of Free Imports, its results as to the
> Trade, External and Internal, the Industries and Wealth
> of the country, and as to the condition of the people. This
> inquiry has been largely carried on in the Press and on
> the platform. It is vigorously asserted that in all these re-
> spects the policy has been . . . relatively—if not abso-
> lutely—a failure. These assertions are equally positively
> denied. . . . Which set of assertions do we . . . believe to
> be the true one?[140]

Devonshire warned against the wisdom of "making a new departure, uncalled for by any existing evils, but based solely on abstract
arguments as to evils which may possibly come into existence in the
future."[141] Charles Ritchie, Chamberlain's nemesis and the chancellor of the Exchequer, was equally unmoved by the evidence presented and claimed that he found nothing in it to alter his original
views. On the contrary, he wrote, the papers distributed to the cabinet tended to confirm his expressed opinion "that there is nothing
in the state of the country which calls for such a momentous change
in its fiscal policy as that which is proposed."[142]

Perhaps the clearest statement of the governmental free traders'
position appears in a Treasury memorandum written just as the debate was about to burst again into public view.

> Though all the evidence on the subject has been diligently
> ransacked by the advocates of a change of policy, it cannot
> be said that they have succeeded in producing more than
> isolated instances of disturbance to particular industries
> . . . which have produced nothing more than surface-
> ripples on the whole volume of industry of the country.
> . . . No forces have been proved to be at work to which
> this country cannot adjust itself easily and advantageously
> as it has hitherto done. The failure to produce contrary
> evidence is in effect admitted by those who try to frighten
> us with visions of the evils with which we may be beset at

---

[140] BM, Add. Mss. 49770, Devonshire
to Balfour, 8/12/03.
[141] Ibid.

[142] PRO, Cab. 37/66/58, "Preferential
Tariffs," C. T. Ritchie, 9/9/03, p. 9.

some future day. In these matters the future may be left
to take care of itself.[143]

What exactly was it that caused Chamberlain and his supporters
such alarm? The stagnation of exports, Devonshire pointed out, "is
the principal, if not only, subject of complaint."[144] Some ministers
were prepared to grant that there might be something to this claim.
"I do not say that there are no features of a disquieting nature in
connection with our trade," Balfour of Burleigh admitted, but certainly nothing to indicate a serious danger to what he termed the
nation's "trading prospects." "I am unable," he declared, "to see
that the information collected by the Board of Trade bears out the
very alarmist view taken on this subject."[145]

The free traders at the Treasury Department approached the
question of Britain's commercial performance with somewhat more
precision. Comparing 1882 with 1902, they concluded that the
value of Britain's imports had gone up 28 percent, twice as much as
the value of its exports over the same period. "Our exports have
lagged," the Treasury confessed, "and they would appear to lag a
good deal more if coal were excluded from the comparison, as
some people contend."[146] The notion that coal exports were bad
because they represented a loss of natural wealth was, however, dismissed as nonsensical.

Still, it had to be admitted that the nation's exports were "not as
buoyant as they might be." Whether this could be taken as "a sign
of lack of prosperity . . . much less of national decadence" was an
entirely separate question.[147] By manipulating price indexes the
Treasury was able to show that a more wholesome situation existed
than appeared at first glance. The Great Depression had been
characterized by a significant drop in average prices; thus, if imports and exports were valued at contemporary prices and compared across time, their growth would seem more sluggish than if
some common index was employed. If trade was measured in constant 1882 prices, for example, imports could be shown to have
risen in total value by 56.6 percent while exports would jump a
healthy 39.4 percent.[148]

Wherever they looked, the Treasury Department's analysts could
find few signs of the problems that so troubled Chamberlain. Trade

[143] PRO, Cab. 37/66/62, "Will Our
Purchasing Power Run Short?" Treasury, 9/25/03.
[144] BM, Add. Mss. 49770, Devonshire
to Balfour, 9/4/03.

[145] PRO, Cab. 37/65/54, pp. 8, 4.
[146] PRO, Cab. 37/66/55, "The Fiscal
Problem," Treasury, 8/25/03, p. 24.
[147] Ibid., p. 25.
[148] Ibid., p. 26.

might be a bit sluggish, but almost every other available measure of national wealth, from savings to coal consumption and numbers of paupers, showed a significant improvement. "In the twenty years compared, there has been an increase in excess of the proportionate increase of population. . . . It will be admitted, even by those who are dissatisfied with our present system, that in spite of it the statistics point to a tolerably satisfactory state of things."[149]

The defenders of free trade in the cabinet and throughout the bureaucracy saw no need for a departure from present policies and nothing to convince them that change would not actually be harmful to British interests. For the most part they admitted to little concern over the direction of events and no fear about what the future might bring.[150] Instead, they concentrated their attention on shooting holes in Chamberlain's plans.

Imperial preference was a relatively easy target. Food duties on selected items would tend to drive up the cost of all grain, whether produced at home or abroad, and would therefore increase the cost of living. This would be politically unpopular, and it would also tend to turn the British working man against his brethren in the colonies.[151] The introduction of preference might also produce friction between the different parts of the empire. Given the range of goods produced in the various colonies, Britain would have to go to great lengths (including perhaps the imposition of a range of additional import duties) to treat each equally.[152]

There was thus a real danger that preference would weaken the empire rather than strengthen it. Whether such a scheme would help British industry was also open to question. Britain already provided its possessions with a good portion of their imports, and it was not obvious that they could absorb much more. Those colonies with high tariff barriers might be either unable or unwilling to lower them enough to have much of an effect on the home country's export business. Others, like India, already had very low duties. If they were cut for British goods, the Indian government would be deprived of much-needed revenue; if they were raised to foreign imports and kept low for Britain, India's substantial European trade would probably be damaged by foreign retaliation.[153]

[149] Ibid., pp. 26–27.
[150] Some supporters of free trade outside the Government were, as will be shown below, either more insightful or more candid.
[151] BM, Add. Mss. 49780, "Preferential Treatment, Notes on Some Points Connected With," E. W.

Hamilton, Treasury, 6/6/03.
[152] On this point see part 1 of the Treasury's review of "The Fiscal Problem" in PRO, Cab. 37/66/55. See also PRO, Cab. 37/65/45, "Preferential Tariffs and Retaliation," Treasury, 7/29/03.
[153] PRO, Cab. 37/65/39, "Preferential

The case against preference was summed up in a memorandum prepared by Edward Hamilton of the Treasury Department in June 1903. "The Preferential system . . . seems to be fraught with danger to the Empire: It may imperil its trade, hamper its finance, lead to strained relations with foreign countries, drag Colonial questions into Party politics, and increase the difficulty of the struggle for life [in] the poorest classes of the community, as well as hinder the prosperity of the mother-country as a whole."[154]

If preference was bad, retaliatory tariffs were worse. In a parliamentary democracy they could not be modulated quite so easily as the protectionists seemed to suggest; once in place they would produce powerful lobbies dedicated to their perpetuation. Imposing tariffs most likely would lead to a commercial war of spiraling duties and counterduties. Given Britain's reliance on trade, there was little reason to expect that the country could succeed at such a competition.[155]

As to the supposed "unfair practices" that were given as justification for protecting British industries, there was no reason to think that they were part of a deliberate plan of attack on Britain.[156] Even if foreign trusts and cartels were dumping cheap goods in the British market, the effects might not be altogether bad. Inexpensive imported steel, for example, could be used to make lower-cost items for export, thereby increasing the competitiveness and the profit margins of domestic businesses.[157] What dumping there was could not go on forever.[158] Nor could it be reliably shown to have caused all the damage for which it was blamed. One Government report on the subject concluded that "it is often in perfect good faith that decay is attributed to dumping while its true cause is to be found in the adoption by other firms of new processes and new mechanical applications which make for economy. . . . They are the legitimate children of competition, whether by the foreigner or by

---

Tariffs in their application to India," India Office, 6/10/03.

[154] See Hamilton's memo of 6/6/03 cited in note 151 above.

[155] As the Treasury pointed out, "A war of tariffs is what two can play at; and, though it is generally assumed that the country which we intend to fight will, as soon as it sees the muzzles of our guns pointed at her, cease to do what we object to her doing, is it not quite possible, if not probable, that we shall come off worsted in the fight?"

(PRO, Cab. 37/66/55, pp. 44–45).

[156] PRO, Cab. 37/66/56, "Most-Favoured-Nation Treaties v. Retaliation," author not indicated, 8/29/03.

[157] PRO, Cab. 37/66/57, "The Export Policy of Trusts in Certain Foreign Countries," Board of Trade, 8/03. The board concluded judiciously that foreign dumping was "neither entirely injurious nor entirely beneficial" to Britain.

[158] PRO, Cab. 37/66/55.

home rivals." [159] In this view, natural causes and not some hideous man-made disease were to blame for what few problems the nation was in fact experiencing.

Balfour's Assessment

The man who approached the whole question of tariff reform and the underlying problem of determining Britain's economic position with something most resembling an open mind was Arthur Balfour. Skeptical both of Chamberlain's sweeping forecasts and of the cheery certainty of the die-hard free traders, the prime minister believed that the entire trade question should be dealt with in what he termed "a spirit of cautious moderation." [160] This was in part a matter of intellectual preference, but it also reflected the reality of the emerging political situation. Balfour had to do what he thought best for the country while holding his party together and keeping the opposition out of power. It was to prove a difficult, and ultimately impossible, assignment.

Like Chamberlain, Balfour believed that increased imperial economic cooperation was a good and perhaps (although he did not usually stress the point) necessary thing. In a speech in Parliament on 28 May the prime minister asserted that *some* scheme of the sort being put forward by Chamberlain would eventually have to be adopted because "if the British Empire is to remain as it is at present, a series of isolated economic units [then] it is vain for us to hope that this branch . . . of the great Anglo-Saxon race is destined to have the great industrial and political future which undoubtedly lies before the United States of America." [161] This was an obvious imitation of the colonial secretary's rhetoric, and it does not reflect Balfour's usual style of argument. In private the prime minister was far more cautious about the idea of imperial preference. "There is much to be said for [it]," he wrote to the king, "but . . . it is most imprudent to attempt to 'rush' it either in the Cabinet or in the Country." [162]

Before his tariff reform inquiry had even gotten under way, Balfour had already reached the tentative conclusion that preference was a political impossibility. Unlike Ritchie he did not oppose it on principle, and, in fact, as he told the duke of Devonshire in early

[159] PRO, Cab. 37/65/42, "Conditions and effects of 'Dumping,'" Treasury, 7/7/03, p. 9.

[160] BM, Add. Mss. 49770, Balfour to Devonshire, 8/27/03.

[161] Speech in the House of Commons, 5/28/03, reprinted in A. Balfour, *Fiscal Reform Speeches, 1880–1905*, p. 38.

[162] Balfour to King Edward, 5/27/03, quoted in Rempel, *Unionists Divided*, p. 34.

June, "If I could have it on my own terms, I am disposed to think I should take it. . . . My hesitation . . . chiefly arises from doubts as to its practicability, rather than its expediency. I question whether the people of *this* country will be sufficiently tolerant of the protective side of the scheme, or the people of the Colonies sufficiently tolerant of its free trade side."[163] Nothing that Balfour heard from the free traders could possibly have weakened his conviction on these points, nor do his initial assumptions about preference appear to have been undermined by consultation with several private economic advisers.[164]

With preference and imperial unity at least temporarily out of reach, most of the prime minister's considerable intellectual energies were concentrated on determining what was happening to British industry. On this question Balfour was inclined, as he told the House of Commons, to believe that Britain's position was "now entirely different" than what it had been sixty years before.[165] Since the adoption of free trade and, in particular, during the last twenty years of the century, a great deal had happened. "We have seen, to begin with, a tariff wall steadily raised against us in every one of the great countries with whom we desire to deal. We have seen . . . an enormous growth of the trust system working behind tariffs."[166] These factors combined to permit the dumping of foreign goods in Britain, a practice that cut into the profits of domestic producers and imperiled "the provision of adequate capital for carrying on great modern industries."[167]

The professional economists whom the prime minister consulted during the summer of 1903 gave him further, although still only partial, support for his pessimism. In July, Percy Ashley wrote that the nation's export trade was, as the protectionists were claiming, "almost stationary." Britain's commerce had been damaged by foreign tariffs and by the industrial development that its own sales of coal and machine tools had helped to stimulate.[168] Where all this

[163] BM, Add. Mss. 49770, Balfour to Devonshire, 6/4/03.

[164] Balfour asked both Percy Ashley and Alfred Marshall about the likely incidence of a tax on imports. Ashley replied that this would depend heavily on the elasticity of demand for the goods being taxed (BM, Add. Mss. 49780, Percy Ashley to Balfour, 6/5/03). Marshall concluded that a preferential duty on foreign grain would drive up the cost of all grain and benefit producers at the expense of consumers (PRO, Cab. T 168/54,

"Memorandum on Fiscal Policy").

[165] Speech in House of Commons, 5/28/03, in Balfour, *Fiscal Reform Speeches*, p. 32.

[166] Speech in House of Commons, 6/10/03, in ibid., p. 49.

[167] Speech at Constitutional Club, 6/26/03, in ibid., p. 61.

[168] "It is an interesting question," Ashley wrote, "how far we are by our exports . . . helping to industrialize our clients, and to make them in the future less our customers" (BM, Add. Mss. 49780, Ashley to Balfour, 7/1/03).

was heading remained uncertain. It seemed apparent that the industrialization of other nations would create "very serious difficulties" before the country was able to "adapt itself to the new order of things." It had become "quite evident that some industries must go. We cannot . . . hope to hold the cotton trade . . . we cannot expect to command (in fact, we have already ceased to command) the iron and steel."[169]

Still, there was no reason to be excessively gloomy. "Taking such indices as we have," Ashley concluded, "the capital of the country is not declining." Great Britain might be losing out in certain sectors and the nation as a whole might be growing relatively more dependent on banking than on manufacturing, but "if scientific and industrial ability remains [in] the country, new industries will develop."[170]

Alfred Marshall, one of Balfour's other consultants, agreed with Ashley that Britain's trade had been hurt by the imposition of overseas tariffs, and he was prepared to grant that exports had not been expanding at their earlier rate. The perfection of technology in which Britain pioneered and its dispersion to areas of the world in which labor costs were lower was putting the country at an increasing disadvantage. Consequently, he advised that "England will not be able to hold her own against other nations by mere sedulous practice of familiar processes. . . . England's place among the nations in the future must depend on the extent to which she retains industrial leadership. She cannot be *the* leader but she may be *a* leader."[171]

It was, in Marshall's view, inevitable that Britain should have lost some of its earlier advantage. But, he continued, "it was not inevitable that she should lose so much of it as she has done." Ironically, "the greatness and rapidity of her loss [was] partly due to that very prosperity which followed the adoption of free trade." The sons of Britain's great midcentury manufacturers had become "content to follow mechanically the lead given by their fathers. They worked shorter hours, and they exerted themselves less to obtain new practical ideas than their fathers had done. And a part of England's leadership was destroyed rapidly."[172]

British businessmen had become too concerned with the mere volume of their trade and too little interested in the kinds of innovations that could increase productivity and preserve their qualitative lead over foreign competitors. If Britain hoped to retain "a high place in the world," it was now "not merely expedient" but

---

[169] BM, Add. Mss. 49780, Ashley to Balfour, 7/4/03.
[170] Ibid.

[171] Marshall, "Memorandum on Fiscal Policy," PRO, Cab. T 168/54.
[172] Ibid.

"absolutely essential" that everything possible be done to increase the "alertness of her industrial population in general and her manufacturers in particular." The best means of accomplishing these ends, Marshall believed, was to keep Britain's home markets open to the new products of innovative countries like Germany and the United States.[173] Free trade was still the best policy, but it would not produce automatically the beneficial results with which Englishmen had traditionally associated it.

After two months of gathering information and listening to disparate opinions, Balfour was ready to formulate his own views for presentation to the cabinet. In August the prime minister circulated a thirty-page memorandum entitled "Economic Notes on Insular Free Trade," in which he laid down the intellectual basis for the policies that he would subsequently pursue. By his own admission the paper was long and abstract, but, he told the duke of Devonshire, "it represents faithfully the point of view from which I approach the subject and I wrote it as much for my own satisfaction as for the benefit of anybody else."[174]

Unlike most of his contemporaries, Balfour began with basic principles rather than with an array of facts and figures. "I am a 'free trader,'" he wrote, but not one of the orthodox variety.[175] Given that the world was made up of many independent nation-states, it was "irrational to suppose that what is good for the wealth-producing capacity of the world must necessarily be good for each particular state." In fact, nations were bound to adopt policies (like protection) that appeared to be in their own best interest, whether or not those measures necessarily increased global welfare.[176] For all their wisdom, this was a possibility that the creators of Britain's free-trade policy had failed to foresee. They never imagined that other countries would not eventually follow their lead in eliminating protective tariffs, and, because of this oversight, they did not take adequate account of the empire's possible commercial importance.[177]

---

[173] Ibid.

[174] BM, Add. Mss. 49770, Balfour to Devonshire, 7/30/03. This document has been much maligned, both at the time and since, as dry and excessively theoretical. In fact it is neither. Writing at the time of Balfour's death (1930), John Maynard Keynes observed that "the 'Economic Notes on Insular Free Trade' is one of the most remarkable scientific deliverances ever made by a Prime Minister in office. It wears well and bears re-reading. I think that econ-

omists today would treat Balfour's doubts, hesitations, vague sensing of trouble to come, polite wonder whether unqualified laisser-faire is quite certainly always for the best, with more respect, even if not with more sympathy, than they did then." (John Maynard Keynes, *The Collected Writings of John Maynard Keynes* 10:44).

[175] A. Balfour, *Economic Notes on Insular Free Trade*, p. 4.

[176] Ibid., p. 5.

[177] Ibid., p. 8.

The question before Britain was "whether a fiscal system suited to a free trade nation in a world of free traders, remains suited in every detail to a free trade nation in a world of protectionists."[178] As a first step toward solving this puzzle, Balfour urged his readers to imagine three types of free-trade states faced with rising tariff barriers. A very small country would quickly be ruined because of its dependence on export earnings, while a very large and more autarkic state might feel little effect from any increased restraint on trade. Medium-sized nations like Britain would be forced to cut prices, wages, and profits so as to maintain export levels. With earnings from trade down, imports would also have to be reduced, and the country would (assuming that foreign tariffs were not raised even further) settle down to a relatively impoverished equilibrium.[179]

Why was it that Britain had not yet suffered such a fate? Why were its exports still increasing, even if not as much as might be desired, while its import trade was "of unexampled magnitude?"[180] Balfour claimed that the nation had escaped worse conditions than those it was already enduring only because of its investments overseas (which, as he explained, caused foreigners to "owe us a great deal of money, which they pay by means of imports into the United Kingdom"[181]), the continued existence of free-trade areas, and the fact that even protected regions were not completely closed to imports. As to the first prop under Britain's prosperity, foreign investments were not an unmixed blessing; while they might help to pay for needed imports, they also drew capital away from the home market. Moreover, as Balfour pointed out, "it must not . . . be forgotten that the magnitude of [our] investments is due rather to the fact that we were first in the industrial field than to the intrinsic merit of our fiscal system."[182] If Britain was losing its lead in industry, then it could not long count on an overwhelming preponderance in world financial markets.

Free-trade areas in South America, the small states of continental Europe, and Turkey, China, and the dependencies of the empire were essential to Britain's continued well-being, yet they too were inherently fragile. Balfour considered it unlikely that the size of those areas not protected by tariffs would increase, but he foresaw several ways in which they might be diminished. The expansion of the British Empire had, "broadly speaking, reached its limits." At the same time, the industrialization of agricultural areas,

---

[178] Ibid., p. 9.
[179] Ibid., pp. 11–14.
[180] Ibid., p. 15.

[181] Ibid., p. 15.
[182] Ibid., p. 17.

domestic political changes in developing countries, and the extension of control by protectionist powers all threatened to eat away at the world's free markets, with harmful consequences for Britain.[183]

As for commerce with the protectionist countries that were still the nation's most important customers, the trends were not promising. Here Balfour, like all of his contemporaries, made reference to the trade returns, but he warned against reading them too narrowly. It was important to consider "not merely what is, but what is to be. The tendency of trade, not its momentary position, is what concerns us." Nevertheless, the returns showed that Britain's export business, "which should, other things remaining the same, have grown with our growth and with the yet more rapid growth of some of our customers, has, in fact, done neither. . . . Absolutely it may have increased, but its rate of increase has on the whole seriously diminished; in some important departments no increase is perceptible, in others there are symptoms of decay."[184] The notion that the slowdown was an inevitable consequence of world industrialization was dismissed as wide of the mark. Under free trade, the growth of Britain's partners should have resulted in a proportionate expansion in British business. Foreign protectionism alone made this impossible.

Looking more closely at the trade returns, Balfour noted another disturbing fact. Exports of coal, machinery, and ships fostered "in an especial degree the competition of foreign protected manufactures," which could only hurt British business in the future. Yet such items made up a significant fraction of total exports, and they could not simply be excluded from the returns. Still, it was difficult to see how their sale could be regarded as, at the same time, "an indication of prosperity and a cause of decline."[185]

Having worked his way from a simple model of the international economy to a review of the statistics, the prime minister summed up his conclusions. "Is our position going to worsen relatively to other nations, or even to worsen absolutely?" he asked. "I see no satisfactory symptoms."[186] It might very well be that "judged by all the available tests, both the total wealth and the diffused well-being of the country [were] greater than they had ever been."[187] This did not mean, however, that the "commercial optimists" were correct. Balfour urged that these people "study tendencies—the dynamics not the statics of trade and manufactures. The ocean we are navigating is smooth enough, but where are we being driven by its

[183] Ibid., pp. 18–19.
[184] Ibid., p. 19.
[185] Ibid., p. 22.

[186] Ibid., p. 23.
[187] Ibid., p. 28.

tides? Does either theory or experience provide any consolatory answer to this question?"[188]

Clearly the prime minister did not believe so. Moreover, he was now prepared to declare that foreign protection must be blamed for all the most serious dangers (both "actual and prospective"[189]) facing Britain's economy. Free (or at least freer) trade was certainly in the national interest, but the only way to obtain it was through negotiation with foreign governments. Without the ability to threaten protective measures of its own, London would be hopelessly handicapped in any such discussions. What Balfour proposed as a solution to Britain's problems, therefore, was an idea to which he had been favorably disposed for over twenty years: the selective imposition of retaliatory tariffs sufficient to force concessions from trading partners. Before this could be done it was necessary that the nation abandon its attachment to the idea that all protection was harmful. "Freedom to negotiate" was the rallying cry that Balfour proposed to his fellow ministers.[190] It was hardly an inspiring slogan. Raising tariffs in order to lower them had a certain awkward logic, but it was not a position likely to generate widespread public enthusiasm.

As far as the free traders were concerned, Balfour's recommendations were just a first step toward outright protectionism. To Chamberlain, the prime minister's stance seemed timid, and his neglect of the colonies and imperial preference, narrow and shortsighted. After a series of cabinet meetings that extended from mid-August to mid-September, the colonial secretary decided that he would have to leave the Government in order to wage a campaign of public education against the ideology of free trade. By withholding his knowledge of Chamberlain's intentions until the last possible moment, Balfour was also able to rid himself of the cabinet's staunchest opponents of tariff reform.[191] Albeit at tremendous cost, the prime minister was now free to pursue the path to which his reason, his reading of the evidence, and his understanding of the political situation had led him.

Public Controversy, 1903–1905

The mass resignations of autumn 1903 marked the beginning of what one historian has called the "death agony" of the Balfour ad-

[188] Ibid., p. 29.
[189] Ibid.
[190] Ibid., pp. 30–31.
[191] Charles Ritchie, Balfour of Burleigh, and secretary of state for India George Hamilton. The widely respected duke of Devonshire, a free trader whom Balfour had been desperately anxious to keep, left soon afterward. For two slightly different accounts of these events, see Rempel, *Unionists Divided*, pp. 49–63, and Gollin, *Balfour's Burden*, pp. 128–88.

ministration.[192] For the next two years the Conservative party and
the country as a whole were wracked by an increasingly bitter debate over tariff reform, which would continue sporadically even
after the general election of January 1906. Balfour clung tena-
ciously to power during these years, determined to finish the work
he had begun on foreign policy and defense reorganization, but his
grip became steadily weaker.

The reopening of public controversy brought with it a vast out-
pouring of pamphlets, books, and speeches that, for all the energy
expended on them, seem to have changed remarkably few minds.[193]
As there had been within the cabinet, so now on the larger stage of
national politics there were three distinct schools of thought. Chamberlain led the supporters of preference and protection (the "whole
hoggers"), while Balfour urged "retaliation" and "liberty of negotiation." Arrayed against both of these was an alliance of Liberals
(including the Liberal Imperialists) and disgruntled free-trade
Conservatives (both Liberal Unionists like the duke of Devonshire
and mainline party members like Winston Churchill and Salisbury's son Hugh Cecil).

Many of the arguments made during the tariff reform controversy were similar to those put forward by the free traders and
fair traders of the 1880s and 1890s. As in the preceding months of
intragovernmental debate, much of what was said had to do with
the presumed impact of the various proposals being advanced—
whether a "food tax" would raise the cost of living, for example, or
if the imposition of retaliatory duties would trigger a full-scale
trade war. In public as in private, however, there was a deeper
problem that had to be addressed. The proponents of change felt
the need to prove the harm that their policies were supposed to
remedy, while the defenders of free trade were compelled to defend the benefits of the status quo. At its most profound level,
therefore, the public discussion of tariff reform, like the internal

[192] Gollin, "Balfour, 1902–1911," in
Southgate, ed., *The Conservative Leadership, 1832–1932*, p. 164.

[193] In addition to volumes of public
addresses by Chamberlain and Balfour,
the prime minister's "Economic Notes
on Insular Free Trade" was published
as a pamphlet in September 1903. Balfour's position received some support,
as for example in Agacy, *Free Trade,
Protection, Dumping, Bounties, and Preferential Tariffs*. It was criticized by such lu-
minaries as the secretary of the Cobden
Club. See Fox, *Mr. Balfour's Pamphlet: A
Reply*. But most writers came out firmly
either for or against Chamberlain. See
books by three of his advisers: Ashley,
The Tariff Problem; Caillard, *Imperial
Fiscal Reform;* Cunningham, *The Rise
and Decline of the Free Trade Movement.*
See also pamphlets by Willoughby, *Sug-
gestions for Securing Fair Play for British
Manufacturers,* and Gaskell, *Free Trade:
A Failure From the First.* On the other
side of the question see, for example,
Perris, *The Protectionist Peril;* Pigou, *The
Riddle of the Tariff;* Strachey, "Free
Trade and the Empire," in *The Empire
and the Century.*

debate that preceded it, centered on contending assessments of Britain's relative economic power, performance, and likely future prospects.

As always, it was the trade statistics that drew the most attention. Here, depending on how one looked at them, could be found "proof" of a wide range of conflicting contentions. In October Chamberlain launched his public campaign with a flourish of figures. "I tell you that it is not well today with British industry," he announced to an audience in Glasgow. Between 1872 and 1902 the population of the United Kingdom had grown by 30 percent while its export trade had increased only 7.5 percent. Extending the calculation that he had made privately in July, Chamberlain now claimed that "our export trade has been practically stagnant for thirty years." [194]

This assertion, absolutely central to the cause of protectionism,[195] was taken up immediately by the opponents of tariff reform. Beginning in the fall of 1903 Herbert Asquith, the Liberal MP and future prime minister, assumed the role of a one-man "truth squad," dogging Chamberlain's steps across the country and offering stinging public rebuttals to his speeches. Two days after the former colonial secretary fired his opening blast, Asquith was ready with a response. The claim that trade was stagnant (and the accompanying implication that Britain's overall economic progress had virtually ceased) was, according to Asquith, based on four related fallacies. In the first place, Chamberlain had entirely ignored the home trade that accounted for five or six times the labor engaged in export industries. Second, he had looked only at exports when it was the total of exports and imports combined that gave the best measure of national progress. Even worse, Chamberlain's estimate made reference only to exports of *goods*, setting aside the services (like the £90-million-per-year shipping business) from which Great Britain profited so considerably. Finally, by chance or design, Chamberlain had selected a base year that made the progress of British trade seem much slower than it had actually been.[196] The year 1872, as Charles Ritchie also pointed out, was one "of great expansion in business, of inflated prices, a tremendously booming year." [197] It

[194] Speech at Glasgow, 10/6/03, in Boyd, ed., *Mr. Chamberlain's Speeches* 2:145.

[195] Sir William Harcourt, the former Liberal chancellor of the Exchequer, complained that, in fact, "the basis of this whole agitation is the assertion of the decaying condition of British trade"

(speech at Rawtenstall, 10/31/03, in Gilmour, ed., *All Sides of the Fiscal Controversy*, p. 238).

[196] Speech at Cinderford, 10/8/03, in Asquith, *Trade and the Empire*, p. 21.

[197] Speech at Croydon, 10/9/03, in Gilmour, *All Sides*, p. 85.

was hardly surprising that the total value of Britain's exports should appear to have grown very little when compared with such an exceptional start. If a more typical beginning point (like 1870 or 1876) had been selected and compared with 1900, the growth in exports would have appeared far greater.[198]

Most free traders probably agreed with Asquith that the export trade was "making very substantial and very satisfactory progress."[199] This did not necessarily mean that they refused to acknowledge a sluggishness in export growth, but they hardly took this as an indication of impending disaster.[200] In the end, no matter how the Board of Trade's much overworked returns were turned and twisted, they could not be used by anyone to score a decisive blow. Having fought Chamberlain to a standstill on the export issue, the free traders sought to move the debate onto a somewhat larger plane. Fluctuations in commerce aside, there was little doubt that the nation had been growing in absolute terms. How much and how fast were questions that could not be answered precisely, but the general direction of things seemed clear.

The fact of absolute increase could be established in various ways. Henry Campbell-Bannerman, the leader of the Opposition, used the Government's own figures to make the point. Official inquiries had "triumphantly vindicated the prosperity and growing wealth of the country," he declared. "The bulk of our trade, the value of our trade, the Income-tax returns, banking returns, rates of wages, . . . and . . . the numbers of persons employed . . . by all of these it is shown that our trade has vigor and elasticity instead of the decadence imputed to it."[201] Similarly, Lord George Hamilton made reference to official decennial figures for total wages and employment (what he called "the real test[s] of the industrial condition of this country") to show that Britain was more prosperous than it had ever been.[202]

Lord Roseberry, the leading Liberal Imperialist, cited Robert Giffen's attempt to fashion a crude measure of national income. Giffen had estimated that the figure was something on the order of £1,750 million per year, and that Britain's capital stood at £15,000

[198] Asquith, *Trade and the Empire,* p. 21.

[199] Speech at Newcastle-on-Tyne, 10/24/03, in Asquith, ibid., p. 43.

[200] Lord George Hamilton, another recent refugee from Balfour's cabinet, declared on reviewing the statistical "Blue Book" issued by the Government that it recorded "gratifying progress in every direction save one—namely, that part of our export trade to foreign countries which consists of manufactured goods" (speech at Ealing, 10/22/03, in Gilmour, *All Sides,* p. 189).

[201] Speech at Bolton, 10/15/03, in ibid., p. 121.

[202] Gilmour, *All Sides,* p. 189.

million. "Those are figures of the Arabian Nights," Roseberry concluded with glee. "If the leading economists of this country . . . put these forward as accurate figures," then it could be declared with certainty "that our country has not suffered very materially."[203]

Those who were less optimistic about Britain's prospects had two responses. In his careful, somewhat tepid pleas for "freedom to negotiate," the prime minister repeated the warnings first annunciated in "Insular Free Trade." The nation's economy might be functioning tolerably well at present, but there was little reason to expect that it would continue to do so. Balfour told a Bristol crowd in November 1903 that he rejected "with profound contempt arguments based merely upon the actual moment in which we live, and which leave entirely out of account tendencies which are moulding and must now more and more mould the commercial fortunes of the world. All these tendencies appear to me to be inimical to the future of this country."[204]

Chamberlain's reply to the free traders' demonstrations of material progress was more profound but also more difficult to express. If one thought not simply in national but in international terms, absolute gains over past performance meant little. "My opponents seem to me intellectually shortsighted," Chamberlain complained. "Throughout this controversy they have failed to seize what I believe is the essential thing to keep in mind—namely, that the greatness of a nation is not to be measured by a comparison with its own past, but by its relative position in the councils of the world."[205]

Here was the heart of the matter. Even as Britain grew, the nation was being surpassed in wealth; yet there was no good way of conveying this harsh truth. In the absence of any reliable comparative measure of national economic power, Chamberlain was reduced to a number of rhetorical ploys. At times he made use of historical comparisons.

> We are richer—there is no doubt that we are richer than we were ten years ago, or fifty years ago . . . but what of other nations? Take the case of Spain. I think in the case of Spain, and I am certain in the case of Holland, that there is more acquired wealth in these countries today than there was in the palmiest times of their history; but that is all. In spite of the growth of their wealth they have fallen from their high estate. The sceptre they once

[203] Speech at Sheffield, 10/13/03, in ibid., p. 110.

[204] Speech at Bristol, 11/13/03, in *Fiscal Reform Speeches*, p. 124.

[205] Speech at the Guildhall (London), 1/19/04, quoted in Amery, *The Life of Joseph Chamberlain* 6:537.

wielded so proudly has passed into other hands and can never return to them. They may be richer, but they are poorer in what constitutes the greatness of a nation, and they count for nothing in the future opinion of the world. Is it wished that we should follow in the same lines?[206]

On other occasions the image of relative decline was driven home with quaint metaphors.

It is not what we have now, but . . . how long we keep it . . . and how much [we shall] keep. . . . We are like a man in a race. He starts with a great advantage; he has been given a hundred yards, perhaps. In the first lap he loses thirty; in the second lap he loses fifty more; and then he is seen by an observer from the Cobden Club and the Cobden Club says, "That is my man; he is still ahead." I think we know better.[207]

Chamberlain may have known better but he was ultimately unable to coax most of his countrymen into the imaginative leap that lifted him above the plateau of the present and allowed a brief, troubling glimpse into the future.

Despite their demonstrations of increasing wealth, the free traders were by no means completely complacent. In private some of them went so far as to suggest that Britain must inevitably lose not only some of its early lead but its supremacy as well. Liberal MP Leonard (later Lord) Courtney wrote to a friend at the beginning of the tariff reform controversy:

We have been doing well and shall continue to do well, but this last truth must be coupled with an acknowledgement that though we are still absolutely going forward we are losing ground and must lose first place. Our national vainglory will not easily acquiesce in being second; and any quack who professes to have a remedy against this loss of supremacy will attract the support of a great many. . . . It seems to be wise not to conceal the unpalatable truth but to try to bring our countrymen to realize it as a fact which tariffs cannot alter.[208]

If they harbored such suspicions, Chamberlain's public interlocutors were wise enough to keep them to themselves. Still, most defenders of the status quo were prepared to admit that certain do-

[206] Ibid., pp. 537–38.
[207] Speech at Liverpool, 10/27/03, in ibid., p. 492.

[208] Quoted in Amery, *The Life of Joseph Chamberlain* 5:319–20.

mestic industries had suffered in recent years. What they would not agree to was the assertion that home producers had been the victims of foul play. Asquith estimated that "in nine out of ten cases at least, where you can show an industry in this country which used to export largely and now exports little or not at all, the explanation is to be found not so much in the operation of hostile tariffs as in other causes, such as their defective methods of production and want of adaptiveness."[209] In Asquith's opinion, some loss of exports was inevitable, with or without protection (and, to some extent, regardless of the quality of British industry), "because countries like the United States and Germany were bound, as time went on, to develop their resources and provide with their own manufactures what was needed for their own domestic consumption."[210]

For the most part the free traders saw Britain's problems (such as they were) as the result of natural processes. If British firms could not become more competitive they would be destroyed—that was the law of the economic jungle. And if comparative advantage shifted from one country to another, there was no point in trying to hold onto businesses that others could now conduct more efficiently. As to claims that the nation's competitors were experiencing faster growth, this too was a perfectly predictable development. Lord Roseberry, for example, scoffed at those who warned that Great Britain was "not getting on half so fast as Germany and the United States. . . . Well, they began with very little. You could not expect to keep the monopoly of the trade of the world, because their populations swelled, and as their energy developed they naturally demanded a share of the trade of the world, and you ought to be pleased and proud that you have kept your position as well as you have."[211]

This was just the kind of self-satisfaction that Chamberlain was determined to dislodge. Britain's apparent defeat in certain crucial sectors was, he insisted, neither inevitable nor natural. To lose out "fairly," according to the laws of comparative advantage, was one thing. "But when I see these industries not leaving us because we are no longer capable of attending to them, but filched from us, stolen by unfair means, then I ask you, . . . How long are you going to take it lying down?"[212]

Despite the soothing assurances of the free traders, Chamber-

[209] Speech at Newcastle-on-Tyne, 10/24/03, in Asquith, *Trade and the Empire*, p. 44.
[210] Ibid., p. 45.
[211] Speech at Leicester, 11/7/03, in Gilmour, *All Sides*, p. 298.
[212] Speech at Liverpool, 10/28/03, in Boyd, ed., *Mr. Chamberlain's Speeches* 2:221.

lain believed that the nation's industrial base was decaying rather than evolving. Men and resources were not simply being shifted easily and painlessly from one line of productive endeavor to another; instead, the country's "principal industries" were disappearing, and not even "secondary and inferior industries" were rising up quickly to take their place. In fact, there was "no evidence whatever that when one trade goes another immediately takes its place."[213]

To the extent that the economy as a whole *was* changing, it was not in ways that would promote national strength. The great iron, steel, and shipbuilding works essential both to the production of arms and to the creation of many skilled jobs were crumbling, and an increasingly large service sector was beginning to take their place. "In the course of another generation," Chamberlain warned, "this will be much less an industrial country inhabited by a race of skillful artisans than a distributive country with a smaller population consisting of rich consumers on the one hand and people engaged in the work of distribution on the other."[214]

At times the transformation seemed already to have occurred. Toward the end of 1904 the former colonial secretary told an audience that

> whereas at one time England was the greatest manufacturing country, now its people are more and more employed in finance, in distribution, in domestic service. . . .
> I think it is worthwhile to consider—whatever its immediate effects may be—whether that state of things will not be the destruction ultimately of all that is best in England, all that has made us what we are, all that has given us prestige and power in the world.[215]

In the short run, the net effect of the changes under way would be to leave Britain more divided between rich and poor and less self-sufficient—in short, "richer and yet weaker."[216] Over the long term the nation could not survive as merely a "hoarder of invested securities" if it was not at the same time "the creator of new wealth." "Granted that you are the clearing-house of the world," Chamberlain told a group of bankers in the City of London, but

> are you entirely beyond anxiety as to the permanence of your great position? . . . Banking is not the creator of our

---

[213] Speech at Birmingham, 11/4/03, in ibid., p. 248.

[214] Speech at Tynemouth, 10/21/03, in ibid., p. 192.

[215] Speech at Limehouse, 12/15/04, in ibid., p. 267–68.

[216] The phrase is from a speech given in Gainsborough, 2/1/05, in ibid., p. 313.

prosperity, but is the creation of it. It is not the cause of our wealth, but it is the consequence of our wealth; and if the industrial energy and development which has been going on for so many years in this country were to be hindered or relaxed, then finance, and all that finance means, will follow trade to the countries which are more successful than ourselves.[217]

Was it inevitable that the new superstates would be wealthier and more efficient than Britain? "When we . . . talk of the prosperity of America and Germany," Chamberlain complained, "[our opponents] say, 'Yes, that is natural. Are they not greater than us, are they not more numerous?' Then, in a sort of despairing fatalism they seem to say, 'What can our little England do but fall a victim to the inexorable decrees of fate?' "[218] To this pessimism there was a familiar answer: empire. Only by binding itself more closely to its colonies could Britain avoid all the horrors that seemed otherwise to lie in store.

To the free traders, Chamberlain's remedies seemed "artificial," unnatural, and unnecessary;[219] in one of Asquith's most memorable phrases, they amounted to an invitation to the nation to "commit industrial suicide" in a "fit of hypochondria."[220] The alternatives to protection, preference, and retaliation were those that had been repeated over and over again since at least the 1880s—"better education, better training, better methods, larger outlook."[221] Roseberry asked, "How are we to fight these hostile tariffs? I believe we must fight them by a more scientific and adaptive spirit—by better education."[222] And a group of antiprotectionists advised that "above all, we have to educate and encourage intelligence, adaptability, and diligence in all ranks of the commercial hierarchy."[223]

All this was unobjectionable, but was it really enough to turn the tide in England's favor? How, in any event, were these noble goals to be accomplished? The seeming airiness of the Liberal platform and the lack of urgency with which it was advanced (education, after all, represented the cure for a disease whose existence was barely acknowledged) made it an easy target for Conservative ridicule. "I notice," said Balfour, "that the only remedy which [the Lib-

[217] Speech of 1/19/04, in ibid., pp. 535–36.

[218] Ibid., p. 538.

[219] Asquith, speech of 10/8/03, in Asquith, *Trade and the Empire*, p. 31.

[220] From a speech at Birmingham, 2/24/05, quoted in BM, Add. Mss.

49780, "Mr. Asquith on Retaliation."

[221] Asquith, speech of 10/8/03, in Asquith, *Trade and the Empire*, p. 31.

[222] Speech of 10/13/03, in Gilmour, *All Sides*, p. 112.

[223] See the introduction to *Protection and Industry*, pp. vii–viii.

erals] . . . propose is education." And "though I do not under-rate education, was anything in this world ever heard so utterly ridiculous as the theory that technical education or any other form of education would neutralise an eighty per cent duty upon your staple manufactures?"[224] Chamberlain had long been a supporter of technical education and, for most of his life, believed strongly in its beneficial effects. It is ironical but, given the heat and frustration of the campaign, probably inevitable that he too should have begun to denigrate it.

Outcome, 1906

Judged by the results of the January 1906 general election, Chamberlain's strident warnings and Balfour's more modest appeals had fallen on not merely deaf but positively hostile ears. After ruling the country for ten years the Conservative Unionist government was subjected to one of the worst defeats in modern British political history. When the ballots were counted the Liberals had won 377 seats (with their Labour and Nationalist allies capturing 53 and 83, respectively), while the Conservatives had 132 and the Liberal Unionists, 25.[225]

There were undoubtedly many reasons for this unprecedented catastrophe, but, in the words of historian Robert Blake, "All the evidence suggests that nothing was more disastrous to his party than Joseph Chamberlain's campaign for tariff reform."[226] To begin with, Chamberlain's efforts reduced the Conservative Unionist alliance to a clutch of squabbling factions while driving together the various segments of the Liberal party. More important, although talk of tariff reform may have stirred enthusiasm in some quarters, it drove away many more voters than it attracted. The predictions of decline that both Chamberlain and Balfour made were not so compelling as to make the likely costs of protection seem worth its supposed benefits.

From early on the Liberals had been able to charge that imperial preference meant a higher cost of living for the average consumer. Chamberlain and his allies admitted that preference required a tax on food, but they offered several additional proposals that were intended to deprive the tax of its sting. Revenue tariffs on certain food imports (tea, for example) could be reduced to offset the burden of a levy on corn. At various times Chamberlain also claimed

---

[224] Speech at Bristol, 11/13/03, in *Fiscal Reform Speeches*, p. 119.
[225] Rempel, *Unionists Divided*, p. 151.

[226] Blake, *The Conservative Party from Peel to Churchill*, p. 180.

that the new tariffs he was suggesting would increase home prices very little and that they might actually be borne largely by foreign exporters. These assertions were based on esoteric calculations that seem to have carried little weight with ordinary voters. What stuck was the charge that preference meant higher taxes and larger grocery bills. To quote Blake again, "The association of Chamberlain's proposals with dearer food was almost certainly a major element in the defeat of 1906." [227]

Preference frightened working-class voters and alienated the large group of employers who benefited from low food costs and the reduced wages that they permitted. A general tariff on imports of manufactured goods did little to offset the potential harm associated with a food tax. It is apparent from looking at the various industrial sectors that, in the short run at least, more people stood to lose from protection than were likely to gain. The industries suffering most severely under free trade simply did not employ a very large portion of the total work force. Thus, as Richard Rempel has pointed out, "although they protested volubly, the 100,000 workers concerned with the production of iron and steel did not count heavily in the balance when compared with the much larger labor forces in industries still attached to free trade." [228]

The latter category included the cotton business, which employed 600,000, coal (which was benefiting from booming overseas demand and provided work for over 800,000 men), and shipping, with 1,000,000 laborers in the dockyards and 200,000 men at sea. Despite Chamberlain's pleas, the financial world also remained firmly committed to free trade. Middle-class bankers, stockbrokers, and insurance agents as well as the majority of working men had reason to fear that the imposition of new tariffs would provoke retaliation, disrupting the smooth flow of goods, services, and money from which so many benefited.[229]

A monumental international disaster on the scale of the Boer War might have persuaded British voters that immediate material sacrifices were needed to preserve national economic power. Barring this, the only thing that could have saved the day for the protectionists was a deep and widespread industrial downturn or at least a collapse in exports of the sort that had occurred periodically since the beginning of the Great Depression. The onset of truly hard times coinciding with the initiation of Chamberlain's campaign could perhaps have convinced a majority of voters that the

[227] Ibid., p. 171.
[228] Rempel, *Unionists Divided*, p. 97.
[229] Ibid., pp. 97–104.

future was not quite so promising as it seemed. Instead, it was at just this time that exports began to pick up. Under the circumstances there seemed little reason to overthrow the conventions of the past and to join in taking what Asquith rightly described as "a leap in the dark."[230]

Conclusion
The Meaning and Measurement of Economic Power

At the close of the nineteenth century, Britain's leaders shared a belief in the importance of "national economic power," but they lacked agreement on exactly what that concept meant or how it should be measured. As a result, their efforts to understand and respond to changes in Britain's position in the world economy were confused, inconclusive, and ultimately inadequate.

In the abstract, all parties could probably have agreed on the importance to the nation of continued increases in total wealth or production. Everyone wanted Britain to stay rich and get richer. Beyond this, however, there was little common ground. The free traders often talked as if all that mattered was that the country's overall wealth expand more rapidly than its population. The composition and distribution of that wealth, as well as its magnitude in comparison with the wealth of other countries, was paid far less attention. Chamberlain, by contrast, believed that Britain's world standing depended on her *relative* wealth. He warned repeatedly that the country could become "richer but weaker" if it allowed itself to be surpassed by the efforts of other states, and he cautioned that a nation whose economy was based on industrial production would retain its international power and domestic stability longer than one that emphasized the mere provision of services.

As has been discussed, there were at the turn of the century no good measures of national income or total industrial production. When the question of Britain's economic performance was raised, those who favored a continuation of existing policies used raw output figures to make crude demonstrations of absolute progress, but they could not show at what rate overall growth was occurring. They were therefore unable to allay fears by proving that the nation's economy was expanding as rapidly as it seemed to have done over the course of the preceding decades.

Advocates of dramatic change were even worse off in the struggle

[230] Speech at Worcester, 11/9/03, in Asquith, *Trade and the Empire,* p. 86.

for analytic high ground than their opponents. An accurate aggregate measure of national income or manufacturing production would have allowed Joseph Chamberlain to argue persuasively that the nation's economic engine had slowed. To support his more alarming claims of relative decline and international erosion he would also have needed a universal index with which to compare Britain to other countries. Such a yardstick would have allowed him to demonstrate not only that competing states were growing more rapidly than Great Britain, but that some of them already had overtaken or were just about to catch up with the country in terms of national income and overall output of manufactured goods.

In the absence of any more sophisticated measurement tool, the trade returns emerged as the accepted indicator of economic advance—a result both of the peculiarities of government record-keeping policy and of the contemporary state of development of economic ideas. The official tables of imports and exports were used to show fluctuations in Britain's trade over time, and similar data collected from foreign governments served as the basis for some limited cross-national comparisons of commercial activity.

The benefits derived from even the most careful use of the trade returns were, however, far outweighed by their disadvantages. In the first place, the available figures provided only a limited window on the functioning of the British economy. They dealt solely with that fraction of the nation's business which involved "visible" foreign trade, overlooking purely domestic activity and ignoring the important "invisible" flows of earnings from international investment and services provided to foreigners. It was perfectly possible that exports could grow while in other respects the British economy languished. Indeed, this is what seems to have happened between the turn of the century and the outbreak of the First World War.[231] People accustomed to judging the nation's overall economic health by the ups and downs of the trade returns were likely to be lulled into complacency by short-term improvements in the performance of their favored indicator.

In addition to this masking effect, the returns also had a subtle impact on the way in which economic questions were formulated and analyzed. By focusing attention on international exchange

[231] As one historian points out, the export boom of 1900–1914 "took place against a background of a sluggish rate of increase of industrial production, stagnant productivity and . . . a fall in real wages" (Cain, "Political Economy in Edwardian England: The Tariff-Reform Controversy," in O'Day, ed., *The Edwardian Age: Conflict and Stability 1900–1914*, p. 46). On the prewar economy see also Offer, "Empire and Social Reform: British Overseas Investment and Domestic Politics, 1908–1914," pp. 119–38.

they reinforced an already existing tendency to translate all doubts about industrial performance into questions about trade. In so doing they strengthened a proclivity for finding the source of Britain's problems outside its own borders. What could have developed into a broadly drawn discussion of the nation's economic future became instead a debate about export growth, and that, in turn, devolved into a disagreement about the alleged harm of foreign protectionism. By their very nature the trade returns encouraged Englishmen to look outward instead of inward and to find fault with their neighbors rather than with themselves.

Whatever else can be said of them, the trade statistics that figured so centrally in the tariff reform controversy were ultimately inconclusive. Their fluctuations drove the debate, but because they were malleable and subject to widely varying readings they also helped to render it unresolvable. Because there was no accepted method for interpreting them, the same figures could be used to "prove" both that the nation's exports were expanding lustily and that their growth had slowed to a virtual crawl. Even if all observers had been able to agree that (as seems in retrospect to have been the case) the trade returns showed some slowdown in export growth, the larger questions of how significant that was, why it was happening, and whether it represented a temporary, cyclical development or a long-term, secular trend would have remained unanswered.

The Eroding Free-Trade Consensus

If (for example) comparative, historical figures for total national manufacturing production had been available in 1900, then at least the issues facing Britain's leaders would have been more clearly drawn. Such figures would probably have shown a slowdown in the growth of the nation's output during the last quarter of the nineteenth century and would most certainly have demonstrated Great Britain's displacement by the United States and its imminent loss of relative position to Germany. With these facts established, the assumption of extreme free traders that Britain was and would always remain the world's leading industrial nation could have been decisively revealed as wishful thinking. The causes of the erosion in the country's relative position and the possible cures for it (if any) could then have received the direct attention they demanded. A continuation of the existing policy of laissez faire might still have emerged as the best available alternative, but the implications of such an approach (and, in particular, the fact that it might well mean simply accepting Britain's displacement as the "workshop of the world") would have been exposed to closer scrutiny.

The absence of decisive evidence of relative decline meant that the intellectual (if not the policy) debate over Britain's future was essentially a draw. For the most part the participants were able to fall back on their preexisting beliefs about what was best for the country and for themselves and to interpret what evidence there was in light of those beliefs. Die-hard free traders usually saw nothing persuasive in the flurry of facts and figures presented by the protectionists. They continued to believe either that all was well or that existing problems were inevitable or, in any case, beyond the reach of protectionist solutions. Convinced proponents of tariff reform were equally unmoved by the protestations of their opponents. They were certain that a grim fate awaited the nation in the new century, even if indications of impending doom were still too faint to be seen by any but the most sensitive observers.

Given the balance of forces that existed before the eruption of the tariff debate, an intellectual draw really meant a political victory for free trade. The consensus that had grown up over the course of the preceding sixty years would not be easily shattered. Both before and after 1903, a majority of the elite and the public clearly continued to believe that protection was bad and that the maintenance of tariffs at the lowest possible level was still crucial to Britain's economic progress. Most people probably also believed that their country was still the world's industrial leader and that, under a policy of free trade, it would be able to continue in that role.

This is not to say, however, that the tariff reform debate was completely without impact. In 1896 and again in 1902–1903, Joseph Chamberlain was able to use external crises to spark a public discussion of national industrial power and policy. While his immediate efforts failed, they did have a number of important secondary effects. First, Chamberlain's arguments changed some minds or, at the very least, they solidified the doubts that were already plaguing skeptical, pragmatic free traders like Arthur Balfour. In the process, Chamberlain forced his party away from its sometimes grudging acceptance of economic liberalism and toward a more openly protectionist stance.

More important than these tactical (and ultimately pyrrhic) victories was the influence of Chamberlain's campaign on the long-term direction of British debate over economic issues. Doubts about the future were now legitimate in a way that they had not been before, and protection, if not popular, was at least a policy that reasonable men could advocate in public. Considering the past strength of the free-trade dogma these were no small accomplishments, and, for better or worse, they helped to lay the groundwork for the adoption in the 1930s of preference and protection.

An Aborted Response

Armed with incontrovertible proof that Britain was slowing down and being overtaken by its competitors, the protectionists might at least have had a chance of winning widespread public and parliamentary support for their proposals. In the near term the only effective alternative to statistical evidence would have been an economic or military catastrophe capable of causing people to change the way they calculated their individual interests or of forcing them to transcend such calculations altogether. As things stood, there was little likelihood that a majority of voters or their representatives would feel the need to undertake any radical changes in national economic policy. The practical result of the tariff reform debate was therefore a continuation of the status quo.

Although a clearer and more widespread perception of the erosion in Britain's position would have strengthened the hand of those who advocated change, it is not at all obvious that the remedies proposed by Chamberlain and Balfour would have worked or even that they would have been better than the disease they aimed to cure. The English people may have been right to reject protectionism, even if they did so partly for the wrong reasons. What would have been the effect on Britain's performance of adopting all or part of the protectionist program? The answer to this question is necessarily speculative, and its full consideration lies well outside the scope of this book. Nevertheless, the issue is an inescapable one, and a few brief comments are therefore warranted.

In retrospect it is apparent that Chamberlain was correct in at least half of his diagnosis of Britain's condition. Size *was* important. The sheer magnitude of the population and raw materials available to the United States, Russia, and (to a lesser extent) Germany gave them at least potential advantages over Britain. These were not always readily exploited but when they were, Britain was quickly caught and surpassed in such categories of production as steel, iron, and coal.

Chamberlain's solution to the problem of insufficient size was, of course, imperial consolidation. Over time he hoped that preferential trading arrangements could be used to mold the British Empire into a single, virtually autarkic commercial organism like Germany or the United States. From the beginning, however, this plan faced serious difficulties. Chamberlain's schemes required, in effect, that the colonies continue as providers of food and raw materials for Britain while purchasing an increasing portion of its manufactured products. For the colonies, "free trade within the Empire" meant losing infant industries to British competition, surrendering a substantial portion of the revenues from import duties, and accepting an increased danger of foreign retaliation against local exports. In return for their loyalty to the mother country the colonies would have been economically frozen or, as Asquith put it, "stereotyped" at their existing level of development.[232]

Chamberlain's proposals clearly amounted to an exceptionally bad bargain for possessions that were increasingly taking on the character of growing and independent states. Even if the British public could have been persuaded to accept import duties and higher food costs, there is good reason to believe that plans for an "Imperial Zollverein" would have foundered on colonial resistance. For this reason alone, economist S. B. Saul concludes, the idea was "nonsensical."[233]

What of the second, protectionist plank in the reform platform? The critics of "one-sided free trade" were probably right that overseas duties did direct harm to Britain's export business. Access to markets was lost, and not always as the result of "fair" competition. Foreign protectionism seems also to have encouraged domestic industry to concentrate on the more easily accessible colonial markets for traditional products like cotton goods.[234] The net result of this movement toward the empire was a blunting of the incentives for Britain to remain adaptive and thus competitive. Ironically, if Chamberlain's preferential schemes had been accepted they would only have served to strengthen this tendency and to worsen its harmful effects.

A general, unconditional, and permanent return to protectionism in Britain seems unlikely to have offset these problems and, indeed, it might well have made things worse by sparking a senseless and damaging global tariff war. Selective import duties might perhaps have defended certain British industries from foreign dumping, but they would also have shielded domestic manufacturers from advanced new products and from the need to adopt more efficient techniques.[235] Alfred Marshall was undoubtedly correct

---

[232] Speech at Cinderford, 10/8/03, in Asquith, *Trade and the Empire*, p. 24.

[233] Saul, *Studies in British Overseas Trade*, p. 228. For a contemporary analysis see Giffen, "The Dream of an Imperial Zollverein (1902)," in *Economic Inquiries and Studies*, pp. 387–404.

[234] S. B. Saul points out that "this was most pronounced with regard to India who, almost alone in the world, had no protection from home textiles and so encouraged Britain in a continued con-

centration on exports of cottons which was eventually to prove disastrous" (*Studies in British Overseas Trade*, p. 229).

[235] For a slightly more favorable assessment of the likely impact of duties on imports of manufactured goods see M. Balfour, *Britain and Joseph Chamberlain*, pp. 286–87. Cain argues that such tariffs "would have made sense only if [they] had been part of a wider government plan designed to encourage the growth of newer sectors of

when he told Balfour that, for purposes of encouraging greater productivity, there was "no device to be compared in efficiency with that of keeping [England's] markets open to the new products of other nations and especially to those of American inventive genius and German sedulous thought and scientific training."[236]

Even while adhering to a general policy of openness, the British government might still have used retaliatory duties in an attempt to coerce other countries into reducing their protective barriers. Where the British market for particular goods was essential to foreign exporters, the threat of discriminatory treatment might have been sufficient to compel a reciprocal lowering of duties. Retaliation might have worked, at least in some cases, some of the time. Although it was not a universal panacea, Balfour's proposal that the government be given freedom to threaten retaliation seems sound in retrospect. If it had been implemented, it might have helped to reduce the general level of protectionism, thereby improving both the short- and the long-term prospects for British industry.

Assuming for a moment that Britain had forced a return to absolute, worldwide free trade, the country would still undoubtedly have experienced some measure of relative economic decline. Part of the reason for this, as has already been suggested, lay with its small size and comparatively sparse endowment of natural resources. But size alone cannot explain why Britain fell behind not only in iron and steel but in the new chemical and electrical technologies that became increasingly important after 1900. Both at the time and more recently, economists have pointed out that turn-of-the-century Britain failed to adapt adequately to changing circumstances. In the traditional sectors British businesses were often not as efficient and productive as those of their competitors; in the new ones the British did not innovate as rapidly or as effectively.[237]

There is a wide range of possible explanations for this phenomenon, all of which center on the inner workings of the British economy. In part the nation's businessmen were suffering the conse-

---

industry, sheltering them from competition in the early stages of their growth" (Cain, "Political Economy," in O'Day, ed., *The Edwardian Age*, p. 49).

[236] PRO, T 168/54.

[237] Marshall's memo to Balfour cited above is one contemporary version of this complaint. For a review of some of the more recent arguments on this question see Kindleberger, *Economic*

Response: Comparative Studies in Trade, Finance, and Growth, 1806 to 1914, pp. 217–36. Some scholars have recently claimed that, in fact, Britain as a whole did about as well as could have been expected. See, for example, Payne, "Industrial Entrepreneurship and Management in Great Britain," in Mathias and Postan, eds., *The Cambridge Economic History of Europe* 7:180–230.

quences of having "gone first"; they had a heavy investment in plants, equipment, and techniques that were being made obsolete by developments in the more recently industrialized countries. The availability of lucrative opportunities overseas and the presence of a finely tuned mechanism for matching the domestic capital supply with foreign demand may have helped to make matters worse by reducing the rate of domestic investment.[238] Because they played so little part in the early phase of the industrial revolution, the professional scientists who were to prove so important in its later stages were not given the respect they deserved.[239] For reasons that seem to lie deep in English culture, there was a certain distaste for education that was not strictly classical, for business and industry as a whole, and for the appearance of excessive effort, planning, or professionalism.[240]

In order for Britain to have done better in the new century some effort was required to overcome or at least to counteract these tendencies. Interestingly enough, the need for such an undertaking was recognized at the time in at least some quarters. Prior to the onset of Chamberlain's campaign there was probably broad agreement on the importance of doing something to improve the level of "national efficiency," although what exactly this meant was often far from clear. During the 1890s what common ground there had been between free traders and fair traders had consisted of their mutual emphasis on the value of practical education and technical training.[241] By 1900 there were growing numbers of Liberal Imperialists, Socialists, and Conservatives interested not only in education but in such disparate ideas as government reorganization, na-

---

[238] See Pollard, "Capital Exports, 1870–1914: Harmful or Beneficial?" pp. 489–514.

[239] Lewis, "International Competition in Manufactures," p. 584.

[240] For a fascinating discussion of these issues see Wiener, *English Culture and the Decline of the Industrial Spirit, 1850–1980.*

[241] William Gastrell, a former commercial attaché and longtime advocate of laissez faire, observed in 1897 that England had been "apathetic, conservative and slow to adapt . . . to new conditions," and he maintained that the future of British trade depended "largely on our present power of learning and rapidly assimilating up-to-date

knowledge of every kind, as also on our capability of adapting ourselves practically, technically and scientifically to the changing conditions of modern commerce" (Gastrell, *Our Trade in the World In Relation to Foreign Competition, 1885 to 1895,* p. 2). Writing at about the same time, the ardent protectionist Ernest Williams maintained that "the great cause of German success is an alert progressiveness, contrasting brilliantly with the conservative stupor of ourselves." England was now engaged in a struggle to defend its position against "the most determined and best equipped foes," and for this warfare, "the best possible training" was needed (Williams, *Made in Germany,* p. 163).

tional military service, and eugenics. After the early disasters of the Boer War, a group of leading figures in British public life calling themselves the "Coefficients" began meeting to discuss possible solutions to the national malaise, and there was even thought given to creating a new "efficiency party," with Lord Roseberry at its head.[242]

All the talk about "national efficiency" did not add up to a coherent program. Much of what was discussed was nonsense, some of it harmless, some more menacing.[243] Amid the chaff, however, there were also the kernels of a number of good ideas. The advocates of efficiency saw Britain as engaged in an ongoing international competition, but they were prepared to look inward to find the reasons for some of the nation's problems. In government and in business Britain could only benefit by discarding the cult of the effortless amateur and placing more emphasis on expertise and long-range planning. There was a need for government support of scientific research. More and better education, both general and technical, was no less desirable for having been urged so often (and neither was a system of providing it that rewarded merit over birth).

Perhaps these measures, along with incentives for productive domestic investment, more aggressive pursuit of overseas markets, and an effort at trade negotiations, could have improved the nation's industrial performance. Britain could not, as Alfred Marshall predicted, be *the* leader of the new century, but it might have done more to remain *a* leader.

Whatever possibility there might have been for the adoption of what would today be called an "industrial policy" disappeared with the beginning of the tariff reform controversy. Joseph Chamberlain's Birmingham speech polarized debate on Britain's economic situation and focused it on a narrow range of issues, split those (like the Coefficients) who shared some common concerns, and, in general, drove discussion to extremes. In the controversy that followed many free traders simply refused to admit that any problems existed, while most tariff reformers blamed foreign governments for all of Britain's woes.

[242] Semmel, *Imperialism and Social Reform: English Social-Imperial Thought, 1875–1914,* p. 168.

[243] There was great interest in developing the "national physique," for example, but also open criticism of party politics and democracy more generally. The Germans and Japanese were admired for their smoothly functioning governments, extraordinary organizational skills, and calculating ruthlessness. Here and in their fascination with racialism and social Darwinism some of the efficiency enthusiasts came close to prefiguring the subsequent fascist critique of liberal democracy. For a discussion see Searle, *The Quest for National Efficiency: A Study in British Politics and Political Thought, 1899–1914.*

Chamberlain believed that, in order to call attention to the nation's problems, he had to issue a spectacular challenge to conventional wisdom. He might have been right, but in doing so he all but destroyed any chance that his warnings would be heeded. Viewed in this light, Chamberlain appears as a truly tragic figure.

Financial Power:
The Growing Burdens
of Empire

The question of Imperial finance may very possibly before long become
a serious problem.
—Edward Hamilton, 24 July 1895

On 13 September 1901, Sir Michael Hicks Beach, chancellor of the
Exchequer, wrote a confidential letter to his prime minister, Lord
Salisbury. Hicks Beach warned that "at the conclusion of the next
financial year we may possibly have to deal with a new financial
situation." After reviewing the trends in spending, taxation, and
debt, the chancellor asked for permission to make "an earnest appeal" for economy to his fellow cabinet ministers. "It seems to me
absolutely essential," he wrote, "that such a financial situation as I
have anticipated for next year should be met by imposing a real
check on the increase of expenditure for which we have been responsible since 1895–6."[1]

Hicks Beach asked only for a reduction in the rate at which
spending was growing. Three years later conditions had taken
a considerable turn for the worse. On 28 April 1904, the new
chancellor of the Exchequer, Austen Chamberlain, warned his
colleagues that they did not "even yet realize the stringency of
the financial situation." Chamberlain called for real reductions in
spending and especially for cuts in the army and navy estimates.
He warned that "however reluctant we may be to face the fact, the
time has come when we must frankly admit that the financial re-

[1] BM, Add. Mss. 49695, Hicks Beach
to Salisbury (enclosed), 9/13/01.

sources of the United Kingdom are inadequate to do all that we should desire in the matter of Imperial defence."[2]

These and other similar declarations by Britain's leading financial authorities were to have a powerful impact on all aspects of national policy. It is, in fact, impossible to make much sense of British strategy and diplomacy after the turn of the century without reference to the presence of a pervasive feeling of fiscal constraint and the widespread fear of financial disaster. Particularly in the second half of the period covered by this study (1900–1905), decisions regarding alliances and the organization and deployment of both the army and navy were profoundly influenced by a desire to control and, if possible, to reduce government spending. The purpose of this chapter is to explain that desire and the fear that produced it.

It is important to note at the outset that visions of imminent collapse were not a simple, direct result of increasingly burdensome government spending. Certainly the costs of ruling Britain and the empire *did* increase in the years before 1900 (see Tables 3-1, 3-2, and 3-3 at the end of this chapter). During the last two decades of the nineteenth century, average annual outlays by the government went from £76.7 million to £89.2 million.[3] For the fiscal year 1888–1889, the total gross expenditure was just over £87 million (down slightly from the year before). Ten years later, on the eve of the new century, that figure had increased over £30 million to £117.7 million.[4] During the same period, however, the gross national product of Great Britain also grew at a substantial rate. The precise dimensions of the increase remain a matter of guesswork for present-day economists, and, as previously noted, they were even less clear to contemporary observers. But it would appear that the rate of overall economic growth was close to the rate at which spending increased. By one estimate the "public sector" (including government expenditure for both civilian and military programs) accounted for between 10 and 11 percent of national income during the 1880s and 1890s. In the first decade of the twentieth century that portion had risen to 14 or 15 percent.[5]

Such an increase in the share of government spending would

[2] AC 17/2/24, cabinet memorandum, 4/28/04.

[3] Mathias, *The First Industrial Nation: An Economic History of Britain, 1700–1914*, p. 463.

[4] Mallet, *British Budgets: 1887–88 to 1912–13*, pp. 476–77.

[5] Hicks, *British Public Finances: Their Structure and Development, 1880–1952*, pp. 12–13. Another calculation puts government spending as a percentage of GNP (all at 1900 prices) at 8.8 percent for 1890, rising to a peak of 14.4 percent during the Boer War and then leveling off at 12.8 percent by 1910 (Peacock and Wiseman, *The Growth of Public Expenditure in the United Kingdom*, p. 42).

not have been trivial, but neither should it have been devastating in its economic impact, especially considering the low base to which it was added. Writing in the 1930s, economic historian J. H. Clapham concluded that, given the growth in national income, the increased outlays of the early 1900s were as easy to bear as the more modestly proportioned budgets of the 1880s had been in their time. The rise in spending, wrote Clapham, "had not been unduly disproportionate to the rise in national capacity to pay."[6]

Some participants in the turn-of-the-century debate over spending and taxation also held this view. One, economist Robert Giffen, observed in early 1902, "As to . . . our ability to meet the increased expenditure of the present time, with no real increase of burden compared with a recent date, there is absolutely no dispute."[7] Comparing 1901 with 1861, Giffen concluded that "notwithstanding the increase of burden, the country is as well able to bear this load as it was to bear the smaller sum of £70 million levied in 1861 and 1871."[8]

Giffen's optimism was not, as will be shown, widely shared, especially within the Conservative Unionist government that held power until 1905. Nevertheless, in a purely economic sense he was undoubtedly correct. Britain was able to afford far greater levels of public expenditure than most Conservatives ever dreamed possible, and in the years preceding the First World War these increasingly vast sums were collected and dispersed without driving the country into ruin.

What this suggests is that the process of measuring what will be referred to here as "financial power" has at least as much to do with subjective factors as it does with objective conditions. Regardless of its political form or of the economic organization of the society it seeks to govern, there are limits on the capacity of a state to mobilize national resources in the pursuit of its various objectives.[9] At the extreme, these limits are "real" or "absolute." In addition to this outermost boundary there are also what might be called "virtual" limits, constraints imposed by the requirements of economic well-being or political stability that have nothing directly to do with the total size of the productive mechanism. Too much government spending for purposes of immediate consumption can divert resources from investment, thereby limiting the scope for future eco-

[6] Clapham, *An Economic History of Modern Britain: Machines and National Rivalries* (1887–1914), p. 410.

[7] Sir Robert Giffen, "A Financial Retrospect, 1861–1901," in Giffen, *Economic Inquiries and Studies* 2:321.

[8] Ibid., p. 325.

[9] This mobilization is what Charles Tilly has called the process of "extraction." For a stimulating discussion, see Tilly, "War Making and State Making as Organized Crime," in Evans, Rueschemeyer, and Skocpol, eds., *Bringing the State Back In*, pp. 169–91.

nomic growth. Too much taxation (whether in the form of levies on earnings, property, transactions, and commodities or the more brutal, direct expropriation of goods and services from unwilling citizens) can produce resistance, evasion, and even political unrest. The assessment of financial power by national leaders is nothing more than the effort to determine where these virtual limits lie at any given moment.

After the turn of the century key British statesmen came to believe that their country was near the end of its financial resources and they acted accordingly. Men like Arthur Balfour and Austen Chamberlain were convinced not that the country had "run out of money" but that bigger budgets and higher taxes would damage the economy, weaken the nation's ability to raise large sums of money in an emergency, and provoke political opposition from either the rich or the poor and perhaps from both. Whether they were right or wrong in these judgments is less important for explaining their actions than understanding what they believed.

Writing in a secret 1904 cabinet memorandum, Balfour put the problem in these words:

> We cannot say that the country could pay so much for its army: that another £100,000 would mean either a violent anti-military reaction or financial ruin. . . . There *is* a point at which the reduction of troops would leave the Empire defenseless. There *is* a point at which expenditure would become unbearable. . . . But long before these various limits are reached they will make themselves felt.[10]

How do such barriers "make themselves felt"? What caused Balfour and his colleagues to believe that they were approaching the limits of Britain's financial power? In order to understand the perception of a collision between strategic needs and fiscal constraints that was so influential after 1900 it is necessary first to refer to certain intellectual and economic developments of the preceding century.

Background
Fiscal Orthodoxy

Writing in 1936 John Maynard Keynes observed that "practical men, who believe themselves to be quite exempt from any intellec-

---

[10] PRO, Cab. 4/1/26B, "A Note on Army Reform and the Military   Needs of the Empire," A. J. Balfour, 6/24/04.

tual influences, are usually the slaves of some defunct economist. Madmen in authority, who hear voices in the air, are distilling their frenzy from some academic scribbler of a few years back."[11] Certainly the men who led Britain in 1900 were far from mad. But there can be no doubt that they were heavily influenced in their thinking about financial matters by the writings of economists and statesmen who were dead if not necessarily intellectually defunct. As much as in the realm of trade, contemporary arguments about fiscal policy were littered with pious references to the wisdom of the "ancients." This was not just a matter of preening for public approval. Secret memoranda from this period intended solely for internal consumption contain frequent references to the authority of past experts, and especially to John Stuart Mill and William Gladstone.[12] The economic historian H. V. Emy has written that the principles of British taxation "had remained the same from Adam Smith to John Stuart Mill" and that the latter was still the principal authority in the last decade of the nineteenth century. An examination of both the public record and intragovernmental sources confirms this assertion.[13]

The first and most important component of the dominant financial orthodoxy was the belief that government ought to limit its interference in the economy to the greatest extent feasible. A precise and absolute demarcation between the public and private spheres was not possible, but all additions to the very basic requirements of defending the nation from external enemies and preserving internal law and order were to be viewed with skepticism. In his *Principles of Political Economy* (first published in 1848) Mill argued against any simple definition of legitimate government responsibility (he pointed out, for example, that the authorities might have to look out for the interests of infants, lunatics, and those "fallen into imbecility"), concluding that the only universal rule in such matters was "the simple and vague one" that interference "should never be admitted but when the case of expediency is strong."[14] Minimal interference meant minimal government spending, which permitted in turn relatively low levels of taxation. Mill and others pointed out that attention had to be paid not just to the rate at which taxes were levied but also to the manner in which they were applied. Arbitrary, unpredictable taxes assessed against profits and savings could

[11] Keynes, *The General Theory of Employment, Interest, and Money,* p. 383.

[12] See, for example, PRO, T 168/52, "The Question of Taxation Discussed," draft, 12/31/01, and PRO, T 168/93, "Financial Situation After War," 12/26/01.

[13] Emy, *Liberals, Radicals, and Social Politics, 1892–1914,* p. 189. See P. Kennedy, *The Rise of the Anglo-German Antagonism, 1860–1914,* p. 324. See also French, *British Economic and Strategic Planning, 1905–1915,* pp. 7–15.

[14] Mill, *Principles of Political Economy,* p. 482.

disrupt the process of economic growth even if they were not imposed at an especially high rate. Still, the greatest danger came
from "excess of taxation," which could "be carried so far as to discourage industry by insufficiency of reward."[15] Even before this
point had been reached, Mill warned, such excess could "[prevent]
or greatly [check] accumulation, or [cause] the capital accumulated
to be sent for investment to foreign countries."[16] For this reason
taxation and the spending that might require it were best kept as
low as possible. In keeping with this dictate, resistance to new government ventures and the imposition of restraints on those which
did exist was a strong and continuous force in British politics. As
one author puts it, "'Retrenchment' was one of the prime political
obsessions of the nineteenth century."[17] It was believed that low public spending would permit continued growth and ever-increasing
prosperity. This faith was reflected in the budget figures for the
fifty years from 1820 to 1870, which increased only slowly while national income soared.

Even in the best of all possible worlds it was recognized that
some government expenditure was unavoidable. To the greatest
possible degree, demands on the public purse were to be met out of
current tax revenues. In this simpler era before the discovery of
miraculous multipliers, deficit spending was considered not only
sinful but impossible in practice over any length of time. The first
job of a chancellor of the Exchequer was to see that the annual budget balanced.[18] If tax revenues were unexpectedly low or some
emergency forced higher-than-anticipated spending, the resulting
deficit could be met by short-term borrowing. Ideally, even the
costs of war should have been defrayed by increased taxation rather
than loans. During the struggle against Napoleon this had proved
impossible, and successive governments spent the rest of the nineteenth century scrupulously paying off the burden of debt that had
resulted. If another emergency arose, Britain's leaders wanted to
be able to have recourse to the vast public money markets of London. Meeting past responsibilities and avoiding unnecessary peacetime borrowing were the two principal means of ensuring the nation's credit.[19]

Any discussion of public spending and finance must come back
eventually to the necessary evil of taxation. Mill had declared in
1848 that "taxes are either direct or indirect." According to his defi-

---

[15] Ibid., p. 532.
[16] Ibid., p. 533.
[17] Porter, *The Lion's Share: A Short History of British Imperialism, 1850–1970*, p. 49.

[18] P. Kennedy, *Rise of the Anglo-German Antagonism*, p. 325.
[19] Ibid. See also French, *British Economic and Strategic Planning*, p. 14.

nition a direct tax was one "demanded from the very persons who, it is intended or desired, should pay it." Such taxes could be imposed on expenditure but fell more typically on the various forms of income, whether rent, profits, or wages. Indirect taxes, by contrast, were those which were "demanded from one person in the expectation and intention that he shall indemnify himself at the expense of another."[20] The most common forms of indirect taxes were those imposed on commodities like tea, tobacco, and alcohol, some of which were imported while others were produced in Britain.

From the middle of the nineteenth century it was generally accepted that, as Mill wrote, "there are some forms of indirect taxation which must be preemptorily excluded." In particular, "taxes on commodities, for revenue purposes, must not operate as protecting duties."[21] If a duty on imports of a commodity was imposed, all sources of that commodity, whether domestic or foreign, would have to be taxed equally, otherwise home producers might be able to earn unfair profits at the expense of consumers. Under Prime Minister Sir Robert Peel (1834–1835 and 1841–1846) and William Gladstone, who served twice as chancellor of the Exchequer (1852–1855 and 1859–1865) and four times as prime minister (1868–1874, 1880–1885, 1886, and 1892–1894), the government eliminated most import duties, and the field of indirect taxation was reduced to a relatively small number of items.

Fiscal orthodoxy also demanded that direct taxes, and especially the levy on incomes, be tightly constrained. Taxes on profits would, Mill warned, be "extremely detrimental to the national wealth"[22] as would any imposition on savings. Wage earners below a certain income should not be taxed lest they be deprived of "what is necessary for healthful existence."[23] It was also generally accepted that the incomes of the wealthy should be left untouched in all but the gravest emergencies. During the Napoleonic and Crimean wars, direct exactions on incomes had been raised, but each time with the intention of lowering them again once the crisis had passed. The income tax (like the government's ability to borrow) was generally regarded as a "reserve engine" to be used only in a crisis.[24]

Whatever their other qualities, the different varieties of taxation did not weigh equally on all segments of the population. As a confidential Treasury Department memorandum pointed out in 1895, indirect taxes tended to fall "on the consuming masses" while direct taxes were those "levied on property or persons, of which (at any

[20] Mill, *Principles of Political Economy,* pp. 495–96.
[21] Ibid., p. 523.
[22] Ibid., p. 497.

[23] Ibid., p. 499.
[24] P. Kennedy, *Rise of the Anglo-German Antagonism,* p. 325.

rate) by far the greater part falls on the propertied classes."[25] This arrangement raised questions of equity that became more controversial with the passage of time. The view of Conservative politicians tended to be that direct taxes should be kept low and that the two classes should essentially contribute in proportion to their numbers. Equality of burdens, by this definition, required that indirect taxes make up the largest fraction of total resources. As the nineteenth century drew to a close this position was criticized by Liberal theoreticians who had begun to experiment with the idea of higher direct taxes, which would increase with the ratepayers' income. It was argued in some quarters that burdens might best be assessed in proportion to ability to bear them or, in other words, that there should be higher direct taxes on the wealthy few and relatively lower indirect levies on the masses.[26] The notion that progressive taxes might be used for the express purpose of redistributing income between rich and poor had not yet emerged as a reasonable position in public debate, but it was not far off.

The men who took power in 1895 tended to be defenders of the accepted wisdom of preceding decades on financial matters. They believed that interference in the economy was bad and that low absolute levels of government spending were good (although new forms of social expenditure might be politically expedient, and increased outlays on defense and colonial development might be necessary for the well-being of the empire). Balanced budgets, low debt, and a preference for nonprotective, indirect taxes as sources of revenue were the order of the day.

Trends in Spending and Taxation

Brief reference has already been made to the increase in public spending that occurred between 1880 and 1900. It is important to point out that this acceleration in the cost of governing followed a long period of comparative stability. Between 1820 and 1850, average annual spending actually decreased from £51.8 million per year in the twenties to £51 million in the forties. Of this, nearly 60 percent went to repayment of outstanding war debt, 30 percent (between £13 and £15 million per year) was devoted to defense, and the remaining 10 to 12 percent was used to fund civil government. During the next three decades spending expanded steadily but still quite slowly. For the 1850s the average annual figure was £59.6 million, growing just under £7 million to £66 million per year

[25] PRO, Cab. 37/39/38, "Some Remarks on Public Finance," E. W. Hamilton, 7/24/95.

[26] See Emy, *Liberals, Radicals, and Social Politics*, pp. 192–95.

in the 1870s.[27] From this point budgets began to grow at an increasingly rapid rate. Between 1884 and 1890 total government spending grew by £4.3 million or 5 percent, an average annual increase of £.7 million. From 1890 to 1896 the budget expanded by £13.8 million or 15 percent in six years, up an average of £2.3 million per year.[28]

The growth of public spending had both internal and external causes. With the extension of the franchise in Britain came demands for higher levels of social spending. The economic historian Eric Hobsbawm has written that "as the working classes got the vote—in 1867, but especially in 1884–5—it became only too obvious that they would demand—and receive—substantial public intervention for greater welfare."[29] Aware of the potential power of the newly enfranchised masses, and fearful that they might be stirred to support radical causes, mainstream politicians of all stripes competed to offer appealing packages of benefits. In some cases these represented honest efforts to ameliorate the conditions of the working man. In others they were no less sincere attempts to ward off the looming specter of socialism. As Arthur Balfour put it in 1895, "Social legislation . . . is not merely to be distinguished from Socialist legislation but it is its most direct opposite and its most effective antidote."[30]

During the last quarter of the nineteenth century both the effective demand for social services and the willingness of ideologically diverse British governments to supply them grew considerably. The net result was a dramatic expansion in "civil expenditures."[31] Of the charges to this account (which included pensions and Post Office and revenue collection costs), government assistance to education grew the most rapidly, increasing four times by one official estimate between the mid-1870s and the mid-1890s.[32]

While the percentage increases in civil and social service outlays were most impressive, the absolute bulk of the growth in spending was due to mounting defense costs. From the Crimean War to 1895 the army had received greater annual attention than the navy. In fiscal year 1887–1888, for example, the navy was allocated £13 million while total expenditure on the army was approximately £17.7 million.[33] By the close of the 1880s the continental European pow-

[27] Mathias, *The First Industrial Nation,* p. 463.

[28] PRO, Cab. 37/58/85, "Growth of Expenditure," unsigned, 9/12/01.

[29] E. J. Hobsbawm, *Industry and Empire,* p. 237.

[30] D. Fraser, *The Evolution of the British Welfare State,* p. 129.

[31] For one set of figures see PRO, T 168/59, "A Provisional Forecast 1903–4," draft, 11/16/02. See also Mallet, *British Budgets,* pp. 508–509.

[32] *Hansard Parliamentary Debates,* 4th ser., vol. 39 (1896), pp. 1071–73.

[33] Mallet, *British Budgets,* pp. 500, 504.

ers, the Japanese, and the Americans posed a collective threat of unparalleled dimensions to England's continued naval supremacy. In an effort to maintain its position, Britain was forced to build more and better ships, and the size of its naval budget grew accordingly. The Naval Defense Act of 1889 boosted spending in 1890–1891 to £18.0 million and to £18.1 million in 1891–1892. The army expenditure for those years was £18.6 million and £18.3 million, respectively. In fiscal year 1894–1895 the naval expenditure consumed a greater relative proportion of the budget for the first time in almost forty years, standing at £18.5 million as compared with £18.4 million for the army.[34]

The explosion in spending that marked the last decade of the century was financed essentially in three ways. First, the general increase in national prosperity meant that indirect or commodity taxes were generating more revenue. Britain's larger and wealthier population was consuming more tea, tobacco, and beer, thereby filling the national coffers with much-needed cash. It had not seemed necessary for some time to tax new items or, for the most part, to impose heavier assessments on those already taxed. The income tax was also yielding a greater return and, despite strong resistance, it had been increased slightly since the middle of the nineteenth century, from $5d.$ per pound after the close of the Crimean War to around $8d.$ in 1895.[35] Finally, in 1894 the Liberal chancellor Sir William Harcourt had created a unified estate tax or "death duty" on inherited property. This amounted to a new direct tax graduated from 1 percent on property worth £500 or less to 8 percent on property over £1 million.[36] Whatever their scruples about the principles on which it was based, the Conservatives found the new death duty too convenient to do without. In 1895 inheritance taxes were almost as important a source of revenue as the income tax.[37]

Taken together, these developments amounted to a significant evolution in national policy. From the 1850s to the 1890s there was a steady shift in the balance between direct and indirect taxes. By one estimate, in 1841–1842 the government collected around £50 million, 73 percent from indirect taxes and the rest through direct means. In 1880 total exactions were £66 million, 60 percent from indirect and 40 percent from direct taxation, and in 1895 £87 million was raised, 54 percent from indirect taxes and 46 percent from

---

[34] Ibid.
[35] Ibid., p. 484. See also PRO, Cab. 37/39/38.

[36] Emy, *Liberals, Radicals, and Social Politics*, p. 191.
[37] PRO, Cab. 37/39/38.

direct levies.[38] The rising overall level of government spending, and the shifting revenue base had begun to put pressure on the financial system well before the crisis of 1901.

Crisis

There can be no doubt that it was the Boer War that precipitated the 1901–1905 financial crisis. Fighting between British forces and Dutch settlers in South Africa lasted well over two years, and the cost of supporting forces in a distant conflict drove government spending to unheard-of levels and caused a sharp increase in taxes. Indeed, it is tempting to see the war as the sole cause of the events that followed.

Undue concentration on the immediate impact of the Boer War would tend, however, to obscure two important points. First, serious concern about England's ability to bear the burdens of empire preceded the outbreak of hostilities by several years. Second, although wartime expenditures may have hastened the day when the virtual limits on Britain's financial power (as seen by its leaders) were reached, they do not explain the presumed location of those limits. The problem for British statesmen was not simply one of objective measurement but of interpretation. Thus the Boer War was a catalytic rather than simply a causative event, and the danger it heralded was perhaps more imagined than real. Subsequent British governments were able to spend more on both defense and domestic services than the Conservatives believed to be either economically healthy or politically feasible. But they did so only by further modifying principles that in 1905 most Conservatives felt had been bent to the very breaking point.

Anxiety and Optimism, 1895–1899

Within one month of the Salisbury government's taking power, warnings of impending difficulty were bubbling up from inside the bureaucracy.[39] On 24 July Edward Hamilton of the Treasury De-

[38] Ibid., and PRO, T 168/51, "Direct v. Indirect Taxation," unsigned, 1902(?).

[39] Within a British government at this time, discussions of fiscal policy centered on the preparation of a yearly budget. Principal responsibility for this document rested with the chancellor of the Exchequer, who was expected to report to Parliament each spring on the state of the nation's finances. The chancellor's budget statement traditionally reviewed the collections and outlays of the year just past and offered a preliminary estimate of the amounts that would have to be raised to meet expenses in the coming fiscal year. Any change in tax or spending policy would be announced by the chancellor in his April speech before the House of Commons. Soon after the completion of one budget cycle the process would begin again,

partment circulated to the new cabinet a memo entitled "Some Remarks on Public Finance." Because of its unusual force and clarity and because it was an early expression of arguments that would be repeated later, this document is worth quoting at some length.

Hamilton began with an ironical reference to the past:

> A little more than twenty years ago we were in the days of "leaps and bounds" of revenue, when Mr. Lowe declared that the chief difficulty of the Chancellor of the Exchequer was to know how to get rid of the money which "persisted in pouring in upon him." We are now in days of "leaps and bounds" of expenditure when the chief difficulty of the Finance Minister of this country is, or soon will be, how to raise money sufficient to cover the demands which "persist in pouring in upon him."[40]

National expenditure had risen to over £100 million per year by 1895. But, Hamilton warned, "large as that sum is, there is every prospect of a still further increase, and a very formidable increase, in the not very distant future." The reasons for this situation were not far to seek:

> Some of the services which the State has undertaken are in their nature services of automatic growth, notably educational services; while the tendency of responsible as well as irresponsible persons is to saddle the State with further undertakings which must be accompanied with heavy cost to the taxpayer. Agriculturalists are pressing to be further relieved from the burden of local rates; school teachers are demanding pensions; the working classes are claiming some provisions for old age—a claim which, if it be freely satisfied, may mean a boundless subsidy from the State;

---

first with a series of consultations between the chancellor and middle-level officials in the Treasury and Customs departments. The views of these civil servants were often very influential in shaping the chancellor's position on how much could be spent in the year ahead. By the late summer or early autumn, the chancellor was ready to begin a series of negotiations with his cabinet-level counterparts who were in the process of preparing their own estimates of future expenditure. For the period under examination here, the most important figures on the "demand" side of the financial equation were the second earl of Selborne (first lord of the Admiralty from 1900 to 1905) and the two secretaries of state for war, St. John Broderick (1900–1903) and H. O. Arnold-Forster (1903–1905). During the private discussions of autumn and winter the prime minister played the role of moderator and referee, attempting to balance the many competing interests at stake. It was his government, after all, that would rise or fall on the result, even though the budget announced in early spring might bear the chancellor's name.

[40] PRO, Cab. 37/39/38, p. 1.

. . . extensions of the Empire cannot be effected without material cost; there is little hope that the War Office and the Admiralty will be satisfied with smaller provisions; and Ireland . . . is "always with us." In view of these considerations, the question of Imperial finance may very possibly before long become a serious problem.[41]

In fiscal year 1895–1896 Hamilton estimated that total expenditures of just over £103 million (of which £36.6 million went to defense and £21 million, to civil services) would be paid for out of direct taxes (£40.2 million), indirect taxes (£47 million), and nontax receipts (mostly Post Office charges amounting to £16 million). The near balance between direct and indirect taxes was the result of a long-term shift away from the latter that had begun over thirty years before. Indeed, since 1897, the only indirect tax to be increased was that on beer and spirits; others had been reduced while the income tax and other direct taxes had risen.[42]

The question, according to Hamilton, was how long Britain would be "able to make ends meet under the present system of taxation."[43] There seemed little prospect of any spending cuts; in fact, the country seemed to have lost all sense of economy. Although in the past the government could "reckon on some natural increase of revenue, owing to the continuous growth of population," it now seemed likely that such increases would be outstripped by the automatic growth in outlays. "If the services which the State has already undertaken grow much more, or if new charges are incurred, the problem of devising some additional method or methods for balancing the account of public revenue and expenditure will ere long have to be faced."[44]

Assuming that spending could not be slowed or cut, there were several ways in which the nation's books might be brought into balance. In the first place it might be possible to suspend the so-called Sinking Fund, diverting to current expenditure that portion of yearly revenue designated for debt repayment. In wartime such a deviation from accepted practice might be possible. "But in normal times to reduce seriously the amount devoted to redeem debt would . . . tell sensibly on our credit and on the financial position which we occupy in the eyes of the world."[45] Hamilton, like most of his contemporaries, believed the Sinking Fund should be held in reserve as an emergency national "war chest."

The second way of dealing with the emerging problem was to

[41] Ibid., pp. 1–2.
[42] Ibid., p. 4.
[43] Ibid.

[44] Ibid., p. 6.
[45] Ibid.

boost existing taxes. Indirect levies might be raised, but the result could easily be a drop in the consumption of taxed items and thus a net reduction in revenue. Higher indirect rates would take up whatever slack was available for use in an emergency as well as create predictable political problems with the working- and middle-class citizens upon whom they weighed most heavily. Thus, Hamilton concluded, "the present duties on commodities, or 'indirect taxes,' either do not admit of being raised, or else . . . it would be highly impolitic to raise them in times of peace."[46]

Existing direct taxes were scarcely more promising as potential sources of greater revenue. A further escalation of the death duties was dismissed out of hand, and "an Income Tax at 8d in the pound seem[ed] already to be at too high a rate for times of peace." Further increases could create serious future problems because the income tax was "the one direct tax of all others to which resort is had most easily, and thus most fittingly if we are involved in war."[47] What Hamilton did not need to say was that direct taxes also fell most heavily on those upper- and upper-middle-class voters from whom the Conservative party drew much of its support.

These considerations led to a third and final alternative—the creation of some new tax. Because a new direct levy seemed to be "almost outside the range of practical politics," Hamilton was forced "by a process of exhaustion" to propose the imposition of more indirect taxes.[48] Here there were several possibilities to be weighed, of which the most obvious was the old levy on corn imports. This duty had been proposed by Peel in 1846, was adopted in 1849, and remained in force for twenty years during the heyday of free trade. Nevertheless, Hamilton warned quite accurately that a new corn duty would raise questions of protectionism and "revive the old controversy about the 'big loaf' and the 'little loaf'" even if the duty had no appreciable impact on the cost of bread.[49] Furthermore, a duty on corn imports would raise the price of all grain, even that produced domestically. In so doing "it would offend against one of the most generally accepted canons of finance, which is, that no tax ought to take out of the pockets of the people more than what it brings into the Exchequer."[50]

The only way of avoiding these problems was to impose a duty on some item like sugar that was not produced at home. Hamilton estimated that a modest tax on sugar imports could raise as much as £4 million each year. Such a duty might arouse some of the same

[46] Ibid., p. 8.
[47] Ibid., p. 9.
[48] Ibid., p. 10.
[49] Ibid., p. 11.
[50] Ibid., p. 12.

consumer complaints as a tax on imported corn, and it would probably raise "awkward questions" regarding the incidence of taxation on rich and poor, but it appeared to be the one means of broadening the existing system without resorting to protective measures.[51]

Hamilton's memorandum reveals the contours of the financial problem as it appeared to him and, as they turned their attention to it, to most of his superiors as well. The nation appeared to have its neck in a gradually tightening noose from which no easy escape was possible. On the one hand it was widely assumed that there was little hope that the growth of spending could be slowed or stopped, let alone reversed. On the other, there appeared to be serious political and economic objections to all means of enhancing revenues. Raising existing direct and indirect taxes meant risking future prosperity and antagonizing voters, wealthy ones in the first instance, the less wealthy (but increasingly numerous) in the second. The one direction in which the tax base might conceivably be extended ran dangerously close to the slippery slope of protectionism. Nothing short of a recognized national emergency could render this safe political ground on which to tread. Barring such a liberating disaster, there seemed no way of avoiding eventual insolvency. "What we have to fear," Hamilton concluded, "is . . . a gradual and insidious growth of public changes outstripping the natural increase of revenue."[52]

After receiving Hamilton's memo Hicks Beach commissioned a study of possible import duties from the Board of Customs. The results echoed Hamilton's analysis. H. W. Primrose of the board's staff reviewed a variety of conceivable import taxes, concluding that "reviving the tax on sugar, possibly the tax on corn, are as much as can perhaps be contemplated in the present day. And even they . . . would bring into acute prominence the controversy . . . in regard to the relative taxation of rich and poor."[53] Within an already limited category, the range of choices available was small, and none was especially appetizing.

In early spring of 1896 the chancellor warned Parliament of difficult times ahead: "The grave question that I think this House and this country ought to consider is this—whether our expenditure is not now increasing faster than our capacity to bear it." If spending continued to increase and revenue did not grow faster, Hicks Beach cautioned, "we shall be within measureable distance of a time when we shall have to choose between diminishing or putting an end to the reduction of our National Debt and an increase

---

[51] Ibid., p. 15.
[52] Ibid., p. 16.

[53] PRO, Cab. 37/40/53, "Possible Registration Duties," H. W. Primrose, 10/95.

of taxation."[54] The chancellor touched on the question of relative taxation, noting that for the last fifty years Britain's ratepayers had borne "the bulk" of new expenditures.[55] No conclusions were drawn from this trend, and Hicks Beach closed by saying simply that further increases in spending were "a cause of great anxiety."[56]

Whatever fears had been aroused during the first year of the new government were largely dispelled by the fortuitous developments of the next three. All major categories of expenditure increased between 1896 and 1899, but renewed prosperity brought in so much revenue that there were substantial yearly surpluses. After announcing the third such surplus in as many reports, Hicks Beach was in an understandably expansive mood. "In a year of unexampled expenditure," he pointed out, "we have been able to provide, not only for the whole of that expenditure without any increase of taxation, but we have also been able to make some remissions to the taxpayers."[57]

Despite some early premonitions, therefore, the closing years of the century seemed to confirm the wisdom of what had gone before. The chancellor put the proposition to his parliamentary audience with a flourish of late-Victorian rhetoric:

> Is there not something in the picture which I have attempted to draw tonight, of a great and wealthy nation meeting necessities far greater than before, from revenue larger, more bouyant and more easily raised than at any previous period of its history, which may strengthen our belief in the soundness of the financial policy which this country has so long pursued?[58]

It was the last moment of tranquil self-confidence that Hicks Beach or his successors would be able to enjoy. The precariousness of existing financial arrangments had been out of sight if not entirely out of mind for three years. Now it was about to reemerge with alarming suddenness.

By early 1899 it had begun to appear likely that revenues for the coming year would not grow as quickly as in those just past. At the same time, both the navy and the army were pressing for substantial budget increases, £3 million in the first case and £1.25 million in the second. This combination raised the nasty prospect of sizable deficits, perhaps as large as £4 million.[59]

[54] *Hansard Parliamentary Debates*, 4th ser., vol. 39 (1896), p. 1073.
[55] Ibid., p. 1074.
[56] Ibid., p. 1075.
[57] *Hansard Parliamentary Debates*, 4th ser., vol. 56 (1898), p. 695.
[58] Ibid., p. 696.
[59] H.H. Mss., 3M/E, Hicks Beach to Salisbury, 1/27/99.

On 27 January Hicks Beach minuted Salisbury, advising him that the prospects for the coming financial year were "very disagreeable." The chancellor complained of the incessant demands of his colleagues and insisted that he could not make up the coming year's deficit by borrowing or by suspending the Sinking Fund. Such steps might suffice to deal with a momentary crisis in which the Exchequer found itself for some reason temporarily short of cash. "But this is no temporary emergency—it is the result of a continuous increase of expenditure which will grow rather than diminish in future years."[60] After the optimism of the three preceding years, Hicks Beach had reverted quickly to the gloomy outlook with which he assumed office. The only responsible way of meeting demands for more spending, he claimed, was through increased taxation. This would preserve the financial integrity of the country while serving as a check on further extravagance. As Hicks Beach put it, "Nothing but increased taxation will turn people's thoughts to some regard for economy."[61]

Salisbury was understandably reluctant to endorse such drastic measures. "I think [first lord of the Admiralty Lord] Goschen is insatiable," he consoled Hicks Beach, "but I am rather disposed towards a loan. An increase of taxation will require justification because it is clearly an alarmist budget."[62] That, came the response from the chancellor, was precisely the point, and borrowing would only diminish the urgency of a much-needed warning.[63]

Hicks Beach used the occasion of his fourth budget speech in the spring of 1899 to make public his renewed concern over the direction of the nation's finances. The chancellor's position could not help but be somewhat awkward. While he complained of the growth of spending in areas "in which, in the old days the Government of the country was never deemed capable of acting at all," he was nevertheless forced to admit that the largest increases had come in defense, not civil or social services.[64] These outlays had been forced on Britain by the "increased and increasing armaments of other nations." To a considerable degree, then, the trend in spending was a reflection of external events to which any government would have had to respond.[65] Still, the growth of recent years could not go on forever. It was reaching the point at which automatic increases in revenue from existing taxes would no longer be able to cover an additional five or six million pounds of spending

---

[60] Ibid.
[61] Ibid.
[62] Hicks Beach, *Life of Sir Michael Hicks Beach* 2:91.
[63] H.H. Mss., 3M/E, Hicks Beach to

Salisbury, 1/30/99.
[64] *Hansard Parliamentary Debates*, 4th ser., vol. 69 (1899), pp. 1004–1006.
[65] Ibid., p. 1025.

per year. Even a higher schedule of rates for existing levies might soon be inadequate to meet the demand for further expenditure. As Hicks Beach put it, "If this [growth in spending] is to continue, Parliament and the country must make up their minds not only to large increases in the existing taxes, but also the discovery of new and productive sources of revenue." But, and here was the rub, "I will venture to prophesy that the result of this would necessarily be a reaction against this great expenditure, which no one would deplore more than I should, for I am convinced that the result of such a reaction would be to reduce the efficiency and the strength of our defensive services."[66]

As attention began to shift toward South Africa, Hicks Beach was already convinced that the nation was walking a thin line between solvency and disaster. Slight increases in existing taxes could cover costs and might help to put a damper on demands for even more spending, but such measures were, at best, palliatives. Some more lasting solution to the nation's predicament would have to be found. Thus, out of public view, the search for a perfect new tax, indirect, nonprotective, undetectable, and capable of rapid expansion, went on.[67] The parameters of this search were imposed by accepted notions of responsible finance and of what the political traffic would bear. Not surprisingly, the range of choices was no wider than it had seemed four years earlier when Edward Hamilton surveyed the situation for his new superiors.

The Shock of War, 1899–1902

The financial impact of the Boer War can be briefly summarized. Early estimates that a conflict in South Africa would cost £5 or £10 million or even £21.5 million were soon swept aside.[68] In 1899–1900 army expenditures rose from £21 million to £44.1 million, and over the next two years they grew to £92.4 million and £94.2 million. Overall government spending went up accordingly, reaching the dizzying figure of £205 million in 1901–1902. Instead of the usual surplus, yearly budgets showed massive deficits, almost £14 million in 1899–1900 and approximately £53 million for each of the next two years.[69]

Emergency conditions were met at first in the time-honored fashion of the early and mid 1800s. The income tax was increased 50 percent from 8*d.* to 1*s.* in 1900–1901 and then by another 2*d.* in

---

[66] Ibid., p. 1004.

[67] See PRO, Cab. 37/50/51, "An Uniform Registration Toll of 1d per Cwt. on All Food Imports," Customs Department, 8/15/99.

[68] H.H. Mss., 3M/E, Hicks Beach to Salisbury, 12/24/99.

[69] Mallet, *British Budgets*, pp. 476–77, 504.

the following year. Duties on tea and tobacco went up, the Sinking Fund was temporarily suspended, and considerable borrowing was undertaken.[70]

From the onset of war to the end of 1900, most eyes focused on the immediate problems of war finance. For a time the exigencies of the struggle for South Africa had the dual effect of worsening Britain's immediate financial position and obscuring the long-term problems that had come to light in 1895 and again in early 1899. As the threat to the physical security of the empire receded, worries about its fiscal soundness became more pronounced. Decisions deferred on several previous occasions could no longer be put aside.

The Search for Alternatives, 1901–1903

Between 1901 and the end of 1903 events moved forward in several stages. Convinced that the moment of truth had finally arrived, those responsible for the nation's finances struggled against their self-imposed bonds, moving first one way and then the other. Initial, gingerly attempts to expand the country's tax base by imposing new customs duties failed to help matters much, and by the end of 1901 there were calls for at least a deceleration in the rate of growth of spending. When these efforts failed the financial authorities, now somewhat less inhibited about new taxes, proposed a duty on corn imports; at the same time they encouraged efforts to push some of the burden of imperial defense off onto the colonies. With the revocation of the corn tax in 1903 and the obvious failure of burden sharing, the virtual limits on Britain's financial power had been reached and indeed to some extent exceeded. As will be shown in the next section, by 1904 the exhaustion of alternatives led to widespread agreement within the Government that spending on armaments would have to be reduced in real terms, regardless of the defensive needs of the empire.

The opening moves in the drama that was about to unfold came, as before, from inside the bureaucracy. On 4 January 1901 Edward Hamilton informed Hicks Beach that his earlier predictions for the coming year had been too sanguine. It now appeared that the deficit would be twice as large as had been estimated only two months before, amounting to £25 million instead of £12.7 million. Even if the Sinking Fund was suspended for another year, almost £20 million would have to be found either from further loans or additional taxation.[71]

At the end of the month Hamilton was permitted to make his

[70] Ibid., p. 484.
[71] PRO, T 168/48, "Possible Financial Position, 1901–2," Edward Hamilton to Hicks Beach, 1/4/01.

case to the entire cabinet. The central theme of Hamilton's 31 January memorandum on "The Financial Problem" was that the country faced challenges extending beyond the war in South Africa. True, that war had already gone on twice as long and been twice as costly as originally expected. To pay for the conflict large loans and sizable tax increases had proven necessary. Indeed, Hamilton suggested, except for the income tax and the duty on tea, all existing levies had been raised to their limit. But this was not the heart of the matter.

> If the present inadequate revenue were solely due to the military operations in South Africa, and were thus of a temporary nature only, it would, in my judgement, be best to confine the fiscal changes of this year's Budget to further increases of [the tea and income taxes] . . . and to retain the [recent] . . . additions to taxation . . . for a fixed period, to enable the deficits of the last three years to be reduced. We are however, I fear confronted with a more serious state of things.[72]

Even if the war (and the much smaller military operations then going on in China) were to cease within the coming year, revenue from existing taxes would barely be sufficient to meet costs. If the Sinking Fund was also restored and the long process of debt repayment was begun again, the bind would be even tighter. Finally, after six years of prosperity there was every reason to fear a cyclical downturn in the country's economic performance. Revenues could thus be expected to fall even if tax rates remained constant, and, meanwhile, demands upon the government would stay high.

In Hamilton's judgment the moment had arrived when the nation's tax structure was no longer adequate to its needs.

> In view . . . of the probable insufficiency of revenues apart from the war . . . one may well ask whether we should be justified in depending any longer on our present resources. . . . The conclusion to which I have, with great reluctance, come is that it is necessary seriously to consider the question of enlarging our sources of revenue and of broadening the basis of our taxation system.[73]

Repeating his analysis of 1895, Hamilton concluded that the only way to broaden the tax base permanently was through the creation of some new indirect levy.

[72] PRO, T 168/52, "The Financial Problem," Edward Hamilton to the cabinet, 1/31/01.
[73] Ibid.

Two such duties were then under consideration at the Customs Board, one on the import of sugar and another on exports of British coal. Neither of the two rather peculiar alternatives put forward by Customs officials was without difficulties, but both had the virtue of at least appearing to be free of protective intent. The problem with a tax on coal exports was that, if it worked, it would decrease foreign consumption and hurt the British carrying trade. A sugar duty did not protect any domestic industry, and it could also be argued that a similar tax had existed in the not-too-distant past.[74] Still, there was no assurance that reimposition would not provoke resistance. As Hamilton warned, "It would be easy to organize a great ado on behalf not only of the 'poor' consumers, but also of the many industries which make extensive use of sugar."[75]

By April of 1901 Hicks Beach was fully committed to the views expressed in Hamilton's memorandum. Indeed, there does not appear to have been any serious opposition within the government to the arguments advanced by Treasury and Customs officials. The annual budget statement for 1901–1902 announced a further 2*d.* increase in the income tax as well as the introduction of new sugar and coal duties. These last two steps were frankly identified by the chancellor as an unwilling "departure of great importance from that system of taxation" to which the country had grown accustomed.[76] Still, the situation would permit no less. "I am afraid," Hicks Beach told the House of Commons, "that the real difficulty before us is not so much the cost of the war in South Africa and China as the increase of what may be called our ordinary expenditure."[77] With the most recent advance in the income tax, direct taxes had been forced about as high as they would go. Further levies on wine and beer would yield little, and increased duties on tea and tobacco were deemed "unwise."[78] Somehow the basis of the entire financial system would have to be broadened in order to meet costs in the years ahead.

One important feature of the 1901 budget statement is that it contained no direct challenge to demands for ever-increasing expenditure. Hicks Beach seems at this point to have regarded the upward trend as a veritable force of nature that could neither be resisted nor controlled. Liberals might favor devoting more money to education, and Conservatives might prefer a larger defense bud-

[74] See PRO, T 168/56, "The New Customs Duties, 1901: Memorandum Descriptive of Their Character and of the Circumstances Attending Their Imposition," G. L. Ryder, 8/16/01.

[75] PRO, T 168/52, 1/31/01.

[76] *Hansard Parliamentary Debates*, 4th ser., vol. 92 (1901), p. 651.

[77] Mallet, *British Budgets*, p. 168.

[78] *Hansard Parliamentary Debates*, 4th ser., vol. 92 (1901), p. 630.

get, but both sides shared a common determination to raise and spend more money.[79] The election of 1900 was taken by Hicks Beach as a rousing vote of support for the particular spending policies of his Government. Now some of the consequences of those policies were beginning to become apparent. With perhaps more confidence than he felt, Hicks Beach closed his address to Parliament by saying, "I will not rate the intelligence of my fellow-countrymen so low as to suppose that when they supported and cheered . . . [the expenditure of the last five years] they did not know that they would have to pay the bill."[80]

The first step away from the safe harbor of fiscal tradition was accomplished with surprising ease. There were objections raised in Parliament to the new duties, but for the most part they passed into law without serious challenge. Initial yields were good; the coal tax brought in £1.3 million in 1901–1902, and sugar duties produced an additional £6.4 million in revenue.[81] Nevertheless, within a matter of months, the overall financial picture appeared bleaker than it had before. Even with the new taxes in place, spending was outrunning revenue and further deficits seemed unavoidable.

During the spring and summer of 1901 Treasury and Customs officials were once again rummaging through their small and uninspiring assortment of options. By the end of the year proposals for a tax on silk, diamonds, food, and all imported goods had been discussed and dismissed.[82] Luxury taxes were unlikely to yield very much, and broad import duties could not help but be protectionist. Frustrated by the inadequacy of his first effort to "broaden" the nation's tax system and fearful of any more radical changes, the chancellor was edging toward a frontal assault on spending as the only remaining remedy.

Hicks Beach was understandably reluctant to make such a move, in large part because he had no direct authority over spending. Reductions in growth or real cuts would have to be wheedled out of the heads of the various government departments. Any major change in budgetary policy on the spending side meant an internal wrangle of major proportions.

On 10 September 1901 Hicks Beach wrote Chamberlain warning that, when the war ended, borrowing would have to stop and debt repayment would have to resume. At that point taxes could probably not even be sustained at existing levels, let alone increased

---

[79] As Hicks Beach put it: "We are of one accord, I am afraid, in this matter—that the money should be spent in some way or other" (ibid., p. 628).

[80] Ibid., p. 651.

[81] Mallet, *British Budgets*, pp. 481, 483.

[82] See PRO, T 168/56 and PRO, T 168/52, "The Question of Taxation Discussed," draft, E. W. Hamilton, 12/13/01.

still further. The conclusion was inescapable: "I am convinced that we must seriously check the increase in our ordinary expenditure, especially on the Army and Navy."[83]

Chamberlain was skeptical of Hicks Beach's claims; by his reckoning the limits on national financial power had not been approached but instead lay somewhere down the road. "I confess that you alarm me," Chamberlain responded on 12 September. "No doubt the normal expenditure on the Army and Navy has been enormous, but has it been more than is necessary—having regard to what other nations are doing?" In the colonial secretary's view the navy must remain inviolable and the army, while more suspect, could not be cut until some conclusions about imperial defense requirements had been reached. Putting defense before expense was not only sound strategically but politically as well. The public would not tolerate a cut in spending "merely to save taxation or to pay debt." This, according to Chamberlain's reasoning, was a reflection of the fact that existing tax burdens were not as heavy as was commonly assumed. Only direct taxes were excessive at the moment, and, Chamberlain advised, although "the reaction may come . . . it has not begun yet and I think you ought to wait for the signs of it before taking any very strong steps to secure economies."[84]

Hicks Beach was not to be put off so easily. The next day he took his case to the highest authority, appealing to Salisbury in the memorandum cited briefly at the beginning of this chapter. The chancellor's assessment was an elaboration of the position that had been developing within the Treasury Department for over six years. As serious as the country's wartime financial problems might be, they were really only the tip of the iceberg. Hicks Beach was at pains, as he had been in April, to point out that long-term trends in national expenditure were the true source of Britain's difficulties. In six years, spending had increased by £42 million or approximately 40 percent. Up until 1901 this expansion had been met "by the unprecedented prosperity of the country, and by taxation imposed for war purposes." But, Hicks Beach warned, "the first is now failing us: the second, even if wholly continued after the war, cannot in my judgement be increased." Even with the new coal and sugar duties and an additional 2*d.* on the income tax, revenue for the coming year would barely exceed expenditure. With the economy flagging it would be useless to raise existing direct taxes. "Heavier direct taxation would not, I think, be borne in time of peace: and the only possible new indirect taxes which would produce any im-

[83] JC 11/18/9, Hicks Beach to Chamberlain, 9/10/01.

[84] JC 11/18/10, Chamberlain to Hicks Beach, 9/12/01.

portant amount, without a complete return to a protectionist policy, would be small duties on corn, or meat, or petroleum, on the
political objections to which I need not dwell."[85] Once peace had
been achieved the Sinking Fund could no longer be suspended
without damaging the nation's credit and, even if it were, it would
produce only a fraction of the revenues necessary to balance the
budget.

The trap into which the nation had been moving for some time
had now swung shut, and its jaws seemed no less tangible for being
composed of political and economic assumptions rather than hard,
undeniable facts. Hicks Beach believed that no more revenue could
be extracted from an already overburdened populace. The only alternative to financial ruin and political unrest was, at the very least,
a cut in the rate of growth of spending.

Proclaiming a reluctance to meddle in matters outside his preserve, Hicks Beach nevertheless went on to offer some suggestions
as to how and where the brakes should be applied. Naval spending
had been increasing so quickly that growth rates could now "be
lessened with perfect safety." To ease matters still further, "a determined attempt" ought to be made to induce the colonies to "take
their share in the Naval Defense of the Empire." Military and civil
service costs could be dealt with even more directly. Higher pay for
soldiers would permit a smaller but more efficient and thus, ultimately, a cheaper standing army. A freeze on further assistance to
education could slow the growth of civilian expenditure. These
steps might not be popular but they were essential if a collapse was
to be averted. In the long run, immediate austerity would reduce
the risk of a damaging popular backlash.[86]

The remainder of 1901 was marked by a high-level intragovernmental debate over the soundness of Hicks Beach's conclusions.
Salisbury, pragmatic as always, privately reassured Hicks Beach of
his sympathy but warned that any immediate action would split the
cabinet.[87] Perhaps to placate his chancellor, Salisbury agreed that
the 13 July memo should be sent to Chamberlain and Balfour. In
letters to both, Hicks Beach repeated his plea not for actual spending cuts but for "a real attempt to stop its increase."[88]

Chamberlain's response to the chancellor's assessment is particularly instructive. Instead of accepting the position toward which

[85] BM, Add. Mss. 49695, Hicks Beach
to Salisbury (enclosed), 9/13/01.

[86] Ibid.

[87] Hicks Beach, *Life of Sir Michael
Hicks Beach* 2 : 152.

[88] BM, Add. Mss. 49695, Hicks
Beach to Balfour, 9/17/01, and
JC 11/18/11, Hicks Beach to Cham-
berlain, 9/16/01.

most of his colleagues were now drifting, the colonial secretary expanded on his earlier argument that the virtual limits on Britain's financial power had barely come into view. In a confidential letter dated 30 September Chamberlain noted that a cooling of popular enthusiasm for great undertakings might eventually force tax reductions and spending cuts. "At the same time," he wrote, "I would observe that, considering the increase of population and of wealth, . . . even our present burdens are very light compared with what our forefathers bore in the beginning of the nineteenth century; and they are moderate in comparison with the estimates of foreign nations at the present time."[89]

This seems a rather obvious argument in retrospect, but at the time it marked a considerable departure from accepted ways of thought. Chamberlain believed that, if properly aroused, the British taxpayer would be far more willing to contribute to great national and imperial projects than was commonly assumed. The only sensible way to calculate the weight of present burdens was therefore to look beyond the confines of the existing tax structure toward some measure of total national wealth. Chamberlain was trying to transcend the accepted terms of the debate over costs in order to arrive at some more realistic judgment about what the country could afford. He thus urged that spending should be compared not to the relatively peaceful closing decades of the nineteenth century but to the darkest days of the struggle against Napoleon. Cross-national comparisons would also, in Chamberlain's view, show the relative lightness of Britain's present burdens.

Approaching the problem in this way, Chamberlain worried more about complaints that the government was spending too little on defense than he did about claims of extravagance. Army inadequacies had been painfully displayed during the recent war, and these in turn had "encouraged doubts as to Naval efficiency." Anticipating public reaction against high defense costs would therefore be a dangerous mistake. Both the opposition and the "malcontents" in the Conservative Unionist alliance would denounce the government "if there were the slightest ground for saying that we put economy before either strenuous prosecution of the war or necessary preparation for future defence. . . . There is no necessity for any declaration of a 'policy of economy' as a supreme object at the present time."[90]

Hicks Beach was unimpressed by Chamberlain's analysis. On 2 October he gave a tart response:

[89] JC 11/18/13, Chamberlain to Hicks Beach, 9/30/01.   [90] Ibid.

It is true that our present burthens are light, considering the increase of population and wealth, compared with those borne by our ancestors one hundred years ago. But they were then engaged in a life-and-death struggle with France; we, on my assumption, will not be at war at all: the cases do not admit of comparison.[91]

Equally dubious was the comparison of British and foreign tax rates:

Very likely . . . our people at large (not the payers of direct taxation) are now more lightly taxed than the people of other European countries. But the lightness of our taxation has been one of the main causes of a far greater increase in the wealth and comfort of our population in the last fifty years than any other European nation has gained.

Continued increases in spending would mean higher taxes and less "wealth and comfort," with the consequent risk of "grave social danger."[92]

Chamberlain eventually agreed that existing rates of growth could not be maintained, but he warned that public opinion and real needs would require some increases in defense spending in the immediate postwar period. These predictions were borne out as ministers prepared their budgets for the coming financial year.

In October Hicks Beach laid his "Appeal for Economy in Estimates" before the cabinet.[93] In responding, the first lord of the Admiralty accepted the need to reconcile navy programs with "the urgent plea of the Chancellor of the Exchequer that a limit should be imposed to the growth of naval expenditure," but he made no promise of immediate cutbacks.[94] Similarly, the secretary of state for war did not defy Hicks Beach directly, but his formal reply emphasized the problems of maintaining rather than reducing army establishments after the war had ended. To accomplish this end, higher pay might be required, and there was thus a strong possibility that peacetime military costs would continue to rise.[95]

[91] JC 11/18/14, Hicks Beach to Chamberlain, 10/2/01.

[92] Ibid.

[93] PRO, Cab. 37/58/109, "Financial Difficulties: Appeal for Economy in Estimates," M. E. Hicks Beach, 10/01.

[94] PRO, Cab. 37/59/118, "The Navy Estimates and the Chancellor of the Exchequer's Memorandum on the Growth of Expenditure," Lord Selborne, 11/16/01. See chapter 4 for a discussion of the extent to which the navy had already begun implicitly to accept financial constraints on its ability to maintain the "Two Power Standard."

[95] PRO, Cab. 37/59/128, "Army Estimates, 1902–3," St. John Broderick, 12/7/01.

By the close of 1901 Britain's tax base had been expanded, if only marginally, and the question of controlling government spending had been elevated to the top of the political agenda. Still, the urgent necessity of raising more money and paying larger bills did not recede. Recording his thoughts in a draft memorandum for the chancellor, Sir Edward Hamilton worried that "it seems almost certain that we shall have to have recourse to further additional taxation."[96] But where to turn and what to tax? The easy steps had already been taken, and all that remained were choices once deemed too risky to undertake.

Inhibitions against new forms of taxation had been eroded somewhat by the successful addition of two new items to the dutiable list. This fact, coupled with the growing belief that the nation's problems were long-term rather than simply war-related, led to an intense internal discussion of available options. This discussion was wide-ranging in the sense that it included consideration of measures that might once have been dismissed out of hand, but it was still hemmed in by a set of unquestionable assumptions. One participant posed the problem in this way:

> The requirements for bringing the war in South Africa to a conclusion and for meeting its consequences, and the certainty of a large and constant increase of normal expenditure on the army and navy, as well as public education, made it necessary to find a new source of permanent income—some tax that would fall on the whole community, inevitably, and would be derived from so wide an area that, even though very low in rate, its yield would be sufficiently ample—an Import Duty that everyone would pay, and no one would be sensible of, which would be inexpensive and unirksome to collect and which would be too low . . . to be fairly open to the charge of protection.[97]

Among the taxes considered and turned down during the winter and early spring of 1902 were a registration duty on all imports, a tax on petroleum, and duties on all imported grain, meat, and dairy produce. The first of these was rejected because it would have raised the cost of raw materials and thus of British manufactured goods. Petroleum provided light and warmth for the poor as well as power for much of the nation's machinery and was therefore deemed an unsuitable object of taxation. Imposing a broad new tariff on all food items at once appeared to be politically inexpe-

[96] PRO, T 168/52, 12/13/01.
[97] PRO, T 171/1, "The Grain and Meal Duties of 1902," G. L. Ryder, 9/7/02.

dient, and it also ran the risk of antagonizing the food-exporting colonies. After much debate, therefore, it was decided to revive the old corn duty, a step that had been toyed with on several previous occasions.[98]

Although Hicks Beach accepted the need for another new tax he was far from enthusiastic about it. Wiser spending policies might have averted the need for such a dangerous new departure, but, as the chancellor noted in his final budget statement, the circumstances were conspiring to make such policies unlikely. The good old days of constant budgets or, more recently, easily financed growth, were gone forever.[99] Under the circumstances a new indirect tax on grain imports was the least of the available evils. Weary after seven years in office and perhaps a little guilty about his role in the burgeoning financial crisis, Hicks Beach followed Salisbury into retirement in the summer of 1902.

Before turning to the final phases of the crisis it is necessary to consider briefly a related but parallel development. Hicks Beach had suggested in September 1901 that the colonies would have to contribute more to the maintenance of the navy. This idea was not a new one, and in fact Hicks Beach himself had made similar proposals at the first Colonial Conference in 1897.[100] At that time the purpose had been only partly to achieve a fairer distribution of costs. Perhaps more important was a desire to encourage greater imperial unity through closer political and military cooperation. As noted in chapter 2, the alternative being urged by some was the far riskier notion of a colonial customs union with its dangerous protectionist implications.[101]

By the summer of 1902, burden sharing was beginning to look like an urgent necessity rather than simply a desirable but dispensable experiment. At the behest of the British, representatives from the so-called self-governing colonies met in London to discuss a range of questions, including possible new arrangements for the sharing of naval costs. In his role as colonial secretary Chamberlain opened the meeting with an emotional plea. "The Weary Titan staggers under the too vast orb of its fate," he told his audience. "We have borne the burden long enough. We think it is time our children should assist us to support it."[102]

---

[98] Ibid.

[99] *Hansard Parliamentary Debates*, 4th ser., vol. 106 (1902), p. 179.

[100] Sir Michael Hicks Beach, *The Colonies and the Navy*, Imperial Federation (Defence) Committee, no. 10, 30 June 1897.

[101] See the discussion in Garvin, *The Life of Joseph Chamberlain* 3:178–94.

[102] Amery, *The Life of Joseph Chamberlain* 5:30.

To illustrate the extent of filial ingratitude, Admiralty officials produced an array of charts and tables comparing the naval contributions per capita of the United Kingdom and its various colonies.[103] The average British taxpayer paid 15*s.* 1*d.* toward maintaining the Royal Navy, while his Canadian and Newfoundland counterparts added nothing. Most generous were the citizens of tiny Natal (4*s.* 5.75*d.* per person), with the Cape Colony, Australia, and New Zealand trailing along behind.[104]

Stirring rhetoric and statistical finger pointing could do little to overcome the divergence of interests separating center and periphery. The British were by now desperate to relieve the mounting pressure on their financial system, but they were prepared to do little more than accept with thanks a larger colonial contribution to maintaining the fleet. Admiralty doctrine held that the navy's principal mission was sea control, which, in time of war, would require the prompt engagement and destruction of all enemy forces. Concentration and rapid mobility were thus the keys to naval success. Any unnecessary scattering of British forces to sooth colonial anxieties in peace or to protect colonial shores in war could be disastrous. The Admiralty position was that all the subjects of the Crown benefited from a strong navy, but, by definition, such a force would have to remain under complete British control.[105] Although some concessions were made to demands for local squadrons, the colonies were essentially invited to pay up and keep quiet.

Predictably, colonial enthusiasm for Britain's proposals was limited. The Canadians simply refused to go along, announcing instead their intention to establish an independent fleet in North American waters.[106] Australia and New Zealand agreed to larger contributions on the understanding that a squadron of ships would be maintained more or less permanently in the South Pacific.[107] The other colonies chipped in varying amounts, but the totals generated were hardly awe-inspiring: £50,000 per year from the Cape Colony, £3,000 from Newfoundland, £35,000 from Natal. Australia, the largest contributor in absolute terms, added about £200,000 to the navy's treasury.[108] In all, the Admiralty succeeded in extracting only half of what it had hoped to obtain.[109] Clearly, cash trans-

[103] See the June 1902 Admiralty memorandum to the Colonial Conference reprinted in Keith, ed., *Selected Speeches and Documents on British Colonial Policy, 1763–1917,* pp. 234–39.

[104] Jebb, *The Colonial Conference,* p. 358.

[105] Keith, ed., *Selected Speeches,* pp. 232–33.

[106] Kendle, *The Colonial and Imperial Conferences, 1887–1911: A Study in Imperial Organization,* p. 52.

[107] Ibid.

[108] Jebb, *The Colonial Conference,* p. 360.

[109] Ibid., p. 375.

fusions from the colonies would not be sufficient to pay for the navy or to restore Britain to good financial health.

With the departure of Hicks Beach in July 1902, the cabinet had lost a weighty symbol of fiscal responsibility. Yet in practice, as has been described, Hicks Beach was somewhat less orthodox than his words suggested. Under pressure he had imposed new taxes, calling for reduced growth in spending only reluctantly and without great effect. Charles Ritchie, the new chancellor of the Exchequer, was a man who made up in the intensity of his convictions what he lacked in political stature. Having served the Government as president of the Board of Trade (1895–1900) and home secretary (1900–1902), Ritchie entered his new assignment as a dedicated free trader and an ardent defender of the financial faith.

By the lights of that faith there were three things wrong with the nation's policies as the Boer War drew to a close. First, income taxes were dangerously burdensome, bringing harmful consequences for the wealthy, investor class and thereby for the nation as a whole. Because they were so high, existing income tax levels also left little room for expansion, thus depriving the country of its usual emergency reserve. Finally, there was considerable concern both in and out of government about the new corn duties. Not only was the grain import tax arguably protective, but it seemed to set a precedent that could be exploited by the enemies of free trade.

Ritchie was determined to set matters straight and to resume what he believed to be sound financial practices. To do that he needed to reduce taxes, and by now it appeared likely that any such reductions could be achieved only by cutting back on existing spending programs. Testing the water, the new chancellor wrote to Lord Selborne in early 1903 that "what is pressing itself on me with added force every day is the necessity of keeping our Expenditure down to the lowest possible limit." [110] For the moment, however, the navy remained outside the reach of would-be budget cutters, and attention focused instead on the less senior and less sacred of the two services.

On 21 February Ritchie circulated his assessment of the current situation to members of the cabinet. Comparing 1899–1900 with 1903–1904, he estimated that ordinary expenditure (excluding war-related costs) had risen by around £30 million while tax revenues had gone up £42 million. Of the latter figure £34 million were due to war taxes while only £8.5 million derived from "the natural

[110] Selborne Papers, 34, Ritchie to Selborne, 1/19/03.

elasticity of revenue." Thus, "if there had been little or no elasticity, practically the whole of the taxation imposed for the war would now be required to meet the present scale of expenditure."[111]

With taxes high and the whole financial system strained to its limits, Ritchie warned, there was a very real possibility that the next economic downturn could provoke some sort of violent anti-Government reaction. Pursuing a line of reasoning much favored by his predecessor, Ritchie argued first that such a reaction would result in damaging defense cuts and second that it could be preempted by prudent reductions in present outlays.[112] But the scope for such cuts was still limited by defensive concerns. While other countries were busy adding to their fleets, Britain could not safely constrain its own. Hence, Ritchie concluded, "the only way of warding off [the danger of a backlash] is to anticipate it by reducing our scale of expenditure and, so far as I can see, there is only one head under which anything like an appreciable reduction can be effected, which is the army."[113]

The belief that cuts in defense (and especially military) spending were becoming necessary was reinforced by the events of 1903. Taking advantage of Joseph Chamberlain's absence from the country, in early spring Ritchie was able to persuade the cabinet to revoke duties on imported corn. The implications of this move and the uproar that followed it have been discussed in chapter 2. Essentially, Chamberlain and his allies had hoped to eliminate tariffs only on grain purchased from Britain's overseas colonies. The system of differential duties thus created would have served as the basis for some kind of imperial customs union that, in turn, would have been better able to compete with the new, federated economic giants like Germany and the United States.

Ritchie and his fellow free traders were more concerned by the remedy Chamberlain was peddling than the disease he purported to cure; for them, protectionism was a far greater danger than long-term industrial decline. But, having headed off the immediate threat of preferential import duties by getting rid of the corn tax, Ritchie found himself with financial problems even more acute than those he had inherited from Hicks Beach. The elimination of corn duties and the reduction in income taxes that orthodoxy required and that the chancellor announced in April 1903 left him with fewer resources without in any direct way easing the demands

---

[111] PRO, T 168/52, "Our Financial Position," C. T. Ritchie, 2/21/03.
[112] Ibid. See also PRO, T 168/52,

"Public Finance," draft, C. T. Ritchie, 12/23/02.
[113] Ibid.

for funds to which he was exposed. Indirectly, however, Ritchie's actions may have strengthened his position by burning an important bridge. One possible source of revenue had been struck off the list of acceptable taxes. If the nation was to live within its reduced means, cuts in spending would now have to be made.

By the time of the 1903–1904 parliamentary budget statement, Ritchie's internal pleas for austerity were receiving support from an unwelcome source. Responding for the Opposition, Sir William Harcourt, the leading Liberal spokesman on financial matters, attacked the Government for its "foolish" policies. The root cause of the nation's difficulties, according to Harcourt, was a foreign policy of "rash new enterprises" and "entangling alliances" that resulted in "wholly unforeseen expenditure" on defense. Naval and military costs were high and rising; yet, for all its talk, the Conservative government had done nothing to shift a greater portion of the burden onto the colonies. "You perorate about the Empire," Harcourt pointed out with some accuracy, "but it is not the Empire that pays. It is little England." [114]

The ultimate consequences of eight years of Conservative rule, the Opposition claimed, could be measured in £159 million of additional debt and more than £30 million per year in new taxation. As Harcourt put it to the unfortunate Ritchie, "You have arrived at an expenditure which, in the judgement of all sober-thinking men . . . it is impossible to continue." What was needed now was "some sort of opinion . . . as to the burden which it is justifiable to put upon the country." With this figure set, expenditure would have to be "arranged accordingly." Harcourt had no doubts that foreign and defense policies tailored to meet the nation's true financial capacity would be more modest than those presently being undertaken. Borrowing a phrase from Disraeli, Harcourt declared, "These bloated armaments . . . are the result of a policy of inflation—a flatulent policy. . . . For dilapidated finance such as yours, there remains only the sovereign remedies of retrenchment and reform." [115]

While he must have chafed at the tone, Ritchie could hardly dispute a claim that he himself had been making for some time. And, although they might have disagreed with Harcourt's analysis of causes, most Conservatives could not help but accept his conclusions.

[114] *Hansard Parliamentary Debates*, 4th ser., vol. 121 (1903), p. 266.

[115] Ibid., pp. 268–69.

Retrenchment, 1903–1905

Ritchie was spared the necessity of dealing with problems he had helped to render more severe by the unintended consequences of his only budget. Revocation of the corn duty provoked a full-dress public controversy over tariff reform, which led in turn to the cabinet crisis of September 1903. After a series of deft manuevers Balfour succeeded in forcing the resignations both of Chamberlain and of the free-trade zealots. As a member of the latter group Ritchie was able to leave office full of righteous indignation over the Government's alleged flirtation with protectionism.

The tangled web of compromises that sent Joseph Chamberlain into the political wilderness helped elevate his son to the position of chancellor of the Exchequer. Austen Chamberlain was just forty when he took office, young, vigorous, and in many ways (including his distinctive monocle) the faithful reflection of his famous father. By 1903 Austen had already held a number of official posts including civil lord of the Admiralty (1895–1900), financial secretary at the Treasury Department (1900–1902), and postmaster general (1902–1903). Intellectually and temperamentally, the junior Chamberlain appears to have been the more cautious and conservative; thus, although he sympathized with his father's fiscal reform campaign, he can hardly be said to have held radical views on most questions of national finance. Politically, Austen saw himself as a link between the two wings of an increasingly troubled and divided Conservative party. Nevertheless, in his role as chancellor, the young Chamberlain accepted the general assessment of Britain's financial position that he had inherited from his two predecessors. Thus it fell to him to insist on the cuts in defense spending that were now increasingly seen to be unavoidable.[116]

Picking up where Ritchie had left off, Chamberlain began an immediate effort to extract pledges of frugality from both civilian defense chiefs. The navy as well as the army was now within reach of the economist's scalpel, or at least of his pen. On 30 September 1903 Lord Selborne wrote Chamberlain that the nation was faced with "two apparently incompatible ideals. . . . To reduce taxation. To maintain the Navy [within] the minimum margin of safety."[117]

Chamberlain responded with a thinly veiled warning of the backlash possible if Selborne failed to meet his requests for economy. "I

[116] Unless otherwise indicated, all further references to "Chamberlain" are to Austen.

[117] Selborne Papers, 34, Selborne to Austen Chamberlain, 9/30/03.

do beg of you most earnestly to consider carefully the position of the Exchequer and the effect which your demands may have, not only on the fortunes of the Party, but, upon the continuity of Naval policy itself."[118] Perhaps because he had heard these arguments before, Selborne was unmoved. He minuted back, "You cannot impose fresh taxation. Moreover, I think you ought to reduce the Income Tax if possible. . . . But on the other hand it is perfectly impossible for me to let the standard of the Navy drop."[119] By December the two ministers had agreed that naval spending would go up by only £2 million in 1904. Even this modest compromise was destroyed at year's end when the Admiralty made a sudden request for funds with which to purchase two additional battleships.[120]

Chamberlain had somewhat better luck in his early dealings with the army. The overall budget for ground forces was shrinking as hostilities in South Africa drew to a close. In 1901–1902 total expenditure on the army stood at £94.2 million. By the next year the figure was £70.2 million, falling to £39.6 million in 1903–1904. The question to be resolved was how low the level of normal peacetime expenditure would be set. Chamberlain wanted more and deeper cuts; the army had, after all, gotten by with only £20 million before the war began.[121]

At first it seemed that Chamberlain had found a valuable ally in the new secretary of state for war. From his arrival in office, H. O. Arnold-Forster accepted the need for a leaner, better-organized army, and he lost no time in making the point to his colleagues. In October, one month after assuming his position, Arnold-Forster wrote Chamberlain that he believed "the country demands, and will insist upon a reduction in Military expenditure. I believe that this reduction can be effected."[122] If cuts were not forthcoming, Arnold-Forster, like his Treasury Department counterparts, feared a damaging popular reaction against what he called "our present, gigantic expenditure."[123] But, fortunately, both the military defenses and the financial needs of the nation could be provided for if the army could be made more efficient.[124]

Arnold-Forster was soon to prove himself to be an ineffective windbag, long on florid memoranda but short on results. What is

[118] Ibid., Chamberlain to Selborne, 11/11/03.

[119] Ibid., Selborne to Chamberlain, 11/13/03.

[120] On the matter of the Chilean battleships, see PRO, Cab. 37/67/90, "Memorandum on Navy Estimates, 1904–05," Selborne, 12/24/03.

[121] Mallet, *British Budgets*, p. 504.

[122] AC 44/3/4, Arnold-Forster to Chamberlain, 10/30/03.

[123] AC 44/2/6, Arnold-Forster to Chamberlain, 11/27/03.

[124] AC 44/2/6, Arnold-Forster to Chamberlain, 12/22/03.

important to note here is simply that, throughout his time in office, the secretary saw his principal goal to be the reduction of military spending. Concern over the limits on Britain's financial power was no longer the exclusive province of those charged with proposing new taxes. Even if it meant readjusting the empire's defensive posture, cuts in the army would have to be made.

By the end of 1903 Chamberlain was preparing to reap the meager harvest that Ritchie had sown. With revenues down and spending not yet under control, deficits were once again the major cause of anxiety.[125] On 7 December the chancellor assessed matters for the cabinet. Whatever its precise size, he wrote, the budget for fiscal year 1904–1905 would have to be met largely through increased taxation. Raising taxes, however, would force the country back into the dangerous predicament from which it had only just begun to emerge. "In view of the gravity of the situation," Chamberlain went on, "I trust that the Cabinet will concur in the necessity for further reductions in our military and naval expenditure. Our defensive strength rests upon our financial not less than upon our military and naval resources."[126]

In early February 1904 Edward Hamilton wrote to Chamberlain regarding the means available for closing the impending budget gap. As always, suspension of debt repayment was an option, but one that would have "the worst possible effect" on the nation's already sagging credit. Higher taxes were thus the sole acceptable way of supplying relief, and the authorities were free only to decide which of the various unpalatable forms of medication they would select.[127]

The range of possible indirect taxes, never wide, had been reduced still further by the eruption of the tariff reform controversy. Proposing a very low duty on all imported goods would have been risky at best before Joseph Chamberlain began his public campaign; it was now completely impossible. That left either new duties on specific items that would irritate out of proportion to their trivial yields or an elevation of existing tariffs. Here too the choices were few. Most customs duties were still at or near their wartime levels. To increase them would, it was felt, drive down consumption and leave the Treasury even worse off than it was before.[128]

Hamilton reasoned that only the relatively new sugar duty provided a margin for expansion, but he also cautioned that such in-

[125] PRO, T 168/61, Edward Hamilton to Chamberlain, 11/11/03.

[126] AC 17/2/17, "The Financial Situation," Chamberlain, 12/7/03.

[127] AC 17/2/29, "The Financial Outlook of 1904–1905," Edward Hamilton, 2/11/04.

[128] Ibid.

creases taken alone would create political difficulties to replace the economic problems they helped solve. Ritchie's actions of the year just past had brought down direct taxes far more than indirect levies. To raise the sugar duty without taking some offsetting steps would therefore "constitute a decided change in the relative burthens of the masses which pay indirect taxes, and of the comparatively limited classes which pay direct taxes."[129]

In order to avoid damaging charges of unfairness, the Government had little choice but to couple a higher sugar duty with renewed high rates on the income tax. Hamilton admitted that such a move would arouse "the strongest opposition on economic as well as on political grounds," and he acknowledged the need for the emergency reserve that low direct taxes could provide. But, he went on,

> I confess I now feel doubtful whether, with our present high standard of ordinary expenditure, we ought not to consider the normal rate of the income tax to be 11d or 1s instead of 7d or 8d, and the reserve which may be drawn upon to consist of the margin between 11d or 1s and 2s instead of . . . between 7d or 8d and 16d.[130]

With all his experience in government, Hamilton concluded, he had never seen a situation more difficult than the one facing the new chancellor of the Exchequer.[131]

In mid-April the budget for the coming year was announced. Blaming a sluggish economy for yielding lower-than-expected revenues, Chamberlain requested higher taxes to cover the projected deficit. This move provoked swift and predictable criticism. Liberal leader Sir Henry Campbell-Bannerman pointed out that, in the second year of peace, the Government was not only restoring war taxes but increasing them. Worse, by its policies the Balfour administration was forcing indirect taxpayers to bear an undue portion of the mounting burden of empire.[132]

Heated parliamentary debate produced two rather different reactions from Treasury officials. Placed on the defensive by their critics, some, like Edward Hamilton, began to question whether the whole financial situation was as dire as the Opposition claimed. This was an interesting and somewhat startling reversal for a man who had long warned against excessive taxation and expenditure.

In a draft paper dated two days after the House of Commons

[129] Ibid. See also AC 17/2/35, "Financial Position," Edward Hamilton, 3/17/04.

[130] Ibid.

[131] Ibid.

[132] *Hansard Parliamentary Debates*, 4th ser., vol. 133 (1904), pp. 568–69.

budget debate, Hamilton pointed out that, while government spending had gone up 125 percent in forty years, the country's population had grown 45 percent over the same period. By very rough estimates national income was £1.75 billion in 1904 as compared with £700 million in 1864. Thus there were at present

> not only many more people to bear the cost of Government . . . but those people are much better off—our total expenditure has, it is true, grown 125%, but our income may be taken to have grown 150% or 25% more: in other words, the total cost of government charged on taxes in 1864–1865 represented 8.6% of the aggregate income of the country and now the total cost of government represents 9.8% of the aggregate income.[133]

Joseph Chamberlain had proposed such a calculation in 1901, and Charles Ritchie had briefly made similar suggestions during the previous year's budget announcement, but neither had pressed the point.[134] Hamilton, like Ritchie, may have simply been playing with the notion of relative burdens as a rhetorical device to use against the Liberals. Too much talk of impending financial ruin was beginning to rebound against the government. Support for budget cuts among voters and in Parliament was beginning to seem excessive and threatening. One way of relieving pressure was to direct attention away from absolute spending figures and toward relative comparisons across time.

Whatever the immediate, tactical purposes of such analysis, the full implications of thinking about the nation's finances in this way, if adopted, could have been considerable. In the first place, there was no obvious reason why 9.8 percent of aggregate income should have marked the highest acceptable level of total government spending. Assuming this *was* the limit, so long as national income continued to grow there would be no need to freeze or reduce present outlays. Even higher taxes might be acceptable on an increasingly wealthy population.

At this point Hamilton pulled back from the conclusions toward which his calculations seemed to be carrying him. Things might not be so bad in some abstract sense, but spending cuts were still desirable. In the real world the virtual limits on the nation's financial resources had been reached, even if there was some theoretical reason for believing they could be pushed back still further.

---

[133] PRO, T 168/62, "1904–5 versus 1864–5," draft, Edward Hamilton, 4/21/04.

[134] *Hansard Parliamentary Debates*, 4th ser., vol. 121 (1903), pp. 247–49.

Whether he indulged in similar speculation or not, Chamberlain showed no signs of deviating from Hamilton's ultimate conclusion. As far as the chancellor was concerned, mounting parliamentary pressure only confirmed the accuracy of analysis rooted in traditional assumptions. The country would tolerate no more taxation and, indeed, prudence required some reductions.

In March Selborne had finally agreed that "even at a further sacrifice of programme" he would not ask for more money in 1905–1906 than he was already receiving.[135] This pledge and Arnold-Forster's promises of a more efficient army were not sufficient to satisfy Chamberlain. On 28 April, with the Commons debate still ringing in his ears, he addressed the cabinet in the sternest possible terms. The heads of the various "spending" departments did not, according to Chamberlain, yet realize how serious the situation had become. Even if the most optimistic Treasury calculations were correct, the best that could be hoped for in the coming year was a barely balanced budget.

> Every member of the Cabinet should, therefore, keep constantly in view the fact that *any* addition to our expenditure involves a further addition to taxation, and it is only by reducing our expenditure that we can make any reduction in taxation. Every scheme or proposal which comes before the Cabinet must be judged in the light of this hard fact.[136]

Even with one budget cycle just closed it was not too soon to consider how future cuts in spending could be brought about. In Chamberlain's view, these would have to be sought "in both the Army and Navy Estimates. Neither alone will be sufficient." This was not a request made lightly. "It is with great reluctance," he wrote, "that I suggest any curtailment of expenditure on the navy; but it would seem clear that we cannot obtain from the army alone all the relief that we require." Only a freeze on civil spending and cuts in the defense budget could "produce that substantial reduction which the state of national finances imperatively demands."[137] The time had come to face facts and to admit frankly that the financial resources of the United Kingdom were "inadequate" to do all that was desirable in providing for imperial defense.[138]

The final year and a half of Conservative rule saw gradual implementation of measures designed to meet Chamberlain's de-

[135] Selborne Papers, 39, Selborne to Chamberlain, 3/22/04.
[136] AC 17/2/24, cabinet memorandum, 4/28/04.
[137] Ibid.
[138] Ibid.

mands. Under strong pressure from the chancellor and the prime minister, Arnold-Forster produced a bewildering series of schemes for army reform. Each had as its essential motive the desire to reduce manpower and thereby costs; each in turn foundered on political objections or resistance from within the military. Proposals to eliminate the home-defense militia were vetoed in Parliament both for sentimental reasons and because they seemed to leave the United Kingdom unprepared for the possibility of invasion. Various suggestions for creating a two-tiered system with short-enlistment battalions for home service and long-term units for deployment overseas were opposed by the General Staff as disruptive and inefficient.[139]

So strong was his desire to achieve economies and so intense was his frustration with Arnold-Forster for failing to do so that, by early 1905, Balfour had practically taken War Office administration into his own hands. In January 1905 Arnold-Forster requested that a joint committee be established to consider the following proposition: "Given that the country cannot afford to pay more than 25 millions a year for the Army, how can that money best be spent upon the maintenance of a force capable of supplying the Military needs of the Empire?"[140] Balfour seized on this suggestion and formed his own small investigatory group (from which Arnold-Forster was excluded) to cross-examine War Office personnel and make recommendations for cost-cutting measures.

In the event, neither a major reorganization of the army nor a £25 million budget proved feasible before Balfour was forced from office. What savings there were, resulted from the withdrawal of a number of colonial garrisons (in the West Indies, Bermuda, Crete, and Canada), the weakening of British forces in Egypt, and the establishment of an effective ceiling on the Government's commitment to the defense of India.[141] The empire's defensive posture was thus significantly influenced by the drive for economy, even if the savings achieved were relatively small. In 1904–1905 the army cost £31.6 million. By 1905–1906 that figure had been reduced to £29.1 million.[142]

While high-level attention concentrated on the ground forces,

[139] See BM, Add. Mss. 50301, "Failed Schemes," and 50302, "Approved Schemes." For more on the problem of military reform see chapter 5.

[140] PRO, Cab. 37/74/10, "Army Reorganization: Correspondence between the Prime Minister and the Secretary of State for War," 1/13/05.

[141] P. Kennedy, *The Rise and Fall of*

British Naval Mastery, p. 215. On the reduction of colonial garrisons see also PRO, Cab. 37/75/45, "Memorandum of the Secretary of State for War Relating to the Army Estimates for 1905–06," Arnold-Forster, 3/6/05. On the Indian defense problem see chapter 5.

[142] Mallet, *British Budgets*, p. 504.

the navy was, on its own initiative, taking steps to eliminate waste and cut costs. In October 1904 Selborne appointed Admiral Sir John Fisher to the post of first sea lord. As commander of the British Mediterranean fleet and then as second sea lord, Fisher had long advocated changes in naval deployment, training, and equipment. Fisher's primary aim was to improve readiness and "fighting efficiency," but he soon saw the possibilities of combining these goals with the politicians' demands for lower budgets.[143]

Fisher quickly named a special Estimates Committee to review naval spending and, within a month, the Admiralty announced far-reaching changes in the distribution and composition of British forces worldwide. Under the new dispensation an assortment of old, slow, and poorly armed vessels were recalled and decommissioned, and the entire system of fleets and squadrons was reorganized. Largely as a result, in 1905 the cost of the navy dropped from £41.0 million to £37.2 million. It was the first time since the Conservatives had come to power ten years before that naval spending had been significantly reduced.[144]

Conclusion
Measuring Financial Power

In a 1905 cabinet memorandum Austen Chamberlain wrote that Britain's "defensive resources" grouped themselves "under three heads. They are naval, military and financial; each of these divisions is of equal importance both to the successful preparation for war and effective conduct of war."[145] This view was one widely shared by Chamberlain's contemporaries, both in and out of government. "Financial power" was considered critical to the nation's survival, and it was held to be something both actual and potential. Englishmen believed that their country was strong because it could afford to spend considerable sums on peacetime preparedness, but also because it had a vast reserve of wealth that could be tapped in an emergency for the prosecution of war. There was naturally a certain tension between these two components: too much expenditure in peace could dry up the reservoir of wartime funds; too little could leave the empire dangerously exposed to the possibility of sudden setbacks. The task of strategists and financial planners was to bring the demands of economy and security into balance.

For purposes of determining the real burden imposed by government (and especially defense) expenditures, the best index

[143] On Fisher's reforms see Marder, *From Dreadnought to Scapa Flow* 1: 21–42.

[144] Mallet, *British Budgets*, pp. 502–503.
[145] AC 43/117, "Army Estimates," 2/3/05.

would probably have been some estimate of that spending as a share of gross national product. This is the kind of measurement that figures prominently in modern debate, and it is the sort of calculation that present-day historians and economists have often made when looking back at the nineteenth and early twentieth centuries. Had they been available at the time, such estimates would have indicated that, although outlays had increased dramatically, the growth of Britain's economy had also been substantial. By the turn of the century the burden of government spending had grown heavier, but it had not done so nearly as rapidly as the growth in absolute expenditure figures seemed to suggest.

As has been noted, some participants in the debate over spending that reached its peak following the Boer War tried to make the case for relative as compared with absolute measurements. Joseph Chamberlain simply asserted that increases in population and wealth must have more than made up for the undeniable expansion in budgets. Economist Robert Giffen tried to make the same point more concretely, using rough estimates of national income as the basis for calculating the change in real burdens.

Equipped with a commonly accepted and widely used index of total national income or gross national product against which to weigh government spending, Giffen and Chamberlain might have been more successful in easing the anxieties of their contemporaries. The absence of such measures has already been noted and explained in chapter 2. Without them it was probably inevitable that absolute spending figures should have come to dominate discussions of the nation's financial condition. As economists Alan Peacock and Jack Wiseman have pointed out, this misleading practice actually represented the continuation of a longstanding tradition. The absolute level of government expenditure at current prices had always been "uppermost in the minds of the nineteenth century Chancellors of the Exchequer."[146] At the turn of the century most Englishmen still thought in these terms. As budgets grew in magnitude, so too did fears of impending fiscal disaster.

Reaching the Limit

Despite the importance of absolute spending figures in the calculations of contemporary observers, there was no single number (whether £100 million or £200 million per year) beyond which all agreed that expenditures could not rise. As long as those taxes already in place could provide revenues to cover the increase, higher

---

[146] Peacock and Wiseman, *The Growth of Public Expenditure*, p. 36.

outlays were tolerated, albeit nervously, by Conservative statesmen. In other words, during the period under study, what were referred to earlier as the "virtual limits" on the nation's capacity to spend were imposed by the structure of the existing tax system. That structure, in turn, was the reflection of a set of longstanding beliefs about what constituted sound financial practice.

Government spending, in the orthodox view, was a necessary evil that was to be kept strictly limited and financed out of taxes rather than through borrowing. All taxes were believed bad, but, because of their harmful effect on the process of accumulation, direct taxes on income and profits were the worst. Indirect levies on imports that acted to protect domestic manufacturers were to be assiduously avoided. Within these constraints resources could safely be generated without disrupting the productive mechanism in peacetime or depriving the nation of a financial reserve in the event of war.

These theoretical underpinnings to the tax system were buttressed in practice by less openly expressed calculations of political interest. Low taxes suited everyone and low direct taxes happened to coincide with the interests of the wealthy and influential. If forced to make changes the Conservatives would certainly have preferred simply to increase levies on consumption rather than risk antagonizing their upper-class supporters by raising taxes on income and wealth. Nevertheless, the growing political power of the less well-to-do made it necessary to preserve at least the appearance of balance in taxation and hence of fairness.

As soon as the Conservatives took power in 1895 some experts within the government began warning that increases in spending would soon exceed the "natural" increase in revenues from existing taxes permitted by economic growth. The worriers cautioned that choices would soon have to be made between higher tax rates and new taxes, on the one hand, and a slower expansion in government programs on the other. From 1896 to early 1899, however, good economic conditions and healthy revenues made it difficult for the pessimists to gain much ground in their crusade for fiscal responsibility. It was only the return of hard times toward the end of the century, followed closely by the outbreak of the Boer War, that produced a decisive change in the balance of forces within the government.

Emergency spending during the period 1899–1902 forced the adoption of higher tax rates and a series of cautious experiments with new taxation. The undeniable short-term problems that the war created also lent credence to the claims of those officials who had long warned of an impending crisis. Michael Hicks Beach,

Edward Hamilton, and others cautioned that the nation's financial difficulties had preceded the onset of hostilities and would persist once the war had been brought to a conclusion. The existing tax system was no longer capable of funding steadily expanding peacetime expenditures. Those few, like Joseph Chamberlain, who continued to defend further increases in spending were now decisively outnumbered. In the wake of the war a new consensus had emerged in favor of the proposition that the limits of Britain's financial resources had been reached and that the government could therefore no longer continue to do business as usual.

A Conservative Response?

In theory, at least, a recognition that change was necessary could have had two kinds of consequences. On the one hand the Conser-

Table 3-1
Gross Expenditures, 1887–1907
(In Millions of Pounds)

Year	Total	Army	Navy	Civil[a]	Debt
1887	87.4	17.7	13.0	30.7	26.2
1888	87.0	16.8	13.8	30.5	26.2
1889	91.2	17.6	15.6	28.1	25.3
1890	94.7	18.6	18.0	29.4	25.2
1891	97.5	18.3	18.1	31.8	25.2
1892	97.6	18.4	17.3	31.8	25.2
1893	98.4	18.7	16.2	32.6	25.2
1894	100.9	18.5	18.5	33.4	25.2
1895	105.1	19.0	21.2	34.5	25.0
1896	109.7	18.5	23.8	35.2	25.0
1897	112.3	20.2	22.4	37.7	25.0
1898	117.7	21.0	26.0	38.6	25.0
1899	143.7	44.1	28.3	39.7	23.2
1900	193.3	92.4	33.2	41.4	19.8
1901	205.2	94.2	34.9	49.1	21.7
1902	194.2	70.2	35.2	55.4	27.2
1903	156.7	39.6	40.0	46.6	27.0
1904	151.7	31.6	41.0	47.7	27.0
1905	150.4	29.1	37.2	49.1	28.0
1906	149.6	28.3	34.6	50.5	28.5
1907	151.8	26.7	32.7	52.9	29.5

Source: All figures from Mallet, *British Budgets: 1887–88 to 1912–13*, pp. 476–77, 500–504, 508–509.
[a]Civil expenditure includes civil and social services, postal services, and spending on revenue collection. Payments to local taxation accounts are not included.

Table 3-2
Gross Revenues, 1887–1907
(In Millions of Pounds)

Year	Total	% Direct[a]	% Indirect[b]	Income Tax Rate[c]
1887	89.8	45.3	54.7	0s. 7d.
1888	89.8	44.1	55.9	0s. 6d.
1889	94.5	44.4	55.6	0s. 6d.
1890	96.5	44.1	55.9	0s. 6d.
1891	98.6	44.3	55.7	0s. 6d.
1892	97.6	44.1	55.9	0s. 6d.
1893	98.3	44.7	55.3	0s. 7d.
1894	101.7	45.4	54.6	0s. 8d.
1895	109.3	47.6	52.4	0s. 8d.
1896	112.2	47.4	52.6	0s. 8d.
1897	116.1	47.9	52.1	0s. 8d.
1898	117.8	48.2	51.8	0s. 8d.
1899	129.8	48.4	51.6	0s. 8d.
1900	140.1	49.4	50.6	1s. 0d.
1901	152.7	52.5	47.5	1s. 2d.
1902	161.3	52.4	47.6	1s. 3d.
1903	151.3	49.3	50.7	0s. 11d.
1904	153.2	49.5	50.5	1s. 0d.
1905	153.9	50.3	49.7	1s. 0d.
1906	155.0	51.4	48.6	1s. 0d.
1907	156.5	51.1	48.9	1s. 0d.

Source: Figures from Mallet, *British Budgets: 1887–88 to 1912–13*, pp. 474–75, 493, 484.

[a]Direct taxes include income tax, estate duties, and land, house, and property taxes.

[b]Indirect taxes include all customs duties and excise duties on goods and commodities.

[c]Rate indicates amount taken by the government from each pound of income above a certain level. One shilling = 12 pence (12d.).

vatives could conceivably have undertaken a major effort at tax reform, breaking out of the confines of the old system in order to sustain continued increases in expenditure. This is exactly what the Liberal party would do only a few years later when it imposed a new "super tax" on incomes and used the revenues to pay for expanded social programs and, eventually, a larger navy.[147] Such a course was unacceptable to the Conservatives, both because it vio-

---

[147]See Emy, "The Impact of Financial Policy on English Party Politics Before 1914," pp. 103–31.

lated orthodox principles and because it ran counter to their immediate political interests. With the onset of the tariff reform debate
in 1903, broad tariffs on imports, always regarded as dubious on
theoretical grounds, were removed from the list of practical possibilities. Other new indirect taxes would have been less revolutionary (if also less productive of revenue), but their exclusive imposition would have seemed unfair and could easily have had harmful
electoral consequences.

Given their assumptions about what the economic and political
traffic would bear, it is not surprising that the Conservatives chose
a second course, the "sovereign remedy of retrenchment." As the
phrase suggests, cutting spending in order to bring budgets into
balance was the time-honored way of dealing with financial dis-
tress. In this sense the Conservative response was traditional and

Table 3-3
Gross Expenditures vs. Gross Revenues, 1887–1907
(In Millions of Pounds)

Year	Expenditure	Revenue	Surplus/Deficit	Natl Debt
1887	87.4	89.8	+2.4	736.1
1888	87.0	89.8	+2.8	704.6
1889	91.2	94.5	+3.2	697.6
1890	94.7	96.5	+1.7	689.0
1891	97.5	98.6	+1.0	683.5
1892	97.6	97.6	+0.02	677.0
1893	98.4	98.3	−0.17	671.1
1894	100.9	101.7	+0.77	667.3
1895	105.1	109.3	+4.2	659.0
1896	109.7	112.2	+2.5	652.3
1897	112.3	116.1	+3.7	645.2
1898	117.7	117.8	+0.2	638.8
1899	143.7	129.8	−13.9	635.4
1900	193.3	140.1	−53.2	638.9
1901	205.2	152.7	−52.5	703.9
1902	194.2	161.3	−33.0	765.2
1903	156.7	151.3	−5.4	798.3
1904	151.7	153.2	+1.4	794.5
1905	150.4	153.9	+3.5	796.7
1906	149.6	155.0	+5.4	789.0
1907	151.8	156.5	+4.7	779.1

Source: Mallet, *British Budgets: 1887–88 to 1912–13,* pp. 474–75, 476–77, 494–95.

truly "conservative." But if retrenchment was inevitable after 1904, its particular form certainly was not. Having decided to make reductions, the cabinet could have chosen to leave the army and navy alone while cutting deeply into civil expenditure. Given their general preferences it is rather surprising that Balfour and his ministers did not even consider the possibility of doing so. This may reflect the fact that defense spending was still seen as abnormally, unnecessarily high two and three years after the close of the Boer War.[148] It is also an indication of the seriousness with which the Conservatives viewed the new social and political forces that were increasingly determining the shape of domestic politics. The danger of military disaster overseas seemed preferable to certain electoral defeat at home. As the next two chapters will demonstrate, the decision for austerity that followed from this calculation would reverberate throughout Britain's defense establishment.

[148] Spending on the army and navy never returned to anything close to its prewar level. The combined total was around £44 million in 1898–1899 and never fell below roughly £58 million for the rest of the period preceding the outbreak of World War I (Mallet, *British Budgets*, p. 505).

Sea Power:
The Surrender of
Worldwide Supremacy

It depends upon what you count to know exactly what your position is.
—Arthur Balfour, House of Commons, 1896

On 6 December 1904, Lord Selborne, first lord of the Admiralty, put before the cabinet a memorandum marked "Distribution of the Fleet (Very Confidential)."[1] In opening his report Selborne declared:

> A new and definite stage has been reached in that evolu-
> tion of the modern steam navy which has been going on
> for the last thirty years, and that stage is marked not only
> by changes in the materiel of the British navy itself but
> also by changes in the strategic position all over the world
> arising out of the development of foreign navies.[2]

To the west, "the United States are forming a navy the power and size of which will be limited only by the amount of money which the American people choose to spend on it." To the east, "the smaller but modern navy of Japan has been put to the test and has not been found wanting." Closer to home the Russian fleet had been in-creased; the navies of Italy, Austria-Hungary, and France were strong, especially in the Mediterranean; and a "new German navy" had come into existence.[3]

---

[1] The first lord of the Admiralty was a civilian and a political appointee, roughly equivalent in stature to the secretary of the navy in the modern American system. The first *sea* lord was the highest ranking naval officer and the most important member of the Admiralty Board responsible for advising the first lord.

[2] PRO, Cab. 37/73/159, "Distribution of the Fleet," Selborne, 12/6/04, p. 1.

[3] Ibid.

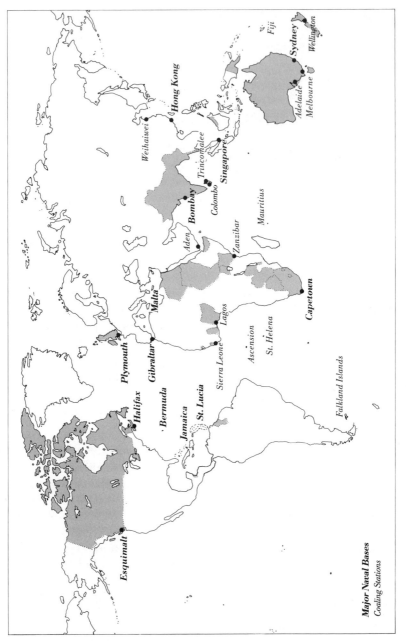

Major Naval Bases
Coding Stations

Esquimalt

Plymouth
Gibraltar
Malta
Halifax
Bermuda
Jamaica
St. Lucia

Sierra Leone
Lagos
Ascension
St. Helena

Aden
Zanzibar
Mauritius

Bombay
Colombo
Trincomalee
Singapore

Weihaiwei
Hong Kong

Fiji
Sydney
Adelaide
Melbourne
Wellington

Capetown

Falkland Islands

British Naval Facilities, 1900

In the face of all this the British navy was distributed on the basis of principles that dated "from a period when the electric telegraph did not exist and when wind was the motive power."[4] Its squadrons were scattered at stations at the four corners of the earth, and many of them included slow, poorly armed, aged vessels that, in the event of war, could "neither fight nor run away." The time had come to eliminate these useless ships and to group those remaining in a peacetime pattern that would also be the "best strategical distribution for war."[5]

Selborne's memo called for the worldwide reorganization of Britain's naval forces. New Channel, Atlantic, and Mediterranean fleets were created (with home ports at Dover, Gibraltar, and Malta, respectively) and the battleship component of the first two was increased at the expense of the third. Meanwhile, the squadrons cruising in distant waters were consolidated and reduced in strength. The Pacific, South Atlantic, North American, and West Indian squadrons were withdrawn, and a Cape squadron was created to take on some of their duties as well as to patrol the west coast of Africa. In Asia an "Eastern warfleet" centered at Singapore was organized out of the Australian, Chinese, and East Indian stations. Both of these flotillas had their numbers "ruthlessly reduced" by the weeding out of old and inefficient vessels.[6]

The intention and eventual result of the scheme that Selborne announced was to permit a permanent strengthening of British naval power in European waters at the expense of the Far East and the Western Hemisphere. This became evident in the following year as five battleships were withdrawn from the China station and assigned to the Channel fleet.[7] In February of 1905 the first lord also announced cutbacks in Britain's dockyards at Halifax, Esquimalt, Jamaica, and Trincomalee.[8]

Looking back, it seems obvious that the changes announced in late 1904 marked a significant shift in the strategic posture of the British Empire. In the three hundred years that followed the defeat of the Spanish Armada, England's trade and her catalog of overseas possessions had grown enormously. The security of Britain's empire, its commerce, and its shores depended on an ability to control the world's oceans. English vessels had to be able to transit safely between the center of the empire, off Europe's shores, and any one of dozens of destinations at the periphery from Alexandria to Bombay, from Capetown to Halifax.

[4] Ibid.
[5] Ibid., p. 4.
[6] Marder, *From Dreadnought to Scapa Flow* 1:41.
[7] Ibid., 42.
[8] Brassey, ed., *The Naval Annual, 1905*, p. 432.

From the close of the Napoleonic Wars the British navy was able to achieve its objective by maintaining superiority in the "narrow seas" around Europe. Until the latter part of the nineteenth century there were no naval competitors outside the Continent, and the European powers were able to devote only sporadic attention to naval development. By blockading enemy fleets in their home ports and by attacking them as they attempted to pass through the confined waters of the English Channel, the North Sea, the Suez Canal, and the mouth of the Mediterranean, British warships could control access to the world's oceans. Writing in 1943, Harold and Margaret Sprout described the situation in these words:

> Through its hold on four narrow seas . . . Great Britain could virtually dictate the terms of Europe's access to the "outer world." Under conditions prevailing until near the end of the nineteenth century, control of these four narrow seas had political and military effects felt around the globe. As long as no important center of naval power existed outside Europe, England's grip on the ocean portals of that Continent constituted in effect a global command of the seas.[9]

During the fifteen years leading up to the period of this study, the fortuitous circumstances on which Britain's worldwide sea supremacy depended had begun to change. In Europe, America, and the Far East new naval powers arose and old ones strengthened their fleets. Between 1895 and 1905 British statesmen were forced to reconsider the assumptions on which the entire empire had been built. By the end of that ten-year period, Britain had acquiesced in the loss of its longstanding control of the world's oceans. Instead of trying to dominate everywhere, the British navy was now directed more narrowly toward retaining its superiority in the waters close to home. Instead of relying only on its own resources to secure the safety of its shipping and empire, Britain was now forced to depend on the continued cooperation of foreign powers. In another fifteen years Britain's navy would just be equal to that of the United States. In twenty-five, England would be the second-ranked naval power.[10]

All this is plain from a vantage point of eighty years. Yet, as

[9] H. Sprout and M. Sprout, *Toward a New Order of Sea Power*, p. 16. For similar arguments see Graham, *The Politics of Naval Supremacy*, p. 23. See also P. Kennedy, "Strategic Aspects of the Anglo-German Naval Race," in P. Kennedy, *Strategy and Diplomacy, 1870–1945*, pp. 129–30.

[10] Jordan, ed., *Naval Warfare in the Twentieth Century, 1900–1945*, p. 14.

Margaret Sprout has noted, the implications of what occurred at the turn of the century "are clearer in retrospect . . . than they were in prospect." [11] Indeed, on first inspection the transition from global to merely local supremacy would appear to have been accomplished with a minimum of turmoil and debate. Is it possible that Britain's leaders did not realize the importance of what was occurring? How did they think about sea power? How did they assess their diminishing ability to control the use of the earth's "great highway"? And what did they think they could do about it?

Background

Discussion of Britain's naval position, official and unofficial, public and private, was shaped around the presence of two deceptively simple and seemingly complementary ideas. These two notions, "command of the seas" and the "Two Power Standard," represented different ways of thinking about sea power. The first involved a functional measure of capability (of what might today be called "outputs" or "outcomes"), and the second involved a straightforward numerical comparison of forces (or "resources"). Where these concepts came from and how they came to be fused together is the first part of this chapter's story. How they became separated at the close of the century, what that separation meant and the confusion it caused, will be the second.

"Command of the Seas"—The Ideology of Sea Power

Historian Paul Kennedy has written that "if there was any period in history when Britannia could have been said to have ruled the waves, then it was in the sixty or so years following the final defeat of Napoleon." [12] Supremacy is seldom conducive to hard thinking. It comes as no surprise, then, that for much of the nineteenth century little intellectual energy was expended in analyzing or justifying Britain's position at sea. The importance of England's continuing preeminence was accepted more as a fact of life than as the result of adherence to any abstract theory. [13]

This is not to say that no one thought or wrote about sea power during these years, but much of what did appear amounted to little more than reheated tales of wartime derring-do. [14] Nevertheless, there was what might be called an "inarticulate navalism" that

[11] M. Sprout, "Mahan: Evangelist of Sea Power," in Earle, ed., *Makers of Modern Strategy*, p. 423.

[12] P. Kennedy, *The Rise and Fall of British Naval Mastery*, p. 149.

[13] Graham, *The Politics of Naval Supremacy*, p. 112.

[14] Schurman, *The Education of a*

found expression in the periodic utterances of politicians and Admiralty officials. In these it is possible to discern the seeds of something that would later grow into a more fully elaborated form.

The existence of Britain's far-flung empire and (for those who were unenthusiastic about that institution) the growing volume of its overseas trade (and especially, from midcentury on, its dependence on imported food) brought home to all but the most obtuse the sea's inescapable importance. The fact that British soil could be reached only by crossing water provided a final proof, for those who required one. There was thus an agreed need for naval supremacy, and demanding it or affirming it was a pastime that, in the words of one author, "could unite the 'economical monomaniacs,' Richard Cobden and Joseph Hume, with Palmerston and Canning." [15]

The precise form of British maritime superiority remained a matter open to discussion. Some commentators concluded that Britain would have to maintain powerful fleets wherever its interests lay, in other words, on all the oceans of the world. Thus Sir James Graham, first lord of the Admiralty between 1830 and 1834, told Parliament that "if the British Navy be not ready at all times and in all places, to sustain our greatness, to assert our rights, and to vindicate our maritime supremacy, then, indeed, is our glory departed." [16] Others, especially those suspicious of imperial expansion and concerned with excessive spending, had a less sweeping vision. Gladstone, for example, set the requirements for Britain's naval policy in these terms: "We are to have a powerful fleet in and near our own waters, and . . . except for this nothing is to be maintained except for well-defined and approved purposes of actual service . . . and not under the notion that there are to be fleets in the various quarters of the world ready when a difficulty arises with a foreign country." [17]

In practice these two positions were less far apart than they seemed. Global supremacy was not an issue. The only real point of dispute was the relative freedom with which the navy should be used for secondary purposes in distant waters—the supression of slavery off Africa, for example, or of piracy in Asian seas. There was no debate over the protection of Britain's trade and possessions from major powers. The command of the seas must rest firmly in

Navy: The Development of British Naval Strategic Thought, 1867–1914, p. 1.

[15] Bartlett, *Great Britain and Sea Power, 1815–1853,* p. 1.

[16] Ibid., p. 57.

[17] Bartlett, "The Mid-Victorian Reappraisal of Naval Policy," in Bourne and Watt, eds., *Studies in International History,* pp. 205–206.

British hands. Given the concentration of the world's naval powers in Europe, this outcome followed inevitably from Britain's command of the "narrow seas" around the Continent.

The only serious challenge to general agreement on the importance of naval supremacy came from those who favored a military buildup at the expense of the fleet. Advocates of militias, conscription, and coastal fortifications both for Britain and for the empire as a whole had nothing against the idea of a strong navy. Their fear was that somehow the navy might fail, that it might be overwhelmed by a combination of opponents, or divided at a crucial moment by its wide-ranging responsibilities, or destroyed as it lay at anchor by some freak storm. In any one of these eventualities the empire would need strong ground forces with which to defend itself. The absence of such forces was an invitation to disaster, and their creation was thus held to be a requirement that exceeded in importance even the maintenance of the navy.[18]

Captain Sir John Colomb's book *The Protection of our Commerce and Distribution of our Naval Forces Considered,* published in 1867, is generally held to be the first serious treatise on naval matters of the Victorian era. Arguing in part against supporters of the army, Colomb sought to show that the security of the empire rested in the first instance on naval supremacy rather than coastal defenses.[19] In the age of steam, when ships required frequent refueling, control of the seas demanded the possession of numerous, far-flung bases. These installations might have to be defended on land, but they should not tie down warships. The fleet would have to be free to move and to engage the enemy wherever he might be found.[20]

Colomb's reasoning won gradual, grudging acceptance even from army enthusiasts, but his ideas were not fully incorporated into official doctrine until near the end of the century. In the meantime the work of an American brother officer had an enormous impact on British naval thinking. With the publication of the works of Alfred Thayer Mahan, the case for naval supremacy generally, for a wide-ranging, powerful, "blue water" navy specifically, and for the primacy of the fleet over the army appeared for the first time in a coherent, persuasive, and accessible form.

There can be no question of the impression that Mahan's writings made upon his contemporaries. *The Influence of Sea Power Upon History, 1660–1783* and *The Influence of Sea Power Upon the French*

---

[18] For a good, brief account of these debates see J. Gooch, *The Prospect of War: Studies in British Defence Policy, 1847–1942,* pp. 3–10.

[19] M. Howard, *The Continental Commitment,* p. 23.

[20] Schurman, *Education of a Navy,* pp. 19–24.

Revolution and Empire, 1793–1812, which appeared in 1890 and 1892, respectively, were widely reprinted, translated, and read (or at least quoted).[21] Nowhere was Mahan received with more enthusiasm than in Britain, where, by the last decade of the century, there was already an upsurge of interest in all things naval. After years of easy predominance, Britain was beginning to face challenges from all sides. "The English people," in the words of naval historian Arthur Marder, "needed *reminding,* not conversion" to the notion that free use of the seas was vital to their survival.[22] Mahan supplied that reminder but, more important, he provided a systematic analysis of the problems of naval power.

Several aspects of Mahan's thought deserve special attention. First, he developed what has been called a "philosophy of sea power," an eloquent defense with historical illustrations of the proposition that "command of the seas" was essential to the acquisition and protection of colonies and trade and thus to a country's success in the harsh competition of international life.[23] All this was hardly new, but it was presented now as the irrefutable result of a "scientific" study of history. Belief in the importance of sea control was no longer an unsubstantiated (if widely held) opinion but a proven "fact."

Beyond this bolstering of conventional notions Mahan also offered a theory of naval strategy. If use of the sea was essential to peacetime prosperity, then denial of safe transit must be the key to success in time of conflict. Mahan maintained that victory in war would result ultimately from the control of the seas. If the enemy could be deprived of use of the ocean highway he could be brought to his knees. Any great nation at war with another would therefore have to "break up the enemy's power on the sea, cutting off his communications with the rest of his possessions, drying up the sources of his wealth in his commerce and making possible a closure of his ports."[24]

Contrary to the views of some, Mahan's belief was that command of the sea could not be achieved either through raids on the enemy's homeland or by protracted harassment of his shipping. The "true end" of an oceangoing navy was to "preponderate over the enemy's navy and so to control the sea." Thus "the enemy's ships

[21] On the reception of Mahan in Europe generally, see Langer, *The Diplomacy of Imperialism, 1870–1890,* pp. 415–45. On Mahan and his ideas see Crowl, "Alfred Thayer Mahan: The Naval Historian," in Paret, ed., *The Makers of Modern Strategy: From Ma-*

chiavelli to the Nuclear Age, pp. 444–77.
[22] Marder, *The Anatomy of British Sea Power,* p. 55.
[23] M. Sprout, "Mahan: Evangelist of Sea Power," p. 418.
[24] Mahan, *The Influence of Sea Power Upon History,* p. 254.

and fleets" were the "true objects to be assailed on all occasions."[25] Only by destroying an opponent's fleet or bottling it up in its home ports could sea control be attained. The achievement of these strategic objectives would require a concentration of superior force, what Mahan called "that overbearing power on the sea which drives the enemy's flag from it, or allows it to appear only as a fugitive, and which, by controlling the great common, closes the highways by which commerce moves to and fro from the enemy's shores."[26]

Mahan's emphasis on concentration and main-force engagements had several logical corollaries. Too wide a distribution of naval resources was a bad thing because it exposed a fleet to gradual annihilation and because it made difficult the accumulation of the great force that would defeat the enemy's concentrated power. Moreover, nature as well as the sound application of strategic principles played a part in determining the outcome of the struggle for sea control. One of the reasons for Britain's great success was that its geographical position permitted a concentration of power at vital points, while that of France, for example, forced the division of its navy into two parts. Finally, because the clash of great fleets would decide control of the seas, the most important units were those which would contribute most directly to a decisive outcome. The ship of the line, in Mahan's day the mighty armored battleship, was therefore the most critical component of naval might.

The "capital-ship-command-of-the-sea doctrine" that Mahan did so much to propagate was latent in earlier navalist thinking.[27] Indeed, one reason for his great popularity in England might have been simply that he was telling people what they already knew or at least what they wanted to hear. Original or not, Mahan's works cast a long shadow over all subsequent discussions of naval matters and of national strategy more generally. His formulations were repeated in the popular press, in naval journals, and in Parliament and quoted in the private correspondence of even so independent a thinker as Admiral Fisher.[28]

In the years that followed the appearance of Mahan's first major works, numerous imitators offered their own gloss on his insights.

[25] Ibid.

[26] Ibid., p. 121.

[27] M. Sprout, "Mahan: Evangelist of Sea Power," p. 434.

[28] In a letter to Joseph Chamberlain dated 10 November 1900, for example, Fisher quotes his favorite Mahanism: "Nelson's far distant storm-beaten ships, upon which the Grand Army never looked, stood between it and the dominion of the world" (in Marder, ed., *Fear God and Dreadnought: The Correspondence of Admiral of the Fleet Lord Fisher of Kilverstone* 1 : 165). The phrase appears again in Fisher's crucial memorandum on fleet redistribution "Organization for War," which is reprinted in Kemp, ed., *The Papers of Admiral Sir John Fisher* 1 : 18.

One noteworthy example, George Clarke, who, as secretary of the newly formed Committee of Imperial Defence, would play a central role in the strategic debates of the Balfour administration, coauthored a book in 1897 entitled *The Navy and the Nation*. In a chapter on "The Command of the Sea," Clarke and journalist James Thursfield defined that concept in unmistakably Mahanian terms. "Strategic freedom of maritime transit is the primary and indefeasible condition of the defence of the British Empire," they argued. "Every fleet capable of impairing that freedom must be defeated or 'contained' in the military sense; so blockaded, that is, that it cannot leave its port of shelter without fighting an action against a superior force."[29]

Such views were not the exclusive preserve of private analysts. As the century drew to a close the Admiralty, which had never gone in much for elaborate theorizing, felt a growing need to rationalize its strategic posture. This it did along the lines that Mahan had laid down in the early 1890s. Thus a 1902 Admiralty document entitled "Memorandum on Sea-Power and the Principles Involved in It" began with a familiar catechism.

> The importance which attaches to the command of the sea lies in the control which it gives over sea communications. The weaker sea-power is absolutely unable to carry to success any large military expedition over sea. . . . The command of the sea is determined by the result of great battles at sea. . . . To any naval Power the destruction of the fleet of the enemy must always be the great object aimed at. . . . It is the battleship chiefly which will have to be concentrated for the decisive battle.[30]

The "Two Power Standard"—Origins and Ambiguities

The schematic formula for supremacy just cited is one with which few informed Englishmen would have disagreed. Yet it clearly lacks one very important component. It is an equation in which the desired result is known but the variables have been assigned no numerical values. Command of the seas may be the object aimed at. An ability to concentrate ships (and especially battleships) may be what gives a fleet the capacity to destroy or blockade its opposition, thereby winning the battle for sea control and with it the war. But what measure of concentration is required to achieve tactical suc-

[29] Clarke and Thursfield, *The Navy and the Nation*, p. 149.
[30] PRO, Adm. 231/36, "Memorandum on Sea-Power and the Principles Involved in It," 6/02.

cess? And, more broadly, what is the overall ratio of forces that must be maintained in order to guarantee the command of the seas? This latter question was at the center of all discussions of the adequacy of Britain's naval power. Into it were collapsed a vast array of assumptions about strategy, tactics, geography, and diplomacy.

In the summer of 1888 a Select Committee on the Naval Estimates reported to Parliament that "no complete scheme had ever been laid before the Admiralty showing apart from financial limits laid down by the Cabinet, what, in the opinion of naval experts, the strength of the fleet should be."[31] Although no generally agreed measure of adequacy existed at this time, there had in the past been periodic declarations about the level of naval strength that the nation should seek to maintain. In 1817 Foreign Minister Castlereagh stated that Britain's objective should be "to keep up a navy equal to the navies of any two Powers that can be brought against us."[32] By the 1830s there were already worries that France and Russia would sign a treaty and effectively fuse their two fleets in opposition to Britain.[33] Anxiety over a possible Franco-Russian alliance intensified in the aftermath of the Crimean War, and an Admiralty minute of early 1858 warned, "When determining upon the number of ships which England should have, it should be borne in mind that the navies of France and Russia may very probably be combined against her."[34]

To some the prospect of an alliance between the French and Russians never seemed very plausible, and concentration on maintaining numerical superiority over one nation alone (presumably France) was widely regarded as sufficient.[35] The fact that no hostile entente did emerge until the 1890s made it easier to sustain the more relaxed position on naval standards. Arthur Marder concludes that, for most of the nineteenth century, Britain was content in practice to maintain a peacetime fleet roughly one-third larger than that of the French.[36] This approach, in the words of another analyst, was "largely determined by a compromise between what

---

[31] Woodward, *Great Britain and the German Navy*, p. 455.

[32] Bartlett, *Great Britain and Sea Power*, p. 23.

[33] Graham, *The Politics of Naval Supremacy*, p. 65.

[34] Bartlett, *Great Britain and Sea Power*, p. 276.

[35] Prime Minister John Russell, for example, told Parliament in 1848, "I do not think that we ought to say so much as was laid down in the Committee of 1817, that it was necessary for this Country to have a force equal to any two foreign Powers: but I think that . . . we ought to be stronger at sea than any one other foreign Power" (quoted in Bartlett, *Great Britain and Sea Power*, p. 274).

[36] Marder, *Anatomy of British Sea Power*, p. 105.

was practicable from the domestic political and financial stand-point, and what seemed desirable in light of Britain's relations with other naval powers."[37] It was not required either by act of Parliament or by any recognized strategic doctrine.

By the end of the 1870s even the traditional British advantage over France was starting to slip away. From England the nations of Europe had learned that power rested on wealth, which depended on empire, which, in turn, could be maintained only with a sizable navy.[38] In 1878 the French began a shipbuilding program that equaled Britain's in cost, and at approximately the same time Italy, Germany, and Russia all stepped up their naval expenditures.[39] For the next five or six years, however, the generally cordial state of diplomatic relations tended to obscure the gradual erosion of Britain's position.

In 1884 there were new disagreements with the French over conflicting imperial claims in Egypt and the Far East, with Germany over the division of Africa, and with Russia regarding the demarcation of spheres of influence in central Asia. "Almost instinctively," as Marder puts it, "the English turned to inspect their first line of defense, and were shocked to find it inadequate for possible contingencies."[40] By a simple count of ships Britain was only narrowly ahead of France, and if, as some feared, a Franco-German naval alliance was concluded, it would bring to bear a superior force of battleships and an almost equal flotilla of cruisers.[41]

In truth it was less "instinct" than a carefully planned program of agitation in the popular press that called attention to the state of the fleet. A series of articles in the *Pall Mall Gazette* entitled "The Truth About the Navy" drew on leaks from inside the government to dramatize the precariousness of Britain's lead and to support calls for increased spending.[42] First Lord Northbrook responded by proposing a £5.5 million program that included money for two first-class "ironclads" and five armored cruisers.[43]

After two years of higher budgets, allocations for warship construction were cut sharply in 1887 and 1888. This might have been

[37] Bartlett, *Great Britain and Sea Power,* p. 276.

[38] For the background to this period see Langer, *The Diplomacy of Imperialism,* pp. 67–100, 415–45.

[39] Marder, *Anatomy of British Sea Power,* p. 120.

[40] Ibid., p. 121.

[41] On the competition between Britain and France at this point see Langer, *European Alliances and Alignments, 1871– 1890,* pp. 476–77. On the overall balance see Sumida, "Financial Limitation, Technological Innovation, and British Naval Policy, 1904–1910," p. 6.

[42] For Fisher's part in the scare see Mackay, *Fisher of Kilverstone,* p. 181.

[43] Marder, *Anatomy of British Sea Power,* p. 122.

partly a reaction to previous increases, but it was apparently also the result of a realization by navy planners that their expensive new battleships might be vulnerable to undersea torpedoes launched from cheap, fast-moving torpedo boats.[44] Whatever the precise reason, British naval activity slacked off while that of the nation's competitors continued. To the navalists this was worrisome enough without the emergence of a threatening new factor. At the beginning of 1888 there were renewed rumors that France and Russia might enter a formal alliance and that, in particular, their fleets might cooperate in an effort to drive British forces out of the Mediterranean.[45]

By the summer, public uneasiness over naval matters had reached such a pitch that Queen Victoria felt compelled to express her concern to the prime minister, Lord Salisbury.[46] A special select committee was formed to consider the question of preparedness, and in the spring of 1889 the first lord of the Admiralty, George Hamilton, made his recommendations to Parliament.[47]

The practical side of Hamilton's plan was the so-called Naval Defense Act, a five-year program of construction with a £23 million price tag. Under the terms of the act, British shipyards were to assemble a total of ten battleships, forty-two cruisers, and eighteen torpedo boats.[48] This was an enormous program, but its ultimate importance lay more in its justification than in its size. For the first time government officials laid out a standard against which their efforts, and those of future governments, could be judged. In the process they also created a compressed, shorthand means of measuring sea power that would figure prominently in all naval debates prior to the outbreak of the First World War.

Having examined the statements of past prime ministers and first lords, Hamilton concluded that the "leading idea" behind Britain's naval preparations had always been "that our establishment should be on such a scale that it should be equal to the naval strength of any two other countries."[49] This considerable "margin of reserve"

[44] Marder suggests that the reason for the cutbacks was concern over costs (*Anatomy of British Sea Power*, p. 123). Another possibility is that British ship designers had to wait until the invention of the quick-firing gun (1889) provided them with a weapon with which to keep torpedo boats out of range of their battleships (Sumida, "Financial Limitation, Technological Innovation, and British Naval Policy, 1904–1910," p. 7).

[45] Marder, *Anatomy of British Sea Power*, p. 131.

[46] Ibid., 132.

[47] For these events see Hamilton, *Parliamentary Reminiscences and Reflections, 1886–1906*, pp. 80–121.

[48] Sumida, "Financial Limitation," pp. 8–9.

[49] *Hansard Parliamentary Debates*, 3d ser., vol. 333 (1889), p. 1171.

was made necessary by the fact that "no amount of foresight or calculation [could] anticipate naval combinations and naval movements."[50] The proposed construction bill would provide Britain with the edge needed to deal with such dangers by bringing its fleet up to a "Two Power Standard." But, the first lord reassured his audience, the requirement itself was neither new nor provocative.[51] The Admiralty was merely taking "the old standard which preceding Governments have set before themselves, and not acted up to."[52]

Hamilton's statement equated Britain's strategic objective, worldwide command of the seas, with a fixed ratio of naval forces. *If* the Royal Navy was equal to that of any two others, *then* sea control was assured. For all its apparent simplicity and precision, however, the two-power standard was riddled with ambiguities.

To take more narrowly military questions first: Assuming that the two powers to be matched were known, what, exactly, should they be equaled in? By the turn of the century some commentators were trying to draw comparisons based on spending, manpower, or total fleet tonnage figures. Hamilton, however, was referring quite clearly to battleships and specifically to those of "the newest type and most approved design."[53] In this he was not much different from most experts on naval strategy, although his stipulation regarding battleship types tended to eliminate from consideration the older, slower craft that both Britain and its enemies possessed in substantial numbers. The essential naval balance was to be measured in terms of modern battleships, but, as subsequent first lords were at pains to point out, other kinds of ships did not fall under the two-power standard. Because of Britain's vast shipping and colonial interests, the Admiralty believed that the country would have to maintain far more than the number of cruisers possessed by its two closest rivals.[54] Other kinds of craft, whether torpedo boats or, later, submarines, played no part in the most important official calculations of naval power.[55] This narrowness of vision was encour-

---

[50] Ibid., p. 1172.

[51] In fact the first lord appears to have been wrong on both counts. In its official form the two-power standard *was* new, and it was followed by an intensification of the programs of France and Russia (Sumida, "Financial Limitation," p. 10).

[52] Lord George Hamilton, statement of 4/1/89, in PRO, Adm. 116/1605, "Pronouncements on the Two Power Standard," 5/09, p. 1.

[53] *Hansard Parliamentary Debates*, 3d ser., vol. 333 (1889), p. 1173.

[54] See statements by Lord Selborne, 3/24/03, and Mr. Runciman, 5/14/03, in PRO, Adm. 116/1605, pp. 8–9.

[55] Arthur Marder concludes that "the relative strength of navies was determined, by the Admiralty and experts, almost entirely by their relative strengths in battleships, especially those of the first-class" (*Anatomy of British Sea Power*, p. 113). According to Brassey's,

aged if not actually caused by the capital ship comparisons institutionalized in the two-power standard.[56]

Equality meant equality in first-class battleships. But what did the word "equality" itself mean? Some participants in the debate were prepared to assume that a simple balance in numbers would be sufficient to ensure victory. Others stressed that what mattered to Britain was not any particular ratio of ships for its own sake but the command of the seas that the ratio presumably provided. "Outcomes" in this view were more important than "inputs" or "resources"; thus the British fleet should not only be equal in numbers to those of any two powers combined but (as some Admiralty officials insisted) "equal to beating them."[57] This, naturally, seemed to require *superior* rather than simply equivalent numbers. How big the margin above a numerical two-power standard should be was a secondary issue of contention among navalists. Some favored a 10-percent edge, others went so far as to suggest a 5 to 3 ratio between Britain and its two closest rivals.[58]

From its inception there were those who criticized the idea that *any* numerical comparison by itself could be an adequate surrogate for some functional measure of sea control. During the debate over the defense act Captain John Colomb had warned that "superiority was the power necessary to keep the enemy's battleships in their harbours" under widely varying conditions. For this reason he believed "all abstract comparisons were absolutely valueless," as "one could not base calculations of superiority merely on the abstract question of numbers."[59] At the same time another skeptic, former fourth sea lord Charles Beresford, objected that "nothing could be more misleading, nothing more ridiculous, than comparing the

---

one of the most respected nongovernmental publications on naval matters, "The relative strength of Navies depends almost entirely on their relative strength in battleships" (Brassey, ed., *The Naval Annual, 1896,* p. 68).

[56] Attempting to explain the lack of attention paid to the submarine before the outbreak of World War I, Bernard Brodie has written, "It is difficult now, looking back, to understand how the . . . danger—or opportunity . . . could have been so completely overlooked. No doubt, part of the reason lay in the tremendous prestige of . . . Rear-Admiral Mahan and of the lessons inculcated in his important works" ("Technological Change, Strategic Doc-

trine, and Political Outcomes," in Knorr, ed., *Historical Dimensions of National Security Problems,* p. 281).

[57] Marder, *Anatomy of British Sea Power,* p. 106.

[58] See statement by Joseph Chamberlain of 12/19/93, PRO, Adm. 116/1605, pp. 2–3. Marder suggests that a 5 to 3 tactical ratio was considered necessary for purposes of maintaining a blockade of enemy ports (*Anatomy of British Sea Power,* p. 107). Chamberlain might simply have been extrapolating from this figure to arrive at an overall measure of force size.

[59] Woodward, *Great Britain and the German Navy,* p. 456.

numbers or tonnage of the fleets of England with those of France or any other Power. What should be compared is the work the respective forces have to do."[60]

This was certainly true. But to get from numbers of ships to combat outcomes with any measure of reliability required the most accurate possible assumptions about the relative effectiveness of the units that would engage one another, and about communications, tactics, the initial distribution of forces, and such imponderables as which side would take the initiative and whether there would be a declaration of war prior to the first engagement at sea. "There were obviously," as Colomb would later say rather regretfully, "details which could not be explained in the House of Commons or to the man in the street; and, therefore, something had to be done to satisfy public opinion . . . and the rough and ready Two Power Standard was adopted."[61]

It would be a mistake, however, to assume that the "rough and ready" standard of 1889 worked its wiles only on the British public. Even within the Admiralty there were no readily available techniques with which to capture the complexities of naval warfare. Strategic planning and the war gaming that went with it were still in their infancy. Indeed, the Royal Navy had no real war plans until well into the 1890s and no detailed scheme for war with France and Russia until after the Fashoda crisis of 1898.[62] At the end of the day *some* decision about the appropriate size of the British naval force had to be made and justified. Even if there had been a more satisfactory (and hence more complex) way of assessing the naval balance, the very simplicity of the two-power standard would have made it difficult to displace. Its longevity as a serious idea in the face of rapidly changing conditions and in both official and public circles would seem to give ample testimony to this assertion.

The equation of a two-power standard with worldwide sea supremacy rested on a number of political as well as military assumptions. In the abstract there was no reason why matching (whatever that meant) the combined forces of any two fleets should produce the desired result. Obviously the limiting case for Hamilton's formula was that in which the two hostile fleets were those of the second- and third-ranked naval powers, whatever their identities. But why assume that Britain would have only two enemies at a time? And, on the other hand, why assume that the two powers after Britain would necessarily cooperate against her?

[60] Ibid.
[61] *Hansard Parliamentary Debates*, 4th ser., vol. 139 (1904), p. 1073.

[62] Marder, *From Dreadnought to Scapa Flow* 1 : 8.

Although the question was always treated coyly in public, it was clear from the outset that the Admiralty had its eye on a Franco-Russian combination. While Italy's fleet was officially ranked third (after that of England and France, but ahead of Russia's), British relations with the Italians were generally good. Thus by matching France and Italy the British could stay ahead of the real threat.[63] From the beginning, then, there was some confusion as to whether the two-power standard was "automatic" (aimed at the number two and three states regardless of who they were) or specifically applicable only to France and Russia.

For geographical reasons the French and Russian fleets could combine only with difficulty. The British navy therefore hoped to defeat its opponents in detail as they moved out of ports on the Baltic and Atlantic coasts and attempted to rendezvous at sea. If (and this was by no means so easily ensured) the Russian Black Sea fleet could be prevented from linking up with the French squadron based at Toulon, then control of the Mediterranean would be guaranteed. So long as a Franco-Russian combination was the worst thing Britain had to fear, there was good reason to expect that it could retain control of the waters around Europe. What this meant in practice was that no substantial hostile force would be able to escape into more distant waters and attack Britain's shipping or its colonies. Under these conditions a two-power standard might very well be taken as a guarantee of worldwide sea control.

By the middle of the 1890s few Englishmen would have hesitated to swear fealty to the idea of a two-power standard in words such as one Liberal MP (and future prime minister) had used in 1889.

> I accept in the fullest and most complete form the doctrine that it is necessary for this country to hold the supremacy of the seas, and . . . further, I accept the doctrine that the test and standard of this supremacy is that our Fleet should be as strong as the combined strength of any two Fleets in the world. That supremacy I believe to be the traditional possession of this country.[64]

Assuming that the Royal Navy remained the most powerful in the world, there were still two possible threats to the reassuring state of affairs in which the standard and supremacy were linked. The first would come if more than two European powers combined

[63] On this period see Taylor, *The Struggle for Mastery in Europe,* pp. 325–45.

[64] Statement by Campbell-Bannerman, 4/1/89, in PRO, Adm. 116/1605, p. 1.

against Britain. The second would result from the emergence of significant non-European navies. Even if they were not ranked in the top three, such forces would compel substantial increases in the British fleet. Covering even small navies at distant ports while matching France and Russia close to home would be a test more rigorous than any Britain had ever faced.

In the closing years of the nineteenth century British statesmen were forced to cope with both these challenges to their "traditional supremacy." Their ability to understand and explain what was happening was constrained by the language available to them, a language devised to describe a situation that was now passing swiftly and decisively away.

Crisis

Between 1895 and 1905 clear-cut naval supremacy slipped from Britain's grasp, and with it went the nation's unique role as the independent, detached arbiter of world affairs (see Table 4-1). This did not occur all at once but it did happen quickly. From 1895 to 1900 Britain's position came under increasing pressure, both in European waters and off the distant shores of the Far East and the Western Hemisphere. In a matter of less than a year, between the months of January and September 1901, Admiralty officials came to the conclusion that past policies and, to a certain extent, past ways of thinking about the naval balance would have to be modified. Although the two-power standard was retained as an index of the adequacy of British naval forces, it was now hemmed in by assumptions that gave it an entirely new meaning. Between 1902 and 1903 the immediate operational significance of the navy's new policy gradually became apparent within the Government. Following the fleet redistribution announcement at the close of 1904, that policy was made public, but the manner in which it was discussed tended to obscure its deeper importance. Even those who had helped to bring the changes about seem to have had difficulty in fully grasping what they would mean for Britain, its empire, and its place in the international system.

Under Pressure, 1895–1900
Center

For most of the nineteenth century, predominance in the waters around Europe was the key to maintaining command of the world's oceans. At least since 1889 Britain had striven to retain a fleet equal in size to that of the next two naval powers combined as the best

Table 4-1
The Diffusion of Sea Power, 1896–1906

Year	Battleships[a]						
	GB	*F*	*R*	*G*	*US*	*J*	*I*
1896	45/12	29/6	10/8	21/3	5/7	0	13/2
1898	51/12	27/9	12/6	17/5	5/8	3/3	15/2
1899	53/17	31/4	12/12	18/7	5/11	3/4	15/4
1901	50/16	28/5	15/10	19/10	7/11	6/1	15/6
1902	52/13	28/8	18/8	25/9	10/8	7/0	17/7
1903	48/15	28/8	18/8	28/8	11/14	7/0	17/6
1904	55/12	30/6	21/9	30/8	12/13	7/2	16/6
1905	59/9	30/6	19/8	29/8	13/13	6/2	16/4
1906	61/6	29/12	12/4	31/8	15/13	11/6	14/4

Source: The Admiralty's "Comparative Tabular Statement of the Numerical Strength of the Fleets of Great Britain, France, Russia, Germany, Italy, United States of America, and Japan," issued periodically before 1900 and each year thereafter and published in *Accounts and Papers* in parliamentary records.

Notes. Because these figures include the smaller second- and third-class battleships as well as those of the first class, they tend somewhat to overstate Germany's naval strength. In 1903, for example, only 12 of the total 28 German battleships were of the first class, and an equal number were third-class vessels. In the same year the British had only 2 third-class and 4 second-class ships out of a total of 48. France and Russia had 1 third-class battleship apiece and 8 and 4 second-class vessels, respectively. Neither the US nor Japan had any third-class ships, and both had only 1 of the second class.

[a] Figure before the slant represents the number of battleships of all classes in service in a given year; figure after slant indicates the number of such vessels under construction.

way of ensuring continued control of the "narrow seas" around the Continent and the open oceans beyond.

During the closing years of the century the Royal Navy's superiority in European waters faced two principal challenges. As the French and the Russians stepped up their naval preparations and moved into closer political and military alignment, there were persistent fears that they would somehow be able to defeat Britain at sea. From the beginning of the 1890s Britain was forced to run harder and harder just to stay even with its two main competitors.

But, the question was asked, what if equality with two powers is no longer enough? Periodically (and especially at moments of diplomatic tension) there was discussion of the possibility of some larger "Continental Coalition" that could field a fleet of overwhelming size. Germany was considered to be the likely third partner in such an alliance, but it was not until after the turn of the century that it would begin to emerge in its own right as Britain's single most dangerous maritime competitor.

Concern that the two-power standard might not be met began almost at the moment of its conception. The problem at first was not so much the overall size of French and Russian forces but the possibility of their cooperation in the Mediterranean, a sea that Fisher (echoing Mahan) would later call "the vital strategic Centre of Britain's position."[65] From the late 1880s the French had been augmenting their Mediterranean fleet, and in 1890 there were also growing signs of Russian preparations for a possible "descent" on Constantinople. According to intelligence reports, the Black Sea fleet was being improved and, particularly worrisome, the number of troop transports available to it appeared to be increasing.[66] In August of 1891 the two powers entered into a formal entente that stopped short of outright military alliance.[67] Just over two years later a Russian squadron called at Toulon, provoking wild demonstrations of Franco-Russian solidarity and associated outpourings of anti-British feeling.[68]

A hostile coalition able to join its forces in the Mediterranean held a sword aimed at the jugular vein of the British Empire. In the event of a conflict in Asia, free use of the Suez Canal would be essential to any British war effort. If Russia moved against India, British forces might have to pass into the Black Sea as they had done during the Crimean War and strike at the enemy's underbelly, thereby disrupting his lines of communication to the east.[69] For this strategy to be successful (or if Britain simply wished to keep Russian ships bottled up in the Black Sea), the Royal Navy would have to act quickly to reach Constantinople and seize control of the Straits of Bosporus. Such a move would have been dangerous enough if it had been opposed by the sultan. Now, with the newly signed entente, the British had to worry about a substantial French force at their backs. Even if they succeeded in forcing their way to the Turkish capital, English ships might find themselves trapped with no easy way of returning to the relative safety of the Mediterranean.

As early as March 1892 the directors of Military and Naval Intelligence had warned that, in light of the Franco-Russian combina-

[65] Fisher Papers, 1/1, Fisher to Joseph Chamberlain, 10/10/00.

[66] Marder, *Anatomy of British Sea Power*, pp. 146, 152.

[67] Taylor, *Struggle for Mastery in Europe*, pp. 335–36.

[68] Langer, *The Diplomacy of Imperialism*, pp. 47–49.

[69] Grenville, *Lord Salisbury and Foreign Policy: The Close of the Nineteenth Century*, pp. 25–26.

tion, "Great Britain unsupported cannot prevent the *coup-de-main* [against Constantinople] without endangering her general naval position."[70] This was undoubtedly a prudent judgment, but it raised some troubling questions. If Britain could no longer be assured of controlling the Straits of Bosporus, then how could it prevent the joining of French and Russian forces in the Mediterranean? If those two hostile fleets were linked in wartime, would Britain be able to hold the "vital strategic Centre"? And, if Britain lost control of the center, how would it be able to retain command of the seas?

Such arcane calculations may have been beyond the reach of ordinary citizens, but the public was by no means unaware that circumstances were changing. After the Toulon port call the English press, nerve endings still tingling from the scares of 1884 and 1889, began to warn again of the inadequacies of the Royal Navy. Public agitation was followed in December 1893 by a heated discussion in Parliament during which the Conservative opposition accused the Government of doing nothing to offset an increasingly unfavorable balance of forces in vital strategic areas. Joseph Chamberlain even went so far as to suggest that the two-power standard might no longer be an adequate index of Britain's needs. "It may be," he urged, "that a better formula would be . . . that for any three battleships built by any naval combination against this country we should build five, and that for every cruiser built by the same combination we should build two."[71]

The Liberal leadership shrugged off Chamberlain's proposal and stood by the more orthodox definition of the two-power standard. Within the Government, however, there were some who worried that even this lesser measure of naval sufficiency was not being adequately sustained. At the time of the Toulon visit the directors of Naval Intelligence and Construction had warned that, if existing programs continued apace, within two years Britain would go from a two-battleship advantage over France and Russia to a three-ship disadvantage. By 1896–1897 the unfavorable margin could be as wide as eight capital ships.[72]

In the face of these figures, First Lord of the Admiralty Spencer proposed a substantial increase in planned construction, including seven battleships and twenty-eight cruisers at a cost of £31 million.[73] Inside the cabinet the aging prime minister William Gladstone resisted this plan with all that remained of his strength, but within a

[70] Marder, *Anatomy of British Sea Power*, pp. 159–60.
[71] Joseph Chamberlain, 12/19/03, PRO, Adm. 116/1605, pp. 2–3.
[72] Marder, *Anatomy of British Sea Power*, p. 191.
[73] Sumida, "Financial Limitation," p. 10.

matter of months he had been forced into retirement and a smaller version of Spencer's plan was adopted.[74] Almost immediately after its passage this program was increased to include a total of nine new first-class battleships, thus ensuring for the immediate future the maintenance of a slight numerical edge over the combined forces of France and Russia.[75]

When the Conservatives returned to power they inherited an ongoing naval buildup combined with a continuing uneasiness about the nation's ability to keep pace with Russia and France. To this there was shortly added the even more troublesome specter of a three-power, anti-British coalition. After Japan's defeat of China in the spring of 1895, France, Russia, and Germany joined together to force the victors to give back some of the territorial concessions they had extracted. Britain stood aside from all this, but the possibility of a three-way combination against its interests and, perhaps, against its fleet had been unmistakably introduced.[76] This theme was replayed with even more menacing overtones following the "Kruger telegram" incident, involving the Kaiser's public attempt to mobilize European opposition to British policy in South Africa while he threatened in private that England would face a "Continental League" if it did not sign a treaty with Germany.[77]

The prospect of such a coalition provoked navalists in Parliament to new heights of anxiety. In the annual debate over the estimates, Sir Charles Dilke cautioned that existing plans were "hand to mouth" and represented merely a "France and Russia programme." The standard of "equality with or superiority over two Powers" was now, Dilke warned, "a fallacious and misleading test." Britain had recently been "within an ace of having demands made upon [it] which would have been supported by a stronger combination than two Powers—possibly by three Powers." There was no assurance that such a situation might not again arise. Under the circumstances, Dilke reasoned, the Government could either enter into an alliance with some other state (a measure that he opposed)

---

[74] Gladstone regarded further increases in British strength as wasteful to the point of madness. At one point in the debate over a new program, he is reported to have exploded, "Bedlam should be enlarged at once, it is the Admirals who have got their knife into me" (Taylor, *Struggle for Mastery in Europe*, p. 348).

[75] Sumida, "Financial Limitation," pp. 11–12.

[76] Langer, *The Diplomacy of Imperialism*, pp. 355–58.

[77] Taylor, *Struggle for Mastery in Europe*, p. 365. The telegram at issue contained a message from Kaiser Wilhelm to Transvaal president Kruger congratulating him on turning aside what appeared to be an English-inspired raid against his territory (P. Kennedy, *The Rise of the Anglo-German Antagonism, 1860–1914*, pp. 220–21).

or follow "the only true policy of this country . . . keeping up such a fleet as would make us safe against any probable combination."[78]

With the South African crisis fading from view and a substantial construction program already in train, the Government was in no mood to alter its naval policies. First Lord Goschen caricatured Dilke's speech as amounting to a proposal that Britain "must have a Navy as large as all the navies of the world combined," an idea that he rightly dismissed as "preposterous."[79] Balfour, in his role as Conservative leader of the House, gave a characteristically more thoughtful response. Dealing first with the question of whether a two-power standard was sufficient, he warned against the temptation of imagining "the extreme case," an unlikely combination "by which [the] nation may be crushed out of existence." Instead, he urged, "we [should] . . . simply contemplate bringing up our fleet to a strength which would enable us to contend on satisfactory terms with the two largest fleets that could be brought against us."[80]

As to whether the fleet was up to even this lesser challenge, Balfour insisted that "it depends upon what you count to know exactly what your position is." Most foreign second-class battleships were not designed to operate very far from their home ports, and there was consequently some question as to their proper weighting in the overall totals. In first-class craft alone, Balfour informed the House, by 1898 Britain would have a five-ship margin over France and Russia.[81]

Dilke was not so easily soothed and he proceeded over the next two years to criticize the Government's building plans whenever they were put before Parliament. A three-power coalition was always possible and, Dilke warned, there was growing evidence that superior French and Russian mobilization procedures had increased the danger of sudden surprise attack.[82]

The official response to all this was rather lame. Goschen claimed that a coalition force with ships of varying design and capability could never defeat the navy of a single nation, even if the opposing fleets were equal in size. As to a combination of three partners, assuming such a thing were possible, the problems of coordination would simply overwhelm whatever advantages might be gained by superiority in numbers. In the first lord's words, the Royal Navy

[78] *Hansard Parliamentary Debates*, 4th ser., vol. 38 (1896), pp. 247–51.
[79] Statement by George Goschen, 3/9/96, in PRO, Adm. 116/1605, p. 5.
[80] Statement by Arthur Balfour,

3/5/96, in ibid., p. 5.
[81] *Hansard Parliamentary Debates*, 4th ser., vol. 38 (1896), pp. 261–62.
[82] Ibid., vol. 47 (1897), p. 69.

must be prepared to meet "any reasonable contingency," but in the face of some "great combination" there would be little choice except to "trust in Providence and a good Admiral."[83]

Having contemplated the worst, most observers could now go back to worrying about the more mundane problem of simply keeping ahead of the Dual Alliance. In May 1898, figures published in Parliament revealed that Britain had fifty-two battleships in commission compared with twenty-seven for France and twelve for Russia. Because the alliance had a total of eighteen battleships under construction, as opposed to England's twelve, the gap between the two sides would narrow from thirteen to seven with the passage of time. Germany, with seventeen battleships built and five building, now clearly held the balance between Britain and its enemies. For the moment, however, this fact did not seem to attract a great deal of attention.[84]

The Admiralty had believed at the beginning of 1898 that three new battleships laid down in the coming year would be just sufficient to keep abreast of France and Russia. During the summer, however, it was announced that the Russians were augmenting their program with six additional capital ships. In response, an unusual emergency supplement of over £2 million was requested from Parliament, and eight more vessels, four battleships and four cruisers, were added to the Royal Navy's construction schedule.[85]

As substantial an undertaking as this was, it could not cover a certain subtle erosion in Britain's position. The Russian navy had now overtaken the Italian in numbers of battleships, thereby changing the significance of the two-power standard. In the past Britain had sustained a comfortable margin over France and Russia by matching France and friendly Italy. But this outcome was a happy consequence of the diplomatic ambiguity in which the standard had always been shrouded rather than the result of any clearly defined policy. With the century drawing to a close, adhering to the two-power standard had come to mean merely keeping pace with the Franco-Russian combination. Even this was beginning to look again like a difficult task.

A report from the director of Naval intelligence to Goschen at the end of 1898 forecast that within six years Britain would have fifty-seven battleships, compared with thirty-four for France and

[83] Statement by Goschen, 3/5/97, in PRO, Adm. 116/1605, pp. 6–7.

[84] Marder, *Anatomy of British Sea Power*, p. 314.

[85] PRO, Cab. 37/49/7, "Navy Estimates, 1899–1900," G. J. Goschen, 1/31/99, p. 4.

twenty-five for Russia.[86] In a memorandum to the cabinet dated 31 January 1899, the first lord apologized for requesting a budget of unprecedented magnitude, one that exceeded "by a very large sum the swollen Estimates of last year."[87] But the activities of other countries and the requirements of the two-power standard left little choice. To stay even, two battleships and five cruisers of various sizes would have to be laid down at an additional cost of over £3 million.[88]

For a brief period at the beginning of 1899 the naval situation seemed to take a turn for the better. The Fashoda crisis, in which England successfully faced down France, temporarily boosted confidence in the fleet at the same time it brought home the continued importance of remaining superior at sea. Some optimists were convinced that Britain's rivals would now be "compelled to withdraw from their conspiracy" against it.[89] Others, more sober, saw only a narrow margin between the nation and its potential enemies, an increasingly costly effort to preserve that edge, and, behind it all, the possibility that German collaboration would upset an already delicate balance.

The onset of the Boer War brought these fears once again to center stage. During the first months of the struggle in South Africa there were persistent reports that the Russians were trying to draw France and Germany into an alliance against Great Britain.[90] This would have been worrisome enough under normal circumstances, but it was particularly frightening with a full-fledged war in progress many thousands of miles from home. To protect movements of reinforcements and supplies, the Royal Navy had been forced to redeploy a substantial portion of its forces along the sea lanes between Southampton and Cape Town, leaving British interests elsewhere dangerously exposed.[91] There was even some concern that the French would take advantage of the relative weakness of the Channel fleet to carry off a surprise invasion of the home islands.[92]

Whatever danger there may have been of a continental coalition passed quickly away but, unlike the situation in 1895 and 1896, the fear of overwhelming opposition seems to have penetrated to the

[86] Marder, *Anatomy of British Sea Power*, p. 345.

[87] PRO, Cab. 37/49/7, p. 1.

[88] Ibid. See also Marder, *Anatomy of British Sea Power*, p. 345.

[89] Sir E. Ashmead-Bartlett, quoted in *Hansard Parliamentary Debates*, 4th ser., vol. 68 (1899), pp. 1045–46.

[90] Grenville, *Lord Salisbury and Foreign Policy*, pp. 271–90.

[91] Nish, *The Anglo-Japanese Alliance*, p. 81. See also Marder, *Anatomy of British Sea Power*, p. 372.

[92] Ibid., p. 378.

highest levels and lingered. In his statement accompanying the estimates for 1900, Goschen appeared to acknowledge the possibility that a two-power standard might no longer be sufficient to meet Britain's needs: "It will require great vigilance and constant sacrifice and attention on the part of the House and the country to keep ourselves abreast of this great development of naval power which is being made, not only in France, Russia and Germany but also in the United States and Japan. In all directions we see this great increase of naval construction."[93]

Just what was to be done about all this Goschen left to his successor, Lord Selborne, who assumed control of the Admiralty toward the end of 1900. Selborne was faced immediately with the problem of maintaining the central balance against France and Russia, a balance that, the new first sea lord Walter Kerr cautioned, might already be worse than it appeared. Kerr advised Selborne on 22 October 1900 that tabulations showing Britain with a slight lead over its two closest competitors did so only because they included some vessels armed with obsolete muzzleloading guns.[94] The French were in the process of converting to the superior breechloaders, where they had not already done so. For Britain, however, the task of modernizing armaments was more difficult because many of the older guns were on ships already approaching the end of their useful lives. If these aging vessels were left out of the account, by 1905 France and Russia would have fifty-seven battleships opposed to fifty-six for Great Britain. Even this position of near parity would be possible only if some of the newer ships with muzzleloaders were included in the fighting line. "If these vessels are excluded," Kerr warned, "our numerical inferiority will be four." From this calculation the naval chief derived his recommendation for a minimal building program of six additional battleships (the two-power standard plus two additional ships), to be completed by the end of 1905.[95]

Some at the Admiralty worried that even this might not be enough. A report by Sir Reginald Custance, the director of Naval Intelligence, calculated that in 1906 France would have thirty-seven battleships, Russia, twenty-six (for a total of sixty-three), and Great Britain, sixty-one. Omitting all ships with muzzleloaders widened the gap from two to seven; the alliance would have sixty battleships with modern weapons versus only fifty-three for England. To just meet this differential a minimum program of seven

---

[93] *Hansard Parliamentary Debates*, 4th ser., vol. 79 (1900), p. 1127.

[94] Selborne Papers, 158, Kerr to Selborne, 10/22/00.
[95] Ibid.

battleships was required. Because he believed that a margin of four over the two leading powers was the least that could be accepted, Custance urged that eleven additional vessels be built.[96]

Within a matter of weeks Kerr had come around to the DNI's figure, although on the basis of somewhat different reasoning. It was learned at the end of December that France was about to begin construction of four new battleships while Russia would add one more to its navy. To preserve what he considered to be the smallest advisable edge over the opposition, Kerr now recommended to the first lord that he request five more ships in addition to the six originally proposed.[97]

Soon after taking office Selborne had been warned by the chancellor of the Exchequer that his department would have to "cut its coat according to its cloth."[98] Now, however, he was being urged to make substantial, costly increases in that very same protective garment if he wished simply to maintain a minimal two-power standard. Budgetary pressures and the rigors of the naval competition in Europe were worry enough. To these was presently to be added a third factor to which Goschen had alluded in his final budget request—the challenge posed by the growth of naval powers outside Europe.

Periphery

West. For some years observers of the naval scene in England had been aware of distant rumblings to the east and west. The United States, which had allowed its fleet to decay after the Civil War, began the slow process of rebuilding in the late 1880s. At around the same time, on the other side of the world, the Japanese were taking the first steps toward acquiring a modern navy.[99] Within a little over a decade these developments were to have the most profound impact on British strategy.

The first stirrings of a renewed American interest in sea power made themselves felt as a potential threat to Britain's imperial possessions in the Western Hemisphere. In 1889, War Office and Admiralty officials undertook one of their periodic (and usually contentious) efforts to agree on plans for defending overseas colonies. The general conclusion of these discussions regarding North America was that existing garrisons were sufficient provided the United States did not increase the size of its navy. As long as this

[96] Selborne Papers, 158, Custance to Selborne, 12/19/00.

[97] Selborne Papers, 158, Kerr to Selborne, 12/27/00.

[98] Selborne Papers, 26, Hicks Beach to Selborne, 11/28/00.

[99] M. Howard, "The Armed Forces," in Hinsley, ed., *The New Cambridge Modern History* 11:237, 240.

did not occur, Britain's control of European waters would prevent
any sizable invasion force from venturing overseas, and relatively
small local squadrons could be relied upon to deal with an American attack. The army's planners agreed that no immediate reinforcements were needed at places like Bermuda and Halifax, but
they expressed the view that the whole problem would have to be
"reconsidered in the event of any serious increase to their Navy
being undertaken by the United States." For the moment this contingency did not have to be faced, but, as the report of the joint
conference remarked, "It should . . . be noticed . . . that the present naval policy of the United States tends in the direction of a considerable increase of strength." [100]

It did not take long for the prophecy of 1889 to be proven accurate. By the next year the United States had three seagoing battleships capable of conducting operations along its coasts, and in 1892
a fourth was added. The Royal Navy, with its overwhelming fleet,
had nothing directly to fear from these developments. There was
now, however, the possibility of yet another hostile collaborator
against British interests at sea. [101]

In late 1895 and early 1896 Britain and the United States were
involved in a dispute over the determination of boundaries in
Venezuela. Partly because this crisis coincided with the Kruger telegram incident, the cabinet decided to give way before American
pressure. Hostilities were avoided but the affair left a bitter taste in
many mouths. [102] On the first day of 1896, after the worst had
passed, Lord Dufferin, former governor of Canada, wrote to Queen
Victoria: "Even if peace is assured for the present, America is sure
now to set about strengthening her navy; and, when she has a
powerful fleet she will be tempted to use it. Consequently . . . England ought to make herself strong enough to confront not two
navies, but three. [103]

Calls for a three-power standard did not, as has been noted, make
much headway, whether the presumed third party was Germany or
the United States. Nevertheless, in the wake of the Venezuelan
scare there was a renewed interest in the defense of the North
American portions of the empire. In April the Joint Naval Military
Committee agreed that "in the case of war with the United States

---

[100] Quoted in PRO, Adm. 1/7322,
"Reinforcements of Colonial Garrisons
in Time of Anticipated War," 7/9/96.
[101] Bourne, *Britain and the Balance of
Power in North America, 1815–1908*,
p. 337.

[102] Grenville, *Lord Salisbury and Foreign Policy*, pp. 55–68.
[103] Bourne, *Britain and the Balance*,
p. 340.

the safety of Canada could be best ensured (if the state of affairs in Europe admitted of such a course) by landing a British force on American territory and making a vigorous offensive movement." [104]

This was an audacious plan and one that the navy accepted with less than heartfelt enthusiasm. During the summer the Admiralty grudgingly acknowledged that landings were still feasible, but it added a crucial caveat: "Their Lordships are of opinion, in view of the rapid increase of the American Navy and the impetus given towards perfecting the defensive arrangements of the country that proposal . . . can only have a temporary value." [105] By the end of the year some navy officers were warning that they had already lost superiority on the western half of the American continent. U.S. forces in the vicinity of the port of Esquimalt were deemed "more than a match for our fleet and the defences existing, and Esquimalt, could be destroyed in a few hours." The fall of the Pacific coast base would lead inevitably to the loss of Vancouver. If these twin disasters were to be avoided, the British government would have to decide to increase both ground and local naval defenses. [106]

Despite this advice there were already high-ranking officials in London who doubted both the wisdom and the feasibility of entering into an open and explicit naval competition with the United States. On 8 January Lord Lansdowne, secretary of state for war and future head of the Foreign Office, recommended against increasing British defenses at Esquimalt. The base itself was not important enough, but, more to the point, the United States was capable of increasing its strength in the area "indefinitely." If Britain tried to keep pace, financial ruin would inevitably result.

> We have already committed ourselves in regard to our Navy to the Doctrine that for every ship of war constructed by certain foreign Powers we should construct another. It is hard to say where this doctrine may lead us. If we include the United States amongst the Powers, whose progress in naval matters is to be met by a similar rejoinder on our part, our Naval Estimates are likely to be a curiosity before we are much older. [107]

[104] PRO, WO 106/40/B1/5, "Defence of Canada," 4/23/96.

[105] Quoted in PRO, WO 106/40/B1/7, "War with the United States," 3/15/01.

[106] PRO, Cab. 37/43/53, "Defence of Esquimalt," Rear Admiral Palliser, 12/11/96.

[107] PRO, Cab. 37/44/2, "The Defence of Esquimalt," Lansdowne, 1/8/97. The notion of potentially limitless American national power generally and naval power in particular was one that took hold increasingly at around this time. See May, *Imperial Democracy: The Emergence of America as a Great Power*, pp. 181–95, 263–70.

At the end of 1897 the first sea lord warned that the American government was making "a supreme effort" to strengthen its coastal defenses "as well as to increase the Navy."[108] With these developments well advanced, the Admiralty was rapidly losing whatever stomach it might once have had for a wartime effort to land forces along America's eastern seaboard. In a characteristically imperious display of bureaucratic independence, the navy simply refused, after March 1898, to respond to the army's requests for comments on its invasion schemes.[109] Turning a deaf ear to War Office fretting and pleading, the Admiralty for its part was becoming less and less willing to contemplate the possibility of a naval clash with the United States.

The decisive event in this regard was clearly the Spanish-American War of 1898. In the course of its brief struggle with Spain the United States demonstrated the fighting power of its new navy and acquired bases both in the Caribbean and the Pacific. The war was also the occasion for a further naval buildup, with three more battleships added to the six in service in 1898, another three laid down during the next year, and an additional two ordered in 1900.[110]

If Great Britain was to retain a superior fleet off the Atlantic coast of North America, it would now have either to redistribute some of its forces in European and Asian waters or undertake an even larger buildup of its own. In February 1899, L. A. Beaumont, the outgoing director of Naval Intelligence, warned that "the United States mean to be the strongest Naval power [along their eastern coast] and it will be difficult to prevent it."[111] The onset of American regional superiority was brought closer by the acquisition of bases once in the ineffectual grasp of Spain. As Custance, Beaumont's successor as DNI, would shortly point out, "with Cuba, Puerto Rico and St. Thomas in the hands of the Americans our position in Jamaica and the Caribbean Sea will be precarious, and will be the cause of much anxiety in the event of war with the United States."[112]

As a final blow to Britain's traditional superiority in the waters of the Western Hemisphere, the United States was now pressing for a canal across Central America that would link the eastern and western portions of its fleet and its new "empire." In March 1900

[108] Bourne, *Britain and the Balance,* p. 338.
[109] PRO, WO 106/40/B1/7.
[110] Bourne, *Britain and the Balance,* p. 338.
[111] PRO, Adm. 1/7550A, "Comment on Foreign Office Request for Admiralty Views Regarding Revision of Clayton-Bulwer Treaty," L. A. Beaumont, 2/6/99.
[112] Bourne, *Britain and the Balance,* p. 346.

Captain C. L. Ottley, naval attache in Washington (and a future director of Naval Intelligence), summarized the situation for his superiors:

> The successful issue of the war with Spain in 1898 has given an added impetus to the policy of naval expansion in the United States, of which the earliest indications were apparent in 1883. That war focussed public attention upon the needs of the fleet. . . . It cannot be questioned that the country in general is in favor of a fleet commensurate with the wealth of the nation and strong enough for all purposes. Closely connected with this question is the proposal for the construction of the Isthmian Canal, of which the strategic importance to the U.S. fleet has been enormously enhanced by the possession of colonies. That such a canal will eventually be built now seems almost certain; and it needs little consideration to show how profoundly the balance of sea power, not only in the Gulf, but also upon the Atlantic and Pacific coasts of North America would be influenced in favour of any country which possessed an unfettered control of the canal in war time.[113]

East. Whereas the emergence of the United States as a naval power seemed an obvious threat to British interests, the growth of Japan was a rather more ambiguous occurrence. In the closing quarter of the nineteenth century there were many European competitors for influence in the Far East. Adding a new, Asian power to the mix could tilt the balance in favor of one or the other of the outside states, depending on the direction that power chose. Britain therefore had good reasons to seek cordial diplomatic relations with Japan and perhaps (although this does not appear to have been clearly thought through) to encourage the growth of the Japanese armed forces. From the early 1870s onward, English officers acted as instructors to their Japanese counterparts and, until 1900, most of the major ships in the Imperial Navy were actually manufactured in Great Britain.[114]

In 1894 the Japanese proved themselves apt pupils in the ways of naval warfare by defeating the larger but less efficient Chinese navy. For all its brilliance this victory alone was not enough to pre-

[113] PRO, Adm. 231/31, "United States, Fleet &c. 1899," Capt. C. L. Ottley, 3/00.

[114] Nish, *The Anglo-Japanese Alliance,* p. 8.

vent the Continental powers from coercing Japan into surrendering much of what it had gained through combat. In the wake of this
humiliation the Tokyo government decided to make substantial increases in the size of its navy and, beginning in 1895, plans were
drawn up for a fleet of six battleships and six modern cruisers.[115]
The Japanese seemed intent on ensuring that they would never
again find themselves at the mercy of European interlopers in Asian
waters, a fact that was not lost on British observers. Reviewing the
relative strengths of the world's navies in its issue for 1896, Brassey's
authoritative *Naval Annual* pointed out that "the Japanese are already building two powerful battleships in England and have drawn
up an extensive programme of shipbuilding, which includes four
battleships of 15,000 tons. It is clear that with this new competitor
in the field, we cannot hope to hold much longer the prominent
position we have hitherto done in the waters of Eastern Asia."[116]

Britain's preeminence in the Far East was threatened not only by
the ambitions of Japan but also, increasingly, by the efforts of its
traditional rivals. In early 1896 Salisbury's advisers were warning
him of stepped-up Russian naval activity in the Pacific.[117] Toward
the end of 1897 the situation took a dramatic turn for the worse
when first the Germans, then the Russians, and finally (in despera-
tion) the British forced the Chinese government to grant them possession of port cities along the strategically important Manchurian
coast.[118] The long-awaited scramble for China seemed about to begin, and in February 1898 Britain dispatched reinforcements to
bolster its territorial and commercial claims. By spring the Royal
Navy had three battleships and ten cruisers of various descriptions
in Chinese waters, while France and Russia together had three
large vessels and twelve smaller ones. In Asia as in Europe, Germany seemed to hold the balance between the two sides with two
battleships and five unarmored cruisers. Japan, for its part, deployed a navy whose entire order of battle contained three battleships and twelve unarmored cruisers.[119] Despite its small size this
fleet was deemed by the first lord of the Admiralty to be already
"very formidable," and there was every prospect that it would expand in the near future.[120]

[115] Ibid., p. 36.
[116] Brassey, ed., *The Naval Annual, 1896*, p. 61.
[117] H.H. Mss., 3M/A 93, W. G. Greene to E. Barrington, 4/2/96.
[118] See Taylor, *Struggle for Mastery in Europe*, pp. 372–76. See also Langer, *The Diplomacy of Imperialism*, pp. 445–85.
[119] Marder, *Anatomy of British Sea Power*, p. 304.
[120] H.H. Mss., 3M/A 93, "British and Foreign Fleets on China Station," G. J. Goschen, 2/1/98.

Even with their existing forces the Japanese were at least theoretically capable of tipping the naval balance whichever way they chose. If Britain was compelled to regard Japan as a potential enemy, it would either have to accommodate one or more of the other powers in the region or increase its forces there unilaterally. If, on the other hand, Japan became an ally, the combined fleets of the two "island empires" might be able to take on those of even the largest Continental coalition.[121]

That Britain was forced in the closing years of the century to consider abandonment of its traditional diplomatic policy of "splendid isolation" was a direct result of the deterioration in its relative naval power.[122] The full extent of the erosion over the course of the preceding decade was cataloged by Reginald Custance in July 1899. According to historian Arthur Marder, the new director of Naval Intelligence wrote that

> the superiority which the British squadrons formerly enjoyed on the North American, West Indies and the Pacific stations had passed away, and they were now "completely outclassed" by the American fleet on the former station and were inferior to [the United States, Argentina, and Chile] in the latter. On the southeast coast of America the British squadron was now inferior to Argentina as well as Brazil. The supremacy formerly enjoyed on the China station had passed to Japan, and the British squadron, considerably superior to the Franco-Russian combination in 1889, was "hardly a match" for them ten years later. Only on the East Indian, the Cape and the Australian stations did the British squadrons remain superior to those of other nations.[123]

The pressures on Britain's naval position had now reached extraordinary, indeed unbearable, levels.

Redefinition, 1901

British statesmen were used to thinking about sea power in terms of the following simple equation:

---

[121] An alliance with Japan might have been logical when seen in these terms, but it was by no means inevitable. On the British efforts to come to terms with either Russia or Germany that preceded the Anglo-Japanese agreement see Grenville, *Lord Salisbury and Foreign Policy*, pp. 127–71.

[122] On the history of "splendid isolation," the phrase and the policy, see C. Howard, *Splendid Isolation*.

[123] Marder, *Anatomy of British Sea Power*, p. 351.

$$two\text{-power standard} = \text{equality with two next-largest fleets}$$
$$= \text{superiority over France} + \text{Russia}$$
$$= \text{control of European waters}$$
$$= \text{command of the seas}$$
$$= \text{security of empire}$$

By the beginning of 1901 there was strong reason to doubt that the first and last expressions in this chain could any longer be considered equivalent. Keeping up with the top two naval powers now meant simply maintaining equality with France and Russia, by itself an increasingly costly undertaking as the century drew to a close. The emergence of a strong German fleet and the acceleration of the Imperial Navy's program in 1900 raised again the possibility that a two-power standard might not be enough to ensure British control of the narrow seas around the Continent. Finally, the growing capabilities of peripheral navies meant that even a firm grip on European waters was no longer a guarantee of worldwide command of the seas. As a result, some of England's far-flung interests and possessions could not be considered as secure as they once had been.

In light of all these changes British strategists had essentially two choices: they could keep the two-power standard and give up on worldwide sea control, or they could continue to pursue that goal and abandon the numerical measure that had always been associated with it. The second course would have required a substantial increase in naval expenditures and the acquisition of a fleet sufficient to meet likely contingencies in the European theater while providing enough ships to ensure supremacy in the Western Hemisphere and the Far East. The first alternative was cheaper but it too had costs, although they were of a rather different sort. Accepting a geographically constrained form of naval superiority implied coming to some accommodation with the peripheral powers and perhaps, as the European states increased their naval strength, with one or more of them as well. This, in turn, seemed logically to require a complete reevaluation of Britain's traditional diplomatic and colonial policies and its entire defensive posture.

Within a remarkably short time, decisions were made that would send Britain down the first path. Considering all the factors pointing in this direction, the choice might have been inescapable. What followed, however, was rather surprising. While they had opted for the two-power standard and supremacy only in European waters, British statesmen continued to talk as if nothing of any significance had really changed, as if, in short, Britain's position was not very much different than it had been thirty years before. This was partly the result of habit and of the fact that the Royal Navy was still larger and more capable than any other in the world. But it was also the expression of conscious deception and, increasingly with the passage of time, of self-delusion. Those responsible for the nation's naval policies did not wish to admit in public the magnitude or the importance of the shift of relative capabilities in which they had acquiesed. They therefore continued to use the same formulas and indexes that had always been employed in discussing sea power. The result, as will be discussed presently, was a high degree of confusion within the Government about the nature of the naval situation and its larger implications. Lacking an easy alternative way of describing what had happened, even those who had decided on major shifts in policy seem to have lost track of how much had changed.

The redefinition of the two-power standard and the abandonment of the national naval strategy that it represented were closely tied to changes in the diplomatic realm. On the one hand, the pressures on Britain's position that have just been described helped to make such changes appear desirable as the twentieth century began. On the other, debate over diplomatic departures within the Government forced a reexamination of some traditional but increasingly questionable assumptions about sea power. This process began almost immediately after Selborne arrived at the Admiralty in November 1900, and it involved first of all the tacit recognition of American supremacy in the Western Hemisphere.

For almost two years the United States and Great Britain had been involved in sporadic efforts to renegotiate the Clayton-Bulwer Treaty of 1850, under whose terms neither party was permitted to build and exert exclusive control over a Central American sea canal. The U.S. government was anxious to remove this restriction on its freedom of action, particularly since it had acquired possessions in the Caribbean and the Pacific whose defense might require the rapid shuttling of naval forces. It was precisely to prevent this enhanced American flexibility that the British had resisted any change in the status quo, and, until the outbreak of the Boer War, negotiations had been slow and indecisive. After the beginning of 1900, and especially after Lord Salisbury handed over his duties as head of the Foreign Office to the more vigorous Lord Lansdowne, circumstances changed considerably. With all their troubles in South Africa, Europe, and the Far East, the British were only too willing to reach some sort of agreement with the United States, even if it meant giving in to a number of American demands.[124]

Since 1899 Naval Intelligence had been warning that there was a high probability that an Isthmian canal would be built and that such a project would benefit the United States at the expense of Great Britain.[125] In December 1900, with a draft agreement already in hand, Lansdowne invited the Admiralty to once again state its views on the subject. Not surprisingly, these had changed very little with the passage of time. In a note to Lord Selborne, the first sea lord, Walter Kerr, summed up the navy's position:

> With the Navy that they are creating, and with the management of the Canal which they seek, the United States will have the means, whatever we may say or think, or make a treaty about, of controlling the traffic that passes through it whether in peace or war. . . . The United States, both commercially and strategically, has much to gain by the construction of the Canal, others much less.[126]

On 5 January the Admiralty responded formally to the Foreign Office request that it evaluate the effect of a canal in a hypothetical war between Britain and the United States. In the opinion of the naval experts, control of any waterway across the Isthmus would reside with the nation that was able to place superior forces at its approaches. If one belligerent controlled either end, then neither could send its ships through without risking their destruction at the opposite side. Even without physical control of the canal itself, whichever power was superior in the Caribbean and the eastern Pacific could deny its opponent access and safe transit.[127]

Given the trend of the past five years, there was little question that the United States would soon have "a fleet sufficiently powerful to insure to her the command of the Caribbean Sea and of American waters on the Pacific Coast. It is difficult to see how Great Britain can prevent this if the latent resources of the U.S. are considered."[128]

Under existing conditions (i.e., before the full latent power of the United States had been realized) Britain could, if it chose to do so, deploy sufficient forces to gain local superiority, but only at the cost of severely weakening its position in other areas. This was a

---

[124] Grenville, "Great Britain and the Isthmian Canal, 1898–1901," p. 60. For a similar account see Bourne, *Britain and the Balance,* pp. 346–51.

[125] See memos by Beaumont and Ottley previously cited.

[126] PRO, Adm. 1/7550A, Kerr to Selborne, 1/2/01.

[127] PRO, Cab. 37/56/2, Admiralty to Foreign Office, 1/5/01.

[128] Ibid.

reflection of the more general dilemma facing naval planners as the result of the growth of potentially hostile powers, both at the center and on the periphery. As the Admiralty's experts warned:

> Great Britain unaided can hardly expect to be able to maintain in the West Indies, the Pacific, and in the North American stations, squadrons sufficiently powerful to dominate those of the United States and at the same time to hold the command of the sea in home waters, the Mediterranean, and the Eastern seas, where it is essential that she should remain predominant.[129]

If during the course of a crisis or war Britain's leaders wished to shift some of their forces away from other theaters toward the Western Hemisphere, they would first have to be "absolutely assured" of the "neutrality of the European Powers."[130] Of course, as the Admiralty knew full well, no such guarantees were possible, and it was therefore extremely unlikely that the Royal Navy could safely spare enough battleships to outnumber the Americans on either side of the proposed Isthmian canal, even if no European power was initially involved in the war.[131] In fact, the canal's very existence would make the task of overwhelming the U.S. fleet even more difficult by increasing its mobility between theaters.

> To sum up the situation from a purely naval and strategic point of view, it appears to my Lords that the preponderance of advantage from the canal would be greatly on the side of the U.S., and that, in the case of war between Great Britain and the United States, the navy of the United States would derive such benefits from the existence of the canal, that it is not really in the interests of Great Britain that it should be constructed.[132]

A canal would hurt British interests because it would virtually ensure American supremacy off U.S. coasts in wartime, a condition that, given the relatively small British deployments there, already prevailed for practical purposes during time of peace. But by all indications the Admiralty had previously reached the conclusion that a canal was inevitable. It followed that the loss by Britain of control in the waters of the Western Hemisphere was inevitable, too. Whatever its official, technical objections to an Isthmian water-

---

[129] Ibid.
[130] Ibid.
[131] See also a memo by the C. in C.

North America, Selborne Papers, 23, Bedford to Selborne, 3/2/01.
[132] Ibid.

way, the Admiralty seems by the beginning of 1901 to have accepted this fact, and there was therefore little complaint when Lord Lansdowne used navy arguments *against* the canal to support his case for a new treaty.[133] With or without it, the buildup of the U.S. fleet made American regional supremacy increasingly likely with each passing year.

In a sense, the decision to acquiesce to an American-built and -controlled canal had more symbolic than practical significance. Still, it seems clear that, in the words of one author, "The importance of the treaty [which was finally signed in November 1901] has not been exaggerated; it committed Great Britain to naval inferiority in American waters and therefore to friendship with the United States."[134] The full implications of this change in posture remained to be worked out, but the effect on naval thinking at the highest levels appears to have been profound and immediate.

Less than two weeks after the Admiralty's analysis of the proposed treaty, Lord Selborne submitted a memorandum to the cabinet regarding the estimates for 1901–1902 in which he suggested for the first time several major modifications in the two-power standard. In theory at least that index had always been flexible or automatic, committing Britain to match the two leading naval nations whatever their identity. Since 1897 the number two and three powers had been England's traditional rivals, France and Russia, but with the increased pace of construction by other states (and especially the United States and Germany), there was now the possibility that Russia would be displaced and the formula's neat symmetry disrupted. Very shortly the question of which nations to track would become a pressing one, and underlying it was the more important problem of whether diplomatic considerations should be included in calculations of naval adequacy.

Fresh from a discussion of the situation in the Western Hemisphere, Selborne had little doubt that such a decision had already, in effect, been made.

> Hitherto, the policy of this country has been stated to be so to build battleships as to maintain an equality of numbers with the combined battleships of the two Powers possessing for the moment the largest fleets. It does not seem to me that this basis of calculation is one that will any longer serve, considering that within the last five years three new navies have sprung into existence—those of the

[133] Grenville, "Great Britain and the Isthmian Canal," p. 67.

[134] Bourne, *Britain and the Balance,* p. 350.

United States, Germany and Japan. It is certain that it
would be a hopeless task to attempt to achieve an equality
with the three largest navies; but I go further, and say
that, if the United States continue their present naval policy and develop their navy as they are easily capable of
developing it if they choose, it will be scarcely possible for
us to raise our navy to a strength equal to that of both
France and the United States combined.[135]

Maintaining an automatic two-power standard once the United
States had achieved third place would be impossible, and the recent
decision regarding the canal had rendered such an effort both
fruitless and unnecessary. At this point Selborne had little to say
about the rise of German or Japanese naval power. Instead he
proposed

to consider our position almost exclusively from its relative strength to that of France and Russia combined, and
from that point of view it seems to me that what we should
aim at is, not a numerical equality, but a strength drawn
partly from numbers but largely also from superiority of
ships, armament, crews and training, such as will enable
us to have a reasonable expectation of beating France and
Russia, if ever unfortunately we should find ourselves engaged in a war with them.[136]

As of the first of the year, Britain had forty-seven first- and second-
class battleships to forty-three for the Dual Alliance. For the time
being, at least, there was no reason to fear losing that margin over
simple equality that "might make just the difference between the
possibility and the impossibility of an invasion of England." What
Selborne had done, however, was to suggest that the two-power
standard be modified so as to provide some as yet unspecified edge
over France and Russia, even if those countries should cease to be
Britain's two leading competitors.[137]

By explicitly excluding the American fleet from the two-power

[135] PRO, Cab. 37/56/8, "Navy Estimates, 1901–1902: Memorandum on
Ship-Building," Selborne, 1/17/01.
[136] Ibid. The need to preserve some
lead over France and Russia combined
was also stressed by the first sea lord. In
one memorandum written at this time,
Walter Kerr observed that "although
equality with the naval power of the

two strongest maritime countries in Europe, has been, in a sense, accepted as a
standard, it is regarded as the *minimum*
to which we should aspire" (PRO, Adm.
1/7516, "Reconsideration of Our Relative Standard of Naval Strength with
That of Foreign Powers," Kerr,
2/14/01).
[137] Ibid.

standard, the first lord was simply acknowledging the cabinet's earlier decision to cede hemispheric supremacy to the United States.
With Britain now reliant on the good will of a foreign power in the
Western Hemisphere, there could be no objection in principle to a
similar devolution in the East. Selborne was eager to derive a verbal
formula that would express the Admiralty's new policy without re-
vealing too much of what was occurring. This second shift would
come soon enough.

For the moment public discussion of naval matters centered on
more familiar, European concerns. During the Commons debate
over the estimates, members worried by the rise of German power
suggested that the country now needed, as Charles Dilke put it,
"to maintain that practical standard which would lead even three
Powers to hesitate before attacking." This meant, at a minimum,
that Britain's existing edge over the Dual Alliance had become a necessity rather than a luxury. Later, during the summer of 1901,
there was another brief scare regarding the adequacy of the Mediterranean fleet and renewed calls for a full-blown three-power
standard. Rising to defend the Government's policy in the House
of Lords, Selborne put forward a cautious reformulation of the
two-power standard along the lines he had worked out several
months before.[138] Demands that the nation build against three opponents were dismissed out of hand. "If a three Power why not a
four Power [standard]?" the first lord asked his listeners, as if the
answer were self-evident. Instead, he said,

> I adopt a totally different method of expressing the needs
> of the country. Without for a moment suggesting that a
> Two Power Standard is too high a one—quite the con-
> trary—I say the Navy should be so strong that it can have
> the *reasonable certainty of success* in performance of any
> duty which it is *reasonably probable* it may be called upon to
> perform [emphasis added].[139]

Exactly which contingencies were now to be considered "reasonably probable" Selborne did not explain, but presumably a war involving the United States was not among them (although one in
which Germany played a part just might be).

At the end of the summer the Government was preparing to enter into serious treaty talks with Japan. Once again, naval considerations played a major role in the decision to pursue a modifica-

---

[138] PRO, Adm. 1/7516, memo by Selborne, 3/23/01.

[139] *Hansard Parliamentary Debates*, 4th
ser., vol. 91 (1901), pp. 957.

tion in the nation's diplomatic posture.[140] And, as with the decision to accommodate the United States, changes at the diplomatic level led to a further refinement in assumptions about the necessary standard of naval preparedness.

On 8 August Lord Salisbury advised the king that an alliance would be pursued and, within a month, the Admiralty had prepared its position on the question of a naval agreement. Selborne was disposed to favor cooperation with the Japanese and, in principle at least, his chief naval adviser was willing to go along. On 2 September Walter Kerr minuted the first lord.

> The course you propose would be from the naval side a very great relief to us. . . . A policy of "splendid isolation" may no longer be possible and . . . great as the disadvantages in other ways may be, an understanding with other Powers may be forced upon us. . . . The strain which is being put upon our naval resources with all our world wide interests is, in view of the feverish developments of other nations, . . . heavier . . . than they can well bear. . . . Any relief that can in reason be obtained would be most welcome.[141]

Selborne laid out his own position in a carefully reasoned paper dated 4 September and entitled "Balance of Naval Power in the Far East." [142] He began by restating the conclusions put forward during and immediately after the treaty negotiations with the United States.

> The recognized standard for the naval strength of Great Britain has hitherto been equality with the ships of the two next greatest naval Powers. I have already given to the Cabinet my reasons for thinking that this standard would be beyond the strength of this country if the United States were to use all their resources to develop this naval strength, and that it is inadequate if applied to a possible war against France in alliance with Russia.[143]

In a war with the Dual Alliance "the decisive battles . . . would certainly be fought in European waters," and the navy should do what it could to bring the strongest possible force to bear there,

[140] See the account by Monger, *The End of Isolation: British Foreign Policy, 1900–1907*, pp. 47–65.

[141] Selborne Papers, 27, Kerr to Selborne, 9/2/01.

[142] For another analysis see Steiner, "Great Britain and the Creation of the Anglo-Japanese Alliance," pp. 29–31.

[143] Selborne Papers, 161, "Balance of Naval Power in the Far East," Selborne, 9/4/01.

"but it does not follow that we should be free to concentrate the whole of our naval strength in those waters and leave the outlying parts of the Empire to await the final issue." Given the abandonment of the Western Hemisphere, the main extra-European theater was now the Far East, and the question was how to balance the defense of British interests there with the requirements of maintaining sufficient power at the center.

> If the British Navy were defeated in the Mediterranean and the Channel the stress of our position would not be alleviated by any amount of superiority in the Chinese seas. If, on the other hand, it were to prove supreme in the Mediterranean and Channel, even serious disasters in Chinese waters would matter little. These considerations furnish, therefore, a sound argument for keeping our naval strength in Chinese waters as low as is compatible with the safety of the Empire. But there is a point below which it would be dangerous to go.[144]

Even if the fleet were victorious in European waters it would be extremely damaging if "British naval power in the Far East were crushed out of existence [because] . . . we could not afford to see our Chinese trade disappear, or to see Hong Kong and Singapore fall, particularly not at a moment when a military struggle with Russia might be in progress on the confines of India."[145]

Obviously, Britain would have to find some way of defending its interests in the Far East while at the same time more than matching its likely opponents in European waters. The problem was that Russia's naval strength in Asia had been steadily increasing. Practically the whole Baltic squadron had been transferred from Kronstadt to Vladivostok and Port Arthur, and, of the eleven battleships now under construction in Russian shipyards, three were believed destined for the Far East.[146] A glance at the figures for the current Asian balance of forces told the story (see Table 4-2).

When the new Russian vessels arrived at their Pacific bases (and they were due there within a few months time), the situation would be even worse. British strength would remain constant while that of the Franco-Russian alliance would increase to nine battleships and twenty cruisers.

> For us the odds of nine battleships to four would be too great, and we should have eventually to add to our battle-

[144] Ibid.
[145] Ibid.
[146] Ibid.

Table 4-2
The Naval Balance in Asia, 1901

	France	Russia	Great Britain	Japan
Battleships	1	5	4	6
Cruisers	9	7	16	31

Source: Selborne Papers, 161, "Balance of Power in the Far East," Selborne, 9/4/01.

ships on the China Station. The effect of this would be two fold. It would leave us with little or nothing more than bare equality of strength in the Channel and Mediterranean. . . . It would strain our naval system greatly, and would add to our expenditure on the manning of the Navy. Every ship on the China Station must be kept in commission, and fully manned in time of peace.[147]

To all these difficulties the first lord had a simple solution. If Britain entered into a naval alliance with Japan, "the case would bear a different aspect." In the coming year the combined battleship strength of the two nations in Asian waters would be eleven, two ahead of France and Russia, and they would also be assured of a "preponderance of cruisers." Under these circumstances

Great Britain would be under no necessity of adding to the number of battleships on the China Station, and at least would be in a position to contemplate the possibility of shortly establishing a small margin of superiority in reserve at home; the number of our cruisers could be reduced on that station, and increased on other stations where badly required; our Far East trade and possessions would be secure.[148]

In return, Japan would "be delivered from the nightmare of seeing her rising power crushed by the combination of the French and Russian fleets." On balance, then, such an agreement "would . . . add materially to the naval strength of this country all over the world, and effectively diminish the probability of a naval war with France or Russia singly or in combination."[149]

By all accounts Selborne's arguments played an important part

[147] Ibid.   [149] Ibid.
[148] Ibid.

in the cabinet's decision to conclude an agreement with Japan. Indeed, according to one diplomatic historian, "consideration of naval policy appears to have tipped the scales in favor of an alliance."[150] The first lord's memorandum is important because it illustrates the further, logical development of his thinking. The earlier and in some ways more painful decision to rely on American good will in the Western Hemisphere had already been made. This freed some resources but not nearly enough to offset developments in Europe and the Far East. If Britain wished to be able to maintain forces in the Pacific superior to those of France and Russia or even of Japan (let alone a coalition of all three), it would either have to weaken itself dangerously in European waters or make substantial increases in the overall size of its fleet.

At the end of the year the first lord presented his latest formulation of Britain's naval requirements to the cabinet. Pressed by the chancellor of the Exchequer to limit the growth of expenditures, Selborne pointed out that he was compelled to do everything he could to thwart the efforts of France and Russia "to establish a naval superiority over" Great Britain.[151] In the past, meeting the two-power standard had ensured that such an unfavorable shift in the balance of forces would not occur. But this was because when Lord George Hamilton had laid down the standard in 1889, France and Italy were the second- and third-ranked naval powers.

By 1894 the distribution of first- and second-class battleships was such that Britain had a margin of six over a possible Franco-Italian alliance, eight over France plus Germany, and fourteen over the real threat of France and Russia.[152] By adhering to the two-power standard Britain was assured of "a large and ample margin of superiority as against any probable combination she might have to face." With the developments of the past eight years, however, "the position [had] completely changed," and, as a result, the meaning of the old catch phrase had been significantly altered.[153] Still, Selborne continued,

> *I would not discard the Two Power Standard, because an avowedly lower standard would be misunderstood and denounced.* Nevertheless . . . if the United States were to build such a navy as they can well afford even the Two

[150] Grenville, *Lord Salisbury and Foreign Policy*, p. 393. See also Steiner, "Great Britain," p. 31, and Nish, *The Anglo-Japanese Alliance*, p. 175.

[151] PRO, Cab. 37/59/118, "The Navy Estimates and the Chancellor of the Exchequer's Memorandum on the Growth of Expenditure," Selborne, 11/16/01, p. 2. For the financial context see chapter 3.

[152] Ibid., pp. 6–7.

[153] Ibid., p. 7.

Power Standard would become beyond our strength. *The standard which I believe now to be the true one is not one which could be publically stated. In Parliament I would always speak, in general terms, of not falling below the Two Power Standard. To the Cabinet I would suggest that if we make such provisions as will offer us the reasonable certainty of success in a war with France and Russia, we shall have fully provided for all contingencies* [emphasis added].[154]

Until the United States, Japan, or (most likely) Germany broke into the top three there was no reason why the changed assumptions on which Britain's naval planning was now based needed to be explained in public. As the director of Naval Intelligence noted at around this time, however, that day was not far distant. Custance calculated that by 1907 Germany would have the same number of battleships as Russia, and, he pointed out, the German fleet would be concentrated in the North Sea rather than divided between the Black Sea and the Pacific. This would mean that

> if we are involved in difficulties with any other Nation, and Germany adopts a menacing attitude, it will be necessary to maintain a force in the North Sea sufficient to mask the German fleet. As the German Navy will be at that date a much greater danger to this country than the Fleet of Russia it is thought that in future all our calculations should refer to France and Germany rather than to France and Russia.[155]

Selborne was not prepared at this point to introduce such complications into the public debate. But there were other more profound reasons for his proposal that the Government be less than candid about the naval situation. Because the two-power standard had long been a symbol, a totem, a formula for worldwide sea control, to admit that the standard no longer had the same meaning would be to acknowledge that the Government had permitted a substantial diminution in Britain's relative power. Giving way on the peripheries in order to concentrate at the center might have been inevitable, but it was not something of which anyone could be particularly proud. For the time being Britain could rely on diplomatic arrangements, both tacit and explicit, to preserve its position in the Western Hemisphere and the Far East. Treaties and agreements were necessarily slender reeds in comparison with the sturdy

[154] Ibid., p. 8. [155] Selborne Papers, 158, Custance to Selborne, 9/24/01.

self-reliance of days gone by, and there was always the possibility
that such understandings would fail, thus exposing the new fragility
of Britain's situation. There is no evidence that Selborne, with his
attention now firmly fixed on Europe and his new, narrowed two-
power standard, gave this disconcerting prospect much thought. In
a note to Custance, First Sea Lord Walter Kerr did express some
concern over what was occurring.

> Our superiority ought to be self-contained and not made
> up of foreign and possibly very unreliable sources. . . .
> While the understanding [with Japan] lasts it would be
> most useful to us in the East and indirectly in European
> waters, but it would be a very unsafe policy to rely on it—
> It would be a great temporary relief while we are pulling
> up our numbers, but it would be imprudent to the last
> degree not to prepare for rupture of the understanding.[156]

Whatever the wisdom of Kerr's admonition it was now sadly out
of date. The days of "self-contained" British naval superiority were
gone forever.

Repercussions, 1902–1903

With the events of 1901, discussion of the emerging naval situation
became increasingly fragmented and confused. At the highest
levels of the Admiralty the decision effectively to abandon worldwide sea control had been made. This was not something that could
be easily admitted but, if the previous year's developments were to
have any beneficial impact on the nation's naval posture they would
have to be followed up in ways that made the change increasingly
apparent. As Selborne moved to reduce the navy's commitments in
the east and the west, he encountered resistance both from his own
service and from the army. Inside the Government the surrender
of supremacy was far from painless.

As long as France and Russia held their positions in the ranking
of world naval powers it was possible to sustain the comforting fic-
tion that Britain was simply adhering to an automatic, apolitical
two-power standard. This, in fact, was the position that Admiralty
officials tended to take in their public declarations on the naval balance. That such a standard could no longer be equated with command of the seas in areas remote from Europe was something that
was not openly discussed.

The Anglo-Japanese treaty signed on 29 January 1902 and pub-

[156] Selborne Papers, 27, Kerr to Custance, 10/5/01.

lished several weeks later committed each country to come to the assistance of the other if it was attacked by two or more hostile powers.[157] What was kept secret was a clause that called for substantial naval cooperation in peacetime, including conversations between officers to work out signaling and basing arrangements.[158] The question of how large a British force should be retained in the Far East to help the Japanese cope with France and Russia was, from the start, a ticklish one. For their part, the Japanese negotiators hoped to commit Britain to a substantial day-to-day presence, perhaps by itself equal to that of Russia. Selborne had no intention of allowing himself to be bound in such a fashion, both on general principles and because he fully intended to use the new agreement to draw down Britain's presence in the Far East to the absolute minimum. Thus, while the terms of the treaty were still being hammered out, the first lord wrote Lansdowne that he "could not consent to . . . such an interpretation as that Japan should hereafter come to us and say 'Russia has . . . seven battleships in Chinese waters. You have only five. We claim that you should send three more.'"[159]

Eventually the question of force levels was sidestepped and the two parties agreed simply that they had "no intention of relaxing [their] efforts to maintain, so far as may be possible, available for concentration in the waters of the Extreme East a naval force superior to that of any third Power." The British resolved "never to neglect the maintenance of supremacy" in Asia, something that was to be measured by the aggregate tonnage of all classes of ships at the China station.[160] Selborne agreed to this index although he dismissed it privately as "worthless" and acceptable "only . . . because its application happens to suit us just now."[161]

The first lord's determination to limit the navy's Far Eastern role was a disappointment to Japan, but it was also something of a shock to his subordinates, who do not seem to have realized the full import of the recently signed agreement. While negotiations were still in progress, Admiral Sir Cyprian A. G. Bridge, commander in chief at the China station, had urged Selborne to maintain a Pacific force at least equal to the Russian Far Eastern fleet.[162] Even after

[157] Langer, *The Diplomacy of Imperialism*, pp. 777–78.
[158] Nish, *The Anglo-Japanese Alliance*, p. 214.
[159] PRO, FO 800/134, Selborne to Lansdowne, 1/2/01.
[160] Nish, *The Anglo-Japanese Alliance*, pp. 218, 214.

[161] PRO, FO 800/134, Selborne to Lansdowne, 1/7/02.
[162] BM, Add. Mss. 49707, Selborne to Balfour, 11/3/01. See also BRI/15, Bridge to Selborne, 2/4/02.

the treaty was initialed, Walter Kerr, echoing Bridge, cautioned the first lord against too hasty a withdrawal of British forces. On 8 February Kerr reminded Selborne that "the Japanese arrangement does not come into force until a second power joins in—Hence the necessity of moving cautiously to see what Russia intends to do with her force in China before we greatly reduce ours."[163]

But the first lord was evidently in no mood for such cautions. Three days later he wrote Bridge informing him that he would soon receive news "which will not make it necessary for us to retain as large a fleet on the China Station as we should otherwise have had to do."[164] First, those light craft which would be "practically useless in Naval war" would be cut. "All the ships which we maintain for political purposes in China may be necessary," Selborne admitted, "but I am not prepared to believe it merely because the Foreign Office . . . says so or because I am told at the Admiralty that 'it has always been considered necessary to maintain these ships.'"[165] In time, even more substantial vessels might be withdrawn. Thus on 14 February Kerr told Bridge, "You must not be surprised if in the course of the year we reduce you by one or more cruisers."[166] Within a month even larger reductions were being considered, and Kerr wrote Bridge, "I want to warn you of the possibility of some reduction in your squadron in China—What is in contemplation is to bring home in due course [four cruisers] without relief—The Anglo-Japanese arrangement facilitates some reduction which for purposes elsewhere is much wanted."[167]

As station commander, Bridge had no choice but to comply with London's directives, but he made little secret of his feelings. In March he lectured Selborne about the twin functions of the China fleet. The first was admittedly political: "to show the Flag . . . and to serve . . . as a direct protection of our fellow-subjects." The second was "more purely naval":

> It is to keep an adequate force of effective cruising ships
> in a sphere in which other naval nations are strongly rep-
> resented . . . and in which it would be a grievous strategic
> error . . . to allow ourselves to be out-numbered by any
> important rival or union of rivals. . . . As long as other
> nations have it in Chinese waters, we too must have also
> a "battleship" force there. Ours ought to be more power-

[163] Selborne Papers, 31, Kerr to Selborne, 2/8/02.

[164] BRI/15, Selborne to Bridge, 2/11/02.

[165] Ibid.

[166] BRI/15, Kerr to Bridge, 2/14/02.

[167] BRI/15, Kerr to Bridge, 3/4/02.

ful than theirs for strategic reasons too obvious to need statement.[168]

Despite these objections Selborne was determined to press ahead with the process of concentration that he believed the altered diplomatic situation now made possible. The existing distribution was "a product of time" and should not be considered absolute and unchangeable. With the expansion of the empire the peacetime tasks of the navy had grown "more and more exacting," and its proper composition had therefore become a cause of some concern.[169] In early February the Admiralty informed the Colonial Office that "in view of the great development which is taking place in certain Foreign Navies, it has become necessary for strategic reasons to concentrate more than is the case at present."[170]

Selborne's interest in redistribution was encouraged by two additional factors. In the first place he was now in increasingly close communication with Admiral Fisher, who would shortly move from his post in the Mediterranean to the position of second sea lord. In his own inimitable fashion, Fisher had begun to bombard the first lord with papers on a whole range of naval issues, including the question of fleet distribution. As always, the thrust of Fisher's letters was that the Mediterranean flotilla needed strengthening, but he argued more broadly that changing conditions required a complete overhaul of the existing naval system. In a February 1902 memo entitled "Strategical Distribution of Our Fleets," Fisher urged that old, weak, and slow vessels be scrapped and that the remaining ships be grouped together into five fighting fleets.[171] This was essentially the scheme that Selborne adopted two years later. The first lord was already convinced that the existing system of distribution was "a relic" that needed drastic rearrangement, but, as he would later note, although his early views on the question were "essentially sound . . . Lord Walter [Kerr] was strongly opposed to them and I held . . . that a disruption of the Board was a greater evil than waiting until I had a First Sea Lord in Fisher who agreed with me."[172]

[168] BRI/15, Bridge to Selborne, 3/02.
[169] Selborne Papers, 161, "Statement Explanatory on the Navy Estimates, 1902–03," Selborne, 2/10/02.
[170] Bourne, *Britain and the Balance*, p. 359.
[171] Fisher Papers, 1/3, Fisher to Selborne, 2/25/02. See also Mackay, *Fisher of Kilverstone*, pp. 257–65. For other letters of this period see Marder, ed., *Fear God and Dreadnought* 1:219–42.
[172] Selborne's comment that the existing system was a "relic" appears in a memo dated 4/4/02. The remark about Kerr is penciled on that memo in Selborne's hand and dated 10/21/04 (Selborne Papers, 158, 4/4/02).

The second factor weighing on Selborne at this time was a growing awareness of the potential strength and importance of the German navy. In April he wrote a skeptical Balfour that when he had
advised the cabinet on naval standards in the autumn of 1901 he
"had not then realized the intensity of the hatred of the German
nation to this country."[173] His own observations as well as consultation with the foreign secretary had made him aware of intensified
German political hostility. Over the next few months Selborne
would also receive intelligence information regarding the expanding capabilities of the kaiser's new war fleet.[174] German activity in
the North Sea was yet another reason to concentrate as much as
possible of the nation's naval power in the waters close to home.

The trend toward redistribution in the Far East might have been
slowed somewhat by the resistance of certain naval officers. In any
case, by the end of 1903 mounting tension between Japan and Russia had forced the temporary shelving of any plans for further reductions in British forces at the China station, and, during the next
year, the battleship contingent under Bridge's command was actually increased in size.[175]

Selborne's initial efforts to reduce the navy's role in the Western
Hemisphere provoked less internal controversy. To begin with,
there were fewer large ships deployed in the western Atlantic and
the Caribbean and, given the assumption of a continuing detente
with the United States, no likely enemies in local waters. Pulling
back further seemed to make perfect sense to most navy men.[176]

This was not, to put it mildly, how matters appeared to the army,
which in the absence of any formal treaty continued to hold itself
ultimately responsible for the defense of Canada and the manning

[173] BM, Add. Mss. 49707, Selborne to
Balfour, 4/4/02. For Balfour's response
see Selborne Papers, 30, Balfour to Selborne, 4/5/02.

[174] One such report from a recent
visitor to the port facilities at Kiel and
Wilhelmshaven warned that the German navy could have no other target
than Britain and that, under the circumstances, it would be "a mere affec-
tation" not to count Germany among
England's possible enemies (PRO, Cab.
37/62/133, "Notes on a Visit to Kiel
and Wilhelmshaven," H. O. Arnold-
Forster, 9/02). See also a report by Custance in Selborne Papers, 158, 9/24/01.
Kerr was skeptical and wrote several
months later, "I do not think that I am

so much impressed as some . . . with
the view that Germany is building
against us" (Selborne Papers, 31, Kerr
to Selborne, 4/28/02).

[175] In the spring of 1901 Britain had
four battleships and thirteen cruisers at
the China station. Two years later it
had the same number of battleships
and only eight cruisers (Marder, *Anatomy of British Sea Power*, pp. 429, 432).
In the winter of 1904 it had five battleships and seven cruisers (Selborne
Papers, 41, Kerr to Selborne, 1/7/04).

[176] Kerr was again less than enthusiastic. He told Selborne that he was "not
prepared to suggest any reductions beyond those already arranged" (Sel-

of the various imperial outposts scattered off the U.S. coast. In the days of unquestioned naval supremacy, Britain had been able to extend a protective umbrella over most of its distant possessions, rendering them unreachable by hostile seaborne forces and readily defensible and reinforceable in the event of local attack.[177] The year 1901 ushered in a new era of vulnerability and uncertainty. As the Admiralty tightened the circle within which most of its forces would operate, it inevitably left its sister service dangerously exposed, and nowhere more so than in North America. This was not immediately apparent, in part because the navy was less than candid about the changes it had in view. As recognition began to dawn, the War Office pressed for a renewal of the strategic guarantees on which its planning had previously been based and which (as it now discovered) the navy was no longer in a position to honor. The result was an interagency tussle of major proportions, a sort of bureaucratic Punch-and-Judy show with bitter and pointed memoranda taking the place of brickbats.

Disagreements about the proper course of action in a war with the United States extended back to before the turn of the century. In May of 1896, following the Venezuelan war scare, the Colonial Defence Committee (CDC) had laid down assumptions on which planning for the protection of overseas possessions was to be based. This document gave the central role to the navy, concluding that "the maintenance of sea supremacy has been assumed as the basis of the system of Imperial defence against attack over the sea. This is the determining factor in shaping the whole defensive policy of the Empire, and is fully recognized by the Admiralty, who have accepted the responsibility of protecting all British territory abroad from organized invasion from the sea."[178] The only attacks over water that the colonies had to fear and to prepare against were small raids of no more than "a few ships."[179]

Canada, with its extended land border, was obviously in a somewhat different position from most other outposts of the empire. The army, as noted, hoped to deal with the danger of an American invasion by planning an amphibious counterattack against the eastern seaboard of the United States. From 1898 to 1901 the navy simply refused to comment on this plan, finally, according to a War Office memo, "intimat[ing] . . . through the Director of Naval In-

---

borne Papers, 31, Kerr to Selborne, 4/29/02).

[177] The other exception, of course, was India. See chapter 5.

[178] Quoted in PRO, Cab. 3/1/1A,

"Military Needs of the Empire in a War with France and Russia," Lieutenant Colonel Altham, 8/12/01, p. 18.

[179] Ibid.

telligence that they [did] not consider that any useful purpose [would] be served by discussing the scheme further." [180]

The reason for the Admiralty's reticence was clearly "the great increase in the American Navy." [181] But this fact raised questions that extended beyond the defense of Canada. Toward the close of 1902 the CDC requested that the Admiralty clarify its position on the balance of naval forces and on the implications of that balance for imperial defense. The committee noted that all of its recommendations were "based upon the assumption that Your Majesty's Navy will hold the seas." [182] Given the growth of American power, this might no longer be possible in the Western Hemisphere if elements of the British fleet were also required to deal with enemies elsewhere. The question of what the navy would do under such circumstances appeared to the CDC "to be a question of grave importance which should be submitted for the consideration of the Lords Commissioners of the Admiralty." [183]

In January 1903 the War Office followed this request for information with one of its own, and, on 24 February, the navy responded. [184] For the first time the Admiralty began to spell out some of the conclusions to which it had come at the highest levels two years before. By the end of 1905 the U.S. fleet would have a total of twenty battleships and eight armored cruisers, of which only a small number would be deployed in the Pacific. Given this fact, along with the "increasing strength of the European Continental Powers," it did not "seem probable that Great Britain would be able to spare a force sufficiently powerful to blockade the Atlantic portion of the United States' fleet in its own ports." [185] The main effort of that portion of the navy which remained in the Western Hemisphere in wartime would probably be devoted to protecting shipments of grain from South America and from Canada to the mother country. Britain's bases at Halifax, Jamaica, Bermuda, and St. Lucia would have to defend themselves from any U.S. invasion force, but, the Admiralty noted cheerily, they would probably not face serious attack because of their relative unimportance. Moreover, the ultimate fate of the empire's western outposts would be determined by

[180] PRO, WO 106/40/B1/1, "Military Policy in a War with the United States, 1902," Lieutenant Colonel Altham, 3/13/02.

[181] Ibid.

[182] Quoted in PRO, Cab. 5/1/3C, "Memo on the Standards of Defence for the Naval Bases of Halifax, Bermuda, Jamaica, and St. Lucia," WO, 9/17/03, p. 5.

[183] Ibid.

[184] Bourne, *Britain and the Balance*, p. 360. For his account of these events see pp. 359–87.

[185] Quoted in PRO, Cab. 5/1/3C, p. 6.

the outcome of the larger war. If Britain was defeated elsewhere (presumably in European waters), the bases would be lost; if Britain won, it would be able to get them back, even if they had been surrendered to the United States in the early stages of a conflict.[186]

The War Office was apparently so stunned by this that it took three months to come up with a suitably outraged reply. On 4 May a memo was sent reminding the Admiralty of its 1896 commitment to defend all overseas possessions from major amphibious attacks. Under the terms of this understanding the army was to provide garrisons capable of dealing only with relatively small raids and landing parties. This suited the War Office, which had no desire to tie up substantial numbers of men in defending what were, for the most part, naval facilities. Now, however, there appeared to be a marked change in strategic conditions. Why did the Admiralty dismiss as unimportant the bases that as recently as 1901 it had described as "essential"? What would happen to reinforcements for Canada if Halifax or Bermuda were lost? How could grain shipments from Latin America be protected if the Royal Navy had no secure ports in the Caribbean? How could Britain ever hope to force the United States to return bases it had already seized? Where, after all, were the Americans vulnerable to any application of British power?[187]

On 29 June the Admiralty responded to the question originally put to it by the cdc and, indirectly, to the increasingly shrill queries of the War Office. In the event of tension in Europe,

> it is unquestionable that . . . It would not be possible for Great Britain to deplete her squadrons in European waters to an extent sufficient to place her on anything like an equality with the American fleet. It follows, therefore, that, at the commencement of hostilities, the United States' naval forces would hold the sea command in the waters of the Western Atlantic and Caribbean Sea, and, as a consequence, would be in a position to make organized attacks on our bases and our seaborne commerce emanating from the Canadian ports, while, at the same time, the despatch of military reinforcements to Canada would be barred to us.[188]

Without sea control Britain's bases would have no real strategic importance. If U.S. forces took them and the Royal Navy regained

---

[186] Ibid.
[187] Ibid., p. 7.

[188] Ibid., p. 8.

local supremacy, then the Americans would be trapped. If the enemy maintained its control of the western Atlantic and the Caribbean, then Britain would lose its bases and not be able to recover them, regardless of how strong its garrisons might be. In the end, as the Admiralty noted laconically, "the consideration of the point raised by the CDC emphasizes the necessity for preserving amicable relations with the United States."[189]

It was all very well for the navy, in its lofty way, to simply declare a war with the United States impossible and then to take its ships and go home. But this left the army high and dry, literally stranded on the doorstep of a nation whose power was growing steadily and whose permanent friendship the War Office was not yet prepared to assume. The army's planners could only sputter in disbelief at a position that was now unmistakably clear, if no less outrageous for being so. "The Admiralty propose to abandon the sea command in the Western Atlantic to the American fleet," they repeated quite accurately, but this would mean the loss of island bases that would be difficult to recover. Moreover "it would entail the abandonment of Canada to the land forces of the United States and it would apparently leave our grain trade with the Dominion and South America at the mercy of American cruisers. Such a condition of affairs might result in our being compelled to sue for peace on humiliating terms."[190]

If all this was true it meant that the pledge of 1896 was null and void, that worldwide sea control could no longer be assured, and that, therefore, the entire strategic posture of the empire must now be in doubt.

> Unless . . . the War Office has misinterpreted the plan for the strategical distribution of our naval forces . . . *the conclusion appears to be unavoidable that the present strength of His Majesty's Navy would not suffice to defend on the high seas the interests of the Empire; in other words, that the Two Power Standard, up to which the country has been given to understand the Navy is maintained no longer exists.* This conclusion so gravely affects the political as well as the military position of the Empire, that it is hoped that the Admiralty will be able to elucidate it [emphasis added].[191]

It was a terrifying flash of insight and one to which the Admiralty had no real response. Regarding the accusation that the

[189] Ibid.
[190] Ibid., p. 3.
[191] Ibid., pp. 3–4.

western Atlantic would be abandoned in the event of simultaneous crises at home and in North America, they would only reply, "This deduction is practically correct."[192] On the new, reduced meaning of the two-power standard, the Admiralty was notably silent.

Obviously, in the narrowest sense, the standard *did* still exist; Britain continued to maintain a lead over the two countries with the second- and third-largest fleets in the world. But, as the army's complaints and the Admiralty's reluctant admissions made abundantly clear, that standard no longer meant control of the world's oceans and guaranteed security for Britain's far-flung possessions.

Selborne had earlier declared his intention to speak always of a two-power standard, regardless of changing political and military circumstances.[193] This he and his aides continued to do, not only in Parliament but within the cabinet. The reluctance to abandon old indexes reveals something of their symbolic power, and, in this case, it also shows how important it was for most Englishmen to believe that their country retained command of the seas. Selborne's lack of public candor may therefore be understandable even if it is not particularly laudable. What is ironical is that the effort to obscure the significance of changes occuring in Britain's position had an effect on thinking inside the government as well as outside. With all that had happened, the nation's naval posture continued to be discussed at the highest levels in terms of a measure that had now lost most if not all of its original significance. From this point forward, official analyses of Britain's position took on an air of incompleteness and unreality.

The assumption that Japan and the United States could be relied upon to support (or at least not to challenge) British interests was quickly absorbed into the Admiralty's world view. What was essential now, as Selborne told the cabinet at the end of 1901, was to build against France and Russia; the rest would take care of itself.[194] The only inkling of a change in official assumptions was the occasional assertion that planning must now take place on a "politically reasonable" basis. This notion tended to be a two-edged sword. On the one hand it allowed for the implicit elimination of contingencies (like the breakdown of relations with the United States or Japan) that might, if considered, have revealed the new vulnerability of Britain's naval posture. On the other it included the possibility of German hostility without seeming to advocate a full-blown three-power standard.

[192] PRO, Cab. 5/1/5C, "Strategic Position of British Naval Bases in Western Atlantic and West Indies," Admiralty, 11/24/03.

[193] See PRO Cab. 37/59/118, p. 8.

[194] Ibid.

By the end of 1902 Selborne's anxiety over the German threat was such that he was prepared to ask the cabinet for a standard of "equality plus a margin." The two-power standard was still to be the basic indicator of adequacy, but now an additional six battleships over and above simple parity with France and Russia were to be retained as a matter of policy. This adjustment resulted directly from the fact that the first lord had "since . . . last autumn . . . studied the naval policy of Germany more closely than . . . previously." Having examined its composition and the characteristics of its ships, Selborne was now convinced that "the great new German navy [was] being carefully built up from the point of view of a war with" Great Britain.[195] Expert opinion held that such a war would follow a major engagement between the Royal Navy and the Dual Alliance from which England would emerge victorious but weakened. The extra numerical edge was needed to deter a potential scavenger rather than to deal with a direct German challenge.[196] A three-power standard would therefore be excessive, but a narrowly defined two-power standard would be less than prudent. This was the position to which Selborne adhered throughout 1902 and to the end of the following year.[197]

Redistribution, 1904–1905

The years 1904–1905 saw the further development of trends that had first become apparent at the end of 1901. The concentration of British naval forces in European waters, which had been going on for several years, was accelerated, and along with it the process of withdrawal from the imperial periphery. These developments continued to produce friction within the navy and between the services, but they went forward nonetheless. Using traditional measures, by the end of 1905 the naval situation looked better than it had for some time. Yet, as some observers pointed out, these measures were deceptive and in fact concealed a major change in Britain's relative power.

[195] PRO, Cab. 37/63/142, "Navy Estimates 1903–1904," Selborne, 10/10/02. The new German ships were reported to have cramped crew quarters and limited coal capacity that together restricted their effective range to the waters of the North Sea and the northern Atlantic.

[196] See, for example, BM, Add. Mss. 49710, Fisher to Balfour, 10/03.

[197] PRO, Cab. 37/67/83, "Naval Policy," Selborne, 12/7/03. As Selborne explained during the 1903 estimates debate: "The Government has never abandoned what has been known as the two-Power standard." At no time, however, had this "been interpreted as a mere equality of battleships with the two next naval Powers." Instead it had been taken as requiring that, "given a war with the next two naval Powers, there should be a reasonable probability of victory for this country" (statement by Selborne, 3/24/03, in PRO, Adm. 116/1605, p. 8).

The first half of 1904 was marked by two events that would lead eventually to a considerable change in the direction of British foreign policy. In February, Japan and Russia came to blows, and, to the surprise of many Western observers, the opening battles of the war proved the Japanese to be more than a match for their Occidental opponents. Initial naval engagements off Port Arthur left the Russian Pacific fleet badly damaged and forced the Czarist government to undertake a long, slow, and ultimately ill-fated movement of reinforcements from the Baltic to the Far East.[198] Meanwhile, the British were free to speculate on the possible effects of a serious Russian defeat.

As indicated in chapter 3, the Admiralty was already under heavy pressure at this point to provide major savings in its estimates, and the presumed "destruction" of Russia's navy could not help but strengthen the hand of the cost cutters. In an attempt to head off any demand for immediate, deep reductions, Lord Selborne wrote the cabinet on 26 February to advise that the extent of damage to the Russian Pacific fleet was not yet fully known. For this reason alone sharp cutbacks were inadvisable. Moreover, even the complete elimination of Russia as a naval power would not diminish the need for a two-power standard.

> It is an error to suppose that the Two Power Standard adopted by this country some fifteen years ago, ratified by every Government since, and accepted as an article of faith by the whole nation has ever had reference only to France and Russia. It has always referred to the two strongest Naval Powers at any given moment. . . . If the Russian navy were to emerge from the present war materially weakened, the result will be that the Two Power Standard must hereafter be calculated with reference to the navies of France and Germany.[199]

This statement was in complete contradiction to Selborne's declarations of 1901. If the two-power standard was once again to be considered an automatic, apolitical gauge of naval adequacy, then there could be no logical reason for excluding the United States should that country's power continue to grow. Questions of consistency aside, however, the first lord's argument suited the bureaucratic needs of the moment while it provided yet another indication of the growing seriousness with which the German threat was being viewed inside the Admiralty.

[198] Monger, *The End of Isolation*, p. 163.
[199] PRO, Cab. 37/69/32, "Naval Estimates 1904–05: Possible Reduction," Selborne, 2/26/04.

The early phase of the Russo-Japanese conflict was also linked to the second major development of early 1904. In part to avoid being drawn into the war by their respective allies, Britain and France came to an agreement regarding spheres of influence in North Africa. Although the entente was limited at first to colonial matters, it indicated a major improvement in relations between the two old rivals and would give way eventually to a virtual diplomatic and military alliance. In the meantime, British planners continued to regard France as a possible enemy, regardless of how unlikely a clash had become.[200]

Taken together, these events formed a fluid pattern that, over the course of the next year, grew gradually more concrete. Germany was being substituted for France and Russia as the principal threat to Britain's control of European waters. This fact did not *cause* the fleet redistribution that was announced at the end of 1904. But the replacement of the Dual Alliance by Germany certainly did nothing to discourage the trend toward concentration, especially given the location and the apparent efficiency of the German fleet.[201]

In May of 1904 Selborne offered the job of first sea lord to Fisher, then serving as commander in chief at Portsmouth. The admiral, who had been thinking of little else since his days in the Mediterranean, quickly accepted, and in October he replaced Walter Kerr as the nation's top naval officer.[202] On the same day that he was asked to become first sea lord, Fisher produced a memo in which he identified "the sufficiency of strength and the fighting efficiency of the fleet" and "absolute instant readiness for war" as his primary objectives. These ends could be achieved, Fisher claimed, and "they can both be got with a great reduction in the Navy Estimates!" but only if his plan was adopted without modifications.[203] "The Scheme! The Whole Scheme!! And Nothing But The Scheme!!" was to be Fisher's bureaucratic battle cry.[204]

---

[200] Thus, two months after the announcement of the entente, the first sea lord requested the Naval Intelligence Department to "work out plans of campaign in every possible naval war—against France, against Russia, against France and Russia, against Germany singly or in any combination, against the United States, &c." (Kemp, ed., *The Papers of Admiral Sir John Fisher* 2 : xxii).

[201] Ibid. Mackay points out that, in their early formulations, Fisher's redistribution schemes were driven by a concern over the balance of forces in the Mediterranean—in other words that they were essentially anti-French rather than, as is often claimed in retrospect, anti-German (*Fisher of Kilverstone*, pp. 263–65). This appears to be correct. Nevertheless, there seems little doubt that by the beginning of 1905 Germany had emerged as Britain's number one concern at sea.

[202] Kemp, ed., *Papers of Admiral Sir John Fisher* 1 : xv.

[203] Ibid., p. 17.

[204] Ibid., p. 20.

The broad outlines of "the Scheme" have already been referred to, and, for the most part, its details are of little importance here.[205] In essence, what Fisher hoped to attain was a smaller, less expensive, more homogeneous, and more highly concentrated and hence more powerful fleet backed by a capable ready reserve. As preconditions for this "momentous change" in existing arrangements, he urged that it was necessary to do four things:

(a) We must reconsider our strategy.
(b) We must eliminate all out-of-date vessels.
(c) We must rearrange all our fleets and squadrons.
(d) We must reduce the number of ships in commission but not the fighting value of the whole.[206]

Having said this, Fisher went on to admit that because "national policy [was] largely involved," the question of strategy could not be "conveniently dealt with" in his May memorandum.[207] This was so despite the fact that the rearrangement of fleets and squadrons that lay at the heart of his proposal was "largely dependent" on prior strategic decisions.[208]

Fisher's evident lack of interest in strategic analysis, both in this and in later variants of his scheme, reflects in part the overriding concern for organizational and technological problems that marked his entire career. As one historian has put it, "His undeniable brilliance as an administrative reformer did not extend to the fields of strategy and tactics."[209] But, more to the point, the new first lord's plan was less an invitation to strategic debate than a statement of policies that followed from previous decisions. The process of concentration that had been set in motion three years before was to continue, leaving the periphery to increasingly powerful and, for the time being at least, friendly nations. This could be seen quite plainly from the table on "Existing and Proposed Distribution of 'Effective Ships'" that was appended to the manifesto Fisher issued on first taking office. The entire battleship fleet at the China station was to be recalled as soon as possible, while the projected British presence off North America was so reduced as to be little more than, in the words of one scholar, "a polite myth."[210]

First reactions to these proposed changes from within the naval establishment were predictably mixed. Fisher loyalists like the di-

---

[205] See the beginning of this chapter.
[206] Kemp, ed., *Papers of Admiral Sir John Fisher* 1:24.
[207] Ibid., p. 25.
[208] Ibid., p. 26.
[209] Haggie, "The Royal Navy and War Planning in the Fisher Era," in P. Kennedy, ed., *The War Plans of the Great Powers, 1880–1914*, p. 129.
[210] Bourne, *Britain and the Balance*, p. 365.

rector of Naval Intelligence Prince Louis Battenberg thought the shifts overdue and urged that they be undertaken as quickly as possible. In April, Battenberg had pressed a plan for the redistribution of armored cruisers on Selborne, writing that his recommendation was "the foundation for further proposals which however I thought inexpedient to mention, as they would not have commended themselves to Lord Walter [Kerr]. Nonetheless they are not only sound but inevitable."[211] In October, with Fisher finally at the helm, Battenberg was among those who favored not only the concentration of heavy cruisers but an immediate recall of the five Far Eastern battleships. These he regarded as "misplaced power," although he was prepared to acknowledge that diplomatic considerations might justify delaying the withdrawal a little longer, "however sound on naval strategical grounds."[212]

Two of Selborne's aging predecessors, former first lords Hamilton and Goschen, voiced their approval for the planned reorganization when they learned of it in December.[213] Kerr, the recently replaced obstructionist, was understandably less enthusiastic. He apparently had little inkling of what was to occur when he handed over his office to Fisher, and was in fact informed of the scheme only days before it was announced in the newspapers. On 11 December he wrote a noncommittal letter of congratulations to Selborne, noting that the key to the new plan was "the reduction of ships in commission on foreign stations which, as you may remember, I was always a bit shy about."[214] Former DNI Reginald Custance was also lukewarm in his praise, pointing out, on the one hand, that he had made the case for redistribution as long ago as 1899, and warning, on the other, against any rapid changes.[215]

In all, there appears to have been little or no concerted resistance to the proposals that Selborne brought forward at the end of 1904; certainly there was no real criticism of the scheme's larger strategic implications. The prince of Wales who, despite his lack of formal authority, took a keen interest in naval affairs, worried that further cuts in the Pacific squadron would weaken the imperial bond between Britain and Canada.[216] But, for the moment, such considerations received little attention from inside the Admiralty.

In one rather limited sense, Fisher's plans for the further con-

[211] Selborne Papers, 44, Battenberg to Selborne, 4/6/04.

[212] Ibid., 10/16/04 and 10/20/04.

[213] Selborne Papers, 42, Goschen to Selborne, 12/12/04, and Hamilton to Selborne, 12/12/04.

[214] Selborne Papers, 41, Kerr to Selborne, 12/11/04.

[215] Selborne Papers, 23, Custance to Selborne, 12/14/04.

[216] Selborne Papers, 44, Selborne to Fisher, 11/21/04.

centration of the fleet were welcomed elsewhere in the Government. The navy's increasing unwillingness to engage U.S. forces had been obvious since at least the end of 1903, and this fact, combined with a general desire for savings, had nudged the War Office away from its insistence on maintaining a number of traditional colonial garrisons. In July the Committee of Imperial Defence had given general approval to a proposal by Secretary of State for War H. O. Arnold-Forster for the withdrawal of some or all of the infantry then based at Halifax, Barbados, Trinidad, Bermuda, and Jamaica.[217] This plan encountered serious opposition from key military men as well as nervous Colonial Office officials, but it was saved by the timely arrival on the scene of Admiral Fisher.[218]

At least concerning some of the smaller colonial installations, Fisher's objectives and those of the War Office hierarchy tended to coincide. In November of 1904 a special committee on the estimates chaired by the new first sea lord reported that it would be possible to realize a savings of over £4 million in the coming fiscal year. The purging of useless ships was largely responsible, but so too was the fleet redistribution, which was about to be formally announced. As the committee explained, "The new strategic concentration of our fleet causes the raison d'être of subsidiary small depots to cease. Ascension, Halifax, Jamaica, Trincomalee and Esquimalt are no longer required to be kept manned and equipped. . . . Similarly, the establishments at Bermuda, Bombay and Simon's Bay can be materially decreased."[219] Backed by these arguments from its powerful new ally, the CID reaffirmed its earlier decisions and ordered infantry battalions withdrawn from Bermuda and Halifax. In addition, the committee accepted the Admiralty's position regarding the abandonment of its base at St. Lucia. This installation was to be given up posthaste, and all of the troops based there were to be brought home.[220]

At this point the marriage of convenience between Admiralty and War Office came to a sudden and unhappy end. The army might be willing, indeed eager, to give up responsibility for the protection of a few naval bases, but it had no intention of abandoning its larger commitment to the defense of Canada. As far as most

[217] Wells, "British Strategic Withdrawal from the Western Hemisphere, 1904–1906," p. 338. For the official record of these decisions see PRO, Cab. 2/1, "Minutes of the 48th Meeting of the CID," 7/8/04.

[218] Wells, "British Strategic Withdrawal," p. 340.

[219] BM, Add. Mss. 49698, "Navy Estimates, 1905–06: Report of Estimates Committee," 11/26/04.

[220] Wells, "British Strategic Withdrawal," pp. 340–41.

navy men were concerned, the same problems that rendered British island facilities in the Western Hemisphere indefensible would make it virtually impossible for Britain to help Canada against the United States. There was no getting around the fact that, as the Admiralty explained, the United States was now a "first class Maritime Power" that was not only a menace to St. Lucia but to "all our possessions on that side of the Atlantic."[221]

As soon as Selborne's memorandum on the distribution of the fleet had been circulated, the army's new General Staff appealed to the CID for a ruling on the whole question of Canadian defense. Because the successful invasion of Canada would be "an Imperial disaster of the very first magnitude," its defense was held by the army to be "one of the most serious problems which the military and naval forces of the Empire are confronted with." Given its advantages in population and geography, the United States would probably have little difficulty in seizing the western portions of the Dominion. The real struggle, however, would be for control of the wealthy and populous central and eastern coastal regions. If the Americans were able to dominate Lake Erie and Lake Ontario, there was little that could be done to prevent them from conquering the surrounding areas and absorbing all of Canada.[222]

In light of its analysis, the General Staff requested that the navy maintain sufficient forces to prevent the United States from seizing control of the two easternmost Great Lakes. And it advised that the control of Lake Ontario should be regarded as "at least as much a part of [the navy's] duty as is control of the [English] Channel." To ensure this, the General Staff urged "the retention of a few fighting ships capable of passing the St. Lawrence and Welland Canals on the North American Station."[223]

By his own account, Fisher had come to the conclusion that Canada was essentially indefensible as early as 1897 during his brief tour as commander in chief of the North American station.[224] This opinion does not appear to have changed much with the passage of time. Shortly before becoming first sea lord he had written to King Edward's personal secretary expressing the view that "we ought to

---

[221] PRO, Cab. 5/1/14c, "Value of St. Lucia as a Naval Base," Admiralty, 11/19/04.

[222] PRO, Cab. 5/1/15c, "The Defence of Canada," General Staff, 12/13/04, pp. 1–5.

[223] Ibid., p. 6.

[224] Fisher wrote to Selborne that an attached memorandum on the question of Canadian defense in which he argued against the entire project contained "an epitome of my views when I was C. in C. in North America" (Selborne Papers, 42, Fisher to Selborne, 12/23/04).

clear out from [the Western] Hemisphere altogether!"[225] Fisher's response to the General Staff memo should therefore hardly have come as a surprise to anyone who knew him well. On 23 December he wrote Selborne that the navy should not send reinforcements to the Great Lakes in time of peace, and that it could not do so once war had begun. The defense of western Canada was therefore "absolutely hopeless. . . . That it would be equally hopeless elsewhere is probably true."[226]

The prospects for any struggle in the open ocean off Canada's coasts were equally bleak. Given the "foregone conclusion" that "sooner or later" the United States would attain supremacy in the western Atlantic, there was no way that Britain could hope for victory without first withdrawing "the whole of her Battle Fleets from European waters." This, as had been pointed out in 1901, would be an extraordinarily risky maneuver, and, even if it permitted the Royal Navy to destroy the U.S. fleet, it "could scarcely have the effect of bringing America to her knees." The vast size of the internal American market and the country's relatively small dependence on foreign trade rendered it virtually immune from even the most complete naval blockade.

Fisher's conclusions were, as usual, blunt to the point of brutality. "The more carefully this problem is considered, the more tremendous do the difficulties which would confront Great Britain in a war with the United States appear to be. . . . That [such a war] . . . would be unpopular and that the outcome of the struggle could only result sooner or later, in the loss of Canada, are the conclusions difficult to avoid."[227] Given the weakness of its position, the policy of the British government ought to be to "use all possible means to avoid such a war." In any case, "it seems an utter waste of time to prepare for it."[228]

This was the outcome toward which all of Selborne's innovations since early 1901 had been pointing, yet, at the last moment, he seems to have recoiled from the product of his handiwork. Without local naval supremacy (and perhaps even with it) Britain could not hope to protect the largest outpost of its empire from invasion. Certainly if the Royal Navy's presence in the Western Hemisphere was reduced still further, there was no chance that such a defense could be provided. Yet Selborne was apparently shocked by Fisher's assertion of these simple truths. On the day after Christmas he

[225] Marder, ed., *Fear God and Dreadnought* 1:327.
[226] Selborne Papers, 42, Fisher to Selborne, 12/23/04.
[227] Ibid.
[228] Ibid.

wrote to Balfour describing a meeting with the volcanic first sea lord. "He said that under no conceivable circumstances could we escape an overwhelming and humiliating defeat by the United States and therefore he would leave Canada to her fate and no matter what the cause of quarrel or merits of the case he would not spend one man or one pound in the defence of Canada. And he meant it."[229] Stunned, Selborne could only reply that he differed "by the breadth of the globe quite as much on the grounds of . . . self-preservation as . . . on those of obligations of honor," but, he admitted, he lacked the arguments with which to overturn Fisher's analysis.[230]

In fact, there could be no decisive refutation of Fisher. On 6 January 1905, the Admiralty made its formal reply to the General Staff, a response that lacked some of Fisher's vehemence but did not differ substantially from his earlier judgments.[231] The navy held that it could do little to help Canada on either the Great Lakes or the high seas. As a result, "The view of the Admiralty is that Canada must primarily rely upon her own resources for defence against invasion by the United States."[232] Having said this, however, the Admiralty warned that the Dominion government should do nothing by way of preparation that might antagonize the Americans.[233] Appeasement was to be pursued by Ottawa as well as by London.

From this point, whether the army realized it or not, the debate over the defense of Canada was essentially finished. The General Staff prodded the Admiralty for some statement of its responsibilities, citing the old promise to the Colonial Defence Committee of 1896, but even this barb had lost much of its sting.[234] Control of the Lakes and their ocean approaches could no longer be assured. The guarantee of protection against invasion by sea still held good, but an attack was far more likely to come by land, and in such a contingency the navy would be of little use. "The conditions which have prevailed in the past exist no longer," the Admiralty explained, and recent developments were "all such as tend to make the direct intervention of the British navy in the local defence of Canada impracticable." There could be no guarantee that "in the event of war with the United States the command of the Western Atlantic will in

---

[229] BM, Add. Mss. 49707, Selborne to Balfour, 12/26/04.

[230] Ibid.

[231] This memorandum was apparently written by Battenberg and Ottley, the outgoing director of Naval Intelligence and his successor (Wells, "British Strategic Withdrawal," pp. 349–50).

[232] PRO, Cab. 5/1/21c, "Defence of Canada," Admiralty, 2/24/05, p. 7.

[233] Ibid., pp. 7–10.

[234] PRO, Cab. 5/1/24c, "General Staff Comments on Cab. 5/1/21c," General Staff, 3/17/05.

future be always maintained." To this comment in an April 1905 memorandum to the cabinet some unnamed reader had appended a footnote: "This is absolutely true, and we must recognise the fact. The difficulty is that we cannot state that fact bluntly to the Canadian government, which would blurt it out all over the world."[235] In July the CID reaffirmed its decision to hand over responsibility for the defense of Halifax and Esquimalt to the presumably unsuspecting Canadians.[236] For all practical purposes the British presence in the Western Hemisphere and the protracted squabbles over it had come to an end.[237]

At the same time as these decisions were being made, crucial events were taking place half a world away off the coast of Korea. The Russian battle fleet, which had been steaming eastward since the end of 1904, had finally reached Asian waters and was about to engage the Japanese. On 27 May, as it was passing through the narrow strait separating Kyushu from the island of Tsushima, the Russian flotilla was set upon and virtually annihilated. The predictions that some strategists had been making for over a year were now proven accurate. Having lost a total of five armored cruisers and fourteen battleships, Russia was reduced to the rank of a minor naval power and forced to sue for peace.[238]

Russia's defeat, as Fisher explained to the cabinet in November, had created "an entirely new Naval situation."[239] A comparison of orders of battle revealed a situation that was "from the British standpoint . . . eminently satisfactory." Whereas before the Japanese victory England alone would have been badly outnumbered by a coalition of France, Russia, and Germany, in its aftermath the Royal Navy could deploy "a force of battleships *considerably superior* to the combined battleship strength of those three Powers. Remember," Fisher told his readers, "it is the battleship that determines victory."[240]

At first blush the new balance of forces appeared so favorable as to warrant "a breathing space" of the sort that had "not occurred in the past generation."[241] Still, as dramatic as the demise of Russian

[235] PRO, Cab. 5/1/25c, "Admiralty Comments on Cab. 5/1/24c," Admiralty, 4/05.

[236] PRO, Cab. 2/1, "Minutes of the 76th Meeting of the CID," 8/20/05.

[237] Wells, "British Strategic Withdrawal," p. 355.

[238] Marder, *Anatomy of British Sea Power*, p. 441.

[239] PRO, Cab. 37/81/173, p. 11.

[240] Ibid., p. 12.

[241] Ibid., p. 13. This was an argument from which Fisher quickly backed away when it became clear that it could be used by those in favor of still greater cutbacks in naval spending. Thus by February of 1906 Fisher was warning that "the superficial plausibility of the notion that money can be saved in consequence of the recent Russian naval collapse has hypnotised men's minds" (PRO, Adm. 115/866B, "The Building Programme of the British Navy," Admiralty, 2/15/06).

naval power undoubtedly was, it really did little to change Fisher's view of the overall strategic situation. By the end of 1904 Germany had already replaced the Dual Alliance in his mind as Britain's most likely enemy. For this reason the concentration of British forces would have to continue, although it was certainly made easier by the weakening of Russia's presence in the Far East and by the virtual disappearance of the czar's fleet.

Fisher spoke of his redistribution plan as one that would ensure Britain's continued dominance of the world's oceans. "Five keys lock up the world!" he wrote in October 1904. "Singapore. The Cape. Alexandria. Gibraltar. Dover. These five keys belong to England, and the five great fleets of England will hold those keys!"[242] The collapse of the Russian navy served to make the job of holding on somewhat simpler. The fact that it was possible at all only because of the forbearance of foreign powers did not seem worth mentioning. Britain, in Fisher's conception, was single-handedly supreme, as it had always been.

In December 1904 former French foreign minister Gabriel Hanotaux observed that, by virtue of their recently announced changes in policy, the British had done something of which neither the Romans nor even Napoleon himself had ever conceived. "She dominates everywhere," he declared. Perhaps too modest to say so himself, Fisher could only concur. "Only the Prime Minister . . . and M. Hanotaux . . . have realised the significance of recent Naval changes," he wrote with satisfaction.[243] Ottley, the new director of Naval Intelligence to whom Fisher passed a copy of Hanotaux's remarks, was equally impressed. "The fact is that it requires a gift of imagination with which Englishmen providentially are not often blessed, to realise all that the new 'reorganization of the fleet' in . . . truth implies," he wrote to Viscount Esher. "It needs the quick intellect of a man of Latin race to express this."[244]

Less-gifted observers reached similar conclusions by more pedestrian means. As Englishmen had been doing for the past twenty years, they looked at the figures, and what they saw there filled them with relief and satisfaction. In February 1905, navalist Archibald Hurd compared the forces of the seven major naval powers and concluded that "not for ten or twelve years has the naval outlook of Great Britain been as cheerful as at present."[245] Hurd maintained

---

[242] Kemp, ed., *Papers of Admiral Sir John Fisher* 1 : 161.

[243] BM, Add. Mss. 49710, "A French Criticism of the Redistribution of the British Fleet," Fisher, 12/28/04.

[244] BM, Add. Mss. 49710, Ottley to Esher, 3/1/05.

[245] Hurd, "The Balance of Naval Power," p. 230.

that it was reasonable to "continue to judge the position of the British fleet" by what he called the "'ready reckoner' method of assessing naval power"—by "'counting noses,' by contrasting the numbers of ships of Powers." This was "the only ready method available." [246] Using it, one could see that "the British supremacy of the seas was never so complete as at this moment. . . . The two-Power standard has been attained by the action of the Admiralty, and Russia, by her misfortunes, has raised the British strength to a virtual three-Power standard." [247]

The existence of such a situation at least in relation to France, Russia, and Germany was something of an embarrassment to Admiralty officials. During the presentation of his final budget request, Lord Selborne felt constrained to point out that the two-power standard referred "only to battleships" and that it had "never . . . applied to any two particular nations, but always to the two strongest naval Powers." The first lord insisted that he did not advocate and had "never . . . advocated a three-Power standard" as a matter of policy because "I do not think the finance of the country could afford it." Nevertheless, he went on, "the spirit of the two-Power standard is not equality. The object is to win." [248] Thus, the British might be able to rest on their oars for a bit, but there was no reason for cuts more substantial than those already planned, nor for accusations of wasteful spending and excessive armament.

By the end of 1905 the idea that Britain's position was stronger than in recent years, perhaps even stronger than it had ever been, had gained widespread acceptance. Certainly if one looked only at the European powers there could be little doubt that the two-power standard had been met and easily exceeded. The diplomatic revolution of the preceding five years and the recent collapse of Russia had permitted an extraordinary concentration of British sea power. Fisher and those around him seemed to believe that this meant the reassertion of the sort of worldwide supremacy that Britain had enjoyed through much of the nineteenth century.

There were some who did not believe that the picture was quite so uniformly rosy, but in the resurgent confidence of the moment they tended to keep their misgivings to themselves; if they did speak out, they were generally ignored. One set of critics worried that reducing the Royal Navy's strength on distant stations would inevitably place British interests in Asia, Africa, and America at greater risk. Without as many gunboats ready to "show the flag," in

[246] Ibid., p. 232.
[247] Ibid., p. 236.

[248] Statement by Selborne, 3/21/05, in PRO, Adm. 116/1605, p. 14.

order to protect its citizens and their possessions, England would lose standing as an imperial power, even if it was not actually forced to give up portions of its empire. This was essentially the case that the Colonial Office (and occasionally the Foreign Office) made whenever the subject of ship withdrawals arose inside the Government.[249]

Following his retirement as commander in chief of the China station, Admiral Sir Cyprian Bridge wrote an article in which he warned that Whitehall had not fully thought through the implications of fleet redistribution. Given that such a reallocation of forces was necessary, Bridge asked, "Can we discern any proof that the ultimate effects of so great a change have been foreseen and allowed for? The redistribution as a whole amounts to little more than a grouping of a great portion of our naval force in the corner of the Atlantic Ocean, which is merely following the old practice."[250] As a result of recent changes, the "mobility and readiness for distant service of considerable groups of ships" had been impaired, and the navy was in danger of being regarded in much the same light as the army once had been, as suitable solely for the defense of the homeland.[251]

That Bridge's comments may have given rise to a certain anxiety among his former fellow officers is suggested by the reaction his article provoked from Fisher. Shortly after the article appeared, the first sea lord wrote an angry and personal response that he marked "not for publication—only meant for colleagues re-assurance." Sidestepping the thrust of Bridge's remarks, Fisher simply asserted that the changing distribution of naval forces—in particular, the recent emergence of a modern German fleet—made concentration essential. There was no increased risk to Britain's trade or to its interests in distant regions. The reasons for Bridge's "literary decadence" could be found in his recent retirement and in an effort on his part to "dispel the ennui of an unpalatable leisure by a dalliance with the editors of newspapers and magazines."[252]

A more profound and telling critique of Admiralty policy came from those who realized that the nation's apparently restored position now rested on appeasement of the new peripheral powers. This might be possible for some time, but if either of the new arrangements broke down, or if (as was eventually to be the case) the

---

[249] Wells, "British Strategic Withdrawal," p. 341. These complaints continued for several years. See 1907 memos by the Colonial Office and the Foreign Office in PRO, CO 537/348.
[250] BM, Add. Mss. 49710, "Remarks on Admiral Sir Cyprian Bridge's Criticisms of Recent Naval Reforms," Fisher, 6/05.
[251] Ibid.
[252] Ibid.

two came into conflict, the relative decline in Britain's naval power
would be dramatically revealed. Simply removing Japan and the
United States from the list of countries against which the two-
power standard was to be measured could not eliminate the forces
they possessed. And, as Fisher would shortly warn those who wanted
to use the improvement in relations with France as an excuse for
not counting its forces, "Ententes may vanish—battleships remain
the surest pledges this country can give for the continued peace of
the world."[253]

Sir John Colomb, who had long been concerned about the inadequacy of existing means of measuring naval power, seems to
have been particularly troubled by the unbridled optimism of those
around him. In March 1905 he addressed Parliament on the question of the recently announced reorganization of the navy. He was
especially uneasy about the withdrawal of forces from the Far East,
for there could be found "the two countries that had made the most
extraordinary developments in naval strength in recent years."

> He could not see anything in [Selborne's published
> memos] . . . showing the scheme to be the result of a
> world wide look at the naval position, for it paid abso-
> lutely no attention whatever to the British position in the
> Pacific. . . . Much as he hoped that amity with the United
> States would long continue, he declined to base the Brit-
> ish naval policy upon pious hopes. With every hope for
> continued amity, they could not ignore the developments
> there, and they must have regard for their own position
> in the Pacific. Take for another example, Japan. Did any-
> body believe that our alliance with Japan was an everlast-
> ing covenant.[254]

The fact was that Britain had vast interests in the Pacific but no primary base there, and, Colomb insisted, the power that controlled
the Pacific would one day be able to control the Indian Ocean as
well. Because it did not consider these unpleasant long-range prospects, "the new scheme was not a calm review dealing with the
whole policy of the Empire in the near future. The policy dealt with
one hemisphere under the conditions of today. . . . This was, therefore, a small scheme rather of the politician than the statesman."[255]

A few observers seemed to understand what had happened but,
seeing no real alternative, they thought it best to keep their own
counsel. Several weeks after Colomb gave his speech in Parliament,

---

[253] PRO, Adm. 116/866B, p. 3.
[254] *Hansard Parliamentary Debates*, 4th

ser., vol. 142 (1905), pp. 1285–86.
[255] Ibid.

George Clarke, secretary of the CID, wrote to Balfour's personal secretary regarding the situation in the Western Hemisphere.

> What is best not to say is that we believe that the idea of opposing the navy of the United States . . . close to its bases must be abandoned. This has naturally altered some strategic aspects of this part of the world. In years not far distant, we shall be quite unable to oppose the navy of Japan in its own waters. It is best to recognize facts but not always to proclaim them from the housetop.[256]

Conclusion
Assessing the Naval Balance

Whatever else may have separated them, most nineteenth-century Englishmen could have agreed on one thing: "command of the seas" was essential to their commerce, their empire, and to their very survival. Ensuring that this critical objective could be achieved in the event of war was the Royal Navy's unaltering task. It was therefore a prime responsibility of the Admiralty and of the nation's political leadership to guarantee that the navy would always have ample forces with which to carry out its vital mission.

To make proper decisions about budgets and fleets, some convenient way of translating back from desired "outcomes" to necessary "inputs" was required. This need, prevailing beliefs about the nature of naval warfare (bolstered from the 1890s onward by the writings of Alfred Thayer Mahan), and the strategic realities of the last quarter of the century (in particular, the hostility of France and Russia and the absence of any significant non-European navies) combined to yield a simple index of sufficiency. As has been described, the two-power standard that came officially into use in 1889 equated worldwide sea supremacy with the maintenance by Britain of a fleet of battleships at least equal in number to that of the next two naval nations combined.

As predictors of war outcomes, numerical comparisons of force strength have certain characteristic deficiencies. Because they usually emphasize only one type of weapon, such comparisons often overlook others that may in fact play an important role in determining the course of a war. Because they concentrate on the observable, concrete components of military power, straight tabulations of ships, guns, or men usually ignore intangible factors like strategy, tactics, weapons technology, communications, leadership,

---

[256] BM, Add. Mss. 49701, Clarke to Sandars, 3/31/05.

and morale. The two-power standard certainly had all of these failings (although it is not obvious that any other equivalent rule of thumb would have been much better). Adhering to it in peacetime was not the guarantee of success in war that many contemporary observers probably assumed it to be.

As a tool for assessing Britain's overall strategic position, the standard had an additional, important flaw. By abstracting from geography and focusing on numbers alone, it tended to conceal a key assumption about the distribution of naval power. Provided that only European nations had navies, controlling Continental waters was the functional equivalent of worldwide sea control. Once extra-European states began to build fleets, even relatively small ones, the situation was bound to change. Britain might still be able to stay ahead of its two closest rivals, but it would not necessarily retain the capacity to dominate in waters far from home. Such a shift could not help but have a far-reaching impact on the security of the empire.

Despite its failings, the two-power standard came increasingly to exercise an important influence on the thinking of citizens, parliamentarians, and naval experts alike. This was a result both of its simplicity and apparent comprehensiveness and, over time, of the power of tradition. All discussions of naval subjects came back eventually to the question of whether the standard was being met. By the end of the century, no one dared suggest that a smaller measure of preparedness might be adequate, and few could muster up the intellectual energy to rethink the assumptions on which the two-power comparison had originally been based. As long as the standard was being adhered to in a narrow, numerical sense, most observers believed that Britannia must still rule the waves.

"New Wine in Old Bottles"

In one of his not infrequent biblical moods, Admiral "Jackie" Fisher admonished his colleagues: "Even the Scripture says 'Don't put new wine into old bottles!'"[257] The remark referred to the need to retire aging and decrepit vessels, but it could just as easily have applied to the continued use by the navy of outmoded rhetoric and methods of assessment. By the late 1890s Fisher and a small but growing group of middle-ranked naval officers had come to believe that Britain could no longer maintain its position in the Western Hemisphere and the Far East while at the same time preserving superiority in European waters. The buildup of French, Russian, and

[257] PRO, Adm. 116/942, "Organization for War," Fisher, 5/04.

German naval forces required that the Royal Navy concentrate its attention on the "strategic center," but the emergence of modern Japanese and American fleets meant that this move would now have to be accompanied by some accommodation of the rising peripheral powers.

With Selborne's appointment as first lord of the Admiralty, advocates of change within the navy acquired a powerful and persuasive ally in the cabinet. In the atmosphere of crisis brought on by the Boer War, Selborne was able in remarkably short order to convince his colleagues of the wisdom of accepting an American-built Isthmian Canal and the positive virtues of entering into an open alliance with Japan. These decisions cleared the way for a substantial redistribution and reconcentration of British naval forces, but the assumptions that underlay Admiralty advice were tightly held, even inside the Government. As a result, subsequent moves to reduce the Pacific fleet and effectively to disengage from the defense of Canada were met with surprise and resistance at the War Office and in some naval circles.

Selborne and his allies hoped to blunt bureaucratic opposition by obscuring their full intentions, and they had an even stronger motivation for misleading Parliament and the public about exactly what was occurring. To admit that the navy was abandoning North America and reducing its strength in Asia would have risked appearing weak and exposing the Admiralty to accusations that it had allowed the nation's all-important naval position to erode. In order to avoid this, Selborne made a conscious decision to continue invoking the time-honored symbols of British supremacy, even though their meaning had already begun to change.

Matching Russia and France (or even, after the events of 1904–1905, Russia, France, and Germany combined) no longer guaranteed control of the world's oceans. Men like Selborne and Fisher seem to have known this at some level or at least some of the time. When they dealt with operational problems in distant theaters they appear to have had few illusions about the widening cracks in Britain's armor. Yet they continued to talk and think most generally in terms of the two-power standard and to measure the overall adequacy of their preparations against it.

What began as an effort at deception seems gradually to have given way to a degree of self-delusion. In a period of dramatic change the old index of naval power was a familiar and comforting, if also an increasingly deceptive, landmark. As long as Japan and the United States failed to penetrate the ranks of the top three powers, it was possible to avoid confronting the political assumptions on which the standard had come to be based and to sidestep the question of what sort of strategic situation its attainment could now produce. Admiralty officials continued to think of themselves as adhering to the tried and true policies of their predecessors and thereby ensuring Britain's continued preeminence. The two-power standard stood between insiders and outsiders. But it also helped to insulate those most responsible for England's security from the far-reaching consequences of the diffusion of naval power.

A Prudent Response?

In retrospect, the abandonment of worldwide sea supremacy may appear as a prudent, sensible, perhaps even a "mature," response to the erosion in Britain's relative naval strength. In fact, as has been discussed, that response was possible mainly because its larger significance was obscured at the time by the language in which it was described. The long-term risks of redistribution were never fully considered, either by the Government or in public debate, nor were the possible alternatives to it given more than passing consideration.

The defeat of Russia by Japan and the improvement of relations between England and France might conceivably have reduced the urgency of concentration, even if they did not permit any real strengthening of Britain's peripheral fleets. By 1905, however, the German navy had come to be perceived as a potent and threatening challenger for control of Continental waters. Assuming the continued primacy of the European theater, the only real alternative to redistribution was therefore an even greater expansion in the Royal Navy's overall size. More battleships and cruisers could conceivably have permitted a buildup close to home while allowing a larger continued presence in Asia and off North America. Even if, on careful reflection, this had appeared desirable on strategic grounds, it seems clear that it would have been dismissed as economically infeasible. Indeed, because prevailing financial assumptions were so strong, the possibility of trying to maintain regional as well as European supremacy was never seriously entertained, and the likely costs of such a strategy were not even estimated.

Redistribution may well have been the best of all the options available to Britain's leaders. It solved some of their immediate problems and did not expose the nation to any obvious, short-term risks. Over the long-run, however, the decisions taken between 1900 and 1905 could not help but weaken Britain's international position and, in particular, the ties that held its empire together. Although the change may not have been obvious at first, Canada and the other colonies and possessions at the empire's extremes were now more fully on their own, in defense as in other matters. After 1902 imperial security depended more heavily than it had before on Britain's ability to maintain friendly relations with the United States and Japan. A portion of the nation's freedom of diplomatic maneuver was thereby lost, and the possibility of further, sudden erosions in its position was created. These risks may have been unavoidable, but they deserved greater and more open consideration than they were ultimately permitted to receive.

FIVE

Land Power:
The Dilemma of Indian
Defense

The story of our proceedings dictated by fear of Russia is an amazing
one. It will have to be written someday.
—George Clarke to Arthur Balfour, 28 April 1905

By the end of 1900 imperial forces in South Africa had begun to
reassert themselves against their Boer opposition. The war was by
no means over, but the risk of disastrous and humiliating defeat at
the hands of a ragtag band of rebellious settlers was quickly reced-
ing. Nevertheless, the early performance of the British army left
little cause for celebration. Virtually all of England's ground forces
were ultimately required to put down a colonial insurrection, and
the training, equipment, and leadership of those forces had been
tested and, in many ways, found sadly lacking. In the finest traditions of the empire, victory had been snatched from the jaws of defeat, but this time the experience was more unnerving than exhila-
rating. As the war wound down to its sordid conclusion, British
strategists began to examine and to question their country's preparedness for ground warfare.

During the summer of 1901 Lieutenant Colonel Edward Altham
of the War Office prepared a study entitled "Military Needs of the
Empire in a War with France and Russia." This paper was described by a future chief of the General Staff as "the first serious
attempt to deal in a comprehensive manner with the problem
of meeting the gravest danger to which the nation is exposed."[1]

[1] PRO, Cab. 3/1/1A, "Military Needs
of the Empire in a War with France and
Russia," Altham, 8/12/01, p. 1. The
comment is by W. G. Nicholson, who in
1901 served as the director of Military
Operations.

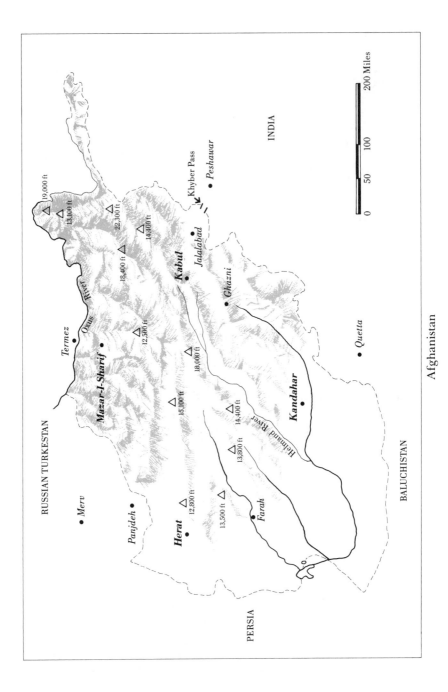

Afghanistan

Altham's memorandum dealt with a whole range of questions, from the defense of the United Kingdom to the security of British colonial bases and the conduct of offensive operations against France and Russia. Regarding what was arguably Britain's most important overseas possession, Altham concluded that "the problem of the defence of India . . . has never been fully faced by the home Government."[2] "Unless," he continued, "we are prepared to accept the loss of India, as an inevitable result of war between this country and France and Russia, it is manifest that drastic measures are necessary to place this portion of our general scheme of Imperial Defence on a safe footing."[3]

That the British government was unwilling to accept the loss of India under *any* circumstances went almost without saying. That it would be willing or able to undertake the drastic steps that Altham believed necessary to provide for Indian security was less obvious. At the turn of the century thoughtful Englishmen were forced to confront the possibility that they might some day have to fight a ground war even larger and more trying than the one being brought to a close in South Africa. Like a premonition of impending disaster, the vision of large-scale land warfare against a modern enemy would haunt British planners from 1900 until the awful day of reckoning arrived in 1914. For nine of those fourteen years the principal problem under investigation would be that of engaging German forces in support of France. But between 1900 and 1905 the most likely enemy was considered to be Russia, and the most probable battlefield, the barren and treacherous terrain of Afghanistan.

It was on India's northwest frontier that the British conjured for the first time with the horrors of total war and, having glanced into the abyss, recoiled. The prospect was too terrifying, the problems too immense, the demands on the will and resources of the empire too extraordinary, to allow a thorough and unflinching examination. As preliminary investigations of the Indian defense dilemma made clear, land war against a sophisticated opponent would require transporting, equipping, supplying, coordinating, and perhaps sacrificing hundreds of thousands (no one yet had the nerve to say millions) of well-trained and well-led men. Britain was simply unprepared both materially and psychologically for such an effort. Making ready for modern war would have required steps that most British statesmen were unwilling to take. It is hardly surprising, therefore, that they preferred to believe such steps were unneces-

[2] Ibid., p. 27.   [3] Ibid., p. 28.

sary, and that they jumped at the chance to overlook indications to the contrary.

In many ways the nation's strategists seem never to have recovered fully from the experience of planning for a struggle over India. After 1905 the geographical focus of attention shifted, but the same unwillingness to face facts carried over from central Asia to the western front. Britain's leaders believed that they could fight and win wars against the vast, conscripted armies of the Continent using only the manpower generated by a modestly proportioned system of voluntary service. In 1914 the nation stumbled into war with little understanding of what would be required to achieve victory. India was a warning of sorts, but in the end it went unheeded.

Background
The Emerging Problem of Large-Scale Land Warfare

Land Power versus Sea Power—the Loss of the "Winning Weapon." If Britain's interests had ended at its own shores, then, given continued control of home waters to prevent invasion, there could have been no conceivable need for the nation to retain a large standing army. In fact, of course, British statesmen had to worry about the security of their country's extensive colonial empire as well as about maintaining the Continental balance of power. Throughout most of the nineteenth century, however, even these problems did not require the application of substantial ground forces for their solution. Most British colonies could be protected with small garrisons of what were often really no more than imperial police. As for events in Europe, Britain could hope to use its capacity for naval blockade to humble any potential enemy, and, if circumstances required, it could threaten to insert relatively small expeditionary forces at places and times of its own choosing. During the Napoleonic and Crimean wars the English had raised substantial armies, but, in the first case and to a lesser extent in the second, these had been largely dissipated after the termination of hostilities.[4]

In the last thirty years of the nineteenth century there were several developments that threatened to expose the empire to military

[4]During 1794–1815 the British army rose to a force of 236,000 men, falling away to 80,000 in 1818 but increasing again to 246,000 in 1856. For most of the rest of the century the total of British forces at home and abroad was slightly under 200,000 (Adye, "Has Our Army Grown With Our Empire?" pp. 1015–16.)

challenges that were both novel and deeply troubling. At base these changes were due to the spread of industrialism that had become evident by midcentury and that grew steadily more significant with the passage of time. The diffusion of naval power and its impact on the physical security of Britain's overseas possessions (especially in the Western Hemisphere) has already been mentioned.[5] Equally significant was the perfection of fast, cheap, and efficient means of land transportation.

Margaret Sprout has noted that "British influence at its peak owed much to the primitive state of overland transport on the continent."[6] Because of the absence of other means, trade between nations was largely conducted over water, but even within states materials could often be transported most economically by circuitous open-ocean routes. Thus, according to Sprout, "goods sent from northwestern to southern Germany, for example, might normally go by ship from the northern ports, through the English Channel, around Gibraltar, through the Dardanelles, and up the Danube to their destination."[7] This meant that even some portion of the internal commerce of many countries and certainly much of their external trade was subject to interdiction by the British navy in wartime.

Measured by its adverse effect on Britain's strategic interests, in retrospect the railroad was, to quote Paul Kennedy, "the real villain of the piece."[8] Its development made possible the creation of secure internal lines of communication where none had existed before. In the short run this rendered other countries less vulnerable to attack at sea and, over the long term, it facilitated the growth of vast, integrated, and more autarkic domestic economies in Russia, the United States, and Germany.[9] As British planners were already beginning to realize in the case of the United States, large land powers with developed systems of domestic transportation were less susceptible to blockade than their more primitive predecessors.

Militarily, railroads made possible the rapid shuttling of forces between widely separated locations, thereby improving the defensive posture of many of Britain's likely opponents. This meant, to quote Kennedy again, that "the traditional British strategy against one power or a coalition dominating Europe, of despatching expeditions to the peripheries, be it in the Baltic or to the Portuguese or Italian coast, would now be a much more risky proposition if the

[5] See chapter 4.

[6] M. Sprout, "Mahan: Evangelist of Sea Power," in Earle, ed., *Makers of Modern Strategy*, p. 424.

[7] Ibid.

[8] P. Kennedy, "Mahan versus Mackinder: Two Interpretations of British Sea Power," in P. Kennedy, *Strategy and Diplomacy, 1870–1945*, p. 50.

[9] Ibid.

enemy could swiftly rush a far greater force to the threatened point by rail instead of having to rely on forced marches along poor roads."[10]

Finally, in addition to calling Britain's preferred method for conducting offensive land operations into question, technological progress also raised the possibility of enemy attack on imperial positions that had once been effectively beyond the reach of ground assault. The defenses of the empire were being subjected to new strains just as those of its rivals appeared to be growing stronger. This was true in North America, but, as will be described, it was even more worrisome in central Asia.

The same techniques of planning and organization that allowed the construction and management of extensive railway networks were also manifest, by the turn of the century, in the increasingly large and sophisticated armies being deployed by most industrialized nations. As early as 1871 the skill of the German army and the efficiency of its General Staff had been the objects of concern and no little admiration among some British military experts. Thirty years later, however, Britain's small volunteer force was still structured and controlled more or less as it had always been. Thus in 1904 a royal commission established in the wake of the Boer War to consider the organization of the British army would describe the prevailing situation as follows:

> Each of the five Great Powers of Europe has abandoned the once prevalent idea that war is the exclusive business of a limited class and has subjected its male population to a thorough training either naval or military. Accordingly, each of these nations is today ready to employ in war the greater part of its able-bodied male population . . . under the guidance of a specially trained body of officers.[11]

As a result, the commission warned, in a war against any major European power Great Britain would be at "a grave disadvantage." By their prior efforts its antagonists would be instantly ready to "devote to the struggle the greater part of [their] resources both in men and in material," while Britain would "not at the beginning have at her disposal in any effective form more than a fraction of her population, and her material resources would be very imperfectly applied."[12]

[10] P. Kennedy, "Mahan versus Mackinder," p. 51.

[11] BM, Add. Mss. 50329, "Report of the Royal Commission on the Militia and Volunteers," 5/20/04.

[12] Ibid.

The Growing Threat to India. At the close of the nineteenth century, England's enemies were better situated to resist blockade and amphibious attack than they had been thirty years before, and better able to mobilize and transport large armies to their own borders and beyond. Whether or not this meant that, as some have argued, in a general sense "sea power was . . . waning in relation to land power," it certainly created new problems for a country that had always had a great deal of the former and relatively little of the latter.[13] These difficulties were felt first and most acutely in the East.

Although their progress was not without fits and starts, between 1800 and the mid-1880s, successive Russian czars had been able to extend control over most of the territory that separated their empire from the northernmost frontiers of British India. From 1830 to 1880 the Russians advanced some 1,200 miles to the southeast, and in the next four years they moved an additional 600 miles from the Caspian Sea to the city of Merv on the Afghan border.[14] In 1884 czarist forces occupied Merv, and during the next year they drove the Afghan army out of Pendjh approximately 100 miles farther south.[15] Russia's borders were now essentially coterminous with those of Afghanistan and Persia, and these "buffer states" were all that kept the two empires apart.

For most of the remainder of the century Russian attention and expansionist energy seemed to be directed toward the Far East rather than toward central Asia. Having reached a logical resting place, the czar's forces paused and went no farther, but to many in India and in England this appeared to be merely a temporary, tactical halt that would be followed some day by a renewed southward march. Feeding fears of an eventual assault on Afghanistan and Persia was the unmistakable evidence of significant improvements in Russia's internal transportation system. By the end of the century a substantial steam mercantile fleet was operating on the Caspian Sea and more than 2,700 miles of railway had been laid in central Asia alone.[16] In 1901 construction was begun on a line that would connect Tashkent to Orenberg and points west, thereby

---

[13] P. Kennedy, "Mahan versus Mackinder," p. 50.

[14] Greaves, *Persia and the Defence of India, 1884–1892*, p. 58. For a brief history of the "Great Game" see Gillard, *The Struggle for Asia, 1828–1914*. See also Morgan, *Anglo-Russian Rivalry in Central Asia, 1810–1895*. On British policy in the first half of the nineteenth century see Yapp, *Strategies of British India: Britain, Iran, and Afghanistan, 1798–1850*.

[15] Gillard, *The Struggle for Asia*, pp. 144–47.

[16] Mahajan, "The Defence of India and the End of Isolation: A Study in the Foreign Policy of the Conservative Government, 1900–1905," p. 169.

bringing the newly acquired provinces into direct communication with the heartland of European Russia.[17]

The combination of territorial acquisitions and infrastructure development resulted in a change in the strategic situation that was distinctly unfavorable to Britain. In theory at least, some portion of the massive Russian army could now be moved by rail to within close range of the Afghan border. Moreover, whether they had been built primarily for peaceful or warlike purposes, the new railroads in central Asia and elsewhere served to reduce Britain's capacity to inflict damage on its most likely future enemy.

In 1885 Lord Roberts, the newly appointed commander in chief of the British Indian Army, wrote a memorandum that began with the question that was to vex imperial strategists for the next two decades. "What are Russia's vulnerable points?" Roberts asked rhetorically. Because the continent of Europe had become "a vast network of railroads," there was little likelihood that a sea blockade would be very effective. Without an ally it would be extremely difficult to strike at Russia over land. "Russia's most vulnerable point," Roberts concluded, was "undoubtedly the littoral of the Black Sea." But in order to repeat the sort of landings there that had eventually led to victory during the Crimean War, Britain would have to rely on the cooperation of Turkey. "If we cannot form an offensive and defensive alliance with her," Roberts wrote, "it appears to me that we must give up all hope of being able to operate against Russia in the Black Sea."[18]

By the early 1890s fears of a Franco-Russian naval alliance in the Mediterranean combined with uncertainty over the loyalties of the Ottoman Empire to persuade most navy and army experts that amphibious attacks on Russia's underbelly were no longer feasible.[19] Even if they had been possible, however, there was reason to doubt that such operations would be decisive. In 1901 the War Office Intelligence Department

> considered what possibility really exists for attacking Russia in Europe, or through Persia or in the Far East and . . . arrived at the conclusion that whatever chance any

[17] PRO, Cab. 6/1/36D, "Strategic Effect of an Extension of the Russian Railway System," War Office, 1/20/04.

[18] This memorandum appears in PRO, Cab. 6/1/7D, "General Kouropatkine's scheme for a Russian Advance upon India, with Notes Thereon by Lord Roberts," which was originally sent from the India Office in 1891 and was reprinted for the CID in March 1903.

[19] See chapter 4 for a discussion of this issue.

of these schemes might have had in the past, none of them . . . [were] now feasible; or, at all events, that they could not be expected so to occupy her military forces as to prevent her from concentrating upon the Afghan border.[20]

This was due in large measure to the fact that Russia now had lines of communication like the Petrovsk to Baku railroad, which lay to the north of the Caucasus mountains and could therefore not be cut by any simple landing on the shores of the Black Sea. The projected Orenberg-Tashkent line would only serve to increase further the security of Russian forces operating in central Asia.[21]

If a European approach was impossible and the Black Sea no longer presented a promising avenue of attack, the only other place where Britain's sea power could be brought to bear was on the Pacific coast. Here too, however, the prospects were dismal. The expanded Russian naval and military presence in the Far East (aided significantly by the construction, beginning in 1891, of a Trans-Siberian railway) and the relative British weakness there meant that the Pacific theater offered few opportunities for offensive action. By the turn of the century, there seemed little cause to disagree with the assessment contained in a letter from Lord Selborne of the Admiralty to the viceroy of India, Lord Curzon. "Compared to our Empire," Selborne wrote of Russia, "hers is invulnerable." In the event of conflict, "we must be on the defensive . . . because there is speaking generally and roughly no part of her territory where we can hit her . . . her communications are secure; she has not even to keep one eye behind her."[22] These conditions gave the czar the luxury of the initiative, something of which he was apparently well aware. In November 1899 Nicholas II wrote to his sister that he had only to mobilize his armies in Turkestan if he wished to paralyze Britain. "The strongest fleet in the world can't prevent us from settling our scores with England precisely at her most vulnerable point," he explained.[23]

If war came there seemed little question as to where the first blow would fall. Britain might not be able to get at Russia, but, through Afghanistan and India beyond, Russia could most certainly get at Britain.

---

[20] PRO, Cab. 6/1/1D, "Report of a Committee Appointed to Consider the Military Defence of India," 12/24/01, p. 15.

[21] Ibid.

[22] Monger, *The End of Isolation: British Foreign Policy, 1900–1907*, p. 7.

[23] Mahajan, "The Defence of India," p. 173.

The Importance of India

As they watched Russia's steel tentacles extend toward the Indian frontier, British strategic planners found themselves caught in a dilemma from which they were never quite able to work free. On the one hand they could not conceive of abandoning the Raj or allowing it to be overthrown by a hostile foreign power. On the other, as they began to consider the prospect of large-scale land warfare with a modern Continental state, they ran up against the obvious but deeply rooted limitations on their peacetime military system. India could not be given up, but if the Russian threat was all that it seemed, there was strong reason to doubt that Britain's eastern empire could be adequately defended. In order to understand the poignancy of this dilemma it is necessary first to reflect on India's special place in the imperial constellation.

The English historians Ronald Robinson and John Gallagher have written that "to all Victorian statesmen, India and the British Isles were the twin centres of their wealth and strength in the world as a whole."[24] Max Beloff, in his book *Imperial Sunset*, goes even further. "Britain without India would not have been the world power that at the time of the Diamond Jubilee [1897] she seemed to be. At that time it could well be argued that she had as much right as Austria-Hungary to be styled a dual monarchy or dual empire."[25]

The importance that British statesmen attached to India is reflected in the pattern of their imperial and diplomatic strategies during most of the period separating the Napoleonic Wars and World War I. Indeed, the whole of Britain's external policy during this period is absolutely incomprehensible without some understanding of the centrality of its eastern empire. Gallagher and Robinson claim that Britain "moved into Africa [in the 1880s], not to build a new African empire but to protect the old empire in India."[26] Certainly this vast undertaking was motivated at least in part by concern over the security of the sea routes through the Suez Canal and around the Cape of Good Hope. Britain's obsession with the Mediterranean and the Straits of Bosporus, and thus with the stability of the Ottoman Empire, was linked directly to a desire to maintain open lines of communication with the East.[27] The Persian Gulf, Persia, and Afghanistan were important almost exclusively

[24] Robinson and Gallagher, *Africa and the Victorians,* p. 17.
[25] Beloff, *Imperial Sunset* 1 : 37.
[26] Robinson and Gallagher, *Africa and the Victorians,* p. 464.
[27] See chapter 4 for more on this issue.

because of their proximity to India.[28] And, by 1900, concern over the Russian threat in central Asia was exerting a profound influence on Britain's dealings with Germany, Japan, and France as well as with Russia itself.[29]

What was it that British statesmen believed themselves to be protecting? In part the answer has to do with economics. Indian markets were essential to the health of Britain's economy, and they became increasingly crucial as protectionism reasserted itself toward the end of the century. By the 1880s India already absorbed about £270 million of English capital or about one-fifth of total British investment overseas.[30] At around the same time, by various counts, Indian consumers purchased 19 percent of Britain's exports,[31] and one-tenth of the total value of British trade was with India.[32] After the onset of the Great Depression in the 1870s, India bought between 40 and 45 percent of all cotton exports from the British Isles, a development so significant that one economist has said that "in this period of difficulty Asia saved Lancashire."[33]

Although the balance was about to shift decisively in the other direction, for most of the nineteenth century India was also a source of military manpower for the empire rather than a drain on its resources. The British Indian Army (consisting of both British and native soldiers) was financed out of local tax revenues, but it was put to use repeatedly for imperial purposes beyond India's borders. Indian troops were employed in the Crimea (1854–1857), in China (1859), Abyssinia (1867), Malta (1878), Afghanistan (1878–1881), Egypt (1882), the Sudan (1885 and 1896–1899), and East Africa (1896),[34] and elements of the British Indian Army would come to the rescue in South Africa in 1899.[35] All of this upset anti-imperialist members of Parliament who feared losing control over foreign policy, but it tended to confirm the assertion of Lord Salisbury that India was an "Eastern barrack in the oriental seas from which we may draw any number of troops without paying for them."[36]

At some point the British attachment to India seems to have transcended reason and to have become an article of faith that

[28] See Greaves, *Persia and the Defence of India,* and Alder, *British India's Northern Frontier, 1865–1895.*

[29] See Monger, *The End of Isolation,* and Mahajan, "The Defence of India." Also Grenville, *Lord Salisbury and Foreign Policy: The Close of the Nineteenth Century.*

[30] Judd, *Balfour and the British Empire,* p. 224.

[31] Ibid.

[32] Beloff, *Imperial Sunset* 1:31.

[33] Hobsbawm, *Industry and Empire,* p. 147.

[34] Thornton, *The Imperial Idea and Its Enemies: A Study in British Power,* p. 111.

[35] Pakenham, *The Boer War,* p. 94.

[36] Thornton, *The Imperial Idea,* p. 111.

most concerned citizens shared. To ties of national and self-interest were added over the years personal, cultural, and religious connections that struck deeply into both societies. If the empire was anything large and noble it was India, and to have abandoned the country in the face of danger would, in the minds of most Englishmen, have been a sin as well as a blunder. As one survey of strategic problems put it in 1892, "We have undertaken the political and moral education of the peoples which inhabit that peninsula, and we have therefore implicitly assumed the duty of guarding our work against interruption. We have made ourselves responsible not merely for the Government, but also for the peace of India." [37]

In the end all this could be reduced to a simple equation that must have been especially comforting in the face of the emergence of gigantic powers possessing vast human and natural resources. With India, Britain could hold her place in the world against all comers; without India the future was bleak indeed. Curzon summed the situation up in a letter to Arthur Balfour in 1901: "As long as we rule India we are the greatest power in the world. If we lose it we shall drop straight away to a third rate power." [38]

Virtual Limits on Britain's Military Power

During the latter part of the nineteenth century the British Indian Army consisted of around 220,000 men, of whom approximately one-third were British. [39] As substantial as these figures were in absolute terms, they seemed paltry when compared with the numbers of men that Russia might be able to mobilize and transport via its new railroads for a thrust into Afghanistan. In 1897 the Russians had a regular army of over one million men, with an additional three million held in reserve. [40] By the turn of the century it seemed apparent that if India's borders were to be defended against an all-out attack, the British would have to find some means of increasing the strength of their forces in central Asia, if possible before, but if necessary immediately after, an invasion had begun.

One way of improving the local military balance would have been to draw on the vast pool of available Indian manpower, filling out the army with an even larger contingent of native troops. The obvious objection to any such scheme was that Britain was an oc-

[37] Dilke and Wilkinson, *Imperial Defence*, p. 97.
[38] M. Howard, *The Continental Commitment*, p. 14.
[39] In 1892 there were 73,000 British and 145,000 native soldiers (Dilke and Wilkinson, *Imperial Defence*, p. 182). In 1901 the figures were 75,000 British and 153,000 Indian troops (PRO, Cab. 6/1/1D).
[40] M. Howard, "The Armed Forces," in Hinsley, ed., *The New Cambridge Modern History* 11:217.

cupying, imperial power that, however noble its aims, had still to be extremely cautious about losing control of its subjects. After the Great Mutiny of 1857 (which had been led by sepoys, British-trained and -equipped soldiers) the British were never free from the nightmare of another bloody uprising.[41] In 1901, over half the total strength of the army in India was considered essential for the maintenance of internal order.[42] An expansion of native forces could only be considered if enough new European troops were available to preserve a satisfactory ratio of "white" to "black" faces.

The other possible source of men was of course the mother country itself. Prior to the outbreak of the Boer War, Britain had roughly 230,000 men under arms (including 74,000 in India).[43] With a population approaching forty million this was hardly a significant fraction. On paper, at least, Great Britain had the capacity to field a far larger army than it had thus far chosen to deploy. That the nation did not do so is an indication of the existence of virtual as opposed to absolute limits on its capabilities. As was the case with financial resources, British statesmen felt themselves confronted by barriers to the generation of national power that were not physically impassable but that could be crossed only at enormous political, economic, and social cost.

Expanding the size of the British army in peacetime would have required either a considerable and costly increase in the monetary incentives for enlistment or the imposition of some form of conscription. Given that the expense of even a slow-growing establishment had gone up disproportionately in the last decades of the century, the probability of the first policy being adopted in peacetime was miniscule. On the other hand the idea of any kind of compulsory service was so unpopular that the British government was unwilling to adopt it even for two years after the outbreak of World War I.[44]

The reasons for this resistance to conscription were many and deep-seated. Service in the army, even when voluntary, had seldom been highly regarded. As the former secretary of state for war H. O. Arnold-Forster explained in 1906, "It is a matter of universal knowledge that, for many generations, the enlistment of a young

[41] The effects of this fear on British planning for a war against Russia will be considered below. For a gorily detailed account of the events of 1857 see Hibbert, *The Great Mutiny.*

[42] Of the 231,000 men in India during that year, 129,000 were stationed at garrisons around the country desig-

nated for use in preserving internal security and were thus unavailable for defensive operations against an external attacker (PRO, Cab. 6/1/1D).

[43] Dunlop, *The Development of the British Army, 1899–1914,* p. 40.

[44] Barnett, *Britain and Her Army, 1509–1970,* p. 397.

man in the Army was looked upon in nearly every home in the country as a sorrow and a disgrace."[45] Choosing to sign up for duty in which one was likely to be "hardly treated, ill-remunerated and often abominably neglected"[46] was bad enough; being forced into such a life as an act of government policy was even worse.

The prospect of maintaining a large standing army on home territory was one that traditionally filled many Englishmen with fear and suspicion. In the first place, such a force meant high levels of taxation, even in peacetime. At the close of the eighteenth century the use of conscription by the French revolutionaries caused "universal military service, an ancient English tradition and obligation [to appear] as an aspect of Jacobin democracy or Napoleonic tyranny."[47] Conversely, within a few years a substantial home army had come to be seen as a potential tool of the aristocracy in reasserting its slowly diminishing authority at the expense of the new middle classes. By the middle of the nineteenth century the growth of a liberal, laissez-faire ideology rendered the notion of enforced service to the state unacceptable to most British citizens, regardless of the nature of that service or of its purpose. After 1871 all the major European countries as well as Japan adopted some form of compulsory service,[48] but by the same time, according to Correlli Barnett, a "long historical process had . . . made conscription unthinkable in Britain."[49]

Without conscription or a drastically increased budget, the size of the army was destined to remain roughly fixed or, if it grew, to do so at a relatively slow pace. Assuming that this was the case, Britain's military planners could only hope to strengthen their position in India by shifting troops from other parts of the world. This might have been appealing in theory to those who were most concerned over the vulnerability of India, and, if war had broken out there, it might even have been possible. In peacetime, however, the wholesale reallocation of forces across the globe would have been an extraordinarily difficult task.

Under the terms of a memorandum issued by Secretary of State for War Edward Stanhope in 1891 the British army was charged with the completion of five missions.[50] It had, first of all, to provide

[45] Arnold-Forster, *The Army in 1906,* p. 145.
   [46] Ibid.
   [47] Barnett, *Britain and Her Army,* p. 257.
   [48] Bond, *War and European Society,* *1870–1970,* p. 32.
   [49] Barnett, *Britain and Her Army,* p. 295.
   [50] On the origins of this document see Beckett, "Edward Stanhope at the War Office, 1887–92," pp. 278–307.

"effective support of the civil power" in the United Kingdom; second, to supply forces for India; third, "to find garrisons for all . . . fortresses and coaling stations, at home and abroad"; fourth, "after providing for these requirements," to mobilize regular and auxiliary forces for the defense of the home islands; and, finally, "subject to the foregoing considerations and to their financial obligations, to aim at being able, in case of necessity, to send abroad two complete Army Corps, with Cavalry Division and Line of Communication."[51]

In order to carry out its many duties the regular British army was organized into pairs of "linked battalions." At any given moment half of these were supposed to be based at home while the others served in India or elsewhere in the empire. Periodically, battalions were to be rotated between the British Isles and assignment overseas, thereby maintaining a balance between center and periphery.[52] In practice, by the 1880s the demands of defending an expanding empire had forced the deployment of a disproportionate number of battalions outside Great Britain[53] (see Table 5-1 at the end of this chapter). Supplementing its regular units at home, the army was able to draw in a crisis on a rather motley collection of auxiliary forces, including the militia, yeomanry, and volunteers.[54] Men serving in the auxiliaries could not be compelled to serve overseas, although they could volunteer to do so.

As big a problem as India might be, therefore, Britain's military planners did not have the luxury of being able to concentrate on it alone. Reinforcing the Indian Army would have meant reducing the level of defense in other colonies (and, in particular, Egypt and South Africa) or drawing down the regular forces available to protect Great Britain against the possibility of invasion. The first move would have aroused opposition from colonial governments that were reluctant to shoulder an even greater portion of the burden of defending their own territory. The second, especially if undertaken at a time of worsening relations with one or more Conti-

[51] Reprinted in Dunlop, *Development of the British Army*, p. 307.

[52] The system of linked battalions had been established under Edward Cardwell, secretary of state for war under Gladstone between 1868 and 1874. The "Cardwell reforms" of that period were intended to improve home defense while lowering military costs by recalling some units and forcing the

colonies to assume more of the burden of their own defense. See Cole and Priestley, *An Outline of British Military History, 1660–1936*, pp. 217–18.

[53] Barnett, *Britain and Her Army*, p. 334.

[54] For a discussion of these forces prior to the outbreak of the Boer War see Dunlop, *Development of the British Army*, pp. 42–66.

nental powers, risked alarming the British public and perhaps (depending on the performance of the navy) even exposing the home islands to sudden attack.

Crisis
Parameters, 1884–1893

The problem of defending India was not one that emerged new and freshly formed after the turn of the century. In fact, to a considerable degree, the terms in which the whole question was discussed after 1900 were set some fifteen years before, following the Russian occupation of the city of Merv. The assumptions formulated in the wake of that traumatic event continued to shape official thinking for at least the next two decades.

With the approach of Russian forces, the precise location of Afghanistan's northern borders became an issue of importance to the great powers and, after several unsuccessful efforts, an Anglo-Russian agreement delimiting the boundary between Russian and Afghan Turkistan was signed in 1887.[55] Despite all the effort that had gone into obtaining it, no one, least of all the British, expected the treaty to last for very long. That summer Lieutenant General Brackenbury, military member of the Viceroy's Council, wrote to the Foreign Office in London to suggest that the Government of India undertake a comprehensive study of its military needs in the light of a possible future Russian advance.[56]

The probability of such an event and the likelihood of its success were both rated extremely high. One officer had warned early in 1887 that England was "powerless to prevent the occupation by Russia of Herat, Afghan Turkestan and Badakshan," the three northernmost provinces of the country that together accounted for about one-third of its territory.[57] The Indian Mobilization Committee, which considered the problem at Brackenbury's request, reached a similar conclusion. If they were ordered to do so Russian

---

[55] Morgan, *Anglo-Russian Rivalry,* p. 199.

[56] Greaves, *Persia and the Defence of India,* p. 39. The viceroy was the embodiment of British power in India. He ruled with authority delegated to him by the Crown (during most of the period of this study, from 1898 to 1905, the post was held by Lord George Curzon) and reported directly to the secretary of state for India (Lord George Hamilton from 1895 to 1903

and St. John Broderick between 1903 and 1905). The commander in chief of British forces in India was Frederick Roberts from 1885 to 1893 and Lord Kitchener between 1902 and 1909.

[57] Memo by Lt. Col. P. J. Maitland, assistant quartermaster general (AQMG) at Simla, March 1887, summarized in PRO, Cab. 3/1/1A, app. 2, "Short Summary of Official Decisions, Opinions, Proposals, &c., Relative to the Defence of India," p. 58.

forces could occupy the city of Herat and take up positions along a line running west to east across the northern part of the country. From here, after a period of consolidation, they would strike out along two axes, one directed at Kabul in the northeast, the other toward Kandahar to the southwest.[58]

Because of the terrain and the considerable distances involved, British forces could not hope to prevent the Russians from achieving their initial objectives. Early advances were therefore conceded to the invader. The question remaining was whether, and if so where, the czarist hordes should be opposed before they descended onto the plains of northern India. In the view of the Mobilization Committee there were "three lines of policy open to England in the face" of Russian incursions into Afghanistan:

I. A policy of inaction: to await, within the limits of our present frontier, the development of events.

II. To acquiesce in the occupation of Herat and Afghan Turkestan by Russia without declaring war, making such forward movements ourselves as may seem desireable for the safety of India.

III. To insist upon the inviolability of Afghanistan, and to declare any infringement by Russia of her boundaries as now laid down a *casus belli*.[59]

The first option was "rigorously vetoed, on both strategic and political grounds" as "altogether too dangerous to be seriously considered."[60] Precisely why this should be so was not spelled out in detail. Presumably, once they had conquered all of Afghanistan the Russians would be able to advance farther when the moment suited them, secure in the meantime behind a wall of mountains.

Another objection to complete inaction was similar to that raised against the second option. The fact of passivity, or even its appearance as manifested in an unwillingness to declare war, would provoke "growing excitement and unrest . . . throughout India."[61] The British feared that if they showed any sign of weakness they would lose their empire through internal upheaval, regardless of what the Russians did upon entering Afghanistan. To some, indeed, the danger of rebellion was more worrisome and more real than the prospect of invasion. As Lord Kimberly put it at the time of the Merv crisis, "I do not . . . at all fear a Russian invasion or

[58] Ibid., memorandum by Indian Mobilization Committee.
[59] Ibid.

[60] Ibid.
[61] Ibid., p. 59.

direct attack upon Herat. The danger will take another form, which I may term 'sap and mine.' "[62]

Fear that Britain's grip on its most prized possession might be tenuous went back thirty years to the Great Mutiny.[63] The sepoy uprising of 1857 had, as previously noted, a lasting impact on the distribution and composition of the Indian Army. More generally it produced a lingering doubt as to whether the Englishman was as welcome in the East as he preferred to imagine. To this not un-realistic concern was added in the latter part of the century a po-tent dash of social Darwinism. The resultant mixture was heady, unsettling stuff.[64]

In 1892 Wilkinson and Dilke explained the situation to their au-dience in terms that would have been familiar to anyone privy to contemporary Government discussions.

> The supremacy of the English rests only to a limited ex-tent upon their own superior force. . . . To a great extent our ascendancy is "moral" resting, that is, upon charac-ter and self-confidence. To this confidence the natives bow. . . . For a century the Englishman has behaved in India as a demi-god. He accounts himself a superior being . . . and the majority of the inhabitants take him at his own valuation. Any weakening of this confidence in the minds of the English or of the Indians would be dan-gerous. . . . The report has gone forth in India that there is another race, the Russian, which faces British audacity with an audacity of its own. If this be true, the English are not the only demi-gods, and for the Indian the test of its truth is rather the behaviour of the British whom he can observe than of the Russians whom he cannot. If he sees that his Englishmen are uneasy, he may interpret it as a sign of their coming doom. He will wait until their time is up, when he will accept new and stronger masters, and per-haps hasten to put himself on the side of the coming race.[65]

[62] Greaves, *Persia and the Defence of India*, p. 16.

[63] The stunning impact of that event may be gauged by the fact that over five hundred books were published on the subject between 1857 and 1862 (Hyam, *Britain's Imperial Century, 1815–1914: A Study of Empire and Expansion*, p. 73).

[64] Hyam reports that, by the begin-ning of the twentieth century, British fears had grown to outlandish propor-tions. In 1903 the viceroy Lord Curzon would not permit "Onward Christian Soldiers" to be sung at a public cere-mony "because it contained the lines 'Crowns and Thrones may perish, Kingdoms rise and wane" (ibid., p. 95).

[65] Dilke and Wilkinson, *Imperial De-fence*, pp. 101–103.

There could be no surer test of the two "races" than would occur after Russia's advance forces had passed into Afghanistan. If it was to retain its aura of omnipotence, Britain would have to go over to the offensive as quickly as possible, and this meant moving visibly and decisively against the invader rather than waiting for him to reach India's frontiers. As Lord Roberts had put it in 1888: "A defensive attitude in India would undoubtedly lead to very grave internal troubles; it would destroy the confidence of the native army and civil population, and undermine our prestige and supremacy in the East."[66]

In Roberts's mind the only question was whether "a vigorous offensive through Afghanistan" would be accompanied by operations elsewhere, such as the Black Sea or the Persian Gulf. Regardless of what happened in those theaters it was essential that British forces move forward across the Indian frontier and toward Russian positions. In early discussions of the problem Roberts had urged the desirability of a single line of advance.[67] Soon, however, military planners were considering more ambitious schemes. A study on "War with Russia," circulated in August 1889, declared that "Russia must never be allowed to occupy Cabul and Candahar. An advance of Russia to Herat and into Afghan Turkestan must be met . . . by a corresponding advance on our part to Candahar and Jellalabad, and possibly Ghazni."[68] By 1891 Roberts was arguing that the appropriate British response to a Russian first move would be the establishment of a line from Kabul to Kandahar.[69] This view seems to have been widely accepted by the early 1890s,[70] and it would dominate all subsequent discussions of the Indian defense problem.

However desirable Kabul and Kandahar may have been as defensive positions to British planners, they were still the cities of a foreign, nonallied country with a long history of independence. There was therefore considerable uncertainty as to the likely attitude of the fierce tribesmen on whose home terrain the great powers would be fighting. The British had suffered more than their

---

[66] Roberts memo, 8/88, in PRO, Cab. 3/1/1A, p. 60.

[67] Ibid., p. 61.

[68] Memorandum by Lieutenant General Brackenbury and Major General Newmarch, 8/89, in PRO, Cab. 3/1/1A, p. 61.

[69] In that year Roberts wrote, "I regard it as impossible to defend India in the event of a conflict with Russia except by the occupation of the strategic front stretching from Kabul to Kandahar" (PRO, Cab. 6/1/7D, p. 9).

[70] Dilke and Wilkinson refer to the desirability of holding "the Kabul-Kandahar line" in their 1892 survey of imperial defense problems (Dilke and Wilkinson, *Imperial Defence*, p. 171).

share of trouble from Afghan warriors in the past and had learned to respect their skill and tenacity. If the local tribes chose to oppose the northern invader and to accept Britain as an ally, the prospects for preserving a buffer zone would be greatly improved. Given the bad blood and mistrust caused by decades of sporadic fighting, however, there could be no guarantee that the Afghans would not concentrate first on their old familiar foe. Roberts, who had led British forces during the Second Afghan War (1878–1880), feared that local hostility would severely hurt any chance that might exist for ousting the Russians.[71] Nevertheless, if India was to be preserved, the counteroffensive would have to go forward, even if it meant fighting tribesmen to get to the real enemy.

Ten years before it would be subjected to truly intense scrutiny, the problem of defending the Raj had thus been boiled down to an exercise in logistics. Strategic questions had been effectively resolved or at least removed from the realm of active contention. At the first sign of aggression Britain would take the Kabul-Kandahar line and prepare to push the Russians back across their borders. The only difficulty that remained was establishing the number of men needed to achieve this end. It was on this seemingly straightforward issue that the debate over Britain's land power would come eventually to turn.

In 1886 the Indian Government had reported that it was studying plans for the mobilization of its two army corps (composed of four infantry battalions and five cavalry brigades) plus a reserve division for use in Afghanistan. According to a later report to the CID, "When this plan reached Home it was found that it depended for its completion upon the assumption that, on the outbreak of war, reinforcements and drafts [to replace casualties from existing units] amounting in all to 700 officers and 13,000 men would be furnished."[72]

One year later the Indian Mobilization Committee drew up a plan of campaign that called for the occupation of Kabul and Kandahar and for a subsequent push from the latter toward the presumed Russian stronghold of Herat. Ninety thousand men would be needed along the main axis, 60,000 for the attack on Herat and for the maintenance of communications from there to Kandahar, and 30,000 in Kandahar itself. An additional 30,000

[71] In 1888 Roberts warned that if "the Afghans and frontier tribes [are] against us . . . any forward movement beyond the Helmud [River] would be well-nigh impossible" (memorandum of 8/88 in PRO, Cab. 3/1/1A, p. 61).

[72] PRO, Cab. 6/3/91D, "Successive Demands for Reinforcements by the Government of India," General Staff, 3/26/06, p. 1.

would be deployed on the Jellalabad-Kabul line for a total force of 120,000 men "of whom half would be British, 30,000 being furnished by the Indian garrison and 30,000 being sent from England."[73]

Such easy assumptions of assistance worried the authorities in London. Early in 1888 the secretary of state for war wrote the Indian Government that a promise of reinforcements might lead to unrealistic expectations and unsound planning. "He therefore considered that any scheme for mobilization of the Army in India should be based upon the actual resources of that Army alone."[74] One year later this position was strengthened in a study endorsed by the secretary that declared that "the present army of India is sufficient for all the requirements of the present time." The Government of India, in the words of Generals Brackenbury and Newmarch, "should clearly understand that for any operations short of actual invasion of her frontiers by Russia it must rely entirely upon Indian resources, and that no reserve for India beyond the drafts necessary to complete the British units to . . . established strength is maintained in this country."[75]

In the event of an actual invasion India could depend "upon every possible assistance," but beyond this general reassurance "His Majesty's Government cannot be expected to give any formal pledge for the supply of a definite number of troops at any particular time or for any specific operation."[76] This was due in part to the problems that would attend any effort to reinforce India from England. Early in 1889 a joint conference of army, navy, and India Office officials had concluded that if Britain was at war with a major naval power no reinforcements could be sent to India without strong escort "until the British Navy had cleared the seas."[77]

Any promise of reinforcements was also opposed by Lord Wolseley, a leading military figure and a future commander in chief of the army.[78] "In the event of any internal excitement [India] could count upon the assistance of all our army," Wolseley wrote in August 1889, but "in the event of a war with Russia she can look for no reinforcement from home as long as the war lasts."[79]

---

[73] PRO, Cab. 3/1/1A, p. 59.
[74] PRO, Cab. 6/3/91D, p. 1.
[75] PRO, Cab. 3/1/1A, p. 64.
[76] Ibid.
[77] PRO, Cab. 6/3/91D, p. 1.
[78] The commander in chief was traditionally the highest ranking officer in the British military system. In 1900

Roberts replaced Wolseley as commander in chief. The decision was made to abolish the position during the period of organizational reform that followed the Boer War, but Balfour asked Roberts to serve out his five-year term.
[79] PRO, Cab. 3/1/1A, p. 64.

London might be unwilling to commit more forces to central Asia, but it had no alternative to the policy of rapid counteroffensive. If that policy was to be carried out, it was becoming increasingly obvious that *some* reinforcements would be required. In June 1891 Roberts advised that "to hold the Cabul-Candahar alignment, without attempting actively offensive operations beyond the Hindu Kush [mountain range]," would require 48,000 British troops and 56,000 Indians. Forty thousand British and 80,000 Indian soldiers would have to be left behind to preserve internal security. Because the number of "white" soldiers in India was only 70,000, "a reinforcement of 18,000 British troops would be required, and a reserve of 12,000 more. Also drafts to keep up to strength the 100,000 British troops which would then be serving in India would then be required."[80] Roberts went on to recommend that the number of native troops be increased by at least 50,000 and that the Government of India be authorized to build railroads across the Afghan frontier, even before hostilities with Russia got under way (and, presumably, regardless of the attitude of the Afghan government).[81] But the most important and lasting feature of Roberts's memo was the specification of a figure for reinforcements. When his paper was forwarded to London in September he wrote, "at the very least 30,000 British troops would be necessary on war becoming imminent."[82]

The Home Government was understandably anxious to throw cold water on Roberts's schemes. In March 1892, a number of "resolutions" were transmitted to the Government of India, including a repeated warning that no reserve for its use was being retained in Britain. As a result, London advised, "no forward line of policy should be laid down in India which contemplates the necessity of reinforcements from England for its accomplishment."[83] To this the "Anglo-Indians" replied by reiterating the urgent need for a quick counteroffensive into southern Afghanistan. Kabul and Kandahar could be taken and held temporarily *provided* that the local Afghan tribesmen were cooperative. But the whole undertaking would be so dangerous that Roberts was reportedly unwilling to risk it "unless he were reassured that reinforcements to the extent of at least 30,000 British troops would be sent to India at the very earliest opportunity."[84]

Within a year the War Office was advising the Indian Govern-

[80] Ibid., p. 65.
[81] Ibid.
[82] Quoted in PRO, Cab. 6/1/31D, "War Office Comments on Curzon and Kitchener Memorandum," 11/11/03, p. 2.
[83] Ibid., p. 66.
[84] Ibid., p. 67.

ment that if it wished to occupy southern Afghanistan it would have to maintain sufficient troops to do so on its own. Delhi responded that, under existing financial and political conditions, the peacetime strength of the British Indian Army would have to remain fixed. With this exchange the discussion reached an impasse and, as a later official history would put it, for the time being "the matter was allowed to rest."[85]

War and Rumors of War, 1900

From 1893 until 1900 the lack of any spectacular Russian advance in central Asia permitted the Indian question to lie unattended and unresolved. A War Office intelligence report written in 1895 concluded that the first five years of the decade had been a time of "consolidation and natural development" during which Russia, "fully conscious of the weak points of her position, . . . confined herself to developing it and securing herself against contingencies in all directions before making any decided step in advance." In the opinion of military analysts, "the centre of gravity of Russian interest" appeared "to have shifted more and more from Central Asia to the Far East."[86] The political authorities were also relatively sanguine, so much so that in 1897 the secretary of state for India wrote that "the danger of a direct attack by Russia upon India yearly lessens, as Russia has other and larger fish to fry."[87]

While anxiety about India diminished during the 1890s, worries about the overall military challenge confronting the empire tended to grow. This was due in part to the fact that the empire itself had expanded substantially during the last quarter of the century while the size of Britain's ground forces remained more or less constant. Since 1870 the army had been fixed at 141 battalions with half originally intended for use overseas.[88] As the territory under London's formal control grew even larger, however, the balanced system of "linked battalions" broke down, and an increasingly sizable fraction of active service units was deployed away from home. By 1897 a total of 77 battalions were on duty in India and various colonial outposts, and only 64 were stationed in the British Isles.[89]

[85] PRO, Cab. 6/3/91D, p. 2.
[86] An important piece of evidence supporting this contention was that the size of Russia's forces deployed in eastern Siberia had increased by 50 percent from 1890 to 1895, while those stationed in central Asia remained constant in number (PRO, WO 33/56/A428, "Russian Advances in Asia,

1890–1895," Captain W. A. Macbean, Intelligence Division, 1895).
[87] Alder, *British India's Northern Frontier*, p. 286.
[88] PRO, Cab. 37/45/42, "Outlines of Army Proposals," Lansdowne, 12/2/97, p. 5.
[89] Ibid., p. 10.

The growing imbalance between home and colonial defense forces raised questions about Britain's security but also about its ability to supply reinforcements to distant outposts in time of need. Both in and out of government there were those who warned that the army was simply too small and too poorly organized to cope with its growing responsibilities. As one writer put it in the wake of the German and American war scares of 1896:

> I think that no one can compare the growth . . . of the Empire, and . . . the growth of the army . . . and say that one has kept pace with the other, or that, in the light of our recent experiences, 300,000 men is a sufficient British regular force for the defence of an Empire comprising one fifth of the surface of the land portion of the globe and one quarter of its estimated population.[90]

The author of this statement, Lieutenant Colonel John Adye, favored an expansion of the reserves in order to avoid the evils of conscription.[91] At around the same time, the commander in chief of the army, Lord Wolseley, was privately pressing Lord Lansdowne (then the secretary of state for war) to add enough regular units to the home army to restore the principle of linkage.[92] Largely for economic reasons, Lansdowne at first resisted any plan that would have enlarged the standing army, but by the end of 1897 he too was forced to acknowledge that "we are unquestionably finding great and increasing difficulty in providing for the whole of the requirements which we have to meet."[93] In January 1898 the secretary proposed to add ten battalions of infantry to the home defense force (a figure two less than that favored by Wolseley), but, under pressure from the Exchequer, Lansdowne agreed to whittle the final number down to six.[94]

Nearly two years before the Boer War began, therefore, serious questions had been raised about the size and efficiency of Britain's armed forces. Nevertheless, when it arrived, the war in South Africa exposed problems that exceeded the imaginings of even the most pessimistic observers. Everything from high-quality strategic planning to adequate field medical care was revealed to be in desperately short supply. Casualties soared to levels seldom seen since

[90] Adye, "Has Our Army Grown," p. 1018.

[91] Ibid., p. 1024.

[92] PRO, Cab. 37/42/32, "Proposed Increase in Army Strength," Lansdowne, 7/10/96, p. 2.

[93] PRO, Cab. 37/45/43, "Outlines of Army Proposals," Lansdowne, 12/15/97, p. 10.

[94] PRO, Cab. 37/46/13, "Notes on Proposals Made by the Chancellor of the Exchequer," Lansdowne, 1/26/98.

the Great Mutiny,[95] and, in order to provide sufficient manpower with which to win the war, the entire British military system was stretched to very near its breaking point. At the onset of hostilities 70,000 regular troops were dispatched to South Africa; by the end of the conflict 180,000 more army regulars (from home and overseas garrisons), 100,000 militiamen, and 15,000 volunteers from England had joined in the fighting, but even this considerable force was not capable on its own of achieving victory. Tens of thousands of colonial volunteers had to be brought in from around the empire before the Boers could be considered completely pacified.[96]

At the most general level the Boer War reduced whatever confidence thoughtful Englishmen may have had in the capabilities of their army and strengthened the hand of those who had been calling for major reforms. More particularly, the war aroused doubts about Britain's ability to mobilize and transport a major expeditionary force while retaining adequate strength at home and in the colonies. As serious as it had been before, this was a problem that was actually worse at the close of the conflict than at its beginning, because of the need to station a large, new peacetime garrison in South Africa.[97]

Whether they favored conscription or a bigger standing professional army or an enlarged reserve, military analysts were now in agreement on one thing: Britain's ground power was inadequate to its needs. As George Clarke, the future secretary of the Committee of Imperial Defence, explained at the beginning of 1900: "We have received a plain warning which we dare not disregard. The responsibilities of the Empire have been allowed to outrun its military strength. The needs of Imperial defence have not been accurately estimated."[98] James Knowles, editor of the journal *The Nineteenth Century,* cast the situation in more vivid terms. Britain, he wrote, had been brought face to face "with a great and grave alternative which has been long approaching . . . and which cannot now be further evaded or ignored. We must either contract the boundaries of our Empire or we must expand our military forces."[99]

This larger strategic question could not be addressed until the war had been brought to a successful conclusion. In the meantime, both indirectly and directly the struggle for South Africa helped to revive the vexing question of Indian defense. The defeats of "Black

[95] Pakenham, *The Boer War,* p. 258.
[96] Cohen, "Systems of Military Service: The Dilemmas of a Liberal-Democratic World Power," p. 102.
[97] See Low, "The Military Weakness of England and the Militia Ballot," p. 17.
[98] Clarke, "The Defence of the Empire and the Militia Ballot," p. 7.
[99] Ibid., p. 1.

Week" in mid-December of 1899 made it difficult to simply assume that British forces would perform adequately in combat. Certainly any thought that an Englishman was worth four Russians or three Frenchmen (or even two Dutch settlers) had now to be completely discarded. In the wake of the Boer War *all* possible sites of military confrontation became potential scenes of disaster, and in central Asia most of all the prospect of even temporary setbacks was deeply disturbing. More immediately, the struggle against the Boers forced a weakening in the Indian and home garrisons while simultaneously antagonizing Russia, France, and Germany. There seemed a real possibility that Britain's enemies would take advantage of its preoccupation and relative weakness on the ground to strike either at the British Isles or, more likely, at India.

According to a subsequent official review of the situation,

> during the winter of 1899–1900, owing to the large numbers of our forces absent in South Africa, it appeared not unlikely that advantage might be taken by Russia of our difficulties, to make a forward move in Central Asia either in the direction of Persia or Afghanistan, and reports and rumours were rife as to large forces being despatched to Transcaspia.[100]

In early February there were intelligence reports indicating that Russian troops had begun once again to advance toward the Afghan frontier.[101] The long-awaited descent on India seemed about to start.

First Steps, 1900–1902

From the beginning of 1900 to the close of 1902 India moved steadily toward center stage in the minds of Britain's strategic planners, gradually forcing South Africa back into its more customary, secondary role. At the end of another year the defense of India had eclipsed every other possible military problem and had emerged as the challenge around which all preparations for ground warfare would have to turn. Indeed, by the beginning of 1904 the reorganization of Britain's entire army had come to depend on some agreement as to the needs of the eastern empire. By this time the threat to Indian security and the difficulties involved in meeting it appeared much larger than they had ever seemed in the past. This

---

[100] PRO, Cab. 6/1/1D, p. 3.
[101] J. Gooch, *The Plans of War: The General Staff and British Military Strategy,* *1900–1916,* p. 198. This study contains an excellent chapter on the Indian defense question.

was due in part to objective indications of danger, in particular, the further extension of Russia's strategic rail network. But the problem also seems to have expanded under examination; like Topsy, it "grew and grew" until it was on the verge of achieving truly frightening dimensions.

Two weeks after receiving reports of Russian troop movements, the secretary of state for India cabled Delhi requesting that complete plans for a possible war be prepared without delay.[102] Ignoring for the moment the accumulated wisdom of all its experts, London ordered that the new war plans were to begin with the assumption that British forces would stay on the defensive, huddling south and east of the Indian frontier rather than advancing directly into Afghanistan.[103] The Government of India responded that it considered the "proper defensive line for India to lie, not on her own border, but beyond it" at Kabul and Kandahar. Reaching these objectives would require active British support.[104] To indicate how much assistance would be needed, the viceroy forwarded a report by his Mobilization Committee that began roughly where Roberts had left off in the 1890s, with a plea for 30,000 reinforcements. These men were to be dispatched from England as soon as the Indian Army mobilized. In addition, should a war become protracted, the committee now believed that 70,000 *more* men would have to be sent out from home and that the sufficiency of even this figure "would depend upon the numbers which Russia could put in the field."[105]

That the viceroy's committee should have settled on a requirement for 30,000 immediate reinforcements seems to have been as much the result of bureaucratic reflex as any kind of sophisticated assessment. Faced with a familiar, if somewhat dusty, problem, the Indian Government reached into its files and pulled out a response that had been rather loosely calculated under very different circumstances almost a decade before. Why the second figure was chosen is less clear, although it did happen to be roughly the size of the expeditionary force mandated in the Stanhope memorandum of 1891. The 30,000/70,000 estimate preceded any real attempt to gauge the size of the Russian threat, but, once it had surfaced, it became an irreducible fraction from which all subsequent calculations proceeded.

In July 1900, the secretary of state for India requested that Delhi check its figures, emphasizing "that he had asked for a scheme of a

[102] PRO, Cab. 6/1/1D, p. 3.
[103] PRO, Cab. 6/3/91D, p. 2.
[104] PRO, Cab. 6/1/1D, p. 4.
[105] PRO, Cab. 6/3/91D, p. 2.

purely defensive nature, and that he had intended that scheme to be based solely on the available resources of India."[106] Curzon's response to this plea must have come as something of a shock: the 100,000-man figure arrived at by his staff was a general, all-purpose estimate *regardless* of "whether a purely defensive or offensive-defensive policy were adopted." Independent of the threat or the strategy chosen to counter it, "India would need a first reinforcement of 30,000 men, another 70,000 in the event of prolonged hostilities, and possibly more to follow."[107] If such essential reinforcements were not forthcoming, the viceroy's telegram concluded, "the only alternative we can see is that India must remain without the means of defending the Indian Empire."[108]

This was strong stuff, even for a man with Curzon's habitual tendency to overstate his case. Over time, however, it would have its intended effect. By the beginning of 1901 the India Office in London was prepared to concede that some number of reinforcements would be necessary in the event of war, but it asked the viceroy's staff to assume that any outside troops would take an indefinitely long time to reach the battlefield. The Indian Government's reply was both obvious and exasperating. If prompt reinforcements could not be relied upon, then the size of the Indian Army would have to be increased, and the cost of such an expansion (naturally) "should be borne largely, if not wholly, by the Imperial exchequer."[109]

Until this point the authorities in London seem to have relied almost exclusively on the analyses of their Indian counterparts. As the South African war drew to a close and Delhi's demands continued unabated, however, the British began to make a more independent examination of their military problems, both in India and across the empire. In August 1901 Lieutenant Colonel Altham submitted his report on the possibility of a war against both France and Russia. Unlike some army officers who worried most about home defense (and who saw in that mission a way for their service to hold its own against the navy), Altham had little fear that the United Kingdom could be invaded. In fact, he regarded the army's concern with insular security as a "radical defect" that encouraged a "flagrant neglect of vital factors, such as the defence of India and Egypt and the power of striking effective blows at the enemy."[110] As long as the navy did its job, Altham concluded,

[106] Ibid.
[107] Ibid.
[108] Quoted in PRO, Cab. 6/1/31D, "War Office Comments on a Memo by Curzon and Kitchener," War Office, 11/11/03, p. 2.
[109] PRO, Cab. 6/1/1D, p. 6.
[110] PRO, Cab. 3/1/1A, p. 49.

the British Empire is impervious to the great land forces of continental nations except in one point—India. Here alone can a fatal blow be dealt us. The loss of India by conquest would be a death blow to our prosperity, prestige, and power. The damaging effects of even a near approach by hostile forces would be incalculable. . . . Second only to the security of the United Kingdom itself, comes the question of the defence of India.[111]

Largely because of the extension of rail lines, India could not be defended by any sort of indirect counterattack through the Crimea, Persia, or the Far East.[112] The full brunt of a Russian attack, as many as 60,000 men within one month of the initiation of hostilities and 200,000 within four months, along with a possible force of 100,000 hostile Afghans, would have to be met head-on.[113] Such a prospect, Altham rightly observed, had "never been fully faced by the home government."[114] As a step toward correcting this oversight he urged the acceptance of two of the Indian Government's most crucial assertions. If war began it was essential that a defensive line be established from Kabul to Kandahar. To ensure that this could be done even before the acquisition of sea control, the number of British troops in India should be increased immediately by the 30,000 men who had been requested as a first reinforcement. Delhi (of course) would pick up the bill.[115]

Altham accepted the Indian Government's assessment of its initial needs in wartime while differing with its judgment as to how these were to be met. On the question of the requirements for a protracted struggle in Afghanistan there was even more accord. The expansion of the "normal British garrison" in India was only a first step toward adequate readiness. "It is therefore recommended," Altham wrote, "that the organization of the forces of the Empire should be such as to permit the despatch to India of two additional Army Corps as soon after the outbreak of war as we attain sea command."[116] The size of such a force was equal to the second half of Delhi's magic fraction, around 70,000 men.

At approximately the same time as Altham was preparing his overview of imperial defense, a special interdepartmental com-

[111] Ibid., p. 51.
[112] Altham believed that "there [could] be no doubt that it was with the idea of some such action that the decision was come to not to reinforce the Indian garrison," which was presumably to "stand on the defensive" (ibid., p. 57).
[113] Ibid., p. 25.
[114] Ibid., p. 28.
[115] Ibid.
[116] Ibid., pp. 28–29.

mittee was beginning work in London on a narrower study of the Indian question.[117] The very existence of such a body reflected the growing belief that, as Arthur Balfour put it in a letter to Lansdowne, "the weakest spot in the Empire is probably the Indian frontier. In a war with Russia our military resources would be strained to their utmost to protect it." The situation was made worse by the fact that "the progress of events" (presumably the expansion of central Asian railways) tended to strengthen "the position of Russia for aggressive purposes in this part of the world," while "no corresponding gain is possible on the side of defence." War might not be as imminent as it had seemed two years before, but, if it came, Balfour was convinced that "a quarrel with Russia anywhere or about anything, means the invasion of India."[118]

In December 1901 the special committee presented its secret report. After allowing for the forces needed to ensure internal tranquility (129,000 regulars plus 13,000 Imperial Service troops) and those which would be unavailable due to the high incidence of various tropical diseases (15,000), it was assumed that there would be some 74,000 men ready for offensive operations in Afghanistan. Such operations would have to be quick and successful because, the committee warned, "any check to our arms, or any long pause, after offensive action had once begun, would tend to excite Native society."[119]

Against 32,000 British and 42,000 native troops the Russians could mobilize immediately 84,000 men, of whom 48,000 would be available for the initial offensive. Within a month 20,000 more could be brought across the Caspian Sea and thence by rail to the central Asian theater. In another month a second increment of 20,000 Russian soldiers would reach the front, and within four or five the hostile force could be as large as from 180,000 to 200,000 men.[120] Because the Russians had only one rail line leading into the area, they would at some point begin to face serious supply problems. "For these reasons," the committee suggested,

> Russia has evidently recognised that a second railroad to Central Asia is necessary, and one, moreover, that will not suffer from the fatal defect of interruption by a sea passage. This will be provided by the line, now under construction, from Orenberg to Tashkent. It is expected to be

[117] The committee consisted of the director general of Military Intelligence, the military secretary of the India Office, and Sir W. Lee-Warner (PRO, Cab. 6/3/91D, p. 2).

[118] BM, Add. Mss. 49727, Balfour to Lansdowne, 12/12/01.

[119] PRO, Cab. 6/1/1D, pp. 7–8.

[120] Ibid., pp. 11–12.

complete in four or five years and will place the Turkestan Military District in direct communication with the European railroad system.[121]

Once this step had been taken the Russians would be able to concentrate even larger forces even more quickly along the Afghan frontier.

On the question of how best to cope with a Russian invasion the committee was in full agreement with Altham that "any hopes of indirectly assisting India by expeditions against Russia in other parts of the world would prove illusory."[122] The forces based in India were clearly too small to deal by themselves with the full brunt of a concerted attack, even before the new rail lines came into service. Given the likely delays in providing reinforcements by sea, the only choice seemed to be some increase in India's permanent garrison along the lines that Altham had already suggested. By the committee's reckoning this strengthening should amount to eighteen new battalions or roughly 18,000 more British troops. With these forces, 30,000 Englishmen would be available to join in the early fighting for control of Afghanistan against 40,000 to 50,000 Russians.[123] As to subsequent reinforcements from the mother country, the committee was silent.

The year 1902 saw little progress toward an agreement on the forces needed to defend India. The Indian Government eventually responded to London's recommendations by saying that it could afford to support only 5,200 more troops out of its own budget.[124] Given that, as one War Office official had recently admitted, "in fighting for India, England will be fighting for her Imperial existence,"[125] it seemed only fair that the empire should foot the bill for any further additions.[126] Moreover, the viceroy's military advisers questioned the assumption that there would necessarily be a long delay before reinforcements arrived. Troops might be brought from South Africa (just as they had recently moved in the opposite direction) or Australia and New Zealand. In any case, the enemy's initial steps into Afghanistan would probably be so slow and cautious that a considerable length of time might precede any major engagement between British and Russian forces.[127]

[121] Ibid., p. 12.
[122] Ibid., p. 15.
[123] Ibid., pp. 16–17.
[124] PRO, Cab. 6/1/2D, "Reply of the Indian Government to Committee Report," Curzon et al., 8/21/02, p. 11.
[125] PRO, WO 106/48/E3/1, "The Military Resources of Russia, and Probable Methods of Their Employment in a War between Russia and England," W. R. Robertson, AQMG, 1/17/02.
[126] PRO, Cab. 6/1/2D, p. 3.
[127] Ibid., pp. 7–8, 11.

Citing the unquestionable authority of the Admiralty (which, in typical fashion, refused to make even a guess as to how long it would take to guarantee safe passage for troop ships), the special committee replied by repeating its request for increases in the Indian Army.[128] Adding 5,200 men was fine, but 18,000 would be even better, especially considering that "the military position of Russia grows stronger every day, and the completion of the Orenberg-Tashkent railway in or about 1905 will add immensely to the danger to which India may be exposed."[129]

More important than these exchanges of paper were the changes in personnel and governmental structure that had occurred in England by the end of the year. In July Balfour took the helm as prime minister, and in December the Committee of Imperial Defence, an organization for which, in its modern form, he was largely responsible, met for the first time.[130] Balfour was, as previously described, already convinced of the importance of the Indian question, and he took office possessed of a strong desire both to deal with it and to set the entire military house of the empire in order. Ever the empiricist, Balfour set out to obtain the best possible information on which to base his decisions, and the new CID gave him just the investigative apparatus he needed. Over the next three years it would coordinate some seventy-five papers on Indian defense and devote over half of its eighty-two meetings to that increasingly pressing subject.[131]

To the Brink, 1903

As the new year opened, Lord Selborne wrote to Curzon summarizing the strategic situation that was emerging in the aftermath of the Boer War.

> Our diplomacy ought to save us from war with the United States, the Dutch republics are eliminated, but we remain with all the difficulties and responsibilities of a military power in Asia. That is the crux for us. . . . It is a terrific task to remain the greatest naval Power, when naval Powers are year by year increasing in numbers and in naval

---

[128] PRO, Cab. 6/1/3D, "Second Report of Committee Appointed to Consider the Military Defence of India," Nicholson, Steadman, Lee-Warner, 12/30/02, p. 14.

[129] Ibid., p. 8.

[130] On the origins and history of the CID see Johnson, *Defence by Committee:*

The British Committee of Imperial Defence, 1885–1959. For an interesting account of the CID's role during the period under discussion here see d'Ombrain, *War Machinery and High Policy: Defence Administration in Peacetime Britain, 1902–1914.*

[131] d'Ombrain, *War Machinery,* p. 62.

strength and at the same time to be a military Power strong enough to meet the greatest military Power in Asia.[132]

Just how terrific the task might be was becoming clearer to other members of the cabinet as well. As George Hamilton, the India secretary, informed Curzon at this time, not only the first lord of the Admiralty but the foreign minister, the chancellor of the Exchequer, and the secretary of state for war were all beginning to acquire "a fuller sense of Britain's liability in the event of war with Russia and the magnitude of the military assistance which India would undoubtedly require."[133]

In March the War Office presented its latest survey of the Indian defense problem to the CID. Without going too deeply into questions of short-term policy, the study's authors revealed that they now favored acceptance of virtually all of the proposals that the Indian authorities had made in 1900. Under existing conditions the Russians could deliver 200,000 troops to southern Turkestan within five months, out of which 120,000 would then be available for prompt deployment into Afghanistan. Once the Orenberg-Tashkent line had been finished, an additional 20,000 men per month could be transported to the theater, creating a total force of 300,000 men after five months had passed.[134]

Comparing the requirements for an India-only defensive strategy with the forces needed to take and hold the Kabul-Kandahar line, the War Office concluded that the former policy would allow the Russians to build up an overwhelming force inside Afghanistan. To meet the invaders whenever and wherever they chose to begin their attack, 163,000 additional British and Indian soldiers would have to be permanently stationed along the northwest frontier. By contrast, an active strategy would require only a 28,000-man increase to the standing British Indian Army. Any thought of passivity was thus laid permanently to rest.[135] The War Office analysts urged acceptance of the Indian Government's request for 70,000 men as reinforcements, although they did not indicate how quickly they thought such a force could be delivered from England.[136]

The War Office report seems to have met with general accep-

---

[132] Selborne to Curzon, 1/4/03, quoted in Monger, *The End of Isolation*, p. 110.

[133] Hamilton to Curzon, 2/27/03, quoted in Monger, *The End of Isolation*, p. 111.

[134] PRO, Cab. 6/1/6D, "Memorandum on the Defence of India," War Office, 3/10/03, pp. 5–6.

[135] Ibid., p. 14.

[136] Ibid., p. 7.

tance on both sides of the imperial divide. Kitchener (former commander in chief of imperial forces in South Africa and now C. in C. India) cabled back that he still could not afford to add 30,000 men to his permanent garrison, but, instead of insisting that Britain pay for them, he simply expressed the hope that they "would . . . be sent out on the first threat of war."[137] Back in London, Lord Roberts, one of Kitchener's predecessors and now commander of all British forces, accepted the need for two corps of reinforcements in the event of a Russian advance. Such a force had been recommended by Sir Charles Dilke as early as 1892. "It must be remembered, however," Roberts wrote Balfour, "that during the last ten years [the] position of Russia has become much stronger and the Trans-Caspian Railway has been completed and greatly improved."[138] Although he did not pursue the thought, Roberts's words contained a clear warning of what was about to happen. As Balfour and his colleagues moved toward accepting the initial substantial demands of the Indian Government (formulated, for the most part, without reference to Russia's recent logistic advances), those demands began to increase.

Over the course of the spring the prime minister, with assistance from the CID and the War Office, continued to refine his picture of what a war in Afghanistan would look like. Balfour was particularly concerned about the probable attitudes of Afghan tribesmen in the face of encroachments on their territory by both British and Russian troops. Afghan forces might join with the enemy or remain neutral or be divided in their loyalties. Even the wholehearted support of local forces could be a mixed blessing; as Balfour astutely pointed out, it could draw Britain into an unwanted war by provoking the Russians. In the end the most likely scenario appeared to be something along the following lines: "Russia invades Afghanistan, . . . the Ameer [the principal Afghan tribal chieftain] calls upon us to assist him, and . . . in fulfillment of our Treaty obligations we pour troops into Kabul and Kandahar."[139]

As the War Office sought to estimate the balance of forces in a possible future war, the attitude of the Afghans came to seem increasingly important. Without support from somewhere it was beginning to look as if the British would be badly outnumbered in their initial engagements with enemy advance elements. In April the War Office Intelligence Department was asked to prepare a

---

[137] PRO, Cab. 6/1/8D, "Military Defence of India," Kitchener, 3/24/03, p. 4.

[138] BM, Add. Mss. 49725, Roberts to Balfour, 3/11/03.

[139] PRO, Cab. 6/1/12D, "Relations with Afghanistan," Balfour, 4/30/03, p. 10.

detailed "Diary of Movements of Russian and British Forces in Afghanistan" based on several assumptions. Mobilization would start on 1 January 1905, with war commencing after only a few days had passed. At that time the Orenberg to Tashkent railroad would have been completed and Russian forces in central Asia would be at their 1903 strength (53,000 in peacetime, 84,000 when mobilized, with an additional 47,000 ready on short notice and 20,000 more per month flowing in along each of two rail lines). The British, meanwhile, would have added the necessary 30,000 men to their Indian garrison. Independent Afghan tribes south of the Hindu Kush mountains would be neutral, and those to the north would support Britain.[140]

Given these rather generous assumptions, within five months the British would be able to deploy 70,000 men in and around Kandahar, 25,000 at Kabul, and 7,000 along the lines of communication back to India. If no reinforcements were forthcoming from England or elsewhere, this would be the maximum force that could be brought to bear in Afghanistan. The Russians for their part would have 60,000 men at Herat, 50,000 at Mazar-i-Sharif (about 175 miles northwest of Kabul), with an additional 140,000 men to the rear. In order to sustain the loyalty of local forces the British would probably have to show an early willingness to engage the enemy rather than follow the militarily preferable course of waiting for him to advance and give battle. Thus, six months after the war began, 65,000 British and Indian troops and, it was hoped, 10,000 loyal Afghans, would clash with 70,000 Russians in the south-central region of the country, and 20,000 British along with 60,000 tribesmen would meet 45,000 Russians in the valleys north of Kabul.[141]

As they looked more and more closely at a possible campaign, the military experts were also becoming increasingly aware of certain peculiar difficulties that a war in central Asia would present. Parts of Afghanistan (especially the mountainous northern provinces) were so barren that they could not long provide adequate food and forage for even relatively small units. One War Office memorandum noted in passing that, while the area around Kandahar was relatively fertile, only 10,000 men could sustain themselves at Kabul for a year without external supplies.[142] Under cer-

---

[140] PRO, Cab. 6/1/11D, "Diary of Movements of Russian and British Forces in Afghanistan," War Office Intelligence Department, 4/20/03, p. 1.

[141] Ibid., p. 7.

[142] PRO, Cab. 6/1/10D, "Explanatory Note on the 'Memorandum on the Defence of India,'" War Office, 3/28/03, p. 6.

tain conditions, feed for the pack animals, which would have to be used to supply troops beyond the railheads, might have to be brought in by train.[143]

Although they would later loom large, these kinds of considerations were treated only as peripheral issues. For the most part the CID concerned itself with various schemes intended to provide rapid reinforcements (of as yet indeterminate size) for use in Afghanistan. One plan would have called for the maintenance of between 10,000 and 15,000 additional men in South Africa available for despatch across the Indian Ocean in the event of an emergency.[144] Another centered on the possibility of sending convoys or fast, single ships from England around the Cape of Good Hope even before sea supremacy had been obtained.[145] The first idea involved expenses that neither Delhi nor London was willing to pay; the second could have resulted in substantial losses of ships and lives. Both died without ever getting very far from the drawing board.

After months of analyzing, calculating, and dickering, by summer Balfour was ready and indeed eager to make at least a preliminary decision on reinforcements. Like the War Office, the prime minister, too, had now, in most important respects, come around to what he understood to be the postition of the Indian Government. In July Balfour drafted a confidential memorandum to Curzon and Kitchener in which he requested their views on a resolution that he intended to put before the cabinet. London was now prepared to accept Delhi's conclusions

> that the present field army in India would, unless obligatory garrisons could be reduced, be less by about 30,000 men than the numbers which might, within a period not exceeding four months, be required to meet the enemy's forces in Afghanistan, that in six months from the outbreak of hostilities, a further force of 70,000 men would have to be landed in India to make good wastage and casualties, as well as to increase the strength of the forces at the front, and that before the end of the first year a third reinforcement would probably be required.[146]

[143] PRO, Cab. 6/1/11D, p. 9.

[144] See minutes of the 9th and 22d meetings of the CID (4/23/03 and 8/5/03) in PRO, Cab. 6/3/94D, "Extracts from Minutes of the Committee of Imperial Defence Regarding Reinforcements for India," 12/06.

[145] The Admiralty estimated that either method would result in a 10-percent loss (PRO, Cab. 6/1/15D, "Memorandum on the Dispatch of Reinforcements from the United Kingdom to India," Admiralty, 5/12/03).

[146] PRO, Cab. 6/1/28D, "Draft of Memorandum to Curzon and Kitchener," Balfour, 7/3/03, pp. 1–2.

"These numbers," Balfour believed, were "based on the supposition that Russia had completed the Orenberg-Tashkent railroad and that India had completed rail communication from Peshawar to the Afghan frontier."[147]

Curzon and Kitchener delayed a full month before firing back their responsive bombshell. Defying history (if not reason), they retorted that the Government of India had, in fact, never made a request of the sort to which Balfour was now acceding, or, at least, that *they* personally had never endorsed such a request. The 30,000/70,000 figure that had first emerged in 1900 did not include any mention of the need for a third reinforcement. More to the point, the calculations on which these earlier estimates had been based did not adequately account for the carrying capacity of the expanding Russian rail network. The assumptions on which the War Office and the prime minister were operating, therefore, probably contained a serious underestimation of what the enemy could accomplish during the first six months of any future war.[148]

The authorities in India were concerned that the reinforcement debate not be brought to a premature conclusion. Kitchener especially had reason to want to slow down the entire process of assessment just as London was preparing to speed it up. Relatively new to his job, the commander in chief was not yet certain of his requirements and was therefore understandably reluctant to accept the calculations of his predecessors. During the summer Kitchener ordered the preparation of an elaborate "Kriegspiel" to test various invasion scenarios and, at the same time, his staff was reviewing plans for a possible reorganization of the entire British Indian Army.[149] Pending the outcome of these studies there could be no definitive position on the question of reinforcements.

In London, meanwhile, the evasiveness of the Anglo-Indians was becoming a source of mounting frustration. With the end of the war in South Africa, public and official attention had turned to ruthless scrutiny of the army and all its failings. Various commissions were created to examine the ground forces and to propose

[147] Ibid., p. 2.

[148] PRO, Cab. 6/1/30D, "Memorandum by the Viceroy and the Commander-in-Chief on the Provisional Report of the Defence Committee on Indian Defence," Curzon and Kitchener, 8/7/03.

[149] The war game was completed by the end of the year, although Kitchener was reluctant to release its results until he had used "back channels" to check its assumptions against those being used by the War Office Intelligence Department in London (PRO, Cab. 30/57/29, Kitchener to Roberts, 12/30/03). The redistribution scheme was first prepared in October 1903 and was transmitted to Britain in March 1904. See PRO, Cab. 6/2/58D, "Scheme for the Re-Distribution of the Army in India," Kitchener, 10/03.

changes in both upper-level and overall organization.[150] In addition, in the words of one author, "the pages of the review and the
Service journals of the time were full of articles advocating various
remedies for the military problems."[151]

In order to get a grip on the slippery problem of army reform
Balfour believed, quite logically, that he had first to provide an answer to the challenge that Admiral Fisher and others were posing:
"Who has yet stated exactly what we want the British Army to do?"
Fisher had asked. *"No one!"*[152] Before offering a response the prime
minister set out to review the various missions for which the army
had traditionally been considered necessary. In February he organized a special subcommittee of the CID to look into the danger of
invasion, long regarded as the principal threat that the ground
forces were intended to meet.[153] Later in the year the standards of
defense for various colonial garrisons were also subjected to rigorous reexamination.[154]

As autumn approached, Balfour's views on the purposes for
which the army existed were becoming increasingly clear. Homeland defense was to be provided principally by the navy; if it was
defeated at sea an enemy could simply starve Britain into submis-
sion without ever landing a soldier on the nation's shores. At worst
the army would have to deal with relatively small amphibious raids.
Maintaining vast ground forces in the British Isles was therefore
both unnecessary and unwise.[155]

Once the navy's position on home defense had been adopted,
decisions regarding other missions followed quite easily. If Britain
held the seas it would be able to protect most of its overseas possessions without manning them with sizable and expensive garrisons.
On the other hand, if it lost maritime supremacy, even the largest
local forces would be of little use. Similarly, control of the seas
should permit Britain to cut off and eventually conquer the over-

[150] The two principal published studies were prepared by the Elgin and Nor-
folk commissions. For a discussion see
Dunlop, *Development of the British Army*,
pp. 146–64. Smaller, more discreet,
and ultimately more influential was the
committee headed by Viscount Esher
(whom Balfour had tried, unsuccess-
fully, to recruit for the job of secretary
of state for war), and consisting only of
Esher, Fisher, and George Clarke.
See d'Ombrain, *War Machinery*, p. 41.

[151] Dunlop, *Development of the British
Army*, p. 151.

[152] BM, Add. Mss. 49710, "A Brief
Precis of the Principal Considerations That Must Influence Our Future
Naval and Military Policy," Fisher,
10/03.

[153] J. Gooch, *The Prospect of War:
Studies in British Defence Policy, 1847–
1942*, p. 10.

[154] See chapter 4.

[155] See PRO, Cab. 3/1/18A, "Draft
Report on the Possibility of Serious
Invasion: Home Defence," Balfour,
11/11/03.

seas possessions of its likely opponents. By this reasoning there was little need for powerful expeditionary forces of the sort that some army officers had proposed for use against enemy colonies.[156]

In November, Balfour summarized the findings of the preceding year. "The investigations we have undertaken on the subject of Imperial Defence," he informed the cabinet, "seem to me to point unmistakably to the conclusion that the chief military problem which this country has to face is that of Indian rather than Home Defence."[157] By a process of elimination the protection of India had emerged as the army's main mission, and preparations for its adequate fulfillment now depended only on a decision about the size of the forces needed to meet a Russian invasion. As a result, the Indian Government's sudden unwillingness to state its needs had become the principal obstacle to army reform. Balfour wrote to the India secretary regarding the now controversial 30,000/70,000 reinforcement figure.

> I have no desire whatever to pin the Indian Government to this, or to any other, estimate of the number of men which they would require in the event of a war with Russia: but it is of the utmost importance that, unless they are prepared to accept the . . . estimate already made, they should supply one of their own. . . . The number of troops required by India is in my view the central element in the whole problem of Imperial Defence so far as this depends upon the Army; and it is quite impossible to form any rational estimate of the military needs of the country, or the burden which should be thrown upon the taxpayer in respect of Army Estimates, until we have in some authoritative shape the conclusions of the Indian Military Authorities.[158]

The whole situation was intensely aggravating, especially for an imperial dog not yet used to being wagged by its own tail. At year's end Balfour wrote to Kitchener expressing his frustrations.

> I am profoundly perturbed . . . at the relations between India and this country. For many purposes we seem to be, not so much integral elements in one Empire, as allied States, one of which though no doubt more or less subor-

[156] Monger, *The End of Isolation,* p. 45.

[157] PRO, Cab. 6/1/34D, "Proposals to Constitute a Headquarters Staff Common to British and the Indian Armies," Balfour, 11/30/03, p. 1.

[158] BM, Add. Mss. 49778, Balfour to George Hamilton, 9/11/03.

dinate to the others has yet sufficient independence to
make effective common action a great difficulty. I fear this
will be more and more felt as common action becomes
more and more necessary. . . . The military relations of
the two Governments, especially in the matter of finance,
may have to be very carefully considered. . . . India pays
nothing for the Navy, without which Indian reinforcements could not be sent, and but little for an Army which
exists chiefly on her behalf. . . . Though India is doubtless
the "brightest jewel" in the imperial crown, as well as an
excellent customer for British manufactures, it is, from a
strictly military point of view, nothing but a weakness.
Were India successfully invaded, the moral cost would be
incalculable, the material loss would be important, but
the burden of British taxation would undergo a most
notable diminution![159]

Over, 1904

The year 1904 was marked by two connected but contradictory
trends, only the first of which will be dealt with in this section.
Pressed to make some definitive statement of its needs, the Indian
Government offered first one and then a series of modifications to
its initial request for 100,000 reinforcements. Within twelve months
the earlier figure had grown by 50 percent, and by early 1905 some
experts were predicting that Britain would have to send close to a
half million men to India if a war there lasted for two years.[160] Such
colossal demands threatened to upset any hope of politically acceptable military reform. Largely for this reason there began to develop
a reaction against further increases in the British commitment to
Indian defense and an accompanying tendency to downgrade the
presumed Russian threat.

On 4 January a telegram was sent to Curzon informing him that
the CID had decided to accept the Indian Government's request for
100,000 reinforcements (thereby simply ignoring the fact that this
figure had already been disavowed informally) and asking in what
order these men were to be sent.[161] As the viceroy's principal military adviser Kitchener was reluctant to be tied to even this substantial figure. Lacking any alternative plan, however, Kitchener and

---

[159] BM, Add Mss. 49726, Balfour to
Kitchener, 12/3/03.

[160] A February General Staff memo
put the figure at 463,000 officers and
men over the course of a two-year war.
See PRO, Cab. 6/3/77D, "Strength in

Which Russia Can Advance towards India—and the Reinforcements Required
by India," General Staff, 2/16/05,
pp. 11–12.

[161] PRO, Cab. 6/3/91D, p. 3.

Curzon had little choice but to make some response to London's direct, official query. On 8 January the viceroy cabled that he would need 21,000 men and 12,000 drafts at the outset of any war and 49,000 men plus 25,000 drafts within six months, for a grand total of 107,000 soldiers of all ranks.[162] These figures were presented on the assumption that they were "based on an intimate knowledge of the power of offence of Russia, and on the probable plan of operations" and "calculated to meet the case of Russian aggression before the completion of the Orenberg-Tashkend [sic] Railway."[163] The latter caveat was especially important because, as Kitchener subsequently wrote Roberts, "we may want *more* when the Russians complete their railway connection in Central Asia."[164]

The timetable for completion of the various Russian construction projects was an issue of contention among intelligence experts, as was the question of the precise impact of railway extensions on the Indian Government's demands for reinforcements. In January the War Office noted that Russia appeared to be preparing to lay tracks between Samarkand (southwest of Tashkent and already linked to that city by rail) and Termez on the Afghan frontier directly south. Once this had been done it might be necessary either "to increase the strength of the army in India permanently or to arrange for sending out reinforcements within less periods of time than those calculated in previous papers on the subject."[165] But, by War Office calculations, the Russians still had three hundred more miles to go on the Orenberg-Tashkent line, and, even if both it and the Samarkand-Termez extension were completed, the maximum force that could be sustained in the region would not rise above 300,000 men.[166]

Kitchener and his staff were dissatisfied with London's appreciation of the emerging logistic situation. "The construction of the remaining 240 miles of the Orenberg-Tashkent railway is being pushed forward with almost feverish haste," they warned. "It is no longer safe or prudent to regard this problem as one which affects merely the distant future."[167] War Office planners had acknowledged the possibility of a new railhead at Termez without allowing the fact of its existence to upset their previous calculations. In fact, Kitchener warned, the carrying capacity of the entire Russian rail network was being too easily and too conservatively assumed.

[162] For a breakdown of units see the minutes of the 32d CID meeting (3/2/04) in PRO, Cab. 6/3/94D, p. 2.

[163] PRO, Cab. 6/3/91D, p. 3.

[164] PRO, Cab. 30/57/29, Kitchener to Roberts, 1/28/04.

[165] PRO, Cab. 6/1/36D, p. 4.

[166] Ibid., p. 2.

[167] PRO, Cab. 6/1/45D, "Comments by the C-in-C India on the War Office Memo on the Defence of India," Kitchener, 2/15/04, p. 4.

Through switching and the use of double engines it might be possible to bring even more enemy forces to bear than anyone had yet been willing to consider.[168] There seemed little doubt that over the preceding thirteen years Russia had "doubled . . . [its] power of offence" by extending its logistic network while the Indian rail system had remained virtually unchanged. "The conclusion is therefore forced upon us," the Indian quartermaster general remarked in an appended note, "that reinforcements which might have proved adequate in 1891 would not suffice under the conditions of next year."[169]

With the arrival of spring, Kitchener was finally ready to share the results of his inquiries into the organization of the Indian Army as well as the war game that his staff had played at Simla several months before. In hopes of reducing the chances of long-distance, telegraph-induced misunderstanding, Colonel Mullaly, the deputy quartermaster general for India, was sent to London to brief the newly created General Staff on "Lord Kitchener's view of the whole question."[170]

As an indication of the seriousness with which he regarded the emerging situation, Kitchener was now prepared to recommend that the British Indian Army be completely overhauled so as to provide more forces for defense against invasion. "The existing distribution and organization of our forces in India dates from before the Mutiny . . . and until recently had regard solely to the preservation of internal order without thought of external aggression." Given that "the problem of external action [had] superseded that of internal defence," plans that permitted the release of only four divisions of British troops for action in Afghanistan were now "obsolete and faulty."[171] What Kitchener proposed instead was to divide India into nine military districts, each of which could provide one division for a mobile field army. In an emergency the Indian Government would decide how many of these units should be sent to the northwest frontier.

Lest anyone conclude that the proposed reorganization would solve all of India's problems, Kitchener hastened to point out that substantial numbers of British troops would still have to be left behind in order to preserve domestic tranquillity. At most, only about 34,000 soldiers would be available for use in Afghanistan, just

---

[168] Ibid., pp. 5–7.
[169] Ibid., p. 9.
[170] PRO, Cab. 6/3/91D, p. 3.
[171] PRO, Cab. 6/2/58D, "Scheme for the Re-distribution of the Army in India, and Preparation of the Army in India for War," Kitchener (originally prepared 10/03; distributed to the Indian civil authorities 3/29/04), p. 185.

enough to plug the old 30,000-man gap and alleviate the need for immediate reinforcements, but nowhere near sufficient to fight a war without assistance. If reinforcements were not forthcoming, Kitchener warned, "British units will become reduced so rapidly that after the first few months we shall practically be fighting Russia, at the most critical stages of the campaign, with an army consisting almost entirely of native soldiers."[172] Things in India might have improved since the Mutiny, but not enough to make that an attractive proposition.

Kitchener's Kriegspiel jumped off from the assumption that his suggestions for reform would be adopted before the outbreak of war. The Orenberg-Tashkent line and its extension to Termez were also taken as given, as was the possibility that an invasion could begin essentially without warning. Under these conditions it was postulated that the Russians could begin to build up a reserve of 300,000 men in central Asia while putting as many as 100,000 troops along the Afghan frontier, all before Britain even began to respond. Having launched an offensive the Russians would presumably lay railroad tracks across their southern border, and these lines, along with an ample supply of pack animals, would permit them to advance toward Kabul and Jalalabad.[173]

With the game structured in this way it was hardly surprising that a satisfactory outcome could be ensured only through the introduction of a deus ex machina—in this case the successful prosecution of operations against Russia in other parts of the world.[174] Still, when the General Staff had examined Kitchener's assumptions, it was able to propose only three important but relatively moderate, quantitative changes. As the aggressor, Russia would have some advantage in preparation but not enough to carry out a surprise attack in full strength. By the time the enemy had increased his central Asian garrison from its peacetime level of 60,000 men to 100,000 (of which 60,000 would be available for immediate field operations), British spies would have sent warning to India. A quick grab of strategic positions in northern Afghanistan (which could not be opposed in any case) might be carried out with little or no warning, but the buildup of forces sufficient to press farther south would take a good deal longer and could not go undetected.[175]

[172] Ibid., p. 156.
[173] For references to the game's assumptions see PRO, Cab. 6/1/50D, "Observations on the Records of a War Game Played at Simla, 1903," General Staff, 5/5/04, pp. 1–11. See also PRO, Cab. 6/2/59D, "Memorandum by the General Staff on the Strength in which Russia can Advance towards India when her Railway System is Extended to Termez," General Staff, 6/20/04.
[174] PRO, Cab. 6/1/50D, p. 10.
[175] PRO, Cab. 6/2/59D, p. 1.

Once an invasion had begun in earnest the pace at which Russian troops could advance would be determined by the speed with which they were able to lay down railroad track. The General Staff assumed that a rate of less than one mile per day on the northern approaches to Kabul and slightly more than a mile per day on the easier terrain south of Herat would be reasonable. The number of men that could be sustained away from the endpoints of these two lines had also to be fixed according to the availability of pack animals for carrying supplies and equipment. Kitchener had been willing to grant the Russians as many such beasts of burden as they required; the General Staff assumed that the enemy would have sufficient transport to sustain a maximum of 150,000 men 150 miles from their railroads within four months of an invasion.[176]

Having made these modifications, the General Staff worked with Colonel Mullaly to prepare a "diary" of troop movements similar to the one that the War Office had developed in the spring of 1903. What had seemed possible in five months then now appeared doable in two. Within six, the Russians could have 90,000 men on the northern line from Mazar-i-Sharif heading toward Kabul and 70,000 men moving south from Herat to Kandahar. In a year they would be in position to lay seige to both ends of the British defensive line, with 70,000 men actually at Kabul and 30,000 strung out along the lines of communication behind them while 80,000 men (backed by another 20,000) attacked Kandahar.[177]

At last it seemed that an authoritative estimate of Russian strength had been agreed to by all parties. On 20 June Field Marshal Roberts wrote, "I doubt if it would be practicable to arrive at a more accurate estimate of what Russia could do, or to obtain more reliable information regarding her position in Central Asia. It seems desireable, therefore, in order to avoid further delay, that . . . the Paper should be forwarded to India."[178]

As the designated representative of the Indian military authorities, Colonel Mullaly set about the task of preparing a request for reinforcements based on the figures that he had helped to derive. On 30 June he submitted a memorandum accepting the General Staff's estimates as "a very moderate basis for calculation" and proposing that "the proportion of our fighting men (British and native) to Russian combatants shall, at least, not be less than five to four. This may be taken as an all-around preliminary approximation for purposes of rough calculation."[179]

[176] Ibid., p. 3.
[177] Ibid., p. 4.
[178] Ibid., p. 6.

[179] Mullaly's memo, "Estimate of the Forces Required, during the First Year of a War, to Oppose Russia Successfully

Deriving the force levels necessary for a successful defense of British positions in Afghanistan was now a matter of simple arithmetic. If within four months the Russians could field 128,000 combatants, then, by the same date, British and Indian forces would have to total 155,000. Given that Russia could have 150,000 men in the front line by the end of one year, they would have to be opposed by a force of 189,000.[180]

Mullaly assumed that the Indian Army would be reorganized along the lines that Kitchener had proposed, but, even if it were, he calculated that its full strength would be committed "within four months from the commencement of hostilities if not before." From that time onward "reinforcements from across the seas" would be necessary both to meet "the further development of strength which Russia will be able to produce by the sixth and eighth months, and to increase the British element as the fighting becomes more severe."[181] Specifically, India would require two infantry divisions, two cavalry brigades, and drafts for units already in combat within four months of the outbreak of war and another four infantry divisions plus drafts by the end of eight months. Counted in men instead of units, the grand total was 113,694 soldiers.[182] As large as the final number might appear, it was, Mullaly believed, "the minimum by which we may be able to obtain moderate security; and if the calculations of the General Staff are over-sanguine—which is not impossible—the reinforcements will have to be much heavier."[183] In particular, if the Afghan tribes were hostile to Britain more troops would have to be sent in order to maintain the "moderate and reasonable prospect of success" that was all that the proposed plan could afford.[184]

Papers by the General Staff and Colonel Mullaly were transmitted to Kitchener for comment, and toward the end of July his response arrived back in London. Although he "accepted generally" the methods of calculation being used, Kitchener feared that the General Staff might still be underestimating "Russia's power of offence," especially the enemy's capacity to lay train lines and provide adequate off-rail transport.[185] Unwilling or unable to challenge the whole analytic structure that had now been built up to deal with the reinforcement problem, the Indian C. in C. fastened instead on as-

---

for the Defence of India," is reproduced in wo 105/42 where it is dated 6/30/04. An apparently identical paper was entered in the Cabinet series under PRO, Cab. 6/24/64D and dated 8/04. Page numbers are taken from the latter version. Quotations cited here are from pp. 3, 4.
[180] Ibid., p. 10.
[181] Ibid., p. 9.
[182] PRO, Cab. 6/3/91D, p. 4.
[183] PRO, Cab. 6/2/64D, p. 10.
[184] Ibid.
[185] PRO, Cab. 6/3/91D, p. 4.

sumptions that had been made about the proportion of field forces that would have to be replaced over time. If the "wastage rate" was as high as 75 percent,[186] then the second reinforcement of four divisions would have to arrive in India within less than eight months, and "at the critical period of the war, namely after the ninth month, two additional divisions" of infantry would be required.[187] All together Kitchener was now asking for eight infantry divisions, two cavalry brigades, and 42,000 drafts for a total of 135,614 men to be delivered from England to India by the end of the first year of war.[188]

With all parties presumably exhausted, the whole question of reinforcements was given a merciful rest at the end of the summer. As winter approached, however, there was increasing concern over the state of relations between Britain and Russia and fear that the ongoing war in the Far East would somehow spill over into central Asia. In late October Russian warships on their way east fired at British fishing vessels off Dogger Bank. Major conflict seemed only weeks, if not days, away.

On 1 November the army informed the India Office that it now intended to base its plans on the request for 107,000 men that had been received at the beginning of the year and suggested that the Indian Government be asked to specify the order in which it wished those reinforcements to be sent.[189] Four days later the viceroy cabled London obstinately confirming his adherence to Kitchener's most recent appeal for 135,000 soldiers. Moreover, he asked that three battalions of infantry be added to that figure to complete the ninth division of the reorganized Indian Army. Several smaller units needed for the advance into Afghanistan, including some railway and telegraph companies and four battalions of mounted infantry, were tacked on for good measure. The Indian Government had now fixed 148,133 officers and men as the bare minimum needed to stave off a Russian invasion for one year.[190]

Back Again, 1904–1905

As if to prove the applicability of Newton's laws to politics, the "action" of India's demands soon began to produce an equal and opposite reaction. During the course of 1904 and into 1905, resistance to Indian requests for assistance grew steadily within the British government. This was due partly to changes in objective cir-

[186] See PRO, WO 105/42, "Precis of the Case Regarding the Despatch of Reinforcements for India," Major Holman, General Staff, 12/21/04.

[187] PRO, Cab. 6/3/91D, p. 4.
[188] Ibid.
[189] PRO, WO 105/42.
[190] PRO, Cab. 6/3/91D, p. 4.

cumstances that seemed to reduce the immediate danger of war (in particular, the humiliating defeat of Russian forces in the Far East and the extension of the Anglo-Japanese treaty to India) and partly to shifts in the way the problem of a possible conflict in Afghanistan was analyzed. Underlying both of these factors was the growing realization that, if the threat was all that it had been made to seem, India could not be adequately defended without major changes in Britain's military system.

Whatever the particular merits of India's demands (and there were reasons to doubt them), they had finally, unmistakably, brought Britain face to face with a terrible reality: in the twentieth century conflict with another major power would almost inevitably involve large-scale land warfare. Technological progress had reduced the effectiveness of Britain's winning naval weapon while exposing previously secure parts of its empire to attack on the ground. The only way of dealing with such threats seemed to be to reply to them in kind by preparing to generate equal increments of land power through the mobilization of huge armies of well-trained and well-equipped men. Most British statesmen were only too happy to put off the day when these facts would have to be faced.

With the outbreak of the Boer War, many observers had been willing to consider a full range of possible remedies to the perceived shortfall in Britain's military power. Some experts went so far as to call publicly for conscription, long regarded as taboo.[191] Inside the government there was also interest in the possibility of a draft, especially among some military officers. At the close of 1901, the director of Military Operations had written to Lord Roberts that

> there is a general impression that the British nation has begun to realize that our Army is too weak numerically, that its organization is capable of improvement, and that it is the duty of all classes to contribute by personal service towards the defence of the Empire. A combination of voluntary enlistment for the Army with conscription for the Militia would rapidly increase our military strength at

[191] For one example, see the article by Sidney Low cited in note 98 above. Low pointed out that at any moment Great Britain might be required to send a force of several hundred thousand men overseas. When the Boer War had ended, he warned, "English statesmanship will be called upon to turn us into a military nation, or at least into a nation that can perform its military duties without unendurable strain and imminent danger of failure. . . . Compulsory service seems the only way of meeting the difficulty" (Low, "Military Weakness of England," pp. 23, 25).

comparatively modest cost. It is possible that the population of the United Kingdom may be disposed to accept
the obligation of compulsory service in order to be secure
at home, and in readiness to uphold British interests and
protect British possessions abroad.[192]

Simultaneously, although rather more reluctantly, St. John Broderick, the secretary of state for war, was being "forced to the conclusion that we must either compel recruits or pay more." Despite his
belief that "by far the most satisfactory and economical solution of
the difficulty, from a military standpoint, would be to establish
compulsion," Broderick resolved to tinker with pay and terms of
service for voluntary recruits before resorting to conscription.[193]

As the panic induced by the Boers began to wear off, so too did
some of the initial enthusiasm for a draft. The long-term problem
of providing adequate manpower for the defense of the empire remained unchanged, but the willingness to consider drastic solutions dwindled. By 1902 many in the Conservative cabinet would
probably have agreed with words which the Indian secretary used
to describe the situation to his viceroy. "I believe that the only solution of our military difficulties is recourse to some form of conscription," Hamilton wrote Curzon, "but I think it is equally clear
that any Government that propose[s] it will fail, and probably be
driven from office."[194]

For two years Broderick struggled to reorganize the volunteer
army into six corps, stationed in Britain, out of which three would
be ready at any time to be sent abroad.[195] But by early in 1903 support for this scheme had collapsed, largely because it would have
resulted in substantial increases in the army estimates.[196] As a result, the nation seemed to be drifting without a military policy, and
conscription appeared once again to be rising up the list of possible
options. In May one high-ranking general noted in his diary, "All
sorts of wild schemes are on. . . . The whole situation is gradually
becoming impossible and we are nearing universal service."[197]

At the close of the year H. O. Arnold-Forster took over the War
Office from Broderick, determined, on the one hand, to avoid conscription[198] (and the potential for political disaster that went with it)

[192] PRO, WO 105/41, Wm. Nicholson to Roberts, 12/16/01.
[193] PRO, Cab. 37/59/128, "Army Estimates, 1902–03," St. John Broderick, 12/7/01, p. 4.
[194] IOL, C126/4, Hamilton to Curzon, 2/6/02.

[195] Dunlop, *Development of the British Army*, p. 132; for a discussion of Broderick's ill-fated plan see pp. 121–45.
[196] Ibid., p. 156.
[197] Ibid., p. 162.
[198] Arnold-Forster later informed Parliament that he had no intention of

and, on the other, to cut costs as much as possible.[199] Without a draft or a greatly increased budget there could be no increase in the size of the peacetime army; indeed, as Arnold-Forster hastened to point out, keeping costs in line would require actual cuts in the number of men under arms.[200] But what would happen once (as seemed likely in any war with a modern power) the full strength of Britain's standing army had been committed in battle? The only possible answer seemed to lie in a system that would permit the rapid mobilization of large numbers of previously trained reserves.

Shortly before Arnold-Forster took office, the Royal Commission of Inquiry into the South African War (the so-called Elgin Commission) had concluded that "the true lesson of the War" was that "no military system will be satisfactory which does not contain powers of expansion outside the limit of the Regular Forces of the Crown, whatever that limit may be."[201] This was a lesson that the new secretary of state for war seems never to have grasped or, if he did, he was never able to put it successfully into practice. In his eagerness to save money, Arnold-Forster sought to institute a three-part program that called for reducing or eliminating as many overseas colonial garrisons as possible, abolishing or substantially modifying the home-based militia and volunteer forces, and dividing the regular army into a Home Service branch (composed of short-term enlistees) and a General Service component for long tours of duty overseas. Each of the two regular army elements was to be backed by a relatively small body of reserves. In the event of large-scale conflict the nation would have to rely on patriotism and the lure of foreign adventure to draw necessary additional recruits.[202]

Although they were open to attack on a variety of grounds,[203]

"mak[ing] any proposals to the House in favour of a system of conscription" (response to a question on 2 June 1904 in the House of Commons, quoted in Dunlop, *Development of the British Army*, p. 176).

[199] For a discussion of the impact of financial considerations on army reform see chapter 3.

[200] As Arnold-Forster explained to the cabinet, "In order to reduce expenditure it is necessary to reduce men. . . . All troops in excess of our requirements in war should be got rid of" (PRO, Cab. 37/71/85, "Revised Proposals for Army Reform by the Secretary of State for War," Arnold-Forster, 6/25/04, p. 4).

[201] Quoted in Dunlop, *Development of the British Army*, p. 166.

[202] For the details of Arnold-Forster's various plans see BM, Add. Mss. 50301, "Failed Schemes," and 50302, "Approved Schemes."

[203] The idea of abolishing the militia turned out to be highly unpopular in Parliament. Splitting the regular ground forces would have created problems of recruitment and organization that professional military men regarded as insuperable. On Arnold-Forster's reign at the War Office see Dunlop, *Development of the British Army*, pp. 165–97. See also Tucker, "The Issue of Army Reform in the Unionist Government, 1903–5," pp. 90–100.

Arnold-Forster's plans would have had a better chance of succeeding had they provided a visible solution to the problem of Indian defense. But, as the demands of the Indian Government for reinforcements increased, it grew clear that neither Arnold-Forster's schemes nor anything resembling them would be equal to the task. Arnold-Forster seems to have realized the danger rather early on. Thus, in March 1904, following the viceroy's request for 107,000 men, the secretary for war wrote a worried note to the chief of the General Staff, General Sir Neville Lyttelton. "It is necessary to make a reply to the request of the Indian Government. . . . It is evident from a perusal of the figures . . . that we cannot at the present time comply with this request, and that if we attempt to furnish anything like the number of troops asked for, we shall be depleting the United Kingdom to a dangerous extent."[204]

As 1904 progressed it became increasingly apparent that, even if they could be met, India's demands would absorb virtually the entire British army. During the spring Lord Roberts warned the cabinet that

> in the existing state of our army, it would be extremely difficult to secure the safety of the United Kingdom, to meet the demands of India, and to be prepared for troubles that might arise in other parts of the Empire. . . . It is evident from the correspondence that has already taken place, that India looks to us for considerably more assistance than we could prudently give her in the first phase of the war.[205]

Roberts wrote in March, before the deluge. By the end of the year, with India's needs set at 148,000 men, it took little more than straightforward addition (or, rather, subtraction) to show that, as one General Staff officer noted, "the entire regular Army at home would not suffice to meet" the viceroy's latest demands.[206]

In December Roberts advised Kitchener that "War Office officials and the members of the Imperial Defence Committee are considerably exercised in their minds as to how your additional demands can best be met." While Roberts had no quarrel with the numbers of men being requested, he did suggest that they might more prudently be provided over a longer period of time.

[204] BM, Add. Mss. 50301, Arnold-Forster to Lyttelton, 3/16/04.

[205] PRO, Cab. 6/1/41D, "What number of troops could be spared for India?" Roberts, 3/23/04, p. 3.

[206] PRO, Cab. 6/2/73D, "Reinforcements for India," Adjutant General, 11/15/04, p. 3. For further General Staff reaction to the viceroy's telegram of 5 November 1904 see PRO, Cab. 6/2/72D, "Despatch of Reinforcements to India," General Staff, 11/04.

> With our comparatively small Army, the public reaction
> after the recent expenditure of something like £200 mil-
> lion sterling on a prolonged war and the urgent necessity
> for limiting the Estimates as much as possible, it would be
> impracticable for any government to keep up a force of
> well trained men sufficiently large to admit of 160,000 of
> them being despatched to India within a very short time.

If such a feat was attempted it would leave Britain in a "crippled
state."[207]

There appeared now to be only two possible positions in the debate over the nation's military power. If one accepted existing assumptions about the Russian threat to India, then it followed necessarily that Britain's small, voluntary army was inadequate and
would have to be overhauled. If, on the other hand, the price of
such change was considered too high to pay, then something would
have to be done to diminish the apparent danger.

Neither Arnold-Forster nor the General Staff, with which he was
increasingly at odds, seemed able to see this essential contradiction.
Well into the last year of Balfour's ministry, both held firmly to the
conventional image of the Russian menace and to the belief that it
could be met with an army not much bigger and not much differently organized than the one already in existence.[208] In the meantime, other, more independent, intellects were prepared to make
the choice and to begin struggling to impose their view of the situation on the Government, and, more particularly, on the prime
minister.

Balfour was inclined to believe that the danger to India was real,
and he was prepared to go to great lengths to see it met. At the

[207] PRO, 30/57, Roberts to Kitchener, 12/23/04.

[208] Arnold-Forster was so preoccu-
pied with the details of his reorganization schemes that he seems to have had
neither the time nor the energy to
make an independent examination of
the reinforcement question. The role
of the General Staff is more open to interpretation. Some authors have argued that, as Nicholas d'Ombrain puts
it, from the beginning "the soldiers for
the most part had almost no interest in
the problem of the Northwest Frontier"
(*War Machinery*, p. 3). J. McDermott
claims that, as reinforcement demands
rose, the General Staff "used the CID
to question the primacy of India in
military planning." In McDermott's
view the army seized on a European
war against Germany as preferable to
the impossible task of preparing for the
defense of India against a Russian invasion ("The Revolution in British Military Thinking from the Boer War to
the Moroccan Crisis," in P. Kennedy,
ed., *The War Plans of the Great Powers,
1880–1914*, pp. 99–117; quote from
p. 106). The General Staff may have
been happy to substitute Germany for
Russia, but it did very little to downplay
the danger to India. In fact, as described below, it appears to have de-
clined the opportunity to do so presented to it by CID secretary George
Clarke.

same time he was the leader of a party and a Government that had been torn by internal disputes and battered by partisan criticism; as such, his tolerance for drastic departures from past policies was necessarily limited. Vying for the prime minister's attention and support were two very different men: Commander in Chief Lord Roberts, the much-decorated septuagenarian hero of Afghanistan and South Africa, and George Clarke, civilian defense analyst, former colonial governor, and recently appointed secretary of the CID.

As a navalist Clarke had always supported a strong fleet as the principal instrument of imperial security and opposed anything that smacked of wasteful spending on excessively large land forces. At the CID he had been a powerful proponent of Balfour's ruling on the minimal dangers of invasion, and, as the debate over Indian reinforcements began to heat up, he approached the claims of the military experts with considerable skepticism. India seemed about to replace home defense as the army's most favored bureaucratic lever; if its demands were upheld, they would mean a bigger and more costly army and less money for battleships and cruisers. Clarke was not initially certain of how the matter could best be handled, but he was convinced, as he wrote to Lord Selborne in May 1904, that "the Indian question is in a very unsatisfactory state and needs reducing to practical form. Many of the papers are purely academic. It seems necessary to throw out proposals which for financial or other reasons are impracticable at the present time." [209]

Russia's preoccupation with Japan reinforced Clarke in his belief that an invasion of India was "outside the region of practical possibilities for some time to come," but he still lacked the analytic means with which to persuade Balfour and others that such an attack "would be an operation of stupendous difficulty." [210] It was the review of studies by Kitchener and the War Office during the sum-

---

[209] Selborne Papers, 45, Clarke to Selborne, 5/25/04.

[210] BM, Add. Mss. 50836, Clarke to Balfour, 7/23/04. Others shared Clarke's suspicions and tried to convince Balfour that his concern over India was misplaced. Fisher bombarded the prime minister's personal secretary with pleas, threats, and warnings. "That d——d Northwest frontier of India is what your Master is suffering from! For God's sake ask him to drop it! You are all being fooled over it!" (BM, Add. Mss. 49710, Fisher to San-dars, 6/18/04). "Get rid of Indian Bogey! . . . Do please look at map of Afghanistan and don't let these . . . idiots fool the Prime Minister! . . . Let the Prime Minister issue an edict . . . that the regular Army is to be reduced by . . . 60,000 odd men. . . . If you don't tell your Master these truths—you will be turned to a leper as white as snow! and we'll sweep the country with the cry 'Down with Balfour and his Bloated Army!' and D——n Sandars!" (BM, Add. Mss. 49710, Fisher to Sandars, 7/29/04 [4:00 A.M.!]).

mer of 1904 that presented the first opportunity for reducing the Indian problem to "practical form." These papers, it will be recalled, focused on the impact of Russia's railway extensions, and they gave strong support to the plausibility of a large-scale invasion.

Lord Roberts, already convinced of the validity of India's claims, saw in the recent spate of staff work a means for promoting one of his own pet projects. To counter Russia's rail-assisted advance, Britain would have to move large numbers of its own men forward into Afghanistan; as Roberts had discovered twenty-five years before, supporting such a force in the field would be no easy matter. Extrapolating from his experience during the Afghan war of 1879–1880, Roberts figured that maintaining five divisions at Kabul would require over 3,000,000 pounds of supplies each day. A single camel could carry 400 pounds, so approximately 7,500 camels would have to complete their 170-mile, one-month journey from the Indian border at the end of each day. Assuming that there were no losses and that each animal could be turned around immediately and headed back to pick up more supplies, a minimum of 234,794 camels (7,574 camels per day × 31 days) would be needed just to support the northernmost portion of the British war effort.[211]

Clearly, it would be virtually impossible to fight a war in Afghanistan if it was necessary to rely on animal transport alone. Roberts's purpose in making the calculations, he told the prime minister, was "to emphasize the great necessity which exists for pushing forward all necessary preparations, and especially the two frontier railroads."[212] If it wished to counter recent Russian moves, Britain would have to assemble a similar logistic system leading up to the northwest Indian frontier. In addition, it would be prudent to begin construction of a rail network inside Afghanistan, regardless of how such a move was received by the local residents.[213]

Unintentionally, unwittingly, Roberts had handed Clarke a stick with which he would now proceed to beat his opponents mercilessly. If Britain faced such logistic difficulties in Afghanistan, why should the Russians have an easier time of it? And, if the attacker's way was strewn with physical obstacles, why was there any reason to fear a massive, sudden "descent" toward India?

[211] Roberts pointed out that fewer animals would be needed in the south where the terrain was easier and local food supplies were more plentiful. On the other hand, as he noted, the camel figure for Kabul did not include spares, nor did it take account of the fact that some animals would have to be used to carry feed for the others (PRO, Cab. 6/2/69D, "Supplies in Afghanistan," Roberts, 8/26/04).

[212] BM, Add. Mss. 49725, Roberts to Balfour, 8/26/04.

[213] PRO, Cab. 6/2/69D.

In September Clarke wrote approvingly of Roberts's calculations to Balfour, but he noted, "I cannot agree that the difficulties of the Russians would be 'nothing like so great' as our own." Even if their early moves were relatively easy, the invaders' subsequent advance over mountains toward Kabul would be more difficult than that of the British. If the English and their Indian "allies" would have difficulty in doing so, then "on Lord Roberts's showing, it would be impossible for the Russians to supply five divisions in the neighborhood of Kabul."[214]

Warming to his theme, Clarke went on to question the entire set of logistic assumptions upon which the invasion debate and, most recently, Kitchener's Kriegspiel had been built. Afghan railways would be absolutely essential to the conduct of large-scale operations, but such lines would be most difficult to put in place. The rates of progress assumed in the Kriegspiel were "preposterous." Railways that might take as long as three years to construct (and that could be safely built only *after* the country had been conquered) were treated as "prairie lines" that would go up almost overnight. "I fear," Clarke wrote, "that the data, on which 136,000 troops are demanded from this country within a year of the outbreak of war, are absolutely fallacious."[215]

The Dogger Bank incident and the further escalation in reinforcement demands that it encouraged seem only to have deepened Clarke's determination to resist. On 14 November he reported to Balfour that he had met with a noted geographer to discuss conditions in Afghanistan. These conversations convinced Clarke that "the Kriegspiel, on which so much is made to depend shows the most deplorable want of geographical knowledge."[216] The assumed speed of railroad construction south of Herat was "ludicrous," and the rates of progress postulated from Termez were "preposterous."[217] The idea that either side could concentrate five divisions at Kabul in the time assumed was therefore "pure lunacy."[218]

Two days after Clarke wrote, the CID met to discuss India's latest request. The secretary's role in this as in other such meetings is not recorded, but at least one member of the group appeared to echo the line of argument toward which Clarke had been pointing in his private correspondence. Chancellor of the Exchequer Austen

[214] BM, Add. Mss. 49700, Clarke to Balfour, 9/27/04.

[215] Ibid.

[216] BM, Add. Mss. 49700, Clarke to Balfour, 11/14/04.

[217] BM, Add. Mss. 50836, "Notes of a Conversation with Sir T. Holdich on November 14, 1904," 11/14/04.

[218] BM, Add. Mss. 49700, Clarke to Balfour, 11/14/04.

Chamberlain drew attention to Roberts's calculations and suggested that they proved that the large numbers of men now being asked for could not be supplied. Logistic problems placed limits on the scale and pace of any possible war in Afghanistan and therefore on the reinforcements that could reasonably be demanded by India. In closing, the committee expressed its "general opinion . . . that we should not be bound to provide more men than can be found under the army scheme now being brought into force." [219]

Clarke's reassessment of the entire Indian problem was now clearly helping those who sought to justify tailoring Britain's response to the capacity of its voluntary military system. On 22 November the CID met again and Arnold-Forster warned that compliance with the viceroy's most recent request would "denude the country of organized troops." Chamberlain, embellishing his earlier remarks, urged that the committee hold to the resolution that it had adopted in June, before the explosion in demands, "that 100,000 men should be regarded as the maximum reinforcement to which the Government should be committed, and . . . the Indian authorities should frame their plans accordingly." [220]

The prime minister's position in the unfolding debate was uncertain. In light of the questions being raised, Balfour tended toward accepting an official limit of 100,000 men pledged, but he wished at the same time to reassure Delhi that "these numbers do not comprehend the whole of the military forces which would be available if Imperial policy permitted their dispatch to India." [221] Sensing an opportunity to press home his case (and willing to exaggerate in a good cause), Clarke wrote Balfour that India's demands had grown from 27,900 men in October 1903 to 158,700 in November 1904. The only possible explanation for this vast increase was "the Kriegspiel played at Simla last year," a game that was "wholly inadequate and even positively misleading."

> The great factors of war—supply and communications—
> are either ignored or absolutely miscalculated. Great
> masses of men are moved across the most difficult country
> in the world as if they were pawns upon a chess board.
> Railways are assumed to be made at prairie speed over
> routes which in some parts prohibit railway construction
> except as an engineering feat requiring a long time, a

[219] Minutes of 57th CID meeting, 11/16/04, summarized in PRO, Cab. 6/3/94D.
[220] Minutes of 58th CID meeting, 11/22/04, summarized in PRO, Cab. 6/3/94D.
[221] Ibid.

great supply of labour, and freedom from all interruption. . . . Similarly the whole question of supplies both for the invading and for the defending army requires to be worked out afresh. Lord Roberts has shewn that the contemplated placing of five British divisions in or in the neighborhood of Kabul in four months is absolutely impossible in present circumstances. It is on data thus hopelessly untrustworthy that the final demand for 158,700 men is based.[222]

"Psychological forces" were to blame for the existing state of affairs, and Clarke warned that "the more men we allow to be hypothecated to the Northwest frontier, the more ambitious will be the plans evolved at Simla." In fact, no case had been made for the large reinforcements being demanded, and, even if it had, the security of the empire as a whole required that no more than 60,000 men be formally pledged. "The military plans of India," Clarke concluded, "should be made to suit the strength of the forces which can be counted upon."[223]

At the very end of the year Clarke reiterated his views to the prime minister. "The alleged requirement of six divisions in four months, together with details," implied, he wrote, "a heavy strain upon our military organization, and goes far in the direction of dictating its form and scope." If the army estimates were to be brought down "to £25 million at the outside," then the Indian problem would have to be contained and the nation would have to rely on a regenerated militia "to form a second line field army." Such an army, Clarke believed, "ought not to be required more than twice in a century."[224]

In January 1905 Kitchener sought to bolster Balfour against the haranguing he was receiving from one of his closest aides. After a fresh examination of local conditions, the Indian commander in chief wrote, "I still think that the Russians, with their trained railway battalions and practice, will advance their railways much faster than is anticipated."[225]

Balfour was not prepared to abandon altogether his hard-won understanding of the Indian situation, but he did accept Clarke's recommendation that another set of reinforcement calculations be made using new, slower rates of advance. A change in assumptions

[222] BM, Add. Mss. 50836, "Notes on the Discussion of the 22 Inst. Indian Reinforcements," Clarke to Balfour, 11/24/04.
[223] Ibid.
[224] BM, Add. Mss. 49700, Clarke to Balfour, 12/28/04.
[225] BM, Add. Mss. 49726, Kitchener to Balfour, 1/17/05.

regarding railway progress would, Clarke predicted, "materially postpone the date at which reinforcements are required."[226] And, indeed, when the General Staff repeated its studies using figures "set forth by the Prime Minister," it found that 100,000 men would be sufficient to hold the Kabul-Kandahar line during the first year of war.[227]

The military men and, ultimately, the prime minister seem to have lacked faith in these modified calculations. In concluding their report the staff officers wrote that "the rate of railway construction—the cardinal ɹactor in the problem—seems to be too low. . . . In the opinion of the General Staff . . . the assumption that a line from the Russian frontier to Herat would take six months to build is not a safe one. . . . Similarly, to the south of Herat the given rate seems too low."[228] The assumed average rates of construction worked out to around a third of a mile per day, considerably less that the one mile per day the Russians had been achieving in Manchuria and with which they had been credited in previous war games. The General Staff preferred its earlier studies, which supported the 143,000-man requirement.[229] Balfour, in a letter to Arnold-Forster dated eight days after these comments were circulated, told him that he still regarded the higher figure "as settled."[230]

Not yet willing to accept the escape that Clarke was offering, the prime minister was finding himself increasingly tangled in the coils of the Indian reinforcement–army reform mess. Arnold-Forster's incompetence and his inability to formulate a plan that would be acceptable either to Parliament or to the army forced Balfour to take matters more directly into his own hands. The problem, however, lay deeper than the personal and intellectual limitations of the secretary of state for war. If the threat to India was real, then there seemed little hope of meeting it within the confines of an all-volunteer force. As Balfour himself admitted, "The inherent difficulty of creating a Voluntary Army adequate to the multifarious responsibilities of this country is so great that in my belief any scheme which it was within the wit of man to contrive will always be open to serious objection."[231]

[226] BM, Add. Mss. 49701, Clarke to Balfour, 1/18/05.

[227] PRO, Cab. 6/3/77D. "Strength in Which Russia can Advance towards India—and the Reinforcements Required by India," General Staff, 2/16/05, pp. 1, 11.

[228] Ibid., p. 12.

[229] Ibid., p. 15.

[230] "Our Present Minimum Military Requirements and Proposals for Fulfilling Them by a Reorganization of the Regular Army and Militia," Balfour, 2/24/05, p. 4, contained in PRO, Cab. 37/77/87, "File of Correspondence on Army Reorganization," 5/16/05.

[231] PRO, Cab. 37/75/54, "Army Reorganization," Balfour, 3/30/05, p. 1.

Balfour agreed with Arnold-Forster that Britain needed a long-service army because it was the only way of ensuring "that we shall be able to maintain the necessary peace garrisons in India and the Colonies." On the other hand, some cheaper force would have to be found to supplement the long-service army, "because no Exchequer is rich enough to maintain, in addition to our peace requirements, the number of long-service soldiers necessary to carry on a prolonged war with a great military Power."[232] Arnold-Forster had provided no such force, and his two-tiered scheme was therefore too expensive as well as numerically inadequate. Balfour placed his trust in some form of revivified militia, an unspecified mechanism for training volunteers after mobilization,[233] and on the hope that, in India at least, there would be a long pause between the outbreak of war and any actual large-scale battles.[234] During such time, presumably, a flood of new recruits could be trained and prepared for the rigors of war in a far-off land.

Even if the nation answered the call to arms without compulsion, and even if there was little reason to fear an attack on Great Britain, Balfour's plan still risked leaving the country virtually disarmed during the early phases of a distant war. Worse, his scheme rested on scantily trained amateurs who could not, by law, be compelled to serve overseas. The militia, as Arnold-Forster kept pointing out, had proved virtually worthless in South Africa. There was little reason to have confidence in men who had "neither the quality nor the training necessary to enable them to contend successfully against foreign troops."[235]

Balfour was obviously, excruciatingly, caught between a pair of imperatives that he could neither reconcile nor safely ignore. Clarke's debunking efforts had not significantly eased the prime minister's fears of Russia, but his debate with Arnold-Forster had failed to free him of his distaste for compulsion. Now, from an unexpected quarter, came the possibility of salvation.

On 29 March Claude Lowther, a Conservative member of Parliament, gave a speech in which he proposed modifying the existing Anglo-Japanese treaty. Lowther made the point that the Indian frontier had become "as vulnerable as the frontier of any European Power," and he asked how it could be possible for Britain to obtain an army sufficient for its defense. "Apart from conscription, a sys-

---

[232] Ibid., p. 2.

[233] PRO, Cab. 37/77/87, p. 3.

[234] PRO, Cab. 37/75/54, p. 5.

[235] "Remarks by the Secretary of State for War upon the Prime Minis-

ter's Proposals for the Reorganization of the Regular Army and Militia," Arnold-Forster, 3/25/05. In PRO, Cab. 37/77/87.

tem which would never be tolerated in this country, because it was wholly alien to the British character," there appeared to be only one solution. The treaty with Japan (which was due to lapse in 1907) should be extended to include as a *casus belli* an attack by any one power on the "Asiatic possessions" of either island empire. In such an instance the two contracting parties would come to each other's assistance, "Great Britain with her Fleet—Japan with her army." By such means Britain "would be relieved of the upkeep of an Army, which if brought to the huge standard of efficiency demanded by the new condition would become an intolerable burden to the British taxpayer."[236]

Lowther's speech helped to trigger a debate on Britain's foreign policy, and it seems also to have filled Clarke with a renewed energy. Seizing on the idea of an extended alliance, Clarke began to press forward again along two seemingly divergent paths; on the one hand he continued to argue that the threat to India was grossly exaggerated, while on the other he urged Balfour to sign a treaty with Japan in order to deter the Russian menace. In fact, given Clarke's desire to wean the prime minister away from the Indian problem, the two approaches were completely complementary.

The prospect of a modified Anglo-Japanese alliance was raised at a 12 April meeting of the CID, along with the still unresolved question of Indian reinforcements and the directly related problem of military reform.[237] Within two weeks Clarke had begun pelting Balfour with memos urging the adoption of Lowther's proposal. Toward the end of April he wrote the prime minister, reviewing the entire history of "Threatened Invasions of India, And Their Effect on British Policy" beginning with Peter the Great and extending down through Napoleon to the present instance. The whole story was one of "supreme futility" on all sides. There had never been any prospect of preventing Russia from conquering central Asia, and, in consequence, Britain should have been willing to settle for an early, accurate delimitation of Afghanistan's boundaries. Drawing comfort from the past, Clarke pointed out that the Crimean War had slowed Russia's advance for twenty-two years, the Russo-Turkish war for another twenty-six. The present war

[236] Nish, *The Anglo-Japanese Alliance*, p. 303.
[237] According to minutes of this meeting, "Mr. Balfour observed that the constant increases which have been made in the Government of India's demands placed considerable difficulty in the way of army reform at home" ("Minutes of the 70th CID, April 12, 1905" contained in PRO, WO 106/44). Nish points out that the "sheer juxtaposition" of the reinforcement and alliance questions led inevitably to consideration of the possible connections between the two (Nish, *The Anglo-Japanese Alliance*, p. 317).

with Japan should give Britain another twenty-year breathing spell. "We have, therefore, ample time for preparation, and for arriving at a clear conception of the problem of the defence of India."[238]

To Clarke an extended treaty with Japan offered a quick and easy way of solving a problem in whose existence he had never truly believed. As a quid pro quo for Britain's continuing naval support, he suggested that "the Japanese in the case of aggression against India . . . agree to provide a force of (say) 150,000 men, for the defence of our frontier." The choice of this figure was clearly no accident, but neither was it the result of any genuine concern with meeting the Indian Government's pleas for assistance in time of war. The mere existence of such a promise from Japan would, Clarke believed, "effectively prevent the realization of any Russian designs upon India—if such designs exist."[239]

With the defeat of Russia's naval forces at Tshushima in late May, there could no longer be any doubt as to who would win the war in the Far East. Clarke was more convinced than ever that an invasion of India was highly improbable, if not physically impossible. On 5 June he submitted a paper to the CID in which he sought to put one final nail into the Indian coffin. Depending on the quantities of food and forage locally available, Clarke calculated that around 400,000 camels would be needed to keep five divisions supplied at Kabul for one year. If local supplies were used up, as many as 545,000 camels might be required to sustain troops seven marches from the nearest railhead; at a distance of fifteen marches, the number might rise to 3,056,000![240]

Although he was inordinately proud of them,[241] there is no evidence to suggest that Clarke's "camel papers" had a decisive impact on the reinforcement debate. What they probably did do was strengthen Balfour's resolve to force through a treaty with Japan, despite the assorted misgivings of Arnold-Forster, the General Staff, and the Indian Government.[242] Russia's humiliation had con-

---

[238] BM, Add. Mss. 49701, Clarke to Balfour, 4/28/05.

[239] BM, Add. Mss. 49701, Clarke to Balfour, 4/29/05.

[240] PRO, Cab. 6/3/83D, "Suggestions as to a Basis for the Calculation of the Required Transport of an Army Operating in Afghanistan," Clarke, 6/5/05, p. 2. See also PRO, Cab. 6/3/89D, Clarke, 11/10/05. These two papers are fascinating examples of early, primitive operations research.

[241] Clarke later told Balfour that he thought it would "do the General Staff good to try and upset" his calculations (BM, Add. Mss. 49701, Clarke to Balfour, 7/8/05).

[242] Arnold-Forster believed that a treaty like the one proposed would be used to justify cuts in the size of the army. See PRO, Cab. 37/78/102, "Japanese Alliance," Arnold-Forster, 6/2/05. He and others worried that Britain's reliance on a non-European power to prop up its empire would be taken by "the natives" as a sign of decadence.

vinced almost everyone, even Lord Kitchener, that war was improbable for the foreseeable future.[243] Clarke's figures now served to buttress what had suddenly become a widely held belief. If Balfour had any doubts about his new, hastily contrived insurance policy, he could comfort himself with the thought that, if Clarke was right, it was extremely unlikely ever to be put into effect.[244] At long last the prime minister could afford to put India (and the possibility of drastic military reform that went with it) to one side.

Balfour was not the only one happy to turn away from a puzzle he could not solve. Five days after the renewed treaty was signed on 12 August, Clarke wrote to the prime minister informing him that the General Staff was about to begin work on a new problem—the delivery of 70,000 men to Belgium in the event of a Franco-German war.[245] "A study of this kind is just what the General Staff would like," Clarke sniffed, "and they might (perhaps) be able to achieve more success than in dealing with the Indian frontier."[246]

Events had conspired to rescue the Conservative government from its uncomfortable dilemma. With the Russian threat presumably diminished, the problem of army reform was suddenly less pressing. The quantities of military power that the nation's leaders were able or willing to generate now seemed once again to approximate the scale of the challenges with which they were faced. But this had more to do with good luck than it did with prudent strategic planning.

One who continued to view the situation with concern after the signing of the Anglo-Japanese treaty was Lord Roberts. From the Boer War Roberts had derived two fundamental lessons: "1. That in future campaigns we must expect demands on a vast scale for

For the views of the General Staff see PRO, WO 106/44, "Anglo-Japanese Agreement of August 12, 1905: Proposals for Concerted Action—Memorandum by the General Staff," General Staff, 11/4/05. See also Nish, *The Anglo-Japanese Alliance*, p. 319.

[243] BM, Add. Mss. 50835, Kitchener to Clarke, 6/15/05.

[244] Nish writes that the military assistance clause was nothing more than a "brainwave" cooked up by Clarke and sold to Balfour "without enough consultation and without enough consideration of the ultimate tactical problems involved" (*The Anglo-Japanese Alliance*, p. 355).

[245] The General Staff had been thinking of such operations as early as the beginning of the year. On 12 January Clarke informed Balfour scornfully that "the General Staff is getting on with the revised Kriegspiel, which I hope they will treat as seriously and as carefully as possible. Unfortunately they are being employed on a huge European campaign in which we are to act in some capacity in Belgium. This is among the least likely of many contingencies" (BM, Add. Mss. 49701, Clarke to Balfour, 1/12/05). On the origins of British planning for a war in Europe see Williamson, *The Politics of Grand Strategy: Britain and France Prepare for War, 1904–1914*, pp. 30–88.

[246] BM, Add. Mss. 49702, Clarke to Balfour, 8/17/05.

Infantry drafts. 2. That our Reserve is not large enough and must be increased. . . . Unless we can arrange for a much larger Reserve than we had in 1899, we might find ourselves in very great difficulty."[247] Unlike most of his colleagues, the commander in chief had actually welcomed the debate over India as a way of bringing home these plain truths and forcing the government to make some appropriate response. "I am thankful that the question of reinforcements for India has been brought prominently to light," he wrote Kitchener in March 1904, "and I trust that it will result in the unpreparedness of this country for engaging in a serious war being realized."[248] "For the first time I imagine, the Prime Minister has been made aware of the real state of the Army and how impossible it would be for it to undertake a war against a great European power."[249]

Roberts believed that it was only through some form of conscription that Britain could prepare itself adequately for the enormous demands of modern ground warfare. But, he conceded in the spring of 1904, "it is difficult to say whether the country are yet prepared for the only way in which we can hope to get anything like a sufficient reserve, *viz:* by some kind of compulsory military training."[250]

If the people were not ready to admit the need for conscription, then it might be the duty of statesmen to persuade them that their responsibilities had exceeded their collective power. The defeat of Russia by Japan could provide a breathing spell in which to repair crucial weaknesses, but such an interlude would not last forever.[251] With the passage of time, Roberts became increasingly worried that fortuitous events in the Far East were being used as an excuse for sweeping the nation's military problems under the rug. The discussion of an extended Anglo-Japanese treaty and the sequential failure of the various plans for army reform could only have served to heighten this concern.

On 10 July Roberts wrote Balfour warning of his intention to begin a public campaign for what he called "Universal Military Training." "I feel that I cannot any longer keep silence as to the condition of our Armed Forces, or allow my fellow countrymen to remain in ignorance of the tremendous risks they run, if they continue to ignore the necessity for their taking a personal share in the

[247] BM, Add. Mss. 49725, Roberts to Sandars, 1/17/03. The two points Roberts makes are quoted from a letter by Lord Lansdowne written in June 1900 while the latter was still secretary of state for war.

[248] PRO, 30/57, Roberts to Kitchener, 3/2/04.
[249] PRO, 30/57, Roberts to Kitchener, 3/30/04.
[250] Ibid.
[251] BM, Add. Mss. 49725, Roberts to Balfour, 4/26/04.

arrangements for the Defence of the Empire." [252] Two weeks later the aging general's mood was even more gloomy. "Army matters cannot be allowed to drift as they are now doing," he wrote Balfour. "At times I despair of any improvement without some national disaster." [253]

The prime minister sought to mollify Roberts by admitting that his efforts to deal with the military situation had been less than completely successful. On the day the renewed treaty with Japan was signed, he confessed that "one of the greatest disappointments I have had to submit to in the last two or three years is the failure to find, or to get adopted, some new organization which would give greater power of military expansion in time of war, and, if possible, bring with it greater economies in time of peace." [254] Nevertheless, *some* improvements had been made, and it would be both incorrect and politically harmful to claim otherwise.

Roberts's response was bitter and frustrated. "If the Nation will not submit to Universal Training, they must take the consequences," he told the prime minister's secretary. It was the duty of the country's political leadership to say frankly where matters stood and not to simply pretend that all was well. [255] As to the prime minister's claim of progress, it was surely true that the army was in some ways better organized than it once had been.

> But to enable a war to be carried on, such as we have been contemplating against Russia in Afghanistan, or to send an Army into Belgium or Holland, as has been once or twice mooted at the Defence Committee meetings, we are most assuredly no better prepared than we were in 1899–1900. . . . Even to meet Kitchener's demands during the first year of the war, it has been found necessary to include several battalions of Militia (every one of which it must be remembered may refuse to volunteer for service in Afghanistan) composed of officers who know but little of soldier's work, and of men unable to shoot and without sufficient training to warrant their being trusted in the fighting line. [256]

By the fall Roberts had decided to quit government and begin mobilizing public support for Universal Military Training. Such a scheme was to be distinguished from conscription because it in-

---

[252] BM, Add. Mss. 49725, Roberts to Balfour, 7/10/05.

[253] BM, Add. Mss. 49725, Roberts to Balfour, 7/23/05.

[254] BM, Add. Mss. 49725, Balfour to Roberts, 8/12/05.

[255] BM, Add. Mss. 49725, Roberts to Sandars, 8/14/05.

[256] BM, Add. Mss. 49725, Roberts to Balfour, 8/28/05.

volved compulsory *training* for all boys and young men, not compulsory *service* (which would be required only in the most extreme emergencies). Whatever its limitations, Roberts believed his plan was the only one that offered hope of providing Britain with the manpower necessary for the defense of its interests. If UMT had been in effect in 1899, it would have supplied "sufficient numbers of men trained to arms" so that "the war in South Africa would never have dragged on for two years and eight months."[257]

The departure of its most respected soldier was an embarrassment to the Balfour administration, but it must also have come as something of a relief. With Roberts gone the Indian problem could be regarded essentially as solved, and the pressure for far-reaching military reform could be dismissed as one among many external irritants. At a CID meeting on 21 November Balfour reassured his colleagues that Roberts's universal training plan was really just another form of conscription, unacceptable to sensible men almost by definition. "I will not ask whether such a scheme is *likely* to be accepted by the people of this country," the prime minister said rather archly. "But we may properly inquire whether it *ought* to be accepted." The army might be "wholly insufficient in point of numbers to carry on a great continental war unaided by continental forces" (something that even the most vigorous military reform advocates had never demanded that it be able to do), but "this . . . is, of course, nothing new. England never has carried on such a war."[258]

The situation in India, Balfour admitted, was "no doubt different."

> The extension of railways up to the Afghan frontier has rendered war with a great Power a military possibility—a new circumstance, whose importance, from the point of view of army organization, is not, as I think, affected either by the Anglo-Japanese Alliance or by the great improbability of a conflict with Russia. It is quite right, therefore, that we should ask ourselves whether an army recruited on the voluntary system is sufficient to meet the new situation, or whether, like the nations of the Continent, we must submit our necks to the yoke of compulsory military service. The reason that I am content to

[257] In the long run Roberts also hoped that universal training would inculcate patriotism, "counteract the physical and moral degeneracy" of crowded city life, and, by increasing "moral and educational discipline," aid "the Nation in the industrial struggle that lies before it" (BM, Add. Mss. 49725, Roberts to Balfour, 10/3/05).

[258] PRO, Cab. 2/1, "Minutes of 81st CID," 11/21/05.

adhere to the voluntary system is based upon long discussions upon Indian frontier defence.[259]

In fact, of course, the prime minister was being disingenuous on at least two counts. What needed to be done and what the nation would accept had not been kept nearly so distinct as his remarks appeared to suggest. Recent events (the war and the treaty) were far more important in setting his mind at ease about India than the "long discussions" that preceded them. As for the prospect of a European war, it seemed for the moment to be almost impossibly remote.

Conclusion
The Assessment of Land Power

In a speech to the House of Commons in August 1902, Arthur Balfour reflected on the difficulties facing the statesmen of a great, insular power as compared with those confronting the leaders of Continental states.

> The problem which other nations have to solve is in most cases one of extreme simplicity. They have not a great Colonial Empire to defend; they know with absolute precision what are their dangers, from what quarter those dangers come, what is the magnitude of them and by what organization of counter-arrangements these dangers can be met. . . . While the problems of foreign Governments may be onerous in respect of the amount of financial contribution required, and may be difficult in consequence of the difficulty of providing an adequate force, the intellectual and speculative elements of those problems are incomparably below those of the problems presented by the British Empire.[260]

Instead of one critical frontier and one enemy (like France) or even two of each (like Germany), England and its imperial possessions presented many, widely separated points of possible ground attack. In order to determine the level of military capability necessary to defend the empire as a whole, British strategists had therefore to make a simultaneous estimate of all the various threats they faced. Historically, no single site had ever seemed vulnerable to the

[259] Ibid.
[260] Contained in PRO, Cab. 37/63/145, "Memorandum on the Need for Organization for War," H. O. Arnold-Forster, 10/20/02, p. 28.

full weight of the land forces of a powerful enemy. By the end of the nineteenth century, however, changes in both the balance of sea power and the development of overland communications appeared to have increased the level of danger in many parts of the empire.

Assuming that the scale of possible attacks could be predicted in advance, Britain's military planners still faced the difficult task of distributing their own scarce resources around the world. Men, even less than ships, could not be moved immediately from one place to another. Indeed, the long sea voyages between imperial outposts and the possibility of naval interdiction meant that there would be inevitable lags in reinforcing garrisons even if some warning of impending attack was available. As a result, the forces stationed at each location would have to be able to fend for themselves in at least the opening stages of any war. A garrison that was too small could be overrun before help arrived. If too many soldiers were tied up in any one place, however, they might leave other prime targets dangerously exposed.

Faced with these complexities and uncertainties, imperial strategists did not try to take refuge in a single, global index of power of the sort that provided at least the illusion of certainty at sea. There was no two-power standard in ground forces that would have required Great Britain to maintain an army equal to those of its largest rivals. Instead the nation's military experts broke their overall problem down into a series of lesser puzzles (defense of the home islands, of India, of Canada, and so on). Within the confines of each of these discrete theaters, manpower figures were accepted as the appropriate indicator of military power.

After the Boer War, Afghanistan came to be viewed as the most probable site of a future land war between Britain and one of its many potential enemies. As this chapter has described, however, the way in which the Indian defense problem was approached after 1900 was largely a reflection of assumptions formulated over ten years earlier. The likely avenues of Russian advance, the need for a prompt British counteroffensive, and the strategic importance of Kabul and Kandahar had all been established during earlier discussions. Subsequent analysis usually took the form of an elaborate counting game.[261] If the Russians could move so many men into

[261] It is interesting to note the importance of certain numbers in this process. Once reinforcements had emerged as the crucial factor, the figures of 30,000, 70,000, and 100,000 men took on a life of their own. The last became an irreducible measure of the minimum British commitment to India. With the passage of time (and the extension of Russia's railroads) the figure sometimes

Afghanistan in a certain amount of time then the British believed that they would have to be able to confront them with a somewhat larger expeditionary force. As some observers would eventually complain, the often fanciful war games played out at the War Office and in India treated units like men on a chessboard, moving them easily from one location to another and stacking them up on opposing squares. The winner at any given site was simply assumed to be the country with the larger accumulation of playing pieces.

This mechanical method of assessing a complex military situation had two important consequences. First, it encouraged what appear in retrospect to have been exaggerated fears of a possible Russian invasion of Afghanistan. Such an attack was not, as historian David Dilks has written, "a vision so remote as to be inconceivable, especially after the Russian railways in Central Asia moved forward." [262] Nevertheless, the geographical, logistic, and local political obstacles to an invasion would clearly have been immense. Straight comparative manpower calculations tended, almost literally, to flatten things out, pushing aside these considerations and making a large, swift attack seem easier than it would probably have been.

The way in which assessments were conducted also guaranteed that the Indian problem would eventually produce a major defense planning crisis. As the presumed enemy invasion force grew, so too did the requirement for more British troops. Through their assumptions about the nature of the battlefield, the capacity of the Russian rail system, and the need to match or better the enemy in numbers of men deployed, the British had brought themselves (on paper at least) to the edge of "absolute war." It was as if, in a few short years, Britain had somehow drifted into contact with a major Continental power, acquiring in the process all the burdens on land that geographical good fortune had previously precluded.

Unstoppable Force Meets Immovable Object

The military crisis of 1901–1905 culminated in the collision of two weighty elements. On the one hand stood the apparently inescapable need for ever larger reinforcements for India; on the other, the seemingly insurmountable political objections to any major changes in the traditional British military system. Fears about

---

went up, but it never went down. When the Liberal government reviewed the question in 1907, the consensus among military experts was once again that 100,000 men would have to be sent from England to India in the first year of a war (PRO, Cab. 6/3/98D, "Report of the Sub-Committee on the Military Requirements of the Empire: India," 5/1/07).

[262] Dilks, *Retreat From Power* 1:4.

the inadequacy of that system and, in particular, about its apparent inability to provide enough trained men to defend the empire went back to well before the turn of the century. These concerns reached a peak following the early setbacks of the Boer War, when high-ranking officials were forced to consider the possibility that conscription might be the only way of providing the army with necessary manpower.

Public and governmental enthusiasm for a draft receded as the war in South Africa drew to a close. From 1902 onward, most military reformers concentrated on developing schemes to reorganize the volunteer army and expand its expeditionary force without actually increasing its overall size. Nevertheless, the option of conscription was now taken more seriously than it had been before. As India's reinforcement demands escalated, there seemed reason to believe that a future war would quickly strip the empire of all its readily available forces. Experts like Lord Roberts began to argue again that a peacetime draft of some sort was the only mechanism capable of creating an adequate standing army and, even more important, a sufficiently large pool of highly trained reservists.

By the end of 1904 Britain's leaders were on the verge of having to choose between a radical overhaul of their military system and the acceptance of what they believed to be an increasingly precarious balance on the Indian frontier. The only escape seemed to lie in some diminution of the Russian threat. This apparent miracle was made possible by a reexamination of the assumptions underlying the entire assessment process and, more importantly, by sheer good fortune.

Following Russia's loss to Japan, the likelihood of conscription being adopted in Britain dwindled and disappeared. The political costs of such a departure were all too obvious, and the military benefits were difficult for most Conservative cabinet ministers to perceive. Like Joseph Chamberlain before him, Lord Roberts despaired of being able directly to change the minds of his colleagues and instead left government to mobilize public opinion in favor of Universal Military Training. As his campaign got under way, Roberts tried to reopen the question of homeland defense, using the danger of a German invasion to arouse popular support for his proposals.[263] The effort was ultimately unsuccessful, and it is hard to imagine that, if a threat to Britain itself was insufficient, anything else would have persuaded the nation of the need for conscription.

[263] See Williamson, *The Politics of Grand Strategy*, pp. 304–11.

Table 5-1
Distribution of British Regular Army
(In Infantry Battalions)

Garrison	1899	1906
Home	71	81
India	52	52
Egypt	2	4
Malta	8	7
Gibraltar	3	3
South Africa	6	14
Mauritius	1	1
Canada	1	0
West Indies	2	1
Ceylon	1	½
China	2	1½
Malaya	0	1
Total	149	166

Source: Dunlop, *The Development of the British Army, 1899–1914,* p. 309.

A Risky Response

Whatever his excesses, Roberts had one very important point to make; regardless of the theater, a future war with a modern power would tax the nation as it had never been taxed before. India might no longer be in danger,[264] but with Britain's small army, its inadequate preparations for emergency expansion, and its long list of defensive commitments (to which France would shortly be added), the nation was still running considerable risks. These risks, in themselves, may have been acceptable and preferable to the alternatives. What was truly dangerous was an unwillingness to recognize the magnitude of the danger and an accompanying tendency to whittle down the threat to match the scale of available resources.

[264] Not everyone believed this immediately. At the beginning of 1905 Clarke relayed to Balfour suggestions from some intelligence experts that the Russians would move into Afghanistan in order "to reestablish their prestige" (BM, Add. Mss. 49701, Clarke to Balfour, 2/15/05). As late as May the British ambassador in Tokyo warned that Russia's "next venture is much more likely to be an attack upon us through India than an attempt to wipe out old scores with [the Japanese]" (Macdonald to Lansdowne, 5/25/05, cited in Williams, "The Strategic Background to the Anglo-Russian Entente of August 1907," p. 302). Still, according to one historian, after the summer of 1907 "India ceased to bulk large, indeed to bulk at all, in the cycles of strategic debate in England" (J. Gooch, *The Plans of War,* p. 2).

At the close of 1905, as the Indian debate was winding down, British military planners were beginning to focus more of their attention on the possibility of a war in Europe. In October a General Staff officer wrote that

> an efficient army of 120,000 British Troops, might just have the effect of preventing any important German successes on the France-German border, and of leading up to the situation that Germany crushed at sea, also felt herself impotent on land. That would also certainly bring about a speedy, and from the British and French points of view, satisfactory peace.[265]

When the Liberal government came to power at the beginning of 1906, the figure of 120,000 men was being formally recommended by the director of Military Operations.[266] Eight years later this was precisely the size of the first British force sent to assist France. It was not nearly enough. Before the war was over, Britain would lose seven times its initial commitment in battlefield casualties alone.[267]

---

[265] "British Military Action in Case of War with Germany," Colonel Callwell, 10/3/05, quoted in Williamson, *The Politics of Grand Strategy*, p. 50.

[266] PRO, WO 106/44/E1.7, "Memorandum upon the Military Forces Required for Over-Sea Warfare," D. M. Grierson, 1/4/06.

[267] Briggs, *A Social History of England*, p. 258.

Change, Assessment, and Adaptation

Without a constant falsification of the world by means of numbers, man could not live.
—Nietzsche, *Beyond Good and Evil*

The first chapter of this study began with three questions: How do statesmen measure relative national power? How do individuals and entire governments become aware of unfavorable changes in the relative power of their own countries? And how do nations seek to adapt to such shifts?

Chapter 1's review of the theoretical literature suggested two alternative sets of answers to these questions in the form of two stylized models. The calculative model assumes a rational process of counting and comparison, and it predicts that both assessments and policies will change smoothly and continuously in response to objective shifts in relative national power. The perceptual model, on the other hand, postulates that assessments are based on images or beliefs. These images are likely to be "sticky"; they will change little (if at all) except as the result of dramatic events. The pattern of national adaptation should therefore be sharply discontinuous, with inaction interrupted by some major crisis that will, in turn, be followed by dramatic changes in overall policy.

The British case does not fit neatly into either of these alternative outlines. In Britain the process of assessment was not unified but divided into a series of debates over the different forms of national power. Each of these parallel discussions was shaped and, in varying degrees, distorted by the presence of simple numerical indicators. Official assessments shifted more quickly in some areas than others, but, in each, change was the result of gradual developments in the thinking of key individuals combined with external shocks. Adaptive policies were also pursued unevenly, with more movement in some sectors than in others. As will be discussed in greater detail below, there are reasons for believing that what was true of Britain at the turn of the century may also be true in other cases.

Assessment
Organizational Fragmentation

At the center of the calculative model is the picture of an individual or an agency of the government coolly measuring the total capabilities of all relevant states. In the perceptual model the unit of analysis is either the consciousness of a single ruler or a collective "official mind" made up of the presumably shared beliefs of a group of statesmen. For reasons that are also likely to apply in other instances, neither of these two unified images adequately captures the reality of the British case.

In Britain during the period under study, government estimates were not the product of a single mind or agency. Instead, the assessment process was fragmented, both intellectually and bureaucratically. People did at times think and talk in terms of "national power" writ large, but they tended for the most part to concentrate on the different forms that the nation's power was assumed to take, whether economic, financial, naval, or military.

This conceptual separation was both reflected and reinforced by the natural division of labor within the government. The military and naval intelligence branches of the two services collected information on the capabilities of foreign armies and navies. Their products were used at irregular intervals by the War Office (and later the General Staff) and the Admiralty to compare Britain's land or sea forces with their opposite numbers in opposing countries. No natural bureaucratic home existed for cross-national comparisons of combined naval and military capabilities, and these were therefore quite rare. Outside the realm of defense, the Board of Trade kept track of British imports and exports, and, under political direction from above, it occasionally tried to measure Britain's economic performance against that of other states. Treasury Department officials monitored government revenues and expenditures and made running comparisons between present and past levels of absolute spending.

Thus, as the twentieth century opened, the British looked both inward and outward with many "eyes" and with more (or perhaps less) than a single "brain." There was no office charged with collecting the full range of available information and formulating all-encompassing appreciations of the nation's position. To the extent that the various strands came together at all, it was only at irregular intervals within the confines of the Committee of Imperial Defence.

Despite Britain's shortcomings in this regard, its contemporaries seem to have been at least as poorly off.[1] Whether in essentially democratic or what might now be called authoritarian regimes, bureaucratization meant compartmentalization. Unless special steps were taken to overcome the resulting separation, intelligence agencies, foreign offices, trade ministries, treasuries, and the armed forces tended to perform their partial calculations in isolation from one another. In imperial Germany, for example, the merging of information about the outside world was inhibited by the navy's flat refusal to exchange intelligence with the General Staff. Despite their much-vaunted efficiency, the Germans lacked even as flawed a unifying body as the British CID. Thus, according to one historian of the period, "the Kaiser's ad hoc councils remained, at least in theory, the only arenas where differences in estimates by the services or by diplomats could confront one another."[2]

This tendency toward fragmentation is not unique to the era before 1914. For Britain the problem of coordinating assessments of foreign powers (the "outward looking" portion of the entire process) persisted well into the interwar period. Indeed, with the creation of an independent Air Ministry intelligence arm and the formation of the so-called Industrial Intelligence Center, it seems to have become even more complex.[3] By one account, during the 1930s the various intelligence staffs "had little to do with each other. No joint staffs existed. . . . The British government had no adequate machinery for the collation and assessment of intelligence."[4]

After the Second World War, the United States sought to alleviate its own coordination problem by creating a Central Intelligence Agency. In theory this should have made it possible to formulate agreed "national" estimates of the capabilities and intentions of foreign states. In practice, of course, there are today still frequent disagreements between different portions of the intelligence commu-

---

[1] Paul Kennedy argues that, as of 1900, France, Russia, Austria-Hungary, the United States, and Germany were all behind Britain in an effort to integrate "strategical, diplomatic and economic factors" (letter to the author, 16 February 1987).

[2] Holger Herwig, "Imperial Germany," in May, *Knowing One's Enemies:* *Intelligence Assessment Before the Two World Wars*, p. 90.

[3] On the organization of British intelligence in the 1930s see Wark, *The Ultimate Enemy: British Intelligence and Nazi Germany, 1933–1939*, pp. 20–22.

[4] Dilks, "Appeasement and 'Intelligence,'" in Dilks, ed., *Retreat From Power* 1 : 141–42.

nity over the significance of external developments. Even if there were none, the question of where and how to draw comparisons between the power of foreign countries and that of the United States would still remain. One participant in the process reports that, as of the midseventies, the CIA's national intelligence officer for the Soviet Union was specifically enjoined to "ignore U.S. capabilities and avoid balance-of-power estimates ('net assessments')."[5] Presumably these estimates were to be performed only by the various military services.[6] Nevertheless, it was at around this time that an Office of Net Assessment charged specifically with the formulation of such comparisons was created for the first time inside the Department of Defense. Despite the apparently unprecedented breadth of its charter, because of its location this bureau was constrained to concentrate on calculations of relative military power. Broader, comprehensive net assessments (like the Carter administration's Presidential Review Memorandum 10) have been attempted, but only on an ad hoc basis.[7]

Although efforts to overcome them are possible, there would appear to be strong organizational forces acting to push modern states away from a unified assessment process and toward a more fragmented approximation of that ideal.

The Importance of Indicators

In its most extreme form, the calculative model suggests the possibility of a single, universal, statistical measure of national capabilities. In the perceptual model, in contrast, groups of statesmen are assumed to possess common, but considerably vaguer, beliefs about other countries (and, in particular, about their strengths and weaknesses) as well as equivalent "self-images."

The British case reveals a complex mixture of calculation and belief. In 1900 most Englishmen probably still shared an overarching confidence in the superiority of their own country, which, as time passed, was based more on faith and habit than on facts. Supporting this larger conception were a number of more specific, partial self-images or beliefs about the different components of British power—about the might of the Royal Navy, for example ("Britan-

[5] Pipes, "Team B: The Reality Behind the Myth," p. 29.

[6] Kaufmann, *A Reasonable Defense*, pp. 109–10.

[7] According to former national security affairs adviser Zbigniew Brzezinski, the PRM-10 study was undertaken at the beginning of the Carter administration because of the need to obtain "not only a narrowly focused accounting of the relative military strength of the two countries but a more sophisticated appraisal of the relative performance— military, political, economic and ideological—of the two competing systems" (*Power and Principle*, p. 177).

nia rules the waves") or the capacity of the nation's economy ("the workshop of the world"). Alongside these were a set of similar beliefs, both whole and partial, about the power of other countries. Russia was feared because of the awesome size of its land army (the "steamroller"), while Turkey was dismissed as the decrepit "sick man of Europe."

These images were probably as common among statesmen and bureaucrats as in the mind of the man on the street. Internal discussions were, however, by no means limited to the repetition of platitudes. Inside the government simple mental pictures coincided and intermingled with a seemingly endless stream of detailed calculations. These, as has already been suggested, did not take the form of an effort to compile some sort of universal index of power, but instead were conducted separately in several distinct realms.

The mix of calculation and belief that characterized official assessments is most readily apparent in the widespread use of a handful of simple, compact indicators of national capabilities. As the preceding chapters have discussed, in each of four functional areas debate centered on a single measure of power, whether the trade returns, absolute government spending figures, numbers of battleships, or infantry reinforcements. These indicators did not emerge freshly minted from a careful attempt at analysis undertaken in 1895 or 1900 by a newly elected government. In fact, most of the intellectual apparatus that the Conservatives brought to bear on the problem of assessing Britain's relative power had been handed down to them in one form or another from previous administrations. The indicators at hand in 1895 had evolved gradually over many years and, in some cases, for much of the preceding century. During that time they had been shaped by a variety of influences, including the exigencies of particular periods, the availability of information, bureaucratic custom, and the assumptions prevailing in public, governmental, and academic circles about the various forms of national power.

By itself each indicator represented the neat condensation of a wide range of considerations into a single, seemingly solid, measure. The two-power standard, for example, was built up out of beliefs about the nature of naval warfare, guesses about the likely political environment that Britain would have to face, and assumptions about the relationship among the various theaters of operations. Taken together, the indicators provided a set of common symbols, a language of sorts, that played an essential role in facilitating the government's collective analytical efforts. Without them each debate over policy would have had to return to a discussion of fundamentals, and communication among officials and between agencies as well as between the government and the public would probably have broken down altogether.

Language may be necessary to promote understanding within groups, but it also seems inevitably to distort the reality it seeks to represent. It should come as no surprise, then, that the strength of the indicators was also their weakness. In simplifying complex problems they narrowed attention to a very small range of familiar, countable factors (concentrating people's minds on numbers of battleships, for example, at the expense of adequate attention to strategic and tactical considerations or to the likely future role of submarines). Because their focus was so limited, the accepted indicators were at times quite misleading (as with the use of the trade returns as surrogate measures of comparative national economic performance). At best (in the calculation of Indian manpower requirements, for example), they conveyed a stylized, flattened picture of processes (like warfare) that were, in fact, multidimensional.

At the deepest level, the use of numerical indicators seems inexorably to have drawn attention away from the more important, functional questions out of which they originally arose and toward the easier but less central task of measuring resources. Government officials may have started out by asking, "How great a financial burden can the nation bear?" or "Can we maintain worldwide sea control?" but they usually ended up answering questions like "How high are our taxes?" or "Are we meeting the Two Power Standard?"

The indicators made discussion possible while simultaneously distorting and ultimately dominating it. Over time they tended to cut deep grooves in the minds of Britain's leaders and to become invested with a symbolic significance that far exceeded their actual usefulness. Their widespread acceptance and repeated use made it difficult and at times even politically dangerous to question the assumptions on which they had initially been based or to examine in a new light the problems at which they had first been directed. As underlying circumstances changed, the existing measures of power remained largely the same, giving those who used them a false sense of stability and security. In the British case, at least, the use of simple numerical measures seems to have encouraged a tendency toward conservatism on the part of decision makers. Because of their narrow scope and their fixative quality, the indicators often obscured the significance of major political, doctrinal, economic, and technological developments, thereby making it more difficult for those who used them to reach a realistic appreciation of ongoing shifts in the distribution of relative national power.

Even a cursory examination of other historical examples suggests that a tendency toward the use of indicators is widespread across time and in different countries.[8] Between the world wars, French strategists were obsessed with manpower and total population figures as indicators of relative military power.[9] During the same period, the British turned a large part of their attention from battleships to long-range bombers and added a requirement for "air parity" to the old naval standard.[10] In the 1960s American intelligence agencies concentrated heavily on numbers of nuclear missile launchers as the best measure of strategic power.[11]

The apparent pervasiveness of simple indicators may help to explain why statesmen are not always able to formulate accurate estimates of the relative power of their own country. Although the impact of such measures will vary from case to case, their use seems likely to inhibit rather than to promote recognition of changes in relative power.

Shifts in Assessment

This last observation raises the question of how assessments do, in fact, change over time. The calculative model that lies, explicitly or otherwise, at the heart of most efforts to construct theories of inter-

[8] Robert Jervis has made a similar observation. He argues that leaders use oversimplified measures as one way of decreasing what he calls the "burden of cognition." In general, Jervis suggests that efforts to simplify calculation tend to encourage inertia and incrementalism in policy making ("The Model of the Drunkard's Search" [mimeo] and letter to the author, 30 May 1986).

[9] Historian Judith Hughes observes that most people at this time were "accustomed to measuring French military strength by comparing French and German birth rates." She goes on to describe how, during the 1920s, Marshall Ferdinand Foch "in a compulsive fashion . . . noted repeatedly the numbers of divisions the new nations of eastern Europe might be able to mobilize in the event of all-out war. He kept juggling the figures until the combined total of their forces and those of France approximated his estimate of German strength" (*To the Maginot Line*, pp. 21, 59).

[10] "Air parity" meant equality in numbers with the largest European bomber force. Until the late thirties, sophisticated analyses of the balance of air power and, in particular, the likely interaction of attacking and defending aircraft, were inhibited in part by the concentration on bomber counting. Formulaic demands for equality were repeated so often that one British official complained of what he called "the parrot-cry of 'parity'" (Shay, *British Rearmament in the Thirties*, p. 188). On the airpower debates of the thirties see Churchill, *The Gathering Storm*, pp. 110–29; Gilbert, *Winston S. Churchill: The Prophet of Truth* 5:485–510, 549–80, 623–76, 717–80, 794–808, 874–920; Bialer, *The Shadow of the Bomber: The Fear of Air Attack and British Politics, 1932–1939;* Wark, "British Intelligence on the German Air Force and Aircraft Industry, 1933–1939," pp. 627–48.

[11] See Wohlstetter, "Is There a Strategic Arms Race?" pp. 3–20. See also Freedman, *U.S. Intelligence and the Soviet Strategic Threat.*

national politics, suggests that shifts in power will be readily detected. If assessments are largely a product of perceptions, on the other hand, they should not be expected to evolve quickly or easily, even in the presence of considerable evidence that objective changes have occurred.

The initial reaction of Britain's leaders, taken as a group, to the events of the late-nineteenth and early-twentieth centuries can fairly be described as having been closer to that predicted by the perceptual model. Certainly there was no swift, accurate, and collective recognition of what appear now to have been significant objective developments. To speak of collective perceptions is always a risky thing, however, and in this case such a convenient simplification would be seriously misleading. Examining a cross-sectional slice of the men in power between 1895 and 1905 reveals that, at any given moment, different people believed different things, and some people clung to their beliefs more firmly than others. In order to understand how and why assessments changed, it is necessary to look at the unfolding debates in which these individuals were engaged.

While the dominant view might have been essentially optimistic, discussion in each of the four areas considered here was influenced by men inside the government who might be called "change agents"—those who, for various reasons, had come to disagree with the prevailing consensus about the different aspects of Britain's power. These men arrived at their opinions over differing periods of time and from a range of distinct personal experiences. Although by the turn of the century they shared certain attitudes and had some overlapping policy preferences, their many differences on tariffs, taxes, and the relative importance of the navy versus the army prevented them from ever forming a dominant alliance within the Conservative party.

Joseph Chamberlain, whose background in manufacturing probably made him more sensitive to industrial problems than many of his eventual Conservative allies, began to worry about Britain's economic future while serving in the 1880s as a Liberal chairman of the Board of Trade. He would later make his critique of free trade into the centerpiece of a campaign to solidify the empire, rejuvenate the British economy, and, coincidentally, promote his own political career. Edward Hamilton's consistent, orthodox views on financial matters and his long experience at the Treasury Department led him to warn of an impending fiscal crisis well before most members of the government were prepared to accept the need either for retrenchment or major tax reform. Admiral John Fisher became convinced of the futility of opposing the United States in its home waters during the 1890s while in command of the North American squadron. Fisher's judgment about Britain's untenable position in the Western Hemisphere was one factor influencing his later conclusion that the Royal Navy should be reconcentrated in European waters. Lord Roberts's worries about the size and readiness of the British army began while he was commander in chief in India during the 1880s and early 1890s, intensified during the Boer War, and subsequently caused him to quit the Government in protest over its resistance to conscription.

The warnings of this handful of worriers did not lead, independently, to rapid, widespread change. Although there was some gradual evolution, official assessments tended to be relatively stable over time. Without an external crisis the efforts of a few individuals to modify the views of their contemporaries would probably not have amounted to much. But, when they came, crises were catalytic rather than simply causative; they did not abruptly change minds but instead opened them, if only briefly, to more pessimistic interpretations of the available evidence that were already "in the air." In the midst of a crisis or in its immediate aftermath, the advocates of change were able to win converts in their own bureaus, among members of the cabinet and, to the extent that there was open discussion, in Parliament and among the public as well.[12] Some of these conversions under fire were permanent; others lapsed with the diminution of a particular crisis. At the peak of the Boer War, for example, a large number of people might have been willing to accept a vision of the future of warfare in which a draft was the only feasible solution to Britain's long-term military problems. Once the war was over, anxiety and acceptance of the need for radical changes diminished rapidly, and the old consensus reasserted itself.

The progress of intellectual evolution was disjointed and uneven in pace across functional areas, with net movement in each a product of the strength of the initial consensus, the intensity and lon-

---

[12] This is a pattern similar to that found in other bureaucracies. Writing of the American executive branch, for example, Morton Halperin notes that at any given moment most of its members "prefer to maintain the status quo, and only a small group is advocating change." This minority is "likely to raise the issue when events, as they perceive them, either provide opportunities for change heretofore absent or increase the cost of continuing to operate without change" (Halperin, *Bureaucratic Politics and Foreign Policy*, pp. 99–100). See also the discussion of the role of "Indians" in persuading their "Chiefs" of the need for change in Allison, *Essence of Decision: Explaining the Cuban Missile Crisis*, p. 176.

gevity of the external shock, and the effectiveness of the agents of change. Thus, between 1895 and 1905, prevailing official assessments of the financial and naval situations had altered more noticeably than those in the economic and military spheres. Even when an old consensus persisted, however (on the state of the economy, for example), it was weaker, shakier, and more susceptible to the effect of future shocks than it had been before the turn of the century. The old platitudes were still heard, but fewer people seem to have believed in them as fervently as before. Nonetheless, a series of setbacks would be needed before the majority view could be eroded and, eventually, overthrown.

The picture that emerges here is of a process that must be explained in intellectual and bureaucratic as well as psychological terms. There was undoubtedly a strong general resistance to accepting evidence of the erosion in Britain's position. At the same time it must be said that "the facts" were not always nearly so obvious at the time as they have come to seem in retrospect. This was not a case of people willfully ignoring a readily apparent, if unpleasant, reality. As has been discussed, data were sometimes hard to come by, and measuring tools were imprecise and sometimes downright deceptive. Nevertheless, due to some combination of experience, temperament, self-interest, and quality of mind, certain individuals inside the government were able to reach a more accurate understanding of what was going on than others; they were, for various reasons, more alert, more skeptical about the existing indicators, and hence more open to signs of change than many of their colleagues. When external events gave them the opportunity, they did what they could to propagate their views.

Official assessments did not adjust steadily, but neither did they shift dramatically and decisively as the result of external shocks. In Britain change went forward as the result of gradual, diffuse intellectual developments that were consolidated and accelerated by periodic crises. If governments are spared some monumental disaster, this may be the way in which they are most likely to come to grips with unfavorable changes in relative national status.

Adaptation

Looked at as a whole, Britain's adaptation to relative decline during the period 1895 to 1905 does not fit into either of the outlines suggested by the two existing models. It was neither smooth, incremental, and continuous, nor in any way binary, completely "off" and then completely "on." Instead, at the level of national policy, the response was partial and, as will be argued in the next chapter, incomplete. In some areas, as in the economic sphere, there was no change at all. In others, like the naval realm, there was considerable movement. In between (as in the financial and military areas) there were relatively modest adjustments to previously existing policies.

This mixed overall response was a reflection both of the pattern of underlying assessments and of the division of domestic political power. A broad intragovernmental consensus would have been the necessary precondition for a coordinated response to the erosion in Britain's international position, but, in and of itself, it would not have been enough. Even if the entire cabinet had been agreed on the need for, let us say, protection, higher taxes, conscription, and a larger navy, it would still have had to win approval for its program in Parliament and in the country as a whole. In fact, there is little likelihood that such a package would have been politically acceptable, and, in any case, there was no such initial, internal agreement, either about the need for or the preferred substance of changes in policy.

If a sweeping, across-the-board reaction to the nation's problems was impossible, attempts at more limited adjustments in particular sectors also ran into considerable difficulty. In some areas key government agencies had the power to act with a certain measure of independence. The Admiralty, for example, could redistribute its ships without the consent of the army. Whatever Joseph Chamberlain might have wanted, on the other hand, the Colonial Office could not unilaterally impose his plan for an imperial customs union on the government or the country (still less on the entire empire).

For the most part, compromise programs that were deemed politically viable had to be worked out by the responsible ministers for presentation to Parliament. Unable to reach some common understanding of the nation's economic problems, the cabinet could not agree either to full-scale protectionism or to absolute free trade and settled instead, after divisive debate and a series of high-level purges, on a proposal for retaliatory tariffs. The result, as registered in the 1906 elections, was resounding popular rejection. Divided over the severity of the military situation and realizing that, even if it was necessary, conscription would probably be rejected by the voters, the Government instead put forward a series of less sweeping plans for army reorganization. Several of these had to be abandoned in the face of harsh public criticism, and the Balfour administration was forced to leave unfinished the pressing task of military reform. Having finally accepted the need for change, but fearing the political and economic consequences of anything too drastic, the cabinet rejected tax increases and cuts in social spending in favor of defense retrenchment. Despite its risks, this approach met with widespread approval, although not enough, in the end, to prop up the Government's sagging popularity.

The results of this initial adaptive phase were therefore spotty at best. Instead of either failing to respond at all or promptly pursuing a single, coherent "national strategy," Britain reacted to the early evidence of relative decline with a handful of partial, and only partially coordinated, measures.

The British example suggests three general prerequisites for an integrated, national response to relative decline: internal consensus on the existence, nature, and extent of unfavorable changes, not just in one area but in several simultaneously; agreement inside the government on the appropriate set of responses to such changes; and, finally, the ability to implement the various parts of a planned response, assuming that one can be agreed upon. Countries in which power is concentrated, both in the state and inside the national government, seem, in theory at least, to have a better chance of responding in a coordinated, centrally directed way to early inklings of relative decline. It would not be surprising, therefore, if liberal democracies failed to do particularly well in this regard.

If this seems an unduly pessimistic note on which to conclude, it should be pointed out that coordination and wisdom are two very different things. The handful of men who ruled imperial Germany in 1914 responded to their own fears of decline by launching a war that brought them and their country to ruin. Factious, uncertain, and in many ways indecisive, democratic Britain certainly did better than that.

Summary

This analysis suggests a number of general conclusions:

First, assessment is clearly a crucial "intervening variable" [13] between objective changes in the structure of the international system and the behavior of individual states. Assessments are related to but not directly determined by reality. They are themselves, in turn, related to but not fully determinative of policy.

---

[13] This term is used by Stephen Krasner to describe the role of international regimes as "standing between basic causal factors on the one hand and outcomes and behavior on the other" ("Structural Causes and Regime Consequences: Regimes as Intervening Variables," in Krasner, ed., *International Regimes,* p. 1).

Second, the process through which modern governments weigh the power of other countries and compare it to their own is likely to be fragmented along bureaucratic and functional lines rather than unified in any central location or focused on any single aggregated measure of power.

Third, simple numerical indicators of capability will be central to most debates over the various components of relative national power.

Fourth, the more divided the process and the more heavily discussion in each area centers on a single indicator, the less likely it is that accurate sectoral or comprehensive assessments will emerge or that real changes in power will be readily recognized.

Fifth, external shocks are a necessary but not a sufficient condition for downward adjustments in assessments. The presence of individual "change agents" ready to capitalize on sudden developments is critical to the process through which such shifts occur.

Sixth, changes in assessments are likely to proceed more quickly in some sectors than in others. The entire process of movement from overall optimism to collective pessimism may take a long time to complete, even if accelerated by a series of shocks.

Seventh, the more widely distributed decision-making power is within a political system, the more likely it is that a nation's initial response to relative decline will be fragmented. Even if some partial responses do occur, they may not be complete or even "strategic" in any meaningful sense of the word.

SEVEN

Britain and the
Experience of Relative Decline

Men make their own history, but they do not make it just as they please.
—Marx, *The Eighteenth Brumaire of Louis Bonaparte*

In the conclusion to his study of the Congress of Vienna, Henry Kissinger writes that "each generation . . . can attempt only one interpretation and a single experiment, for it is its own subject. This is the challenge of history and its tragedy; it is the shape 'destiny' assumes on the earth."[1] What can be said, in retrospect, about the "experiment" performed between 1895 and 1905? Was it, even in some limited sense, successful? And, if it failed, was there any conceivable way that it might have been conducted so as to turn out differently?

A "Remarkable Feat"?

Most recent students of the period have concluded that Britain's late-Victorian and early-Edwardian leaders saw clearly what was happening to their country. Max Beloff, for example, writes of the 1890s that "there is little evidence of complacency at the top. . . . [Yet] those in whose hands power lay were for the most part undaunted by the new challenges to Britain's position that they sensed. They believed that measures could be devised to meet them; and they believed that they had the right to take such measures."[2] Similarly, Ronald Hyam observes that "the relative decline in world influence and the new pessimism led to a realisation that many

[1] Kissinger, *A World Restored*, p. 232.   [2] Beloff, *Imperial Sunset* 1:5.

changes would have to be made in Britain. The late Victorians did not whine about their problems but tried to find solutions."[3]

As was suggested in chapter 6, such generalizations about the quality of thought of Britain's leaders are too highly aggregated to be truly accurate. Some people did not see or refused to acknowledge the extent of the erosion in their national position. Others understood what was happening in one area but not elsewhere. Still others had moments of lucidity and concern, followed by a relapse into complacency. The picture is a varied one, with considerable disagreements inside the government about what was occurring and what, if anything, needed to be done, and even larger ones within the political system as a whole. As Paul Kennedy aptly notes in his study of both England and Germany during this period, "what emerges . . . more than anything else was the existence of *conflicting* schools of thought within the governmental machine."[4]

Britain's leaders were less than uniformly farsighted; not surprisingly, therefore, the policies they pursued also fell far short of lasting success. This is a conclusion that differs from much of what has already been written about the years 1895 to 1905. The common understanding of Britain's overall performance during this time, and, indeed, for much of the period from the turn of the century until the outbreak of the First World War, is that it represented a triumph of prudence, realism, and sound diplomacy. According to Michael Howard, the series of treaties into which Britain entered after 1900 "added up to quite a remarkable feat of diplomatic pacification."[5] The 1902 agreement with Japan alleviated British anxieties in the Far East and, together with an informal but no less important policy of appeasing the United States, freed naval resources for concentration in European waters. Despite years of mutual suspicion, the British were also able gradually to compose their differences with France and Russia. Failure to reach a similar accommodation with Germany was not the result of any lack of effort.

In addition to their diplomatic moves, Britain's leaders took other steps to improve their strategic position. London simply shed some of its lesser defensive commitments and elsewhere (as with Canada and India) encouraged its dependencies to take on a greater share of their own defense. There were also efforts aimed at im-

[3] Hyam, *Britain's Imperial Century, 1815–1915: A Study of Empire and Expansion*, p. 102.
[4] P. Kennedy, *The Rise of the Anglo-German Antagonism, 1860–1914*, p. 433.
[5] M. Howard, *The Continental Commitment*, p. 30.

proving imperial solidarity and extracting financial contributions from the self-governing colonies, and internal reorganizations intended to increase the fighting efficiency and reduce the costs of both the army and the navy. In all, Robert Gilpin concludes, in the decades prior to the First World War Great Britain was able to bring "its resources and commitments into balance."[6]

This account is not entirely inaccurate, although it does tend to overstate the extent to which British policy was the result of some coherent and careful strategic design. In fact, as has been described, the various agencies of the government often did not cooperate and at times did not even communicate with one another. Even the nation's diplomacy, which in retrospect gives the impression of coordination and calculation, was largely ad hoc and opportunistic. Thus historian J. A. S. Grenville writes of the developments of the period 1900–1905 that, while it is tempting to regard them "as the inevitable and logical outcome of some plan," in fact, "there was no 'master plan.' Although [Foreign Secretary] Lansdowne inaugurated the 'new course,' he had no clear conception of what the final outcome of his policy would be. The great change of British policy was the consequence not of one but of a number of piecemeal decisions."[7]

The standard view also overlooks the role of simple good fortune in improving Britain's prospects. If not for developments largely outside of its control, the situation after the turn of the century might have appeared entirely different. Japan's defeat of Russia lessened the pressure on Britain's eastern empire. Germany's erratic and heavy-handed initiatives served to drive France and Russia closer together and to push both of them toward accommodation with Great Britain.

Nevertheless, there can be no doubt that the strategic situation in 1905 was markedly better for Britain than it had been only ten years before. By the time Balfour left office there was no immediate need to fear a clash with Russia in the Mediterranean, Afghanistan, or the Far East. The probability of a war with France over African possessions or with the United States over developments in the Western Hemisphere had been considerably reduced. Britain now seemed free to concentrate the full weight of its attention on Germany. This, it is usually assumed, was the desirable end result of all British maneuvering from roughly 1900 onward. What most (but not all) contemporary and many modern observers have

[6] Gilpin, *War and Change in World Politics*, p. 194.
[7] Grenville, *Lord Salisbury and Foreign Policy: The Close of the Nineteenth Century*, p. 434.

tended to downplay, however, is the way in which the policies pursued at the turn of the century simply ignored or papered over serious underlying weaknesses in Britain's position or, in solving certain problems, created new and perhaps more dangerous ones.

An Untended Engine

The deepest source of all Great Britain's subsequent difficulties was, quite obviously, its economy. As the country's early lead eroded and eventually disappeared, its people ceased to enjoy their accustomed advantage in relative prosperity over all the other nations of the world. With the rise of overseas competitors, several key industries fell on hard times, and predominance in many of the old and most of the new sectors of production passed into the hands of foreigners. These changes had strategic as well as economic consequences. With the passage of time Britain found it more difficult to maintain its place in the peacetime military competition and became less capable of waging sustained, intensive warfare than several of its rivals. This was not simply a matter of differences in total wealth but also of relative technological sophistication. By 1914 Britain's backwardness in chemicals, electrical machinery, and precision engineering was so marked as to cause serious problems in its prosecution of the war against Germany.[8]

The question of how things might have been different has already been discussed at some length in the conclusion to chapter 2. Certainly protectionism and imperial unification were not the answer; if adopted, they would in all probability have only made matters worse. The great tragedy of the tariff reform debate, however, is that the warnings of the protectionists and their sometimes telling criticisms of liberal economic dogma were rejected along with their dubious remedies. Arthur Balfour's crucial recognition of the "general truth that there is no pre-established harmony between economic world interests and national well-being" was ignored or forgotten.[9] Yet, in a system of independent and some-

[8] Correlli Barnett reports that, at the outbreak of the war, Britain was almost entirely dependent on Germany for ball bearings, magnetos, optical glass, and many of the chemicals used in manufacturing dyes, drugs, poison gas, and high explosives. A heavy importer of German clocks and toys, England lacked the precision machinery needed to produce shell casings. Worst of all, the country had virtually no modern machine-tool industry. Shortages of engines, aircraft, and ammunition were the inevitable result, and, Barnett concludes, it was only "the purchase of American, Swedish and Swiss machine tools that prevented a total breakdown of the British effort to create new industries between 1914 and 1916" (*The Collapse of British Power*, pp. 84–88).

[9] Balfour, *Economic Notes on Insular Free Trade*, p. 5.

times hostile states, governments had reason to be concerned about the relative as well as the absolute performance of their national economies. The requirements of military preparedness also demanded that states take some interest in the composition of their industrial base, a fact that even Adam Smith had been quick to acknowledge.[10]

For the most part these insights were lost in the heat of debate over protectionism. After 1903 Englishmen tended to divide into those who clung to laissez faire and refused to acknowledge any difficulties and those who blamed all their country's woes on foreigners. A smaller and more discreet group recognized the onset of relative decline but believed that nothing could be done to arrest its progress. The possibility that limited government action could have improved the nation's overall economic performance by promoting research and development, encouraging domestic investment, and seeking better access to overseas markets was not given serious consideration. Nor was there sufficient recognition of the need for more active efforts to preserve and develop Britain's defense industrial base. Steel and shipbuilding were allowed to deteriorate, chemicals and electromechanical devices lagged far behind. Britain was fortunate, in the trials that lay ahead, to have more advanced friends on whom it could rely.

The Acceptance of Financial Limits

After the turn of the century the shape of Britain's foreign and defense policies was heavily influenced by a widespread belief that the nation could no longer afford to expend increasing sums on defense. As illustrated in chapter 3, that belief was the product of an excessive concentration on absolute spending figures (as compared with the more realistic estimate of burdens that could have been obtained by measuring spending as a portion of increasing national income) and an underlying fear that changes in the tax structure would have catastrophic economic and political consequences. Instead of imposing new taxes, the Conservative government under-

[10] In his *Wealth of Nations*, Smith argued in favor of protection "when some particular industry is necessary for the defense of the country," and he pointed out that "it is of importance that the kingdom depend as little as possible upon its neighbours for the manufactures necessary for its defense; and if these cannot be maintained at home, it is reasonable that all other branches of industry be taxed in order to support them" (quoted in Earle, "Adam Smith, Alexander Hamilton, Friedrich List: The Economic Foundations of Military Power," in Paret, ed., *Makers of Modern Strategy from Machiavelli to the Nuclear Age*, p. 224).

took a policy of retrenchment, seeking to reduce threats through diplomacy while improving the efficiency of the armed forces and trying to get the colonies to bear a greater portion of the total imperial defense burden.

The efficacy of British diplomacy will be considered below. The results of the other two efforts in this overall approach were decidedly mixed. The various defense reforms introduced after 1900, the creation of a General Staff, the strengthening of the CID, the consolidation of naval facilities and fleets, the attempts to simplify and rationalize army organization—all represented improvements over what had come before. Taken together they probably did produce some increase in the efficiency of Britain's overall defensive efforts in the sense that they generated more fighting power for each pound of expenditure. If, however, a significant increase in that power was necessary to sustain Britain's many far-flung commitments, then reorganization was a poor substitute for a real expansion in forces. Defense reform made a limited budget go further, but it could not create capabilities out of thin air.

The attempts at burden sharing undertaken between 1895 and 1905 were even less successful. Despite the dropping of heavy hints from London, the colonies refused to contribute much toward their own protection. In part this was a reaction against Britain's unwillingness to allow them a greater say in defense planning. Distant possessions were expected, for example, to help pay for the Royal Navy without being able to demand that it station ships in their vicinity. Most of the colonies did not seem to have much fear that Britain would abandon them in a crisis, no matter how stingy they were in peacetime. On balance, therefore, the effort to disperse defense burdens produced more friction than financial relief. In the end it may actually have helped to accelerate the growing divergence of outlook and interests between the center and the imperial periphery.

From a purely economic standpoint, Britain could have afforded to spend more. As the Liberals would demonstrate after 1906, the nation's growing productive base could easily sustain increases in both civilian and defense expenditures, although not without changes in the tax system and considerable accompanying political turmoil. In retrospect the financial crisis of 1901–1905 really marked the beginning of a process that would extend well into the twentieth century.[11] With the rise of modern powers in Asia and

[11] For an extremely useful overview see H. Sprout and M. Sprout, "The Dilemma of Rising Demands and Insufficient Resources," pp. 660–93.

North America as well as in Europe, it was inevitable that the British Empire should have become more difficult and more costly to defend. The burden of providing for adequate imperial protection would probably have increased even if Britain's economy had continued to grow at the rates it had achieved during the nineteenth century, but instead growth slowed before and especially after the First World War. At the same time, in response to rising popular demand, government spending on social services underwent a considerable expansion.

From the turn of the century onward, successive British governments found themselves faced with an increasingly sharp dilemma.[12] On the one hand it seemed that some fairly high level of social spending had become essential to maintaining a decent and stable society. On the other, to those who were willing to view the problem dispassionately, it was apparent that increasing amounts would have to be spent on ensuring the safety of the empire. Assuming limited budgets, there appeared to be only two real choices: to sharply reduce the scope of the nation's global responsibility or to increase defense outlays, even at the expense of slower growth in social services. Instead, starting in 1904, Britain's political leaders began to follow a third course, one that would not finally arrive at its dangerous destination until more than thirty years had passed. Through a combination of treaties, appeasement, and wishful thinking, the threats to which the empire was exposed were deemed to have been miraculously reduced, so much so in fact that they could be met with quite modest defense expenditures. Britain, therefore, did not have to adjust its world posture in any serious way; at the same time, the growth in domestic spending could continue apace. It was a comfortable solution, so long as it lasted. But it left Britain with a long list of commitments from which the country would find it ever more difficult to retreat without humiliation, and a vast array of vulnerable points, most of which it was increasingly ill-prepared to defend.

Surrendering Supremacy

Throughout the nineteenth century, the security of the empire had depended on British superiority in what was then the dominant form of military technology. Provided that the Royal Navy could

---

[12] For a somewhat different view of the same general problem see P. Kennedy, "Strategy versus Finance in Twentieth-Century Britain," in P. Kennedy, *Strategy and Diplomacy, 1870–1945*, pp. 89–106.

maintain worldwide command of the seas, the safety of the nation's insular possessions was all but guaranteed. So long as hostile powers had only a limited capacity to project their forces over land, a preponderance in sea power was sufficient also to protect Britain's great mainland colonies and to support its interests on the European continent. Britain's naval mastery served to deter the country's opponents and reassure dependents while providing a "winning weapon" in the event of war. Better yet, it did all this at relatively low cost and without need of a large standing army.

By the turn of the century the growth in foreign navies and the extension of vast railroad networks across Europe and North America as well as into Asia had combined to eat away at the bases of Britain's traditional maritime strategy. The advent of serious naval competitors on the periphery meant that controlling European waters would no longer be all that was needed to guarantee command of the world's oceans. The proliferation of rail lines lessened the vulnerability of Britain's enemies to blockades and small amphibious operations and rendered many of its own possessions more susceptible than they had ever been to attack over land. As will be discussed in a moment, these developments seemed to increase the need for Britain to maintain large or readily expandable ground forces if it wished to defend its colonies or to make its influence felt on the Continent.

After 1901–1902 Britain's leaders simply gave up on trying to retain worldwide supremacy and traded it in for a lesser form of European sea control. This transition, momentous as it appears in retrospect, was eased both by changes in objective conditions and by confusion (some of it deliberate) over the meaning of the accepted measures of naval power. The decision to appease the United States taken in 1901 and the Anglo-Japanese treaty of 1902 allowed Britain to concentrate on retaining its grip in home waters without having to acknowledge that this no longer ensured worldwide sea control. Russia's defeat by Japan and the improvement of relations with France made the task of preserving superiority in Europe seem easier, even in the face of a growing challenge from Germany.

Appeasement of the United States would prove eventually to be a winning gamble; considering America's vast potential and Canada's extreme vulnerability to invasion, it was in any case an unavoidable one. Nevertheless, it was not a decision in which anyone familiar with the past history of Anglo-American relations could have had overwhelming confidence at the time. In the Far East, as some contemporary observers pointed out, Britain had chosen to place its fate increasingly in the hands of the Japanese. Here, perhaps predictably, the coincidence of interests turned out to be less long-lasting. Given the underlying differences between the two island empires, the geography of the region, and the distribution of their interests within it, the British would probably have been wiser to do what they could to maintain their independent position in Asian waters. Prevailing financial assumptions rather than any unchanging law of nature prevented Britain from expanding its fleet still further and trying harder to retain at least a part of its wider global supremacy.

As suggested in the conclusion to chapter 4, Britain's reliance on diplomatic props to its naval position carried two inescapable and interlocking dangers. The visible reduction of the British presence in (and, presumably, commitment to) Asia and North America could only serve to speed a process of imperial dissolution that was already well under way. So long as relations with the emerging regional power in both areas remained cordial, Britain could afford to focus on Europe. Should the new arrangements falter, the nation would find it extremely difficult, with the naval forces at hand, to hold onto its empire while providing for its own defense. Intellectual honesty and simple prudence demanded that this risk be acknowledged. To have done so openly, however, would have further aroused the anxieties of the colonies about Britain's commitment to their security.

Certainly the day could not have been held off altogether; perhaps it could not even have been significantly delayed. But from the moment Britain surrendered naval supremacy, its empire was living on borrowed time.

Preparations for Total War

By the end of the nineteenth century changes in the strategic environment demanded that Britain improve its capacity for mobilizing, transporting, deploying, and supporting large ground forces if it wished to preserve its world role. The weakness of the traditional military system, with its reliance on a small core of professional soldiers backed by a ragged assortment of volunteers, had been clearly demonstated during the Boer War. In South Africa the British army had been hard pressed to defeat a relatively unsophisticated opponent. In central Asia the enemy's forces would be larger and presumably better equipped. As the Indian defense problem received renewed attention after 1900, it began to appear that all-out war against a modern land power would simply exceed the capacities of Britain's existing military structure. Without a larger standing army or, at the very least, a far more substantial pool of well-trained and highly organized reserve manpower, Britain would be unable to sustain the necessary level of effort much beyond the opening phases of a future war. The only plausible answer to the nation's military frailty seemed to lie in some form of mandatory training or compulsory service.

After 1904 good luck and a fortuitous increase in geographical awareness combined to lessen the perceived danger of a Russian descent on Afghanistan and with it the felt need for conscription. Illusory or not, horrific visions of invasion had at least helped to concentrate the minds of Britain's strategic planners on the demands of modern, large-scale land warfare. With Russia's defeat in the Far East the immediate threat might have diminished substantially, but the larger danger had not. Especially in Europe, the combination of railways, conscription, and opposing alliances guaranteed that the next war would be larger in scale and geographical scope than anything that had come before. There was little likelihood that Britain could exert a decisive influence on the outcome of such a conflict through timely use of its chosen instruments of blockade, light intervention, and financial assistance to one or another of the fighting powers.

If Britain's leaders intended to participate in a meaningful way in any future European war and, in particular, if they hoped to play a significant role in containing German expansion, they would have had to increase considerably their country's military capabilities. Rather than incur the domestic political costs of doing this before it was too late, they chose instead to rely on a less strenuous policy of alliance and deterrence. By aligning themselves ever more closely with France they hoped to stiffen the resolve of their new-found friend while dissuading the Germans from any thoughts of aggressive war. The military calculations underlying this approach seem to have been marked by the same kinds of assumptions that had emerged at the close of the Indian defense debate. Britain's available expeditionary force was deemed just sufficient to ensure victory against a much larger enemy. As if by some miracle, the necessary and the possible turned out to be identical with one another.

This equation proved, of course, to be a false one. With a larger, more capable, and more readily expandable army, the British might have been able indefinitely to deter a German assault on France.

Failing that, they might at least have been better prepared to play a decisive role in the early stages of a Continental conflict.[13] Instead the British got the worst of both worlds. Their commitment to France was not sufficient to prevent a war or to win quickly once one had begun, but it was more than enough to draw them into a struggle for which they were woefully unprepared. France was meant to provide a counterweight to German ambition. Insufficiently supported, that country acted in the end more as an anchor, pulling Britain irresistibly over the edge into an enervating European war.

The Balance of Risks

The policies just discussed (some expansion in the Government's economic role, moderately higher taxes, a fractionally larger fleet, some form of conscription) share a common feature. To one degree or another each of them would have required the extraction or redirection of an increased fraction of the resources of British society. The state mechanism capable of imposing such measures, whether separately or as a package, would have had to be more powerful than the one that existed at the turn of the century. Such power could conceivably have been granted by a democratic polity more convinced of the need for sacrifice in order to uphold its international stature. On the other hand, Britain could have become (as certain contemporary critics hoped that it would) a less democratic, more authoritarian country. The first alternative was improbable in the absence either of more farsighted and persuasive leadership or of some danger even larger, more obvious, and more pressing than those faced in the years leading up to the First World War. The second outcome, given the traditional moderation and gradual democratization of British politics, was, fortunately, even less likely.

Some historians have argued that there was no way, short of a radical and undesirable domestic transformation, for Britain to get

[13] For an analysis that reaches similar conclusions see Kagan, "World War I, World War II, World War III," pp. 24–25. Kagan writes that, if the British had been willing to swallow "the bitter pill of introducing conscription, and in time of peace, at that," they might have been able to render "the Schlieffen Plan or any conceivable German plan of war obviously absurd and certain to fail." However painful the sacrifices might have been in terms of cost and the abandonment of cherished traditions, Kagan insists, "they could have spared Britain four terrible years of war, horrendous casualties, and the rapid loss of its place in the world" (ibid., p. 25).

out of its deepening predicament. Bernard Porter, for example, has written that

> the only way Britain could adequately safeguard her vital national interests against external dangers was by undermining those same interests from inside. It was like a man threatened by burglary having to sell his valuables to buy protection against the burglar. . . . There was no way through this paradox, and no way, therefore, that British foreign policy from the 1890s on could possibly "succeed."[14]

It is not evident, however, that the choices were really as stark as this. There were steps that could conceivably have been taken to enhance Britain's power without destroying the nation's domestic institutions. Comparatively small changes in accepted practices might, as has already been suggested, have paid reasonable and perhaps even disproportionate long-term strategic dividends. Certainly a modest degree of government intervention in the economy, somewhat higher tax rates, greater proportionate levels of defense spending, and even peacetime conscription were, if not inherently desirable, at least not fundamentally incompatible with democracy or, necessarily, with economic growth. Such measures, together with continued, patient efforts to gradually reduce and restructure Britain's imperial defense burdens might have improved the nation's performance in the opening decades of the new century.

By 1900 a return to primacy was clearly impossible, and any policy that aimed at such a chimerical goal would have been both self-delusory and self-defeating. Still, more could have been done to preserve Britain's position and to prepare the country for what was to come. There would surely have been dangers involved in following such a course, not least among them the possibility of a public backlash against the increased effort required to sustain a global role.[15] But there were dangers, too, in trying to continue to play the part of a world power without being willing to pay for the privilege.

---

[14] Porter, *Britain, Europe, and the World, 1850–1982: Delusions of Grandeur*, pp. 56–57.

[15] Paul Kennedy has argued, for example, that "the decision of both Tory and Liberal governments to refuse the demands of Lord Roberts' National Service League and all later pressures for conscription was, paradoxically, a good way of keeping the Empire going—and keeping it reasonably popular at home" (see his stimulating essay, "Why Did the British Empire Last So Long?" in P. Kennedy, *Strategy and Diplomacy*, p. 204).

Bibliography

Documents

Official Papers (Public Record Office [PRO])

Cabinet (Cab.)

Cab. 2, minutes of Committee of Imperial Defence (CID)
Cab. 3, CID papers on home defense
Cab. 4, CID miscellaneous papers
Cab. 5, CID papers on colonial defense
Cab. 6, CID papers on Indian defense
Cab. 37, cabinet memoranda

Admiralty (Adm.)

Adm. 1, Admiralty and Secretariat papers
Adm. 116, secretary's casebooks
Adm. 231, Naval Intelligence Department reports

War Office (WO)

WO 33, reports and miscellaneous papers
WO 106, director of Military Operations, director of Military Intelligence

Treasury (T)

T 171, budget and finance bill papers

Private Papers

H. O. Arnold-Forster (British Museum, Add. Mss. 50301–50329)
Arthur J. Balfour (British Museum, Add. Mss. 49695–49780)
Admiral Cyprian A. G. Bridge (National Maritime Museum Library)
Austen Chamberlain (Birmingham University Library)
Joseph Chamberlain (Birmingham University Library)
George Clarke (Lord Sydenham) (British Museum, Add. Mss. 50835–50836)
Admiral John Fisher (Churchill College Library, Cambridge)
Edward W. Hamilton (PRO, T 178)
Lord George Hamilton (India Office Library)
Lord Kitchener (PRO, 30/57)
Lord Lansdowne (PRO, FO 800/134)
Lord Roberts (PRO, WO 105)
Lord Salisbury (third marquess) (Hatfield House)
Lord Selborne (Bodleian Library, Oxford)

Parliamentary Records
Accounts and Papers
Hansard Parliamentary Debates
Parliamentary Papers

Books and Articles

Adams, Robert M. *Decadent Societies.* San Francisco: North Point Press, 1983.

Adye, John. "Has Our Army Grown With Our Empire?" *The Nineteenth Century,* no. 232 (June 1896): 1012–24.

Agacy, Henry A. *Free Trade, Protection, Dumping, Bounties, and Preferential Tariffs.* London: Longmans, Green, 1903.

Albertini, Luigi. *The Origins of the War of 1914.* 3 vols. New York: Oxford University Press, 1952.

Albrecht-Carrie, René. *A Diplomatic History of Europe Since the Congress of Vienna.* New York: Harper and Row, 1973.

Aldcroft, D. H., ed. *The Development of British Industry and Foreign Competition, 1815–1914.* London: Allen and Unwin, 1968.

Aldcroft, D. H., and H. W. Richardson. *The British Economy, 1870–1939.* London: Macmillan, 1969.

Alder, G. J. *British India's Northern Frontier, 1865–1895.* London: Longmans, 1963.

Allison, Graham T. *Essence of Decision: Explaining the Cuban Missile Crisis.* Boston: Little, Brown, 1971.

Almond, Gabriel A., and Stephen J. Genco. "Clouds, Clocks, and the Study of Politics." *World Politics* 29, no. 4 (1977): 489–522.

Andrew, C. A. *Théophile Delcassé and the Making of the Entente Cordiale.* New York: St. Martin's Press, 1968.

Arnold-Forster, H. O. *The Army in 1906.* New York: E. P. Dutton, 1906.

Aron, Raymond. *Peace and War: A Theory of International Relations.* New York: Doubleday, 1966.

Ashley, W. J. *The Tariff Problem.* London: P. S. King and Son, 1903.

Asquith, H. H. *Trade and the Empire.* London: Methuen, 1903.

Axelrod, Robert M., ed. *Structure of Decision: The Cognitive Maps of Political Elites.* Princeton: Princeton University Press, 1976.

Bairoch, Paul. "Europe's Gross National Product: 1800–1975." *The Journal of European Economic History* 5, no. 2 (1976): 273–340.

Baldwin, David A. "Power Analysis and World Politics." *World Politics* 31, no. 2 (1979): 161–94.

Balfour, Arthur J. *Essays and Addresses.* Edinburgh: David Douglas, 1893.

———. *Economic Notes on Insular Free Trade.* London: Longmans, Green, 1903.

———. *Fiscal Reform Speeches, 1880–1905.* London: Longmans, Green, 1906.

———. *Chapters of Autobiography.* London: Cassell, 1930.

Balfour, Michael. *Britain and Joseph Chamberlain.* London: Allen and Unwin, 1985.

Barnett, Correlli. *Britain and Her Army, 1509–1970.* New York: William Morrow, 1970.

———. *The Collapse of British Power.* New York: William Morrow, 1972.

Barraclough, Geoffrey. *An Introduction to Contemporary History.* Harmondsworth, Eng.: Penguin, 1967.

Bartlett, C. J. *Great Britain and Sea Power, 1815–1853.* Oxford: Clarendon Press, 1963.

———. "The Mid-Victorian Reappraisal of Naval Policy." In *Studies in International History,* edited by K. Bourne and D. C. Watt, 198–208. London: Longmans, 1967.

———, ed. *Britain Pre-eminent: Studies of British World Influence in the Nineteenth Century.* London: Macmillan, 1969.

Beckett, Ian F. W. "Edward Stanhope at the War Office, 1887–92." *The Journal of Strategic Studies* 5, no. 2 (1982): 278–307.

Beloff, Max. *Imperial Sunset.* Vol. 1, *Britain's Liberal Empire, 1897–1921.* London: Methuen, 1969.

Benians, E. A., Sir James Butler, and C. E. Carrington, eds. *The Cambridge History of the British Empire.* Vol. 3, *The Empire—Commonwealth, 1870–1919.* Cambridge: Cambridge University Press, 1959.

Bialer, Uri. *The Shadow of the Bomber: The Fear of Air Attack and British Politics, 1932–1939.* London: Royal Historical Society, 1980.

Bignold, H. B. *The Burden of Empire: By an Australian.* Imperial Federation (Defence) Committee, no. 15. London, 1901.

Blainey, Geoffrey. *The Causes of War.* New York: Free Press, 1973.

Blake, Robert. *The Conservative Party from Peel to Churchill.* London: Eyre and Spottiswoode, 1970.

Bodelsen, C. A. *Studies in Mid-Victorian Imperialism.* London: Heinemann, 1960.

Bond, Brian. *The Victorian Army and the Staff College, 1854–1914.* London: Methuen, 1972.

———. *War and European Society, 1870–1970.* Leicester: Fontana, 1983.

Booth, Ken. *Strategy and Ethnocentrism.* New York: Holmes and Meier, 1979.

Boulding, Kenneth E. "National Images and International Systems." *Journal of Conflict Resolution* 3, no. 2 (1959): 120–31.

———. "The Learning and Reality-Testing Process in the International System." *Journal of International Affairs* 21, no. 1 (1967): 1–15.

Bourne, Kenneth. *The Foreign Policy of Victorian England, 1830–1902.* Oxford: Clarendon Press, 1970.

———. *Britain and the Balance of Power in North America, 1815–1908.* Berkeley and Los Angeles: University of California Press, 1976.

Boyd, Charles W., ed. *Mr. Chamberlain's Speeches.* 2 vols. London: Constable, 1914.

Brassey, T. A., ed. *The Naval Annual.* Portsmouth: J. Griffen, 1895–1905 (various years).

Bremer, Stuart A. "National Capabilities and War Proneness." In *The Correlates of War.* Vol. 2, edited by J. David Singer, 57–82. New York: Free Press, 1980.

Briggs, Asa. *A Social History of England.* New York: Viking, 1984.

Brodie, Bernard. *Sea Power in the Machine Age.* Princeton: Princeton University Press, 1940.

———. "Technological Change, Strategic Doctrine, and Political Outcomes." In *Historical Dimensions of National Security Problems,* edited by Klaus Knorr, 263–306. Lawrence: University Press of Kansas, 1976.

Brown, Benjamin H. *The Tariff Reform Movement in Great Britain, 1881–1895.* New York: Columbia University Press, 1943.

Brown, Seyom. "The Changing Essence of Power." *Foreign Affairs* 51 (January 1973): 286–99.

———. *New Forces in World Politics.* Washington, D.C.: Brookings Institution, 1974.

Browne, Harry. *Joseph Chamberlain: Radical and Imperialist.* London: Longmans, 1974.

Brzezinski, Zbigniew. *Power and Principle.* New York: Farrar Straus Giroux, 1983.

Bueno de Mesquita, Bruce. *The War Trap.* New Haven: Yale University Press, 1981.

Bull, Hedley. *The Anarchical Society.* New York: Columbia University Press, 1977.

Bullock, Allan, and Maurice Shock. *The Liberal Tradition.* New York: New York University Press, 1957.

Burn, Richard. *The Darkening Cloud: Or England's Commercial Decline and the Depression of Our National Industry from the Inroads of Foreign Competition.* Liverpool: T. Kaye, 1856.

Busch, Peter A. Appendix, "Mathematical Models of Arms Races." In *What Price Vigilance? The Burdens of National Defense,* by Bruce Russett, 193–233. New Haven: Yale University Press.

Buzan, Barry, and R. J. Barry, eds. *Change and the Study of International Relations: The Evaded Dimension.* New York: St. Martin's Press, 1981.

Cain, Peter. "Political Economy in Edwardian England: The Tariff-Reform Controversy." In *The Edwardian Age: Conflict and Stability, 1900–1914,* edited by Alan O'Day, 35–59. London: Macmillan, 1979.

Calliard, Vincent. *Imperial Fiscal Reform.* London: Edward Arnold, 1903.

Campbell, Alexander E. *Great Britain and the United States, 1895–1903.* London: Longmans, 1960.

Campbell, Charles S. *Anglo-American Understanding, 1898–1903.* Baltimore: Johns Hopkins University Press, 1957.

Carnegie, Andrew. "British Pessimism." *The Nineteenth Century and After* 49, no. 212 (1901): 901–12.

Carr, E. H. *The Twenty Years' Crisis, 1919–1939.* New York: Harper and Row, 1964.

Cecil, Lady Gwendolen. *Life of Robert Marquis of Salisbury.* 4 vols. London: Hodden and Stoughton, 1922–1931.

Chamberlain, Austen. *Down the Years.* London: Cassell, 1935.

Churchill, Rogers P. *The Anglo-Russian Convention of 1907.* Cedar Rapids, Iowa: Torch Press, 1939.

Churchill, Winston S. *The Gathering Storm.* Boston: Houghton Mifflin, 1977.

———. *Great Contemporaries.* Chicago: University of Chicago Press, 1973.

Cipolla, Carlo M., ed. *The Economic Decline of Empires.* London: Methuen, 1970.

Clapham, J. H. *An Economic History of Modern Britain: Machines and National Rivalries (1887–1914).* New York: Macmillan, 1938.

Clarke, George S., and James R. Thursfield. *The Navy and the Nation.* London: John Murray, 1897.

Clarke, Sir George Sydenham. "The Defence of the Empire and the Militia Ballot." *The Nineteenth Century,* no. 275 (January 1900): 2–13.

Cline, Ray S. *World Power Assessment, 1977.* Boulder, Colo.: Westview Press, 1977.

Cobden, Richard. *Speeches on Free Trade.* London: Macmillan, 1903.

Cohen, Eliot A. "Systems of Military Service: The Dilemmas of a Liberal-Democratic World Power." Ph.D. diss., Harvard University, 1982.

Cole, Major D. H., and Major E. C. Priestley, *An Outline of British Military History, 1660–1936.* London: Sifton Praed, 1936.

Colomb, John. *The Defence of Great and Greater Britain.* London: E. Stanford, 1880.

Colomb, Philip. *Naval Warfare.* London: W. H. Allen, 1895.

The Concise Dictionary of National Biography: Part II, 1901–1970. Oxford: Oxford University Press, 1982.

Condliffe, John B. *The Commerce of Nations.* New York: W. W. Norton, 1950.

Coppock, D. J. "The Causes of the Great Depression, 1873–1896." *The Manchester School of Economic and Social Studies* 29, no. 3 (1961): 205–32.

Crowl, Philip A. "Alfred Thayer Mahan: The Naval Historian." In *The Makers of Modern Strategy: From Machiavelli to the Nuclear Age,* edited by Peter Paret, 444–77. Princeton: Princeton University Press, 1986.

Cunningham, W. *The Rise and Decline of the Free Trade Movement.* London: C. J. Clay and Sons, 1904.

Cyert, Richard M., and James G. March, *A Behavioral Theory of the Firm.* Englewood Cliffs, N.J.: Prentice-Hall, 1963.

Dahl, Robert A. "The Concept of Power." *Behavioral Science* 2, no. 3 (1957): 201–15.

Davis, Lance E., and Robert A. Huttenback. "The Political Economy of British Imperialism: Measures of Benefits and Support." *Journal of Economic History* 42, no. 1 (1982): 119–32.

Dehio, Ludwig. *The Precarious Balance.* New York: Alfred A. Knopf, 1962.

De Rivera, Joseph. *The Psychological Dimension of Foreign Policy.* Columbus, Ohio: Merrill, 1968.

Deutsch, Karl. *The Nerves of Government.* New York: Free Press, 1966.

Dilke, Charles W. *Greater Britain.* New York: Harper and Brothers, 1869.

———. *Problems of Greater Britain.* New York: Macmillan, 1890.

Dilke, Charles W., and Spenser Wilkinson. *Imperial Defence.* London: Macmillan, 1892.

Dilks, David, ed. *Retreat from Power.* Vol. 1, *1906–1939.* London: Macmillan, 1981.

d'Ombrain, Nicholas. *War Machinery and High Policy: Defence Administration in Peacetime Britain, 1902–1914.* Oxford: Oxford University Press, 1973.

Doran, Charles F. "War and Power Dynamics: Economic Underpinnings." *International Studies Quarterly* 27, no. 4 (1983): 419–41.

Downs, George W., David M. Rocke, and Randolph M. Siverson. "Arms Races and Cooperation." *World Politics* 38, no. 1 (1985): 118–46.

Dugdale, Blanche E. C. *Balfour: A Life of Arthur James Balfour.* New York: Putnam, 1937.

Dunlop, Colonel John K. *The Development of the British Army, 1899–1914.* London: Methuen, 1938.

Earle, Edward M. "Adam Smith, Alexander Hamilton, Fredrich List: The Economic Foundations of Military Power." In *Makers of Modern Strategy from Machiavelli to the Nuclear Age,* edited by Peter Paret, 217–61. Princeton: Princeton University Press, 1986.

Eckstein, Harry. "Case Study and Theory in Political Science." In *Handbook of Political Science.* Vol. 7, *Strategies of Inquiry,* edited by F. I. Greenstein and N. W. Polsby, 79–138. Reading, Mass.: Addison-Wesley, 1975.

Egremont, Max. *Balfour: A Life of Arthur James Balfour.* London: Collins, 1980.

Emy, H. V. "The Impact of Financial Policy on English Party Politics Before 1914." *The Historical Journal* 15, no. 1 (1972): 103–31.

———. *Liberals, Radicals, and Social Politics, 1892–1914.* Cambridge: Cambridge University Press, 1973.

Fay, Sidney B. *The Origins of the World War.* 2 vols. New York: Free Press, 1966.

Fergusson, Thomas G. *British Military Intelligence, 1870–1914: The Development of a Modern Intelligence Organization.* Frederick, Md.: University Publications of America, 1984.

Ferris, Wayne H. *The Power Capabilities of Nation-States.* Lexington, Mass.: D. C. Heath, 1973.

Fieldhouse, D. K. *The Colonial Empires: A Comparative Survey from the Eighteenth Century.* New York: Delacorte Press, 1966.

———. *Economy and Empire, 1830–1914.* London: Weidenfeld and Nicolson, 1973.

Fisher, John A. *Memories and Records.* New York: George H. Doran, 1920.

Fox, Harold. *Mr. Balfour's Pamphlet: A Reply.* London: T. Fisher Unwin, 1903.

Fraser, Derek. *The Evolution of the British Welfare State.* London: Macmillan, 1973.

Fraser, Peter. "The Liberal Unionist Alliance: Chamberlain, Hartington, and the Conservatives, 1886–1904." *The English Historical Review* 77, no. 302 (1962): 53–78.

———. *Joseph Chamberlain: Radicalism and Empire, 1868–1914.* London: Cassell, 1966.

Freedman, Lawrence. *U.S. Intelligence and the Soviet Strategic Threat.* Princeton: Princeton University Press, 1986.

French, David. *British Economic and Strategic Planning, 1905–1915.* London: Allen and Unwin, 1982.

Froude, James Anthony. *Short Studies on Great Subjects.* New York: Charles Scribners, 1872.

Fuller, J. F. C. *Imperial Defence, 1588–1914.* London: Sifton, Praed, 1926.

Gallagher, John, and Ronald Robinson. "The Imperialism of Free Trade." *The Economic History Review* 6, no. 1 (1953): 1–15.

Garvin, J. L., and J. Amery. *The Life of Joseph Chamberlain.* 6 vols. London: Macmillan, 1932–1969.

Gaskell, Thomas P. *Free Trade: A Failure from the First.* London: Macmillan, 1903.

Gastrell, William S. H. *Our Trade in the World in Relation to Foreign Competition 1885 to 1895.* London: Chapman and Hall, 1897.

George, Alexander. "The 'Operational Code': A Neglected Approach to the Study of Political Leaders and Decision-Making." *International Studies Quarterly* 13 (1969): 190–222.

———. "The Causal Nexus Between Cognitive Beliefs and Decision-Making Behavior: The 'Operational Code' Belief System." In *Psychological Models in International Politics,* edited by Lawrence S. Falkowski, 95–124. Boulder, Colo.: Westview Press, 1979.

———. "Case Studies and Theory Development: The Method of Structured, Focused Comparison." In *Diplomacy: New Approaches in History, Theory, and Policy,* edited by Paul Gordon, 43–68. New York: Free Press, 1979.

———. *Presidential Decisionmaking in Foreign Policy: The Effective Use of Information and Advice.* Boulder, Colo.: Westview Press, 1980.

Giffen, Robert. *Essays in Finance.* London: G. Bell and Sons, 1880.

———. *The Use of Import and Export Statistics.* London: E. Stanford, 1882.

———. *Statistics.* London: Macmillan, 1913.

———, ed. *Economic Inquiries and Studies.* 2 vols. Shannon: Irish University Press, 1971.

Gilbert, Martin. *Winston S. Churchill: The Prophet of Truth.* Boston: Houghton Mifflin, 1977.

Gillard, D. R. "Salisbury and the Indian Defence Problem, 1885–1902." In *Studies in International History,* edited by K. Bourne and D. C. Watt, 236–48. London: Longmans, 1967.

———. *The Struggle for Asia, 1828–1914.* London: Methuen, 1977.

Gilmour, T. L., ed. *All Sides of the Fiscal Controversy.* London: Lawrence and Bullen, 1903.

Gilpin, Robert. *U.S. Power and the Multinational Corporation: The Political Economy of Foreign Direct Investment.* New York: Basic Books, 1975.

———. *War and Change in World Politics.* Cambridge: Cambridge University Press, 1981.

Goldhammer, Herbert. "The U.S.-Soviet Strategic Balance as seen from London and Paris." *Survival* 19, no. 5 (1977): 202–207.

———. *Reality and Belief in Military Affairs,* R-2448-NA. Santa Monica, Calif.: The Rand Corporation, 1979.

Goldmann, Kjell, and Gunnar Sjostedt, eds. *Power, Capabilities, Interdepen-*

dence: Problems in the Study of International Influence. Beverly Hills, Calif.: Sage Publications, 1979.

Gollin, Alfred. *Balfour's Burden: Arthur Balfour and Imperial Preference.* London: Anthony Blond, 1965.

Gooch, G. P. *Before the War: Studies in Diplomacy.* 2 vols. New York: Russell and Russell, 1967.

Gooch, G. P., and A. W. Ward, *The Cambridge History of British Foreign Policy, 1783–1919.* New York: Macmillan, 1923.

Gooch, John. *The Plans of War: The General Staff and British Military Strategy, c. 1900–1916.* London: Routledge and Kegan Paul, 1974.

———. *The Prospect of War: Studies in British Defence Policy, 1847–1942.* London: Frank Cass, 1981.

Gopal, Sarvepalli. *British Policy in India, 1858–1905.* Cambridge: Cambridge University Press, 1965.

Gordon, Donald C. "The Admiralty and Dominion Navies, 1902–1914." *Journal of Modern History* 33, no. 4 (1961): 407–22.

———. *The Dominion Partnership in Imperial Defense, 1870–1914.* Baltimore: Johns Hopkins University Press, 1965.

———. *The Moment of Power: Britain's Imperial Epoch.* Englewood Cliffs, N.J.: Prentice-Hall, 1970.

Gourevitch, Peter. "International Trade, Domestic Coalitions, and Liberty: Comparative Responses to the Crisis of 1873–1896." *Journal of Interdisciplinary History* 8, no. 2 (1977): 281–313.

Graham, Gerald S. *The Politics of Naval Supremacy.* Cambridge: Cambridge University Press, 1965.

Greaves, Rose Louise. *Persia and the Defence of India, 1884–1892.* London: Athlone Press, 1959.

Grenville, J. A. S. "Great Britain and the Isthmian Canal, 1891–1901." *American Historical Review* 61 no. 1 (1955): 48–69.

———. *Lord Salisbury and Foreign Policy: The Close of the Nineteenth Century.* London: Athlone Press, 1964.

Gulick, Edward Vose. *Europe's Classical Balance of Power.* New York: W. W. Norton, 1967.

Haggie, P. "The Royal Navy and War Planning in the Fisher Era." In *The War Plans of the Great Powers, 1880–1914,* edited by Paul Kennedy, 118–32. London: Allen and Unwin, 1979.

Halevy, Elie. *A History of the English People.* Vol. 1, *1895–1905.* London: Ernest Benn, 1929.

Halperin, Morton H. *Bureaucratic Politics and Foreign Policy.* Washington, D.C.: Brookings Institution, 1974.

Halpern, Paul P. *The Mediterranean Naval Situation, 1908–1914.* Cambridge: Harvard University Press, 1971.

Hamer, W. S. *The British Army: Civil Military Relations, 1885–1905.* Oxford: Clarendon Press, 1970.

Hamilton, Lord George. *Parliamentary Reminiscences and Reflections, 1886–1906.* London: John Murray, 1922.

Hargreaves, J. D. "The Origins of the Anglo-French Military Conversations in 1905." *History* 36 (October 1951): 244–48.

Harsanyi, Jack C. "Measurement of Social Power, Opportunity Costs, and the Theory of Two-Person Bargaining Games." *Behavioral Science* 7, no. 11 (1962): 67–79.

Hart, Jeffrey. "Three Approaches to the Measurement of Power in International Relations." *International Organization* 30, no. 2 (1976): 289–305.

Hayes, Carlton J. H. *A Generation of Materialism, 1871–1900.* New York: Harper and Row, 1941.

Hewins, W. A. S. *The Apologia of an Imperialist,* 2 vols. London: Constable, 1929.

Hibbert, Christopher. *The Great Mutiny.* Harmondsworth, Eng.: Penguin, 1980.

Hicks, Ursula K. *British Public Finances: Their Structure and Development, 1880–1952.* London: Oxford University Press, 1954.

Hicks Beach, Sir Michael. *The Colonies and the Navy.* Imperial Federation (Defence) Committee, no. 10, London, 1897.

Hicks Beach, Lady Victoria. *Life of Sir Michael Hicks Beach.* 2 vols. London: Macmillan, 1932.

Hinsley, F. H., ed. *The New Cambridge Modern History.* Vol. 11, *Material Progress and World-Wide Problems, 1870–1898.* Cambridge: Cambridge University Press, 1979.

Hobsbawm, E. J. *Industry and Empire.* Harmondsworth, Eng.: Penguin, 1981.

Hoffman, Ross J. S. *Great Britain and the German Trade Rivalry, 1875–1914.* Philadelphia: University of Pennsylvania Press, 1933.

Hoffmann, Stanley. *The State of War.* New York: Praeger, 1965.

———. "Notes on the Elusiveness of Modern Power." *International Journal* 30, no. 2 (1975): 183–206.

———. "An American Social Science: International Relations," *Daedalus* 106, no. 3 (1977): 41–60.

———, ed. *Contemporary Theory in International Relations.* Englewood Cliffs, N.J.: Prentice-Hall, 1960.

Holsti, Ole. "Cognitive Dynamics and Images of the Enemy: Dulles and Russia." In *Enemies in Politics,* edited by D. J. Finlay, O. R. Holsti, and R. R. Fagen, 25–96. Chicago: Rand McNally, 1967.

Holsti, Ole R., P. Terrence Hopman, and John D. Sullivan. *Unity and Disintegration in International Alliances: Comparative Studies.* New York: John Wiley, 1973.

Holsti, Ole R., Randolph Siverson, and Alexander George, eds. *Change in the International System.* Boulder, Colo.: Westview Press, 1980.

Howard, Christopher. *Splendid Isolation.* New York: St. Martin's Press, 1967.

———. *Britain and the Casus Belli, 1822–1902.* London: Athlone Press, 1974.

Howard, Michael. *The Continental Commitment.* London: Temple South, 1972.

———. *War in European History.* Oxford: Oxford University Press, 1976.

Hughes, Judith M. *To the Maginot Line.* Cambridge, Mass.: Harvard University Press, 1971.

Humble, Richard. *Before the Dreadnought: The Royal Navy from Nelson to Fisher.* London: Macdonald and Jane's, 1976.

Hurd, Archibald S. "The Balance of Naval Power." *The Nineteenth Century* 336 (February 1905): 228–37.

———. "The Contest for Sea-Power: Germany's Opportunity." *The Nineteenth Century* 342 (August 1905): 308–19.

Hyam, Ronald. *Britain's Imperial Century, 1815–1914: A Study of Empire and Expansion.* London: B. T. Batsford, 1976.

Imlah, A. H. *Economic Elements in the 'Pax Britannica.'* Cambridge, Mass.: Harvard University Press, 1958.

Jeans, J. S. *England's Supremacy.* London: Longmans, Green, 1885.

Jebb, Richard. *The Imperial Conference.* London: Longmans, Green, 1911.

Jervis, Robert. *The Logic of Images in International Relations.* Princeton: Princeton University Press, 1970.

———. *Perception and Misperception in International Politics.* Princeton: Princeton University Press, 1976.

Johnson, Franklyn Arthur. *Defence by Committee: The British Committee of Imperial Defence, 1885–1959.* London: Oxford University Press, 1960.

Jonsson, Christer, ed. *Cognitive Dynamics and International Politics.* New York: St. Martin's Press, 1982.

Jordan, G. H. S. "Pensions not Dreadnoughts: The Radicals and Naval Retrenchment." In *Edwardian Radicalism, 1900–1914,* edited by A. J. A. Morris, 162–79. London: Routledge and Kegan Paul, 1974.

———, ed. *Naval Warfare in the Twentieth Century, 1900–1945.* London: Croom Helm, 1977.

Judd, Denis. *Balfour and the British Empire.* London: Macmillan, 1968.

Kagan, Donald. "World War I, World War II, World War III." *Commentary* 83, no. 3 (1987): 21–40.

Kaplan, Morton A. *System and Process in International Politics.* New York: John Wiley, 1957.

Kaufmann, William W. *A Reasonable Defense.* Washington, D.C.: Brookings Institution, 1986.

Keith, Arthur B., ed. *Selected Speeches and Documents on British Colonial Policy.* Vol. 2, *1763–1917.* London: Oxford University Press, 1918.

Kelman, Herbert C., ed. *International Behavior: A Social-Psychological Analysis.* New York: Holt, Rinehart and Winston, 1965.

Kemp, P. K., ed. *The Papers of Admiral Sir John Fisher.* 2 vols. London: Navy Records Society, 1960.

Kendle, John Edward. *The Colonial and Imperial Conferences, 1887–1911: A Study in Imperial Organization.* London: Longmans, Green, 1967.

Kennedy, A. L. *Salisbury, 1830–1903: Portrait of a Statesman.* London: John Murray, 1953.

Kennedy, Paul. *The Rise and Fall of British Naval Mastery.* London: Allen and Unwin, 1976.

———. *The Rise of the Anglo-German Antagonism, 1860–1914.* London: Allen and Unwin, 1980.

———. *The Realities Behind Diplomacy: Background Influences on British External Policy, 1865–1980.* London: Fontana Paperbacks, 1981.

————. "The First World War and the International Power System." *International Security* 9, no. 1 (1984): 7–40.

————. *Strategy and Diplomacy, 1870–1945.* London: Fontana Paperbacks, 1984.

Kenyon, J. P. *A Dictionary of British History.* New York: Stein and Day, 1983.

Keohane, Robert O. "The Theory of Hegemonic Stability and Changes in International Economic Regimes, 1967–1977." In *Change and the International System,* edited by Ole Holsti, 131–62. Boulder, Colo.: Westview Press, 1980.

————. "Theory of World Politics: Structural Realism and Beyond." In *Political Science: The State of the Discipline,* edited by Ada W. Finifter, 503–40. Washington, D.C.: American Political Science Association, 1983.

————. *After Hegemony: Cooperation and Discord in the World Political Economy.* Princeton: Princeton University Press, 1984.

Keohane, Robert O., and Joseph S. Nye. *Power and Interdependence: World Politics in Transition.* Boston: Little, Brown, 1977.

Keynes, John Maynard. *The Collected Writings of John Maynard Keynes.* Vol. 10, *Essays in Biography.* London: Macmillan, 1972.

————. *The General Theory of Employment, Interest, and Money.* London: Macmillan, 1973.

Kindleberger, Charles P. *The World in Depression, 1929–1939.* Berkeley and Los Angeles: University of California Press, 1975.

————. *Economic Response: Comparative Studies in Trade, Finance, and Growth, 1806 to 1914.* Cambridge, Mass.: Harvard University Press, 1978.

Kissinger, Henry A. *A World Restored.* Boston: Houghton Mifflin, 1957.

————. *American Foreign Policy.* New York: W. W. Norton, 1974.

Knorr, Klaus. *Power and Wealth: The Political Economy of International Power.* New York: Basic Books, 1973.

————. *Military Power and Potential.* Lexington, Mass.: D. C. Heath, 1973.

————. "Threat Perception." In *Historical Dimensions of National Security Problems,* edited by Klaus Knorr, 78–119. Lawrence: University Press of Kansas, 1976.

Knorr, Klaus, and James N. Rosenau, eds. *Contending Approaches to International Politics.* Princeton: Princeton University Press, 1969.

Krasner, Stephen. "State Power and the Structure of International Trade." *World Politics* 28, no. 3 (1976): 317–43.

————, ed. *International Regimes.* Ithaca: Cornell University Press, 1983.

Landes, David S. "Technological Change and Development in Western Europe, 1750–1914." In *The Cambridge Economic History of Europe.* Vol. 6, *The Industrial Revolutions and After: Incomes, Population, and Technological Change,* edited by H. J. Habakkuk and M. Postan, 353–576. Cambridge: Cambridge University Press, 1965.

————. *The Unbound Prometheus.* Cambridge: Cambridge University Press, 1970.

Langer, William L. *European Alliances and Alignments, 1870–1890.* New York: Alfred A. Knopf, 1950.

————. *The Diplomacy of Imperialism, 1890–1902.* New York: Alfred A. Knopf, 1956.

League of Nations. *Industrialization and Foreign Trade.* New York, 1945.

Lebow, Richard Ned. *Between Peace and War.* Baltimore: Johns Hopkins University Press, 1984.

Leites, Nathan. *The Operational Code of the Politburo.* New York: McGraw-Hill, 1951.

Levy, Jack S. "Theories of General War." *World Politics* 37, no. 3 (1985): 344–74.

Lewis, W. Arthur. "International Competition in Manufactures." *The American Economic Review* 47, no. 2 (1957): 578–87.

———. *Growth and Fluctuations, 1870–1913.* London: Allen and Unwin, 1978.

Lilly, W. S. "Collapse of England." *The Fortnightly Review* 425 (1 May 1902): 771–84.

Lippmann, Walter. *U.S. Foreign Policy: Shield of the Republic.* Boston: Little, Brown, 1943.

Low, Sidney. "The Military Weakness of England and the Militia Ballot." *The Nineteenth Century* 275 (January 1900): 14–28.

Lowe, C. J. *Salisbury and the Mediterranean, 1884–1896.* London: Routledge and Kegan Paul, 1965.

———. *The Reluctant Imperialists: British Foreign Policy 1878–1902.* New York: Macmillan, 1967.

Lowe, C. J., and M. L. Dockrill. *The Mirage of Power: British Foreign Policy, 1902–1922.* 3 vols. London: Routledge and Kegan Paul, 1972.

Luterbacher, Urs. "Arms Race Models: Where Do We Stand?" *European Journal of Political Research* 3 (1975): 199–217.

Luttwak, Edward N. "Perceptions of Military Force and U.S. Defence Policy." *Survival* 19, no. 1 (1977): 2–8.

Luvaas, Jay. *The Education of an Army: British Military Thought, 1815–1940.* Chicago: University of Chicago Press, 1964.

McCloskey, D. N., ed. *Essays on a Mature Economy: Britain After 1870.* London: Methuen, 1971.

McDermott, J. "The Revolution in British Military Thinking from the Boer War to the Moroccan Crisis." In *The War Plans of the Great Powers, 1880–1914,* edited by Paul Kennedy, 99–117. London: Allen and Unwin, 1979.

Machray, Robert. "The Collapse of Russia." *The Nineteenth Century* 441 (July 1905): 51–61.

MacKay, Ruddock F. "The Admiralty, the German Navy, and the Redistribution of the British Fleet, 1904–05." *Mariner's Mirror* 56, no. 3 (1970): 341–46.

———. *Fisher of Kilverstone.* Oxford: Clarendon Press, 1973.

McKenzie, F. A. *The American Invaders: Their Plans, Tactics, and Progress.* New York: Street and Smith, 1901.

McKeown, Timothy J. "Tariffs and Hegemonic Stability Theory." *International Organization* 37, no. 1 (1983): 73–91.

Mackintosh, J. P. "The Role of the CID Before 1914." *English History Review* 77, no. 304 (1962): 490–503.

Maddison, A. "Economic Growth in Western Europe, 1870–1957." *Banca Nazionale del Lavoro, Quarterly Review* 48 (March 1959): 58–102.

———. "Growth and Fluctuation in the World Economy, 1870–1960." *Banca Nazionale del Lavoro, Quarterly Review* 61 (June 1962): 127–95.

Mahajan, Sneh. "The Defence of India and the End of Isolation: A Study in the Foreign Policy of the Conservative Government, 1900–1905." *The Journal of Imperial and Commonwealth History* 10, no. 2 (1982): 168–93.

Mahan, Alfred Thayer. *The Influence of Sea Power Upon History*. New York: Hill and Wang, 1983.

Mallet, Bernard. *British Budgets: 1887–88 to 1912–13*. London: Macmillan, 1913.

March, James G., and Herbert A. Simon, *Organizations*. New York: John Wiley, 1958.

Marder, Arthur J. *The Anatomy of British Sea Power*. New York: Alfred A. Knopf, 1940.

———. *Fear God and Dreadnought: The Correspondence of Admiral of the Fleet Lord John Fisher of Kilverstone*. 3 vols. Cambridge: Harvard University Press, 1952.

———. *From Dreadnought to Scapa Flow*. Vol. 1, *The Road to War, 1904–1910*. London: Oxford University Press, 1961.

Marshall, Andrew W. *Problems of Estimating Military Power*, P-3417. Santa Monica, Calif.: The Rand Corporation, 1966.

Mathias, Peter. *The First Industrial Nation: An Economic History of Britain, 1700–1914*. New York: Charles Scribner's Sons, 1969.

May, Ernest R. *Imperial Democracy: The Emergence of America as a Great Power*. New York: Harper and Row, 1973.

———, ed. *Knowing One's Enemies: Intelligence Assessment Before the Two World Wars*. Princeton: Princeton University Press, 1984.

Mill, John Stuart. *Principles of Political Economy*. London: Longmans, Green, Reader and Dyer, 1875.

Milward, Alan S. *War, Economy, and Society, 1939–1945*. Berkeley and Los Angeles: University of California Press, 1977.

Mitchell, B. R. *European Historical Statistics, 1750–1975*. London: Macmillan, 1980.

Monger, George. *The End of Isolation: British Foreign Policy, 1900–1907*. London: Thomas Nelson and Sons, 1963.

Morgan, Gerald. *Anglo-Russian Rivalry in Central Asia, 1810–1895*. London: Frank Cass, 1981.

Morgenthau, Hans. *Politics Among Nations*. New York: Alfred A. Knopf, 1973.

Morris, James. *Heaven's Command*. London: Faber and Faber, 1973.

Morse, Edward L. *Modernization and the Transformation of International Relations*. New York: Free Press, 1976.

Murray, Williamson. *The Change in the European Balance of Power, 1938–1939*. Princeton: Princeton University Press, 1984.

Musson, A. E. "The Great Depression in Britain, 1873–1896: A Reappraisal." *The Journal of Economic History* 19, no. 2 (1959): 199–228.

———. "British Industrial Growth During the 'Great Depression' (1873–96): Some Comments." *The Economic History Review* 15, no. 3 (1963): 529–33.

Nagel, Jack H. "Some Questions About the Concept of Power." *Behavioral Science* 13, no. 2 (1968): 129–37.

Neale, R. G. *Great Britain and United States Expansion, 1898–1900.* East Lansing: Michigan State University Press, 1971.

Nish, Ian H. *The Anglo-Japanese Alliance.* London: Athlone Press, 1966.

Oakeshott, W. F. *Commerce and Society: A Short History of Trade and Its Effect on Civilization.* Oxford: Oxford University Press, 1936.

Odell, John S. *U.S. International Monetary Policy: Markets, Power, and Ideas as Sources of Change.* Princeton: Princeton University Press, 1982.

Offer, Avner. "Empire and Social Reform: British Overseas Investment and Domestic Politics, 1908–1914." *The Historical Journal* 26, no. 1 (1983): 119–38.

Olson, Mancur. *The Rise and Decline of Nations: Economic Growth, Stagflation, and Social Rigidities.* New Haven: Yale University Press, 1982.

Organski, A. F. K. "The Power Transition." In *International Politics and Foreign Policy,* edited by James N. Rosenau, 367–75. New York: Free Press of Glencoe, 1961.

———. "The Costs of Major Wars: The Phoenix Factor." *American Political Science Review* 71 (December 1977): 1347–66.

Padfield, Peter. *The Great Naval Race: The Anglo-German Naval Rivalry, 1900–1914.* London: Hart-Davis, MacGibbon, 1974.

———. *Rule Britannia: The Victorian and Edwardian Navy.* London: Routledge and Kegan Paul, 1981.

Pakenham, Thomas. *The Boer War.* New York: Random House, 1979.

Payne, Peter L. "Industrial Entrepreneurship and Management in Great Britain." In *The Cambridge Economic History of Europe.* Vol. 7, *The Industrial Economies: Capital, Labour, and Enterprise,* edited by Peter Mathias and M. M. Postan, 180–230. Cambridge: Cambridge University Press, 1978.

Peacock, Alan T., and Jack Wiseman, *The Growth of Public Expenditure in the United Kingdom.* Princeton: Princeton University Press, 1961.

Pelling, Henry. *Modern Britain, 1885–1955.* New York: W. W. Norton, 1960.

Perkins, Bradford. *The Great Rapprochement: England and the United States, 1895–1914.* New York: Atheneum, 1968.

Perris, G. H. *The Protectionist Peril.* London: Methuen, 1903.

Phelps Brown, E. H., and S. J. Handfield-Jones. "The Climacteric of the 1890's: A Study in the Expanding Economy." *Oxford Economic Papers,* n.s. 4, no. 3 (1952): 266–307.

Pigou, A. C. *The Riddle of the Tariff.* London: R. Brimley Johnson, 1903.

Pinto-Duschinsky, Michael. *The Political Thought of Lord Salisbury, 1854–68.* London: Constable, 1967.

Pipes, Richard. "Team B: The Reality Behind the Myth." *Commentary* 82, no. 4 (1986): 25–40.

Platt, D. C. M. *Finance, Trade, and Politics in British Foreign Policy, 1815–1914*. Oxford: Clarendon Press, 1968.

———. "Economic Factors in British Policy During the 'New Imperialism.'" *Past and Present* 39 (April 1968): 120–38.

———. "The Imperialism of Free Trade: Some Reservations." *Economic History Review* 21, no. 2 (1968): 296–306.

———. "National Economy and British Imperial Expansion Before 1914." *Journal of Imperial and Commonwealth History* 2, no. 1 (1973): 3–14.

———. *Britain's Investment Overseas on the Eve of the First World War: The Use and Abuse of Numbers*. New York: St. Martin's Press, 1986.

Polanyi, Karl. *The Great Transformation: The Political and Economic Origins of Our Time*. Boston: Beacon Press, 1944.

Pollard, Sidney. "Capital Exports, 1870–1914: Harmful or Beneficial?" *The Economic History Review* 38, no. 4 (1985): 489–514.

Porter, Bernard. *The Lion's Share: A Short History of British Imperialism, 1850–1970*. New York: Longmans, 1975.

———. *Britain, Europe, and the World, 1850–1982: Delusions of Grandeur*. London: Allen and Unwin, 1983.

Protection and Industry. London: Methuen, 1904.

Quester, George H. *Offense and Defense in the International System*. New York: John Wiley, 1977.

Ranft, Bryan, ed. *Technological Change and British Naval Policy, 1860–1939*. London: Hodder and Stoughton, 1977.

Rattinger, Hans. "Econometrics and Arms Races: A Critical Review and Some Extensions." *European Journal of Political Research* 4 (1976): 421–39.

Read, Donald D. *Edwardian England, 1901–1915: Society and Politics*. London: Harrap, 1972.

Rempel, Richard A. *Unionists Divided: Arthur Balfour, Joseph Chamberlain, and the Unionist Free Traders*. Devon, Eng.: David and Charles, 1972.

Ricardo, David. *On the Principles of Political Economy and Taxation*. London: John Murray, 1817.

Robinson, Ronald, and John Gallagher, *Africa and the Victorians*. New York: St. Martin's Press, 1961.

Rosecrance, Richard N. *Action and Reaction in World Politics: International Systems in Perspective*. Boston: Little, Brown, 1963.

Rosenau, James N. "Capabilities and Control in an Interdependent World." *International Security* 1, no. 2 (1976): 32–49.

———. *The Study of Political Adaptation*. London: Frances Pinter, 1981.

Russett, Bruce. "International Interactions and Processes." In *Political Science: The State of the Discipline*, edited by Ada W. Finifter, 543–53. Washington, D.C.: American Political Science Association, 1983.

———. "The Mysterious Case of Vanishing Hegemony." *International Organization* 39, no. 2 (1985): 207–31.

Sandler, Stanley. *The Emergence of the Modern Capital Ship*. Newark: University of Delaware Press, 1979.

Saul, S. B. *Studies in British Overseas Trade, 1870–1914*. Liverpool: Liverpool University Press, 1960.

————. *The Myth of the Great Depression, 1873–1896.* New York: St. Martin's Press, 1969.

Schurman, D. M. *The Education of a Navy: The Development of British Naval Strategic Thought, 1867–1914.* London: Cassell, 1965.

Seaman, L. C. B. *From Vienna to Versailles.* New York: Harper, 1963.

Searle, G. R. *The Quest for National Efficiency: A Study in British Politics and Political Thought, 1899–1914.* Oxford: Basil Blackwell, 1971.

Seeley, John. *The Expansion of England: Two Courses of Lectures.* London: Macmillan, 1899.

Semmel, Bernard. *Imperialism and Social Reform: English Social-Imperial Thought, 1875–1914.* Cambridge: Harvard University Press, 1960.

Shannon, R. T. *The Crisis of Imperialism, 1865–1915.* London: Hart-Davis, MacGibbon, 1974.

Shay, Paul, Jr. *British Rearmament in the Thirties.* Princeton: Princeton University Press, 1977.

Short, Wilfrid M. *The Mind of Arthur James Balfour.* New York: George H. Doran, 1918.

Simon, Herbert A. "Notes on the Observation and Measurement of Political Power." *The Journal of Politics* 15, no. 4 (1953): 500–16.

Singer, J. David. "The Level-of-Analysis Problem in International Relations." *World Politics* 1, no. 1 (1961): 77–92.

Smith, Adam. *An Inquiry into the Nature and Causes of the Wealth of Nations.* London: Longmans, 1846.

Smith, Paul, ed. *Lord Salisbury on Politics.* Cambridge: Cambridge University Press, 1972.

Smith, Tony. *The Pattern of Imperialism: The United States, Great Britain, and the Late-Industrializing World since 1815.* Cambridge: Cambridge University Press, 1981.

Snyder, Glenn H., and Paul Diesing, *Conflict Among Nations: Bargaining, Decision Making, and System Structure in International Crises.* Princeton: Princeton University Press, 1977.

Southgate, Donald, ed. *The Conservative Leadership, 1832–1932.* New York: St. Martin's Press, 1974.

Sprout, Harold, and Margaret Sprout. *Toward a New Order of Sea Power.* Princeton: Princeton University Press, 1943.

————. "Retreat from World Power: Process and Consequences of Readjustment." *World Politics* 15, no. 4 (1963): 655–88.

————. *An Ecological Paradigm for the Study of International Politics.* Center for International Studies Research Monograph, no. 30. Princeton: Princeton University Press, 1968.

————. "The Dilemma of Rising Demands and Insufficient Resources." *World Politics* 20, no. 4 (1968): 660–93.

Sprout, Margaret. "Mahan: Evangelist of Sea Power." In *Makers of Modern Strategy,* edited by Edward Meade Earle, 415–45. New York: Atheneum, 1966.

Stein, Arthur A. "The Hegemon's Dilemma: Great Britain, the United States, and the International Economic Order." *International Organization* 38, 2 (1984): 355–86.

Steinbruner, John D. *The Cybernetic Theory of Decision: New Dimensions of Political Analysis.* Princeton: Princeton University Press, 1974.

Steiner, Zara. "Great Britain and the Creation of the Anglo-Japanese Alliance." *The Journal of Modern History* 31, no. 1 (1959): 27–36.

———. *The Foreign Office and Foreign Policy, 1898–1914.* Cambridge: Cambridge University Press, 1969.

———. *Britain and the Origins of the First World War.* London: Macmillan, 1977.

Stoessinger, John. *Nations in Darkness: China, Russia, America.* New York: Random House, 1971.

Strachey, John St. Loe. "Free Trade and the Empire." In *The Empire and the Century,* 144–59. London: John Murray, 1905.

Strang, Lord. *Britain in World Affairs.* New York: Frederick A. Praeger, 1961.

Strauss, William L. *Joseph Chamberlain and the Theory of Imperialism.* Washington: American Council on Public Affairs, 1942.

Sumida, Jon J. "Financial Limitation, Technological Innovation, and British Naval Policy, 1904–1910." Ph.D. diss., University of Chicago, 1982.

Sydenham, Lord. *My Working Life.* London: John Murray, 1927.

Taylor, A. J. P. *The Struggle for Mastery in Europe, 1848–1918.* Oxford: Oxford University Press, 1977.

Thomson, David. *England in the Nineteenth Century.* Harmondsworth, Eng.: Penguin, 1978.

Thornton, A. P. *The Imperial Idea and Its Enemies: A Study in British Power.* New York: Anchor Books, 1959.

Thucydides, *The Peloponnesian War.* Harmondsworth, Eng.: Penguin, 1980.

Tilly, Charles. "War Making and State Making as Organized Crime." In *Bringing the State Back In,* edited by Peter B. Evans, Dietrich Rueschemeyer, and Theda Skocpol, 169–91. Cambridge: Cambridge University Press, 1985.

Towle, Philip, ed. *Estimating Foreign Military Power.* London: Croom Helm, 1982.

Tuchman, Barbara. *The Proud Tower.* New York: Macmillan, 1967.

Tucker, Albert. "The Issue of Army Reform in the Unionist Government, 1903–5." *The Historical Journal* 9, no. 1 (1966): 90–100.

Tyler, J. E. *The Struggle for Imperial Unity (1868–1895).* London: Longmans, Green, 1938.

Walt, Stephen M. *The Origins of Alliances.* Ithaca: Cornell University Press, 1987.

Waltz, Kenneth N. *Theory of International Politics.* Reading, Mass.: Addison-Wesley, 1979.

Wark, Wesley K. "British Intelligence on the German Air Force and Aircraft Industry, 1933–1939." *The Historical Journal* 25, no. 3 (1982): 627–48.

———. *The Ultimate Enemy: British Intelligence and Nazi Germany, 1933–1939.* Ithaca: Cornell University Press, 1985.

Wells, Samuel F., Jr. "British Strategic Withdrawal from the Western

Hemisphere, 1904–1906." *Canadian Historical Journal* 49, no. 4 (1968): 335–56.

Wiener, Martin J. *English Culture and the Decline of the Industrial Spirit, 1850–1980.* Cambridge: Cambridge University Press, 1981.

Wight, Martin. *Power Politics.* New York: Holmes and Meier, 1978.

Williams, Beryl J. "The Strategic Background to the Anglo-Russian Entente of August 1907." *The Historical Journal* 9, no. 2 (1966): 360–73.

Williams, Ernest E. *Made in Germany.* Sussex, Eng.: Harvester Press, 1973.

Williamson, Samuel R., Jr. *The Politics of Grand Strategy: Britain and France Prepare for War, 1904–1914.* Cambridge, Mass.: Harvard University Press, 1969.

Willoughby, F. S. *Suggestions for Securing Fair Play for British Manufacturers.* Manchester, Eng.: James Collins and Kingston, 1903.

Wilson, Keith M. "To the Western Front: British War Plans and the 'Military Entente' with France Before the First World War." *British Journal of International Studies* 3 (1977): 151–68.

Wish, Naomi Bailin. "Foreign Policy Makers and Their National Role Conceptions." *International Studies Quarterly* 24, no. 4 (1980): 532–54.

Wohlstetter, Albert. "Is There a Strategic Arms Race?" *Foreign Policy,* no. 15 (Summer 1974): 3–20.

Wolfers, Arnold. *Discord and Collaboration.* Baltimore: Johns Hopkins University Press, 1979.

Woodward, E. L. *Great Britain and the German Navy.* Hamden, Conn.: Archon Books, 1964.

Wright, Harrison M., ed. *The "New Imperialism": Analysis of Late Nineteenth-Century Expansion.* Lexington, Mass.: D. C. Heath, 1976.

Wright, Quincy. *A Study of War.* Chicago: University of Chicago Press, 1942.

Yapp, Malcolm. *Strategies of British India: Britain, Iran, and Afghanistan, 1798–1850.* New York: Oxford University Press, 1980.

Young, Kenneth. *Arthur James Balfour.* London: G. Bell and Sons, 1963.

Zebel, Sydney H. "Fair Trade: An English Reaction to the Breakdown of the Cobden Treaty System." *The Journal of Modern History* 12, no. 2 (1940): 161–85.

———. "Joseph Chamberlain and the Genesis of Tariff Reform." *The Journal of British Studies* 7, no. 1 (1967): 131–57.

———. *Balfour: A Political Biography.* Cambridge: Cambridge University Press, 1973.

Index